CW00797117

Martyrdom in Moc

The Islamic resurgence in modern times has received extensive treatment in scholarly literature. Most of this literature, however, deals with the concept of jihad and disputes between radicals and their rivals over theological and political issues, and far less with martyrdom and death. Moreover, studies that do address the issue of martyrdom focus mainly on "suicide" attacks – a phenomenon of the late twentieth century and onward – without sufficiently placing them within a historical perspective or using an integrative approach to illuminate their political, social, and symbolic features. This book fills these lacunae by tracing the evolving Islamic perceptions of martyrdom, its political and symbolic functions, and its use of past legacies in both Sunni and Shi'i milieus, with comparative references to Judaism, Christianity, and other non-Islamic domains. Based on wide-ranging primary sources, along with historical and sociological literature, the study provides an in-depth analysis of modern Islamic martyrdom and its various interpretations while also evaluating the historical realities in which such interpretations were molded and debated.

Meir Hatina is Associate Professor of Islamic and Middle Eastern Studies and director of the Levtzion Center for Islamic Studies at the Hebrew University of Jerusalem.

Martyrdom in Modern Islam

Piety, Power, and Politics

MEIR HATINA

The Hebrew University of Jerusalem

CAMBRIDGE
UNIVERSITY PRESS

CAMBRIDGE
UNIVERSITY PRESS

32 Avenue of the Americas, New York NY 10013-2473, USA

Cambridge University Press is part of the University of Cambridge.

It furthers the University's mission by disseminating knowledge in the pursuit of education, learning and research at the highest international levels of excellence.

www.cambridge.org
Information on this title: www.cambridge.org/9781107635470

First published 2014
First paperback edition 2015

A catalogue record for this publication is available from the British Library

Library of Congress Cataloguing in Publication data
Hatina, Meir.
Martyrdom in modern Islam : piety, power, and politics / Meir Hatina.
pages cm
ISBN 978-1-107-06307-5 (hardback)
1. Martyrdom – Islam.   2. Terrorism – Religious aspects – Islam.   I. Title.
BP190.5.M3H38   2014
297.2'7–dc23   2013048023

ISBN 978-1-107-06307-5 Hardback
ISBN 978-1-107-63547-0 Paperback

To Emmanuel Sivan,
a pioneer in the study of modern Islam

For the martyr the touch of death is like
a mosquito bite to each of you

– Abu ʿAbdallah Muhammad ibn Yazid ibn Majah,
Sunan ibn Majah (Cairo: Ihyaʾ al-Kutub al-ʿArabiya, n.d.),
Vol. 2, p. 937

Contents

Figures

Acknowledgments

The present study explores the evolving perceptions of Islamic martyrdom in modern times and its reliance on past legacies in both Sunni and Shiʿi milieus, with comparative references to Judaism, Christianity, and other non-Islamic cultures. Based on a vast array of primary sources and the use of methodological and sociological literature, the volume reveals a vibrant picture of martyrdom in the discourse of Islamist ideologies and movements, closely reflecting sociopolitical settings. In this, the book offers new insights and reappraisals that suggest areas for further research.

I am indebted to a number of institutions, as well as to colleagues and students who assisted me in the process of preparing this volume. The research was made possible by a generous grant from the Israel Science Foundation (ISF). Special thanks are also due to the Hebrew University's Levtzion Center for Islamic Studies, the Faculty of Humanities, and the Research and Development Authority. An earlier draft of the book was completed while I was a visiting scholar at the Institut für Politische Wissenschaft, Friedrich-Alexander-Universität Erlnagen-Nürnberg, Germany, in 2010, and I remain deeply grateful to the late Professor Christoph Schumann, director of the institute, for offering a stimulating environment in which to pursue my research there.

My deepest appreciation also goes to the following mentors and colleagues for their valuable assistance, advice, and critiques: Muhammad al-Atawneh, Meir Bar-Asher, David Commins, Daphna Ephrat, Diego Holstein, Etan Kohlberg, Meir Litvak, Nico Prucha, Emmanuel Sivan, Michaʾel Tanchum, and Itzchak Weismann. I wish to thank the two anonymous reviewers found by Cambridge University Press for their expertise and insightful comments about the manuscript. Thanks are also due to Yoni

Sheffer, who helped locate and collect valuable material, and to Judy Krausz, who edited the book with skill and integrity. Last but not least, I am indebted to the editorial staff at Cambridge University Press, especially to William M. Hammell and Sarika Narula, for their invaluable professional guidance.

A Note on Transliteration

The English transliteration of Arabic words in this volume follows standard academic rules as established by the *International Journal of Middle East Studies*. Arabic names and terms commonly used in the English-language literature appear in their English version.

Arabic terms are italicized, except for those that recur often, such as 'ulama', fatwa, shaykh, and shari'a, and ' is used for the Arabic letter 'ayn and ' for hamza. No subscripts or superscripts are used.

All translations of Qur'anic verses are those of M.A.S. Abdel Haleem, *The Qur'an: A New Translation* (Oxford: Oxford University Press, 2004), with occasional slight alterations. Verses cited follow the numbering of the common Egyptian edition.

Introduction

The study discusses the important role of convictions and the belief in a cause to the point of dying for them, as manifested in modern Islamic discourse, while exploring their sociopolitical and cultural contexts. Martyrdom in this context is to be understood mainly as a violent death in response to religious or other persecution, by execution, or in the battlefield during wartime.

Conviction is necessary in human life. It gives meaning to human conduct and provides answers to the central questions of life.[1] Western thought, however, has tended to minimize the ideal of self-sacrifice for a higher goal or perception. Rationalism, together with an individual-centered focus, evoked a perception of self-sacrifice as a form of mental disturbance or as stemming from a sense of futility. Arnold Toynbee observed that the hedonistic approach to life, symbolized by the adage "eat, drink and be merry, for tomorrow we may die," points to the centrality of the ego in human purpose, which he viewed as the main source of evil. By contrast, he wrote, altruism and working for the benefit of the collective has become the province of a minority who possess a strong sense of self-discipline.[2]

Another rational approach, put forward by Freud, was a refutation of the notion of immortality, namely that upon dying the human being passes on to another sphere of being. Death, he held, is final. Afterward there is nothing. Religion is a false and deceptive magic, he argued, and the notion of immortality that it harbors reflects the height of human vapidity in its

---

[1] See Eugene Weiner and Anita Weiner, *The Martyr's Conviction: A Sociological Analysis* (Atlanta, GA: Scholars Press, 1990), pp. 1–2.
[2] Richard L. Gage (ed.), *Choose Life: A Dialogue – Arnold Toynbee and Disaku Lkeda* (London: Oxford University Press, 1976), pp. 23, 245–246, 304–309.

effort to deny the fact of termination in death.[3] Ironically, however, instead of fading, the phenomenon of martyrs, and the commemoration of them, has survived in modern times.

Martyrdom appeared in earliest human history. The religions of Egypt, Mesopotamia, and ancient Greece contained the seeds of the notions of good and evil, and of heroism. Judaism in the Maccabean period adopted the notion of a struggle against evil for the sake of monotheism. Hellenism introduced a personal dimension to this ideology in the image of the ascetic philosopher. Eastern Christianity created the model of the warrior-hero, as did Islam, which promised immortality, absolution from sins, exemption from Judgment Day, and the attribute of communicating with the prophets.

Manifestations of martyrdom continued well into the modern era. Random examples are kamikaze pilots who dived into American fleets and exploded with their planes during the Second World War, self-immolation by Buddhist monks in Vietnam in protest against the American occupation in the 1960s, soldiers in the Irish Republican Army (IRA) who died in hunger strikes in British jails in the 1970s and early 1980s, and activists in liberation movements in the Middle East and the Third World.

Various theories explain why people die for their beliefs. One centers on the presence of persecution and tyranny, especially in reference to classic martyrdom. This theory holds that martyrdom appears where rulers make extreme demands on their subjects, evoking anger and opposition. Another theory – the theory of honor – focuses on social degradation. When people are degraded, their dignity and self-esteem become a primary priority. Other, essentially psychological explanations include the theory of group imitation and competition, as well as the theory of psychological aberration – that is, self-destruction. Yet another theory, emphasizing cultural heritage, views martyrdom as a built-in cultural norm influenced by faith, rituals, folk art, literature, and symbols. Lastly, the theory of social control points to the ability of the group to retain the loyalty of its members and preserve their allegiance to collective norms.[4]

DEFINING MARTYRDOM

Etymologically, a martyr is a witness. In the Christian context, the apostles were witnesses to Christ's acts and sayings, and in early Christian history

---

[3] Quoted from Israel Oron, *Death, Immortality and Ideology* (Tel Aviv: Ministry of Defense, 2002), p. 33 (in Hebrew).

[4] Weiner and Weiner, *The Martyr's Conviction*, pp. 13–24.

the term related to the significance of testimony to religious belief. In the wake of persecution by the Romans, the term became associated with persons who were executed or otherwise died for their faith. It had a purely religious meaning: it did not apply to ethnic or political strife or to criminals who were executed. Only in the sixteenth-century Reformation period did the term take on a broader meaning, applying to persons who died or were tortured either for a religious or a political cause.

Every culture, whether ancient or modern, has a pantheon of heroes who can fit the notion of martyr. Martyrdom can be attained in various ways, including choosing suffering or death over giving up faith or a principle, torture or execution for holding a defiant view, or painful suffering for a long time. The term "martyr" thus embraces a range of behaviors and motivations. Some martyrs actively choose suffering and death, whereas others passively accept death that is forced on them. Some martyrs have a clearly articulated viewpoint; others do not.

Socialization and group pressure, which support the martyr in a steadfast ratification of a goal and a readiness for self-sacrifice to attain it, play an important role in motive. In this respect, norms of self-sacrifice are more influential in collectivist cultures than in other cultures. Additionally, model leaders and other charismatic figures contribute to social influence. The more numerous the acts of self-sacrifice, the greater the likelihood that such acts will become a norm. From the collective point of view, the self-sacrifice of the individual adds quality, morality, and positive values to the group.[5]

Methodologically, such reciprocity between micro and macro history – between the personal and the collective – as reflected in social and cultural norms provides the context in which every individual functions, adopting all or some of its cultural attributes or building an alternative version based on them.[6] This is also true of martyrs, who are witnesses to the viability of their community and thereby also fill the role of social overseer.

Martyrdom is an effective tool for the formation of groups or the reinforcement of existing groups. In a confrontation with another, stronger group, martyrs can unify their community, heighten its coherence, and

---

[5] Ibid., pp. 72–76; Riddle, *The Martyrs*; also Ariel Merari, *Driven to Death: Psychological and Social Aspects of Suicide Terrorism* (New York: Oxford University Press, 2010), pp. 263–269.
[6] Edmund Burke and David N. Yaghoubian, "Middle Eastern Societies and Ordinary People's Lives," in idem (eds.), *Struggle and Survival in the Modern Middle East* (London: I.B. Tauris, 1993), pp. 1–32; also Carlo Ginzburg, "Microhistory: Two or Three Things That I Know About It," *Critical Inquiry* 20/1 (1993), pp. 10–35.

reinforce its resistance. Martyrdom engenders a politicization of the relationship between rival groups while imbuing the political contest between
them with lofty significance. Such an example of dramatic persuasion in
the public space creates a convictional community, expanding the potential for the recruitment of more members and delegitimizing other ideologies, especially that of the rival group. In short, martyrs function as a
mechanism for the ideological erosion of the other.

In this sense, the act of martyrdom must be a public act, or at least highly
publicized thereafter, so as to reinforce the members of the group while
challenging the legitimacy of the empowered side. Stories or legends about
the martyrs become a canonical tradition utilized for solidarity and indoctrination even after the attainment of political gains.

Martyrdom represents an attempt to break through the ideological and
social boundaries between rival groups through an act of heroism. Death is
depicted as a victory in battle, for although the hero's body has been
defeated, his/her spirit was not broken.

The heroism of martyrdom is closely associated with the notion of
altruism. Self-sacrifice is an altruistic act that runs counter to the human
instinct for survival. The martyr could avoid death, but accepts it with
determination and even seeks it. The contribution of the individual who
sacrifices him/herself for the collective is reflected in his/her readiness to fill
a double role: as sacrificer and sacrifice. His/her altruistic death harbors
two symbolic aspects: strength and purity. It represents self-discipline and
self-mastery, as well as redemptive suffering, with the venue of the act of
obliteration located in the public space for all to see. In this sense, the lives
of saints or ascetics are often less dramatic than the deaths of martyrs.

The sociologist Émile Durkheim, the first topologist in the field of
suicide, emphasized group processes and the importance of cultural institutions as determinants of behavior, perceiving self-sacrifice as a radical
expression of group solidarity. In his seminal work, *On Suicide* (1897), he
coined the term "altruistic suicide," by which the individual, as an organic
part of the social group, sacrifices self and individual needs for the sake of
the group out of a sense of identification with its collective values. By
placing ideology above physical survival, martyrdom ratifies the superiority of values over personal being and signifies the ultimate assimilation of
a truth that is perceived as the true essence of life. This perception differs
from egoistic suicide, which results from unfulfilled narcissist yearnings or
from discouragement resulting from a failure to find a raison d'être in
life. It also differs from anomic suicide stemming from loneliness and
alienation from society, especially in periods of economic disaster, family

catastrophe, or cultural disorientation. Whereas in the egoistic and anomic cases society is an insufficient presence in life, in the altruistic case society regulates life effectively.[7] The philosopher Bertrand Russell perceived self-sacrifice as part of an impersonal view of the world in which "man feels his ego to be but a small part of the world," a view that is one of the components of bravery. In this outlook, Russell observed, "unknown both to the voluptuary and to the ascetic, personal death appears a trivial matter," with the borders of the "I" expanding to encompass the collective.[8]

In repressed societies with little political power, such as the Jews during the Hellenist period or the early Christians in the Roman era, martyrdom forges authority, escalates the struggle, reinforces the ranks, legitimizes the alternative culture, and creates a sense of differentiation and animosity vis-à-vis the enemy. Moreover, martyrs motivate their society to adopt a position of self-determination regarding political and cultural freedom. Martyrdom induces a social pact sealed in blood. Historically, to quote Samuel Klausner, a minority and powerless society "that values individual life above group survival and above its cultural survival is not ready to become self-determining."[9]

Although some martyrs, such as in early Christianity, refused to use physical violence against their enemies, martyrdom is not generally passively submissive. The nonviolent martyr uses psychological warfare against the enemy, seeking to challenge the legitimacy of the enemy's authority.[10] The early Christians prompted violence against themselves but responded only by exerting psychological and moral pressure against the enemy. However, there were also combative Christian communities, such as the Christians in the wake of Constantine's victory in the fourth century. The Muslims under the Umayyads in the eighth century are another example of combative religious communities. Martyrs in such societies were activists who helped the group expand its influence and authority, contesting their rivals.[11]

The community, for its part, imbues such acts with an ideology that focuses on the significance of life with an affinity for death, emphasizing

---

[7] Émile Durkheim, *On Suicide: A Study in Sociology*, trans. by John A. Spaulding and George Simpson (new ed., New York: The Free Press, 1966), mainly pp. 145–240, 271–276, 297–300.

[8] Bertrand Russell, *On Education* (London: Unwin Books, 1964), pp. 38–39.

[9] See also Samuel Klausner, "Martyrdom," in *The Encyclopedia of Religion* 9 (1987), p. 233.

[10] Ibid., p. 231.

[11] Ibid., pp. 232–234; also Karl Rahner, *On the Theology of Death* (New York: Herder and Herder, 1961).

the sanctity of the mission and the satanic character of the enemy. The community also controls martyrdom, setting the rules for acts of martyrdom and defining the values that merit self-sacrifice, so as to prevent it from spreading beyond what is required.[12]

A loss of control over martyrdom, such as in the Judean provinces at the end of the first century BC, was destructive for Jewish autonomy, while a similar loss of control during the Bar-Kokhba uprising of 132–135 led to the destruction of the Temple. These destructive events shifted the center of Jewish population to the Diaspora. During the Middle Ages, Jews were a minority group in Islamic lands from the Arabian peninsula to Spain, as well as in the Christian states of Europe. Periodically, pressure was exerted on them to convert, prompting rabbinical disputations on the topic of martyrdom. The Talmudic rabbis constricted martyrdom, limiting it only to situations of forced violation of the prohibition of idol worship, incest or adultery, and murder. In a similar vein, Maimonides, warning that the death of a martyr is an automatic death sentence for all his relatives, sought to limit the possibilities of martyrdom. Maimonides' view was that only under extreme pressure was self-sacrifice allowed. Otherwise, he advised submission.[13]

Islam, too, forbade the believer to seek death. A death wish (*talab al-shahada*) even on the battlefield was viewed as too similar to suicide in the opinion of Muslim jurists. Rules were set for martyrdom. For example, candidates who could not stand up to the mission or to the enemy, or could not be trusted regarding whether their motivation was purely voluntary, should not be encouraged. Ibn Rushd (d. 1198) set formal parameters for participation in jihad: age, marital status, and attitude toward danger, namely a *shahid* is forbidden to recoil from battle or danger in cases when the enemy force is up to twice that of his own soldiers, but should withdraw if the proportion is any larger.[14] In modern times Shaykh al-Azhar Mahmud Shaltut (d. 1963) ruled that jihad should be mounted in three circumstances only: to repel aggression, defend the mission of Islam, or defend Muslims' freedom of religion in non-Muslim lands.[15]

---

[12] Yael Zerubavel, "Battle, Self-sacrifice, Sacrifice: Recompense in the Ideology of Patriotic Self-sacrifice in Israel," in Avner Ben-Amos and Daniel Bar-Tal (eds.), *Patriotism: Homeland Love* (Tel Aviv: Hakibbutz Hameuchad, 2004), pp. 61–62 (in Hebrew).

[13] David Hartman, *Crisis and Leadership: Epistles of Maimonides* (Philadelphia: The Jewish Publication Society of America, 1985), pp. 13–207.

[14] Klausner, "Martyrdom," pp. 235–236; Donald W. Riddle, *The Martyrs: A Study in Social Control* (Chicago: University of Chicago Press, 1931).

[15] Shaltut quoted in Rudolph Peters, *Jihad in Classical and Modern Islam* (Princeton, NJ: Markus Wiener Publishers, 1996), pp. 59–101.

During wartime, death on the battlefield elicits glorification. Men who die in this way are viewed as perfect – young, unstained heroes honored by commemorative ceremonies. Heroic self-sacrifice distinguishes not only the individual but also the entire social body by differentiating the "we" (the men) from "them" (the women). Thus, a political community molded by gender division and male dominance is created based on fallen men who sacrificed themselves while displaying military prowess.[16] In some cases, martyrdom can also be viewed as part of a contest over political supremacy in the community, with the death of martyrs in the struggle against the external enemy serving the struggle against political rivals from within as well. The martyr thus fills a dual purpose by delegitimizing the enemy outside while consolidating the status of his/her group in the community.[17]

As the preceding discussion shows, the martyr reinforces communal and national identity, especially in crisis situations. Since the martyr can no longer speak, his/her mission now shifts to his/her representatives, who deal with the politics of martyrdom. The martyr becomes part of the community's official memory. He/she is presented as someone who, by a publicly witnessed death, conveyed a deterrent message of determination, commitment, and non-submission to the enemy while simultaneously serving as a model worthy of imitation and a recruitment agent of future martyrs.

The martyr becomes a mythological figure who stimulates the commemoration of revolutionary goals and stirs deep feelings. These feelings provide legitimation and significance to the declared goal.[18] Indeed, the martyr has no existence without memorialization, commemoration, and narration. In fact, most of the people who sacrifice their lives are not necessarily martyrs. Most do not acquire, or do not retain, an implacable faith in the face of a threat to their life. Total commitment is not widespread in reality. Often, martyrs are hesitant, and the circumstances of self-sacrifice are forced on them. Their faith might be weakened by torture and imprisonment. Narratives are therefore necessary. They imbue martyrs

---

[16] Carolyn Marvin and David W. Inge, "Blood Sacrifice and the Nation: Revisiting Civil Religion," *Journal of the American Academy of Religion* 64/4 (1996), pp. 767–780.

[17] Klausner, "Martyrdom," pp. 231–232. See also Valérie Rosoux's examination of the political use of national martyrs in France, "The Politics of Martyrdom," in Rona M. Fields et al. (ed.), *Martyrdom: The Psychology, Theology and Politics of Self-sacrifice* (Westport, CT: Praeger Publishers, 2004), pp. 83–116.

[18] Christian Szyska, "Martyrdom: A Drama of Foundation and Tradition," in Friederike Pannewick (ed.), *Martyrdom in Literature: Visions of Death and Meaningful Suffering in Europe and the Middle East from Antiquity to Modernity* (Wiesdanden: Reichert, 2004), pp. 29–46.

with significance and influence. As sociologist Ronald Kassimer writes, "Martyrs are made not simply by their beliefs and actions but by those who witnessed them, remembered them and told their story."[19] In the same vein, some scholars pointed to "cult and discourse," in which the concept of martyrdom is bound up with the narratives and literature that have shaped and been shaped by people's memories.[20]

A great deal depends on the persuasiveness of the narrative and on the group's knowledge systems and modes of transmission. These determine the importance of the martyr. The narrative is molded, as in every story, by the oral and written traditions of the community. If the cultural tradition is prone to the tragic (as the Shi'a's), the narrative will reflect this tendency. If the tradition is liturgical, the martyrdom will assume liturgical conventions. Notably, the narrative is not necessarily written at the time of death of the martyr or during the lifetime of his/her contemporaries. Several successful narratives were created by martyrologists who were not witnesses to the events. Some narratives were even imagined. Thus, secondary source material that memorializes martyrs, which constitutes the bulk of the corpus available for researchers, should be examined with caution. It tends to divulge the writer's world view more than the martyr's.[21]

The writer or commentator belongs to what Stanley Fish has termed "interpretive communities" who can freely impose their viewpoint on the texts and use them as polemical ammunition. As a rule, while historical literature is a legitimate research category, it is an open category that contains truth and facts but is imbued with input by interpretive communities. They mold the meaning of the text and define how these texts should be understood. Martyrdom, therefore, may be viewed as a discourse – a form of death for God that changes and develops over time in accordance with the aims and goals of the community.[22]

---

[19] Rosourx, "The Politics of Martyrdom," p. 83 (quotation), pp. 83–87; Ronald Kassimir, "Complex Martyrs: Symbols and Catholic Church Formation and Political Differentiation in Uganda," *African Affairs* 90 (1991), p. 362.

[20] Richard Finn and Michael Smart, "Christian Martyrdom: History and Interpretation," in Brian Wicker (ed.), *Witnesses to Faith? Martyrdom in Christianity and Islam* (Aldershot, Hants: Ashgate, 2006), mainly pp. 41–44.

[21] Weiner and Weiner, *The Martyr's Conviction*, pp. 8–9, note 1, 27–29; on the social and cultural functions of martyrdom writing, see ibid., pp. 87–127; also Elizabeth A. Castelli, *Martyrdom and Memory: Early Christian Culture Making* (New York: Columbia University Press, 2004).

[22] Stanley Eugene Fish, *Is there a Text in this Class? The Authority of Interpretive Communities* (Cambridge, MA: Harvard University Press, 1980), pp. 1–17; Daniel Boyarin, *Dying for God: Martyrdom and the Making of Christianity and Judaism* (Stanford, CA: Stanford University Press, 1999), pp. 94–95, 117–126.

MARTYRDOM IN MODERN TIMES

War heroes in ancient times were commemorated in folk epics recounting their heroic acts. The biblical book of Judges, for example, is devoted to a description of the acts of bravery of ancient Hebrew heroes. In ancient Greece ritual ceremonies are known to have been dedicated to fallen heroes in patriotic wars, especially in the wars against the Persians in the fifth century BC and in the Peloponnesian War (431–404 BC). Lewis Farnell, a scholar of hero commemorations in ancient Greece, described them as "a reward for patriotism, for a noble death against the national foe," involving ritual funeral and burial rites.[23]

Patriotic self-sacrifice also became a major value in the ethos of the modern national state. Its roots lay in the French Revolution as a secular revolution heralding a shift in martyrdom from the religious to the national sphere. The tradition of martyrdom was nurtured to serve the goals of secular national movements such as in France and Germany in the nineteenth and early twentieth centuries.[24] The fighters in this context belonged to citizen rather than mercenary armies, in contrast to the custom in the Roman Empire, in the Italian city states, and in the absolutist regimes in Europe in medieval times. Side by side with the shift during the nationalist era to the notions of "subject" and "citizen," the ancient Greek and Roman concept of the "patriotic war" reappeared, with citizens assuming the burden of defense, and their self-sacrifice reflecting national partnership. As part of the mourning process, the private aspect of loss was nationalized and the nation as a whole became indebted to the memory of the fallen.[25]

Symbols play a prominent role in patriotic martyrdom and are vital in the nation-building process. In the view of historian George Mosse, political ideas are molded and projected not by rational argument but by means of a symbolic process that provides an additional means of social control over the masses and instills a sense of community. People perceive reality entirely through symbolism and myths, he claimed, without which individuals have no identity. Their identity is forged by symbols.[26]

[23] Lewis R. Farnell, *Greek Hero Cult and Ideas of Immortality* (Oxford: The Clarendon Press, 1921), pp. 362–363.
[24] Weiner and Weiner, *The Martyr's Conviction*, pp. 88–91; Rosourx, "The Politics of Martyrdom," pp. 86–112.
[25] Avner Ben-Amos and Daniel Bar-Tal, "Patriotism as a Psychological-Sociological Phenomenon," in idem (eds.), *Patriotism*, pp. 13–28.
[26] George L. Mosse, *The Nationalizations of the Masses: Political Symbolism and Mass Movements in Germany from the Napoleonic Wars through the Third Reich* (New York: H. Fertig, 1975), pp. 6–7.

This is all the more true of national liberation movements, which require symbols, rituals, and myths to gain as much support as possible. Without its own distinctive symbols, a liberation movement has little chance of succeeding, for if one has no flag of one's own, it is difficult to oppose the flag of the oppressor.[27]

Modern patterns of memorial ceremonies for fallen soldiers were consolidated primarily after the First World War in Germany, Britain, and France. The events of the Second World War entrenched them further. The ghosts of the dead became embedded in Europe's politics and public life. Monuments, cemeteries, and memorial days were part and parcel of the commemorative repertory of the fallen in war. The fallen were also documented by official memorial bodies in compilations and albums, providing a kind of detailed and methodical roadmap that traces the history of self-sacrifice in specific countries.[28] An instructive example is *Scenes of Fighting and Martyrdom Guide: War Years in Poland 1939–45*, produced in Warsaw by the Council for the Preservation of Monuments in 1964–1968. Its first section, *Resistance and Martyrdom*, documented 500 memorial sites established throughout Poland where acts of resistance and martyrdom against the Nazi occupation during the Second World War occurred. A survey of the compilation reveals a broad use of the term martyrdom, with no differentiation between soldiers and civilians or between passive and active death, suggesting a sense of shared fate and unity built around love of homeland and freedom.[29] The dual function of memorialization in the Polish public space, namely molding historic awareness and entrenching national values, is clearly expressed by the head of the Council in the introduction:

This publication seeks to bring to life for young people the years of occupation, to explain to them those years in our history, which were the most significant, the most illustrious, the most replete with sacrifice.... The inhuman character of fascism can best be grasped at the scenes of its crimes. Even so, it is precisely at those places of heroism displayed by the Nazis' victims that the best lessons can be

---

[27] Amikam Nachmani, "The Palestinian Intifada: The Dynamics of Symbols and Symbolic Realities – The Role of Symbols, Rituals and Myths in National Struggles," *Alpayim* 24 (2002), p. 77 (in Hebrew).

[28] See, e.g., George L. Mosse, *Fallen Soldiers: Reshaping the Memory of the World Wars* (Oxford: Oxford University Press, 1990); Avner Ben Amos, *Funerals, Politics and Memory in Modern France 1789–1996* (Oxford: Oxford University Press, 2000); also Emmanuel Sivan, *The 1948 Generation: Myth, Profile and Memory* (Tel Aviv: Ministry of Defence, 1991), mainly chapters 8, 9, and 10 (in Hebrew).

[29] Council for the Preservation of Monuments, *Scenes of Fighting and Martyrdom Guide: War Years in Poland 1939–45* (Warsaw: Sport Turystyka Publication, 1968).

learned as to the boundless love of motherland, as to uncompromising struggle for humanity's highest ideals – liberty and social justice.[30]

In discussing the rise of modern nationalism in Europe between 1870 and 1914, Eric Hobsbawm notes that the political and social changes of the time, and the ascent of the political power of the masses, demanded new tools by which to attain control, loyalty, and group cohesion. Alternatives had to be found for the traditional unifying elements that had been provided by church and monarchy. A new tradition of national holidays, festivals, ceremonies, monuments, symbols, and heroes was created both by establishment organs and vernacular social agents. This new network of rituals and symbolic elements, promoted by repetition, aimed at establishing continuity with a suitable historical past, thereby preserving, or in some cases remolding, the social order.[31]

Martyrdom and its commemoration in modern times was not exclusively the province of the state and its official agents. It was nurtured as well by secular opposition movements such as the Narodnaya Vola in Czarist Russia, the Syrian Social Nationalist Party (SSNP) in Lebanon, the Front de libération nationale (FLN) in Algeria, and the Kurdish Workers Party (PKK) in Turkey, as well as by various religious groups. These groups sought to restore the metaphysical dimension to human experience that, in their view, had been trapped in a web of hedonism and secularism. The most prominent role in the restoration of the religious dimension was that of Islamist protest movements.

Notably, the use of the term "Islamism" throughout the volume refers to movements that were actively involved in the politics of dissent and sought to apply Islamic precepts to all spheres of life. As such they differentiated themselves from other religious agents such as the establishment of 'ulama' or Sufi shaykhs.[32]

THE ISLAMIC DIMENSION

Self-sacrifice constituted an important component of modern Islamism throughout the twentieth century and beyond. It projected virtue, piety, and power and served two purposes: revealing the authentic essence of

[30] Ibid., pp. 8–9.
[31] Eric Hobsbawm, "Introduction: Inventing Traditions," in E. Hobsbawm and T. Ranger (eds.), *The Invention of Tradition* (Cambridge: Cambridge University Press, 1983), pp. 1–14; idem, "Mass-Producing Traditions: Europe 1870–1914," ibid., pp. 263–307.
[32] Michaelle Browers, "The Secular Bias of Ideology Studies and the Problem of Islamism," *Journal of Political Ideologies* 10 (2005), pp. 75–93.

Islam as a religion that fights against sociopolitical injustice, and demonstrating Islam's superiority over other cultures that sanctify the value of life over the worship of Allah. However, despite its assertiveness, the ethos of martyrdom cloaked a religious culture on the defensive, which in its heyday had been a world power but in the modern era lagged behind Christian Europe and North America increasingly in terms of material progress and political power. Shifting from words to deeds, Islamist martyrdom acquired varying interpretations during the twentieth century, from engagement in communal activity to launching "suicide" attacks.[33] This diversity reflected the historical and political contexts in which Islamist movements functioned and provided further evidence of the multifaceted nature of modern Islamist thought.

The present volume seeks to explore the contentious theme of martyrdom in twentieth-century Islamist thought and practice by focusing on its main spokesmen and by tracing its links both to the legacy of the past and to contemporary sociopolitical reality. Curiously, these issues have not been investigated comprehensively in the research literature, and constitute the main contribution of the study.

Most of the extant literature is devoted to the perception of jihad in modern Islam, or to disputes between radicals and their rivals over theological and political issues, yet it barely relates to the perception of self-sacrifice or willing death.[34] Researchers who have dealt with martyrdom have done so in the specific context of "suicide" bombers, who appeared only in the last two decades of the twentieth century and ignited the imagination of the public and the research community. However, the

---

[33] "Suicide" attack has become a term commonly used in Western parlance. The quotation marks are meant to signify this reality without taking a stance on the issue.

[34] See, e.g., Peters, *Jihad in Classical and Modern Islam*; Umar F. Abd-Allah, *The Islamic Struggle in Syria* (Berkeley: Mizan Press, 1983); Gilles Kepel, *The Prophet and the Pharaoh* (London: Dar al-Saqi, 1985); idem, *Jihad: The Trail of Political Islam* (Cambridge, MA: Harvard University Press, 2002); Emmanuel Sivan, *Radical Islam* (New Haven: Yale University Press, 1990); Seyyed Vali Reza Nasr, *Mawdudi and the Making of Islamic Revivalism* (New York: Oxford University Press, 1996); Johannes J. G. Jansen, *The Dual Nature of Islamic Fundamentalism* (Ithaca, NY: Cornell University Press, 1997); Fawaz A. Gerges, *The Far Enemy: Why Jihad Went Global* (New York: Cambridge University Press, 2005); Augustus R. Norton, *Hezbollah: A Short History* (Princeton NJ: Princeton University Press, 2007); Philipp Holtmann, *Abu Mus'ab al-Suri's Jihad Concept* (Tel Aviv: Moshe Dayan Center, 2009); Thomas Hegghammer, *Jihad in Saudi Arabia* (Cambridge: Cambridge University Press, 2010); Daniel Lav, *Radical Islam and the Revival of Medieval Theology* (Cambridge: Cambridge University Press, 2012); Joas Wagemakers, *A Quietist Jihadi: The Ideology and Influence of Abu Muhammad al-Maqdisi* (Cambridge: Cambridge University Press, 2012).

phenomenon has not been sufficiently discussed in a broad historical perspective or in the context of its ideological, symbolic, social, and political aspects. Instead, a significant and at times obsessive research effort, especially by social scientists, psychologists, and specialists in the field of terror, has been devoted to analyzing the personal motivations of the "suicide" bomber, group influence, and decision-making processes.[35] Some scholars, for example, Stephen Holmes and Diego Gambetta, avoided ideological interpretations of the "suicide" phenomenon, positing instead a purely secular/political rationale of combating injustice and tyranny.[36] Still other scholars, such as Ariel Merari and Adam Landkford, attributed mental health problems and suicidal tendencies to "suicide" bombers.[37]

An important contribution to the discussion of self-sacrifice was made by research on modern Shi'ite activism, especially in Iran, for example, by Haggai Ram (1994), Nader Nazemi (1997), Karman S. Aghaie (2004),

---

[35] See, e.g., Martin Kramer, "Sacrifice and Fratricide in Shiite Lebanon," *Terrorism and Political Violence* 3/3 (Autumn 1991), pp. 30–47; Marc Sageman, *Understanding Terror Networks* (Philadelphia: University of Pennsylvania Press, 2004); Mohammed M. Hafez, *Manufacturing Human Bombs: The Making of Palestinian Suicide Bombers* (Washington, DC: U.S. Institute of Peace Press, 2006); idem, *Suicide Bombers in Iraq: The Strategy and Ideology of Martyrdom* (Washington, DC: U.S. Institute of Peace Press, 2007); Diego Gambetta (ed.), *Making Sense of Suicide Missions* (Oxford: Oxford University Press, 2005); Farhad Khosrokhavar, *Suicide Bombers: Allah's New Martyrs* (London: Pluto Press, 2005); David Cook and Olivia Allison, *Understanding and Addressing Suicide Attacks: The Faith and Politics of Martyrdom Operations* (Westport, CT: Praeger Security International, 2007); Eli Alshech, "Egoistic Martyrdom and Hamas' Success in the 2005 Municipal Elections: A Study of Hamas Martyrs' Ethical Wills, Biographies and Eulogies," *Die Welt des Islams* 48 (2008), pp. 23–49; Merari, *Driven to Death*.

[36] Stephen Holmes, "Al-Qaeda, September 11, 2001," in Gambetta (ed.), *Making Sense of Suicide Missions*, pp. 131–172; Diego Gambetta, "Forward," in ibid., p. v; also idem, "Can We Make Sense of Suicide Missions?" pp. 279–283.

[37] See Ariel Merari "The Readiness to Kill and Die," in Walter Reich (ed.), *Origins of Terrorism* (Cambridge: Cambridge University Press, 1990), pp. 192–207. Notably, in later writings Merari largely revised his view of "suicide" attacks as the product of personality factors, as more data (mainly in the Palestinian context) became available, pointing to more interactive motivations such as social milieu, group influences, and personal reasons. Merari, *Driven to Death*, mainly pp. 261–277. Adam Landkford advocated a purely psychological explanation, arguing that the September 11 hijackers and other "suicide" perpetrators experienced personal crises such as unwanted pregnancies, HIV, or other ailments, physical problems, and the death of loved ones, resulting in suicidal tendencies. Landkford, "Ten Years after 9/11: The Suicidal Angel," in: dam-landkford/ten-years-after-911-the-s_b_956462.html (accessed date March 4, 2013); idem, *The Myth of Martyrdom: What Really Drives Suicide Bombers, Rampage Shooting and other Self-Destructive Killers* (New York: Palgrave Macmillan, 2013).

and Roxanne Varzi (2006). Their focus, however, was mainly on the commemoration project of the fallen in the Iran-Iraq War, and, moreover, lacked a comparative perspective of Sunni activism.[38] Sunni activism was discussed to some extent by historian David Cook in his book, *Martyrdom in Islam* (2007), although most of the volume deals with the earlier history of the topic, with only a single, somewhat generalized chapter devoted to the modern period. Moreover, most of the discussion in the book is theological and textual, with no methodological or sociological insights provided. These and other lacunae, including a tendency to stray from a historical analysis of the contemporary "suicide" attacks to ways of dealing with them, are prominent as well in another volume by Cook, written together with Olivia Allison, *Understanding and Addressing Suicide Attacks* (2007).[39] Another researcher, the anthropologist Talal Asad, in a book titled *On Suicide Bombing* (2007), provides a more anthropological view, but also includes a polemical dimension in its attack against Western critics of the phenomenon. In Asad's view, violence and cruelty, including harming civilians, are a universal phenomenon in which the liberal and secular West has played a significant role.[40]

The present study offers a broad perspective of martyrdom in modern Islamist discourse – both Sunni and Shi'i – analyzing the political, symbolic, and pedagogic functions of self-sacrifice, with comparative references as well to its status in Judaism and Christianity. The book discusses four main themes: the importance of conviction and the willingness to die for it; the importance of social networks in offering moral, psychological, and material incentives for martyrdom acts; the function of the martyr as a cultural agent; and the abiding link between religion and politics and between history and collective memory, thus positing martyrdom as a vital component of identity politics and of power-struggle relationships.[41]

---

[38] Haggai Ram, *Myth and Mobilization in Revolutionary Iran* (Washington, DC: American University Press, 1994), mainly chapter 3; Nader Nazemi, "Sacrifice and Authorship: A Compendium of the Wills of Iranian War Martyrs," *Iranian Studies* 30 (1997), pp. 263–271; Kamran S. Aghaie, *The Martyrs of Karbala: Shi'i Symbols and Rituals in Modern Iran* (Washington, DC: University of Washington Press, 2004), mainly chapters 6, 7, and 8; Roxanne Varzi, *Warring Souls: Youth, Media, and Martyrdom in Post-revolutionary Iran* (Durham: Duke University Press, 2006), mainly chapters 2 and 3.

[39] David Cook, *Martyrdom in Islam* (New York: Cambridge University Press, 2007); Cook and Allison, *Understanding and Addressing Suicide Attacks*.

[40] Talal Asad, *On Suicide Bombing* (New York: Cambridge University Press, 2007), mainly chapter 2.

[41] On the affinity between violence and power, see, e.g., Hannah Arendt, "On Violence," in idem, *Crises of the Republic* (New York: Harcourt Brace, 1972), pp. 105–112, 134–146; J. E. Seery, *Political Theory for Mortals* (Ithaca, NY: Cornell University Press, 1996).

The volume is based on wide-ranging primary sources that include Islamic chronicles, juridical literature, ideological manifestos, memoirs, written and recorded wills, leaflets, periodicals, sermons, and fatwas (legal opinions). Careful analyses of these sources reveal a multifaceted religious discourse on martyrdom ranging from unity to dispute and voices of restraint alongside extremism and the anticipation of salvation. Secondary methodological and historical sources help shed light on the broader sociopolitical context in which the concept of martyrdom was molded and debated in Islamist discourse. Sociological literature on the themes of sacrifice and suicide is also used.

THE STRUCTURE OF THE BOOK

The basic purpose of any religion is to provide meaning to a given reality. Through it the believer acquires existential purpose and a guide to a moral life – in other words, authenticity. The most extreme and ultimate expression of this conviction is self-sacrifice for the sake of God and faith.[42] The willingness to give up one's life for God exists in all three monotheistic religions: Judaism, Christianity, and Islam. However, the early history of each religion dictated a specific kind of death on the part of the believer. The first two chapters trace these theological and historical foundations.

Chapter 1 reviews martyrdom in Judaism and Christianity, the two monotheistic traditions that preceded Islam and in some ways affected its concept of death, for example, as a confessional act of faith in God and paradise. In Judaism, the defensive context in which the Jewish people found itself, especially in terms of persecution by the Greek and Roman Empires, fostered the notion of martyrdom for God in the face of forced conversion or the violation of the prohibitions of idolatry, incest, and murder. In the case of Christianity, the model presented by Jesus as a lamb led to the slaughter – thereby atoning for mankind's sins – evoked a willingness for passive death among the believers persecuted by the Roman Empire during the first four centuries AD. By comparison, Islam, as shown in Chapter 2, glorified the death of martyrs on the battlefield who fought infidels and apostates. Any other self-inflicted death, such as suicide prompted by illness, imprisonment, or despair, was perceived as sinful, punishable by the torments of hell.

---

[42] See Søren Kierkegaard, *Either/Or*, trans. by David F. Swenson and Lillian M. Swenson (New York: Doubleday, 1959), Vol. 1.

Viewed historically, the ideal of martyrdom was not necessarily actual-
ized in the Muslim community. The ongoing war against unbelievers
(*kuffar*) proved to be impractical and was frequently neglected in favor
of armistices and peace agreements.

As a result, the parameters of martyrdom were expanded to include not
only fallen warriors but also ascetics, or those who died while carrying out
the duties of worship. Nevertheless, the elevated status of military martyrdom in Muslim religious literature created a decisive difference between
Islamic society and other societies. Martyrdom was lauded as well by key
molders of modern Islamist activism, who exalted heroic episodes in Muslim
history and positioned self-sacrifice as an important concept in the struggle
between truth and falsehood and between purity and defilement.

This ethos acquired new interpretations and emphases during the twentieth century. Chapter 3 explores and analyzes the modern evolution of
martyrdom through comparative perspectives. Thus, whereas the Muslim
Brethren in Egypt, Syria, and Jordan in the first half of the century associated self-sacrifice mainly with communal activism and working for the
public good, radical groups associated it with a violent struggle against
"apostate" regimes. In this sense, radical Sunnis defied the Muslim taboo
against opposing local rulers and enthusiastically adopted the Islamic
literature praising jihad and self-sacrifice (*fada'il*). Still, they were cautious
in the matter of the type of the martyr's death, which had to be circumstantial and unplanned lest it be viewed as suicide, thereby constituting
weakness and submission to Satan. They were cautious, too, regarding the
prohibition of not harming Muslim civilians, whose lives are blessed by
Islam. This guarded position revealed theological and moral prohibitions
against both self-immolation and the killing of innocent people. However,
under the impact of the modern Shi'i model of initiated or offensive death,
the appearance of "suicide" attacks from the early 1980s onward largely
altered the accepted understanding of martyrdom until then. This was
reflected in at least two basic aspects: the death of the perpetrator, which
was a premeditated act, and indiscriminate damage caused by the attack
to enemy civilians, including children, and sometimes to Muslim believers
as well.

Chapter 4, dealing with the modern phenomenon of "suicide" attacks,
explores various forms of martyrdom in the latter twentieth and early
twenty-first centuries, focusing on ethno-national conflicts. Whereas
Iranian martyrdom was officially promoted and supported by the state,
elsewhere, such as in Lebanon, Palestine, Chechnya, Afghanistan, and
Kashmir, it was fostered by dissident Islamist movements whose agenda

was twofold: military, aimed at foreign conquerors, and political, aimed at rival groups in their communities. Other non-Islamist movements as well adopted the weapon of "suicide," demonstrating that a secular cause, too, could serve as a motivation for death.

In both the Shi'i and the Sunni orbits, however, martyrdom was national in character, reflecting particular geographical settings. The appearance of al-Qa'ida changed this and introduced a transnational character that replaced the local enemy with a global enemy and further radicalized the perception of martyrdom, including the legitimization of attacks against Muslims. Chapter 5 focuses on al-Qa'ida's perception of death, revealing an assertive and uncompromising outlook aimed at setting new moral standards for Muslim conduct.

Chapter 6 presents a view of the martyr as preacher and saint, imbued with supernatural attributes, whose mission is twofold: calling for martyrdom for God and defying oppressors and preaching a religious way of life. The martyr's self-sacrifice was presented not only as an effective combat tool but also as a theological and political statement in the name of a supreme authority, with the goal of providing an effective representation of the option of protest and opposition over the option of compromise, convergence, and synthesis. In this respect, martyrdom serves as a means of attaining distinction, advocating a willingness to die and not only to kill. Martyrs' wills became one of the nuclei of a pedagogic enterprise aimed at creating a commemorative community that cherishes the fallen and embraces the message of revolution and liberation. The chapter offers an analysis of the image of the martyr and his role in the drama as projected in the written and video-recorded wills prepared before embarking on the mission from which there was no return. It also provides an additional glimpse of the ideological mind-set of Islamist movements in their effective use of print, electronic, and Internet media to advance their cause.

Chapter 7 highlights disputes and polemics within the Islamic spectrum over "suicide" attacks, namely between critics who argued that these were pure acts of violence and suicide and advocates who held that such acts were the ultimate realization of God's will. Focusing mainly on the scholarly 'ulama' community, the chapter reveals a nuanced Islamic legal discourse contending with a new and challenging phenomenon and the need to define its permitted and forbidden parameters, as well as power struggles for religious authority and guidance.

"Suicide" acts, which appeared for the first time in the West in the late 1990s, intensified disputes among Western observers regarding the link between Islam and violence and generated a range of psychological explanations ranging from nihilism and self-destruction to sexual frustration. Chapter 8 critically examines these observations, while laying greater emphasis on an ideological reading of the phenomenon and its sociopolitical, symbolic, and pedagogic functions.

The book traces the evolving religious perceptions of martyrdom, its political and symbolic functions, and its use of past legacies in both the Sunni and the Shiʿi orbits, providing an innovative basis and new insights for future research on the issue of self-sacrifice and death in modern Islam.

I

Defying the Oppressor: Martyrdom in Judaism and Christianity

Martyrdom was a common heritage in settled societies throughout the East and in the Mediterranean Basin. The practice per se began with the coalescence of various ancient philosophical streams, especially stoicism. The philosopher manifested the superiority of wisdom over feeling, and his own superiority over a corrupt and corrupting world, by putting an end to his life or assisting others to do so. Exemplars were philosophers and holy men toward the end of the Roman Empire who chose this dramatic practice as a symbol of opposition to unjust authority. The practice was adopted by the monotheistic religions as well.[1] Inasmuch as it conveyed courageous conviction and dissent, a logical outcome was to refer to its victims as martyrs, or witnesses (the literal meaning of the Greek term *martus*). However, the three monotheistic religions – Judaism, Christianity, and Islam – linked the term "martyr" to another concept, namely confession, thereby creating a new, broader semantic field. The willingness to give up one's life for God existed, and exists, in all three religions, yet the early history of each dictated a specific kind of death on the part of the believer.

JUDAISM: SANCTIFYING THE NAME OF GOD

The defensive position in which the Jewish people found themselves, in light of persecution by the Greek and Roman Empires, fostered the notion

---

[1] Arent Jan A. Wensinck, *The Oriental Doctrine of the Martyrs* (Amsterdam: Koninklijke Akademie van Wetenschappen, 1921), pp. 1–28; also Michael Bonner, *Jihad in Islamic History* (Princeton, NJ: Princeton University Press, 2006), pp. 73–74.

of martyrdom for God in the face of forced conversion or violation of the prohibitions of idolatry, incest, and murder. The death of Hannah and her seven sons during persecutions by the Greek ruler Antiochus of Syria in 167, and similar acts of self-sacrifice in the Bar-Kochba rebellion during persecutions by Hadrian in the province of Judaea in 132–135, became cornerstones in the historical ethos of Jewish martyrdom.[2] This was also true regarding the dramatic execution of Rabbi Akiva following the suppression of the Bar-Kokhba rebellion, as he persisted in reciting the prayer *Shema Israel* ("Hear O Israel, the Lord is our God, the Lord is one") while his executioners raked his flesh with iron combs. These accounts gained a place of honor in molding the concept of Jewish self-sacrifice – namely that the authority of the Caesar is temporary and is overpowered by the eternal power of God. Death is temporary and is accompanied by resurrection and eternal life in the Garden of Eden.[3]

The readiness of Jews to die rather than compromise their religion during this period was perceived as worthy and logical, nurtured by a religious world view of observing the commandments and worshipping God as providing meaning, order, dignity, and holiness to life. The neglect of these commandments, however, will lead to chaos and defilement. Moreover, persecution was perceived as the final drama before the redemption, with those who died in the defense of religion described as resurrected to life.[4]

Rabbinic Judaism spoke in terms of the sanctification of God vis-à-vis the defamation of God, rather than of martyrdom. A traditional legal and ideological tension exists in Judaism between the sanctification of life and risking one's life. On the one hand, there is the duty to protect life, as the sages emphasized: "You shall keep my laws and my rules, by which one shall live" (Leviticus 18:5). On the other hand, major prohibitions against

---

[2] On these episodes, see Moshe D. Herr, "Persecution and Martyrdom in Hadrian's Days," pp. 85–125; Shemuel Safrai, "Martyrdom in the Teachings of the Tannaim," in Th.C. de Kruijf and H. van de Sandt (eds.), *Sjaloom* (Arnhem: B. Folkertsma Stichting voor Tamudica, 1983), pp. 145–164; J. W. van Henten (ed.), *Die Entstehung der Jüdischen Martyrologie* (*The Emergence of Jewish Martyrology*) (Leiden: Brill, 1989) idem, *The Maccabean Martyrs as Saviours of the Jewish People* (Leiden: Brill, 1997); Boyarin, *Dying for God*, pp. 95–114.

[3] See Michael Berenbaum and Reuven Firestone, "The Theology of Martyrdom," in Fields et al. (eds.), *Martyrdom*, pp. 120–125.

[4] However, there was also a more passive version of self-sacrifice, advocated by the Hellenistic Jews of Alexandria, that was embodied in the notion of vicarious atonement through ritual animal sacrifice to placate God's anger against sinners. Weiner and Weiner, *The Martyr's Conviction*, pp. 27–48.

idolatry, incest, and homicide call for self-sacrifice rather than violating such taboos.

Certain rabbis added various restrictions to these prohibitions. For example, a Jew must never commit a sin in public to save his life. The Talmud sages also began to differentiate more definitively between suicide and fatalities resulting from oppression. In cases where the legal tradition ruled that a person should choose death rather than violate a major commandment, the rabbinical commentary was always worded passively, namely, "should be killed," rather than implying a premeditated death.

The rabbinic prohibition against suicide, however, coalesced only gradually.[5] Eventually, suicide was viewed as a serious crime in the Jewish tradition and as a clear and definitive religious and moral violation. Several reasons were given for this acute prohibition: the value of life is higher than all else, which dictates the duty to preserve life; man is not the master of his body and thus does not have the right to take his life or to harm it, for his body is given to him as a deposit by the Creator for the purpose of discharging his duties ethically according to the Torah; and suicide denies the Jewish principles of reward and punishment and the next world. A suicide cannot repent, and his death does not grant him absolution – in contrast to a murderer – according to a later legal ruling that a suicide has no place in the next world. Morally, therefore, there is strong opposition to suicide in the Jewish tradition and support for the sanctity of the value of life.

Sanctions that developed against suicide were aimed at minimizing burial rituals, eulogies, and mourning in such cases. Nevertheless, in extreme conditions, especially in the face of hopeless situations, suicide was considered a legitimate option, as can be learned from the attitude of Jewish law in cases of suicide in the Biblical period, for example, toward Avimelekh (Judges 9: 52–54), and Saul and his spear-bearer (Samuel I, 31: 3–6). These events were depicted as the acts of heroes who were vanquished in war and took their own lives rather than fall into their enemies' hands alive. Such an act – choosing death with dignity over life, or over death in disgrace – was viewed as heroic. Similarly, during the Second Temple period (516 BC–AD 70) individuals, families, and whole groups committed suicide as a result of persecution by the Romans, and these acts were acceptable, recorded without censure or reservation.[6]

---

[5] Jeremy Cohen, *Sanctifying the Name of God: Jewish Martyrs and Jewish Memories of the First Crusade* (Philadelphia: University of Pennsylvania Press, 2004), pp. 16–19.

[6] Yechezkel S. Lichtenstein, *Suicide: Halakhic, Historical and Theological Aspects* (Tel Aviv: Hakibbutz Hameuchad, 2008), pp. 17–50 (in Hebrew).

The appearance of suicide among Jews during the Second Temple period overlapped with similar acts in the surrounding gentile world. Conceivably, it might have been influenced by the widespread practice of suicide among the Greeks and Romans. The stoic philosophy supported suicide as an expression of free will and of complete control over one's fate. It entitled the individual to decide when to respond to a sign by God that the time had come to depart from life, described as "self-removal from life."[7]

The status of *kiddush hashem* – the sanctification of God's name – differed from suicide. This practice was well illuminated by the Essenes, who viewed themselves as chosen by God and as children of light. The notion of suffering and death as a positive religious attribute played an important role for the Essenes. During the Roman wars they were known to have accepted death with joy, prepared to die for the sanctification of God's name. They adopted the idea of the happiness of the righteous after death and the grant of everlasting life, as was written in the Talmud: "And the righteous wear crowns on their heads and enjoy the divine splendor of the revelation."[8] The motif of celestial attire appears in other sources of Jewish literature as well.[9]

A large body of commentary about death and the sanctification of God's name appeared at the time of the edicts issued by Antiochus. This material also relates to death as an act of atonement, such as the death of the righteous at the hands of gentiles, which serves as absolution for the sins of Israel. Such literature reveals a Jewish influence on early Christianity and on the interpretation of Jesus' self-sacrifice as atonement for mankind.[10]

Although the principle of the sanctification of God was more fully realized at a later stage in the wake of persecutions that demanded practical decisions regarding life and death, ultimately this concept was institutionalized as an obligatory command. Some of the sages discerned that a person's merit could be judged by exemplary behavior during his entire life, or even by a single act – the sanctification of God. Jewish history is

---

[7] Ibid., pp. 51–56.

[8] *Masekhet Brakhot*, 2: 17, col. 1.

[9] Hillel Newman, *Proximity to Power and Jewish Sectarian Groups of the Ancient Period* (Leiden: Brill, 2006).

[10] David Flusser, "Martyrdom during the Period of the Second Temple and Early Christianity," in *Holy War and Martyrdom* (Jerusalem: The Israeli Historical Society, 1968), pp. 61–71.

replete with martyrs for the sanctification of God who perceived their death as a form of spiritual resistance.

Mass self-sacrifice occurred at Masada in 73, three years after the destruction of the Second Temple, replicated by similar acts at Yodfat and Gamla during the same period. Approximately a thousand years later, in 1096, mass self-sacrifice occurred in the Rhine Valley during the First Crusade, when the Jewish communities in Mainz and Worms were forced to choose between baptism or death, marking the first and most significant anti-Jewish acts of violence in Christian Europe during the Middle Ages. Many Jews chose death in the sanctification of God, taking the lives of their families and themselves rather than submitting to slavery, torture, forced conversion, or slaughter by the enemy. They preferred a spiritual existence to a physical one. Some also chose baptism and life, as shown in research by Jeremy Cohen, but the martyrdom paradigm of the events of 1096 was enshrined in Ashkenazi Jewish culture for generations to come, preserving its distinctive heritage as reflected in liturgical poetry (*piyyut*) and later chronicles.[11]

During those persecutions Jews killed themselves by their own hand, which ignited rabbinical debate. Although choosing death by the enemy to prevent the violation of the three commandments against idolatry, incest, and murder was commended, taking one's own life was another matter entirely. The Torah and the Holy Scriptures explicitly forbid and deplore suicide even in the name of the sanctification of God. Modern scholars have approached this issue from two points of view. One focuses on the importance that Ashkenazi Jews attributed to legendary history, including the suicides at Masada, stressing these accounts as shaping Jewish tradition and legal norms. Rabbinic traditions commemorating Jewish martyrdom in the Land of Israel reinforced this legacy. The other approach in explaining the choice of death during the events of 1096 focuses on the ideological climate of the first Crusades, namely the fanaticism of the Christians to the point of rejecting bribes that were offered so that the only choice left to the Jews was death or conversion. Many Jews chose suicide as a more meaningful alternative, taking the initiative themselves and controlling their fate rather than leaving it to the enemy. The Jews thereby

---

[11] Cohen, *Sanctifying the Name of God*, pp. viii–ix, 1–9. Cohen stresses the importance of analyzing the historical context in which the chronicles were written, rather than the historical documentation they contain. The greater the importance attributed by a culture to an episode in its past, the more elusive the raw data of that event becomes. The accounts of death thus reflected an ideology of martyrdom adopted by the Jewish survivor rather than the actual death of the martyr.

challenged the threatening ideology of the Crusades, fortifying Jewish communal identity by choosing self-martyrdom.[12]

Accounts in the chronicles leave no doubt that these acts were performed with complete awareness and with the intent to bear witness to the truth of the faith held by the Jews and the lie of Christianity in whose name they were forced to sacrifice their lives. Christianity was perceived by the Jews in Germany and France in the eleventh century as a sworn enemy of God and as a force that blocked the revelation of His kingdom on Earth. The chronicles echo the perception of the Jews that Christianity's conception of the holy trinity was nothing but idol worship in disguise. Statements by the sanctifiers of God emphasize the total distinctiveness of God and the gap between Jewish monotheism and Christian polytheism. The recitation of *Shema Israel*, proclaiming the unity of God, was the last utterance of the sanctifiers of God. By contrast, the church sacraments were foreign to the Jews and were viewed as paganism. Their animosity toward Christianity thus served as a factor that spurred the acts of martyrdom by the Jews of the Rhineland. Ashkenazi martyrdom literature shows that a status of honor was accorded to those born in the image of God and who were expected, therefore, to meet higher demands.[13]

The act of the sanctification of God had various aspects, such as demonstrating the highest degree of the love of God or bearing witness to the true religiosity of the martyr, but above all it reflected the belief in the eternity of the life of the spirit following physical life. Similarly, increased asceticism and mysticism following the expulsion from Spain in 1492 laid special emphasis on love of God and cleaving to His Torah. However, although the rabbis of the time preached the absolute sanctification of God, clearly, a significant proportion of the Jews did not meet this demand. Many of the forced converts during the early Middle Ages, especially in Portugal, did remain loyal to Judaism to a certain degree but not all of them. They created a new kind of Jewish theology to justify their dubious position. They permitted idolatry, when threatening edicts were issued, to stay alive, relying on Torah verses and sayings of the sages regarding the importance of preserving life. Their position regarding religion and martyrdom was thus distant from that of Ashkenazi Jewry. They were loyal to Judaism but on their own terms.[14]

---

[12] Ibid., pp. 13–16, 22–30; also Lichtenstein, *Suicide*, pp. 128–176.

[13] Lichtenstein, *Suicide*, pp. 156–160.

[14] Cecil Roth, "Religion and Martyrdom among the Conversos," in *Holy War and Martyrdom*, pp. 93–105.

Jews in the Islamic countries also perceived the sanctification of God differently from the Ashkenazi Jews. Although in northern Europe many Ashkenazi Jews killed their families and themselves rather than be forced by the Christians to convert, this practice did not take hold in the Islamic countries at that time. A relatively small number of deaths for the sanctification of God are known to have occurred in the Islamic lands as compared to the Ashkenazi communities. When forced to decide between conversion and death, Sephardi Jews during the Middle Ages mainly chose conversion. Many Sephardi Jews became Muslims, including learned scholars and community leaders as well as ordinary people, for example, during the middle of the twelfth century under the rule of al-Muwahhidun in North Africa. The reason is linked mainly to the religious ideals of the non-Jewish environment where the Jews lived and worked, as well as their own attitude toward the Christian and Muslim creeds.

In Christianity, death for the sanctification of God was viewed as a lofty value, and formative Christianity generated many martyrs, thereby influencing Jewish thought. Islam was more restrained in this respect. Moreover, Christianity was perceived as idolatrous, with its belief in the holy trinity and in such rituals as the bread of communion interpreted as pagan. Islam, by comparison, was perceived as monotheistic; Maimonides himself ruled that Islam was not pagan. The practical significance was that conversion to Christianity was tantamount to paganism, whereas conversion to Islam was not. Clearly, Maimonides' ruling applied only to someone who faced a choice between conversion and death. However, he sought to restrict the inclination toward martyrdom and reinforce the prohibition against suicide by ruling that choosing martyrdom when the circumstances do not necessitate it is tantamount to suicide. Additionally, the Ashkenazi Jewish communities developed a deep antipathy for Christianity and its symbols in light of systematic attempts to force them to convert. Lastly, the Jews in Islamic lands were open to Muslim culture, especially in Muslim Spain, whereas the Ashkenazi Jews had a distant and meager acquaintance with Christian culture.[15]

In modern times, with the appearance of the Zionist movement and the establishment of the State of Israel, the traditional significance of the sanctification of God and of the readiness of Jews to die for their religion

[15] Avraham Grossman, "Martyrdom in the Early Eleventh and Twelfth Centuries: Between Ashkenaz and the Muslim World," *Pe'amim* 75 (Spring 1998), pp. 27–46 (in Hebrew); Hartman, *Crisis and Leadership: Epistles of Maimonides*, pp. 13–207; Lichtenstein, *Suicide*, pp. 249–271; Bat-Zion Eraqi-Klorman, "Muslim Society as an Alternative: Jews Converting to Islam," *Jewish Social Studies* 14/1 (Fall 2007), pp. 89–118.

in an atmosphere of persecution changed, replaced by an activist approach to self-sacrifice for national revival.[16] In the early days of Zionism, death for the sanctification of God was perceived as a reflection of helpless Diaspora passivity. Instead, Zionism encouraged Jews to take action once again, as in biblical times, and not wait for the redemption. This activist stance also constituted the moral justification for demanding sacrifice on behalf of the nation. The change introduced by Zionism mandated a rejection of any resemblance between death for the sanctification of God and death for the cause of the territorial nation. It posited a readiness for sacrifice aimed at national sovereignty, a choice made by individuals in a community with a secular moral character.[17]

CHRISTIANITY: "YOUR CRUELTY IS OUR GLORY"

Christianity, like premodern Judaism, experienced persecution, but the early Christian martyrs died a passive death at the hands of their captors and oppressors rather than self-inflicted death. Martyrdom and persecution were constants during the early centuries of Christianity, called the "era of martyrs." The model establishing Jesus as the sacrificial lamb who thereby atones for the people's sins nurtured the willingness for passive death by persecuted believers in the Roman Empire over the first four centuries AC.[18]

An apt explanation for the acceptance of martyrdom as a key for salvation was provided by Quintus Tertullian of Carthage (d. 225), often depicted as "the father of Latin Christianity," who explained to a Roman governor: "Your cruelty is our glory." Tertullian thereby signified that the vocation of the Christian is to suffer, with his execution harboring his victory.[19] Thus, victory is the result not of defeating the enemy on the

---

[16] Maoz Azaryahu, *State Cults: Celebrating Independence and Commemorating the Fallen in Israel 1948–1956* (Beer-Sheba: The Ben-Gurion Research Center, 1995), pp. 103–131.

[17] Uri S. Cohen, *Survival: Senses of Death between the World Wars* (Tel Aviv: Resling Publishing, 2007), mainly pp. 17–36, 221–242 (in Hebrew).

[18] Aviad Kleinberg, *Flesh Made Word: Saints' Stories and the Western Imagination* (Cambridge, MA: Belknap Press of Harvard University Press, 2008), pp. 9–34; Mahmoud Ayoub, "Martyrdom in Christianity and Islam," in R. T. Antoun and M. E. Hegland (eds.), *Religious Resurgence: Contemporary Cases in Islam, Christianity and Judaism* (New York: Syracuse University Press, 1987), pp. 67–70; Glen W. Bowersock, *Martyrdom and Rome* (Cambridge: Cambridge University Press, 1995), pp. 1–39; Frances M. Young, *Sacrifice and the Death of Christ* (London: SPCM Press, 1975).

[19] Tertullian quoted by Bowersock, *Martyrdom and Rome*, p. 20. See also Robin Daniel, *This Holy Seed: Faith, Hope and Love in the Early Churches of North Africa* (Chester: Tamarisk Publications, 2010), pp. 46–60.

battlefield but of cleaving to faith in the presence of the enemy's violence. For Tertullian, martyrdom was primarily an ethical exercise in obeying God's will. God's will tests the resilience of the Christians' faith and loyalty by persecution and execution. Satan, therefore, is not the rival of Christianity; he is an agent of God by which Christian loyalty is tested. On the opposite side, both Jesus and the Holy Spirit are celestial messengers of support who help the Christian remain loyal.[20]

Martyrdom is thus a definitive link in the eschatological struggle between God and Satan. The martyr is resilient to pain, functions in Jesus' name, and rises above physical weakness by his determined spirit. Moreover, the martyr personifies the Church in microcosm and thereby performs the work of the Church. This identification goes hand in hand with another statement by Tertullian, namely "the blood of the martyrs is the seed of the Church."[21]

Tertullian's observations explain the readiness of many Christians in the Roman Empire to sacrifice their lives and, in fact, to seek opportunities to do so. Viewing eternal salvation as a higher value than physical survival, the Christian martyrs were prepared to undergo barbaric torments. The higher the number of martyrs reached throughout the empire, the more widespread the public commemorations of them became. Commemorative martyr literature (*acta martyrum*) became the most popular literary genre during the formative period of the Church. Churches and ritual sites became destinations for pilgrimages. Touching a grave or nighttime prayers in monasteries to restore health or induce holy visions were widespread. Another practice reflecting the power attributed to martyrs was the burial of the faithful close to a martyr's grave so that they would be resurrected to life together with him. High points were commemorative festivals and public processions in memory of a martyr, ending in gatherings in a monastery, shrine, or at a ritual site associated with the martyr. Not only did the martyr acquire honor but so did his family and even their town. Potential martyrs who withstood torture and lived on were granted prestigious positions and high status.

The oath of belief in Christianity – "I am a Christian" (paralleled by Judaism's "Hear O Israel") – became the central component in the accounts of martyrdom and was perceived as a "second baptism," this time of blood, which promised purification from all sins and immediate

[20] William C. Weinrich, *Spirit and Martyrdom* (Washington, DC: University Press of America, 1981), pp. 253–267.
[21] Ibid., pp. 187–203, 236–242.

entry into paradise. Self-sacrifice was an act of great significance both in Judaism and Christianity. If suffering were involved in the act, this had a higher purpose. Each religion provided a different justification for such suffering. In Judaism, the answer to Job's questioning of the suffering of a righteous man is the limitations of human understanding of revelation. In Christianity, suffering reveals the limitless love, compassion, and atonement for the sins of humanity that are bound up with self-sacrifice, as demonstrated by Jesus on the cross.[22]

In essence, early Christian martyrdom constituted a passive protest against the use of violence, thereby challenging the power structure of the oppressor. Its guiding principle was that there is an authority higher than human authority, for which death is worthwhile. Acting on behalf of this higher authority places the individual beyond good and evil and determines one's fate. Although some Christians had served in the Roman army, thereafter they refused to use violence to protect themselves or their fate. The execution of Christians became a theatrical event, and their acts became widely known, functioning for their admirers as symbols of struggle by "athletes of God."[23] A significant number of martyrs were women. They played a subordinate role (they were listed separately in the compilations of martyrs) but still a heroic one; their achievements were perceived as elevating them to the status of their male counterparts. Women who were subject to cruel treatment by the courts and were condemned to execution gained attention and empathy.[24]

Notably, early Christian martyrdom was a largely urban phenomenon in the Roman Empire. The locations of acts of martyrdom in prisons and in central plazas before large crowds of spectators afforded publicity and elicited discussion, thereby serving the interests of the Christian Church while exposing the Roman administration to a measure of consternation.[25] Apparently, acts of martyrdom served as an opportunity for pagans to be exposed to Christianity during the first and second centuries AD. The zeal of the early Christians to die at the hands of their oppressors gave pause to the pagans. This voluntary willingness for death was closely related to suicide carried out with the help of an outside agent, yet it was clearly

---

[22] Ayoub, "Martyrdom in Christianity and Islam," p. 69.
[23] Bonner, *Jihad in Islamic History*, p. 74.
[24] Stuart G. Hall, "Women among the Early Martyrs," in Diane Wood (ed.), *Martyrs and Martyrologies* (Cambridge, MA: Blackwell Publishers, 1993), pp. 1–21; Chris Jones, "Women, Death, and the Law during the Christian Persecutions," ibid., pp. 23–34.
[25] Bowersock, *Martyrdom and Rome*, pp. 42–45.

hastened by the victim him/herself, a reflection of the elevated value of suicide in Roman society (and, notably, its prohibition for slaves).

The Christians' zeal in fact evoked dispute in early Christian theology. Although the personal redemption of the martyr and his path to paradise were always viewed as assured, the particular search for spiritual security by drastic means was not always supported by the Church, which reasoned that true martyrdom must result from God's will, not man's. This dispute was led by Clement of Alexandria (d. 215), who argued that martyrdom in the true etymological sense of the term means "bearing witness," constituting a confession of faith in God. Every person who believes in God and obeys his laws is a martyr, whether in words or deeds. Martyrdom thus does not necessarily obligate death. Moreover, forced martyrdom by the Romans, he held, is only one way, but not necessarily the optimal way, of attaining martyrdom. Bearing witness could be achieved by confessing the faith in a far less sanguinary manner.

Clement was thus influenced by Greek philosophy in which a violent death was perceived as suicide. In this respect his viewpoint was identical to that of Judaism, which preceded him, and Islam, which came after his time. It was only under the leadership of Augustine (d. 430) that the Church consolidated a clear and firm position opposing suicide. Augustine's purposefulness in adopting this position suggests that the controversy over suicide was still ongoing, especially in the Latin West. He ruled that a person who kills him/herself has committed murder, a condemnation of suicide reflecting the Greco-Jewish ethic. This ended the practice of voluntary martyrdom, and from then on the ritual of confession represented the aspiration for martyrdom without spilling blood.[26]

The martyrdom ritual remained an important component of Christian religious life in the late ancient era during the second half of the fourth

---

[26] Ibid., pp. 59–74. A quite different stance was later adopted by Thomas Aquinas (d. 1274), who praised the value of martyrdom as part of his emphasis on the value of courage and resistance in the face of oppression. He rejected Augustine's position, citing evidence from the New Testament that sacrificing one's life for God is a blessed act. The value of courage was described by him as one of the four cardinal virtues. His stance was revolutionary and granted importance to the Aristotelian view that highlighted the importance of human rationality in all exalted acts, including courage. Aquinas reached the conclusion that martyrdom was the highest form of courage. "Thomas Aquinas on Martyrdom," Appendix 1 in Wicker (ed.), *Witnesses to Faith?* pp. 139–146; Bernard K. Freamon, "Martyrdom, Suicide and the Islamic Law of War: A Short Legal History," *Fordham International Law Journal* 27 (2003), pp. 311–312.

century. Sermons about martyrs were a main means of re-contextualization
to the present and future. Historical accuracy was not the primary interest
of the audience listening to the sermons, nor were eulogies, but rather
adherence to the belief in the very act of sacrifice. The historical core was
blended with hagiography, which sought to present the martyr as both
holy and human, whose behavior embodied the highest Christian virtues.
History was turned into hagiography adorned with stylistic elements and
quotations from holy texts.

In evaluating the historic significance of martyrdom, the martyrological
literature is more interesting than the main actors in the drama. The blood
of the martyrs became the seed of the Church, as Tertullian argued,
describing how the seed was planted, watered, and nurtured by a supportive pedagogic system. Sometimes it was not even important whether the
martyrs existed, and so they were invented to provide the Church with
status or to strengthen the identity of the congregation.

Not surprisingly, then, Roman Catholicism developed a certified martyrology, namely, a well-organized list of martyrs with dates of birth and
brief biographies – a kind of martyrological lexicon. Thus, a consciousness
of the blood tie between Christians of the present and those who suffered
and gave up their lives for the holy kingdom was officially preserved.[27]
Written and unwritten testimonies in the hagiographic tradition, liturgical
passions, miracle books, sermons, poems, plays, paintings, sculptures, and
letters reinforced this memory. Similarly, the bodily relics and garments of
martyrs who were perceived as miracle workers were preserved. An additional impetus to the hagiographic discourse was provided by rituals
surrounding saints and their often elaborately constructed graves from
the second century onward. As shown by Peter Brown, martyrs' tombs
were viewed as public property, accessible to all and the focus of rituals
attended by the entire community.[28] Above and beyond commemorating
the martyr in words, images, and ritual, hagiographic literature aimed at
presenting him/her as *hagio* – holy. The accounts of the martyrs became
larger than life, whereas grains of authentic historic information about
them shrank or disappeared.[29]

What were the aims of the martyr narratives, in light of the secondary
importance accorded to historical veracity? The first aim was to transform

---

[27] Cóilín Owens, "A Literary Preamble," in Fields et al. *Martyrdom*, pp. 3–6.

[28] Peter Brown, *The Cult of Saints: Its Rise and Function in Latin Christianity* (Chicago:
University of Chicago Press, 1981), mainly pp. 1–22.

[29] Ibid.; Bowersock, *Martyrdom and Rome*, pp. 26–39; Klienberg, *Flesh Made Word*,
pp. 26–28.

the martyr into a living memory rather than a dim figure from the distant past, so as to induce the faithful to follow in his/her footsteps. The second aim was the construction of the Christian identity.[30] The martyr embodied the Christian virtues worthy of imbuing. Moreover, the hagiography was fashioned by the congregation itself, thereby contributing to the coalescence of its own identity, reinforcing theological or legal themes to which the members of the congregation adhered. At the same time, martyrdom provided Christians with ammunition for disputation in their relationships with other religions or with other sects within Christianity itself. Sometimes, one Christian group would justify its persecution of a rival Christian group by claiming that the rival's martyrs were not true martyrs but merely desperate fanatics who committed suicide by sacrificing themselves to their enemies.[31]

While the two traditional foundations of the martyr's testimony – faith and a stoic disregard of pain – continued to mold Christian thought, the categories of martyrdom widened to include asceticism and holiness attributed to persons who spread the gospel or who led the Church in a spirit of asceticism. Heroic attributes such as piety, pilgrimage, and miracles proliferated, while martyrdom in the old, more brutal pattern became rare.[32] The image of desert ascetics such as St. Anthony (d. 356), St. Athanasius (d. 373), and St. Martin (d. 397) provided the model for centuries of hagiography to come. St. Anthony was the classic ascetic who pushed the devil to the edge with ability to bear self-abnegation, profuse prayer and fasting. The ascetics were said to have undergone "white" martyrdom through their lives of mortification, in contrast to those who underwent the "red" martyrdom of death through the shedding of their blood.[33]

The cult of saints penetrated the social fabric and dominated the calendar of the masses, featuring such attributes as healing, mediation with God, and ensurance of fertility. Saints and their names were adopted by churches, schools, and colleges; pilgrimages were made to their graves; children were named after them as a guarantee of safekeeping; paintings

---

[30] Johan Leemans, "Martyr, Monk and Victor of Paganism: An Analysis of Basil of Caesarea's Panegyrical Sermon on Grodius," in Johan Leemans (ed.), *More than a Memory: The Discourse of Martyrdom and the Construction of Christian Identity in the History of Christianity* (Leuven: Peeters, 2005), pp. 61–62.

[31] See, e.g., Brad S. Gregory, *Salvation at Stake: Christian Martyrdom in Early Modern Europe* (Cambridge, MA: Harvard University Press, 1999), mainly chapters 1 and 3.

[32] Aviad Kleinberg, *Prophets in Their Own Country* (Chicago: Chicago University Press, 1992), mainly chapters 1–3; Leemans, "Martyr, Monk and Victor of Paganism," pp. 45–79.

[33] Lawrence S. Cunningham, "Cause Non Poena: On the Contemporary Martyrs," in Leemans (ed.), *More than a Memory*, p. 462.

and sculptures of their images were displayed; and hagiographic literature was written about them, all aimed to stimulate faithfulness and provide models of asceticism. The saints were depicted as sharing a part of Jesus' greatness, portrayed as seated on royal thrones and wearing crowns.[34]

Not only was the formative Christian concept of martyrdom devaluated, thereby paving the way for other forms of devotion, but also it underwent a weakening of the boldness that had typified it. In the Latin West, while authorizing Christian doctrine, with its aim of reforming evil and restoring harmony to the world, as a justification for war, St. Augustine, as discussed earlier, and other theologists, nevertheless warned against a lust for violence. They emphasized that not every wrongdoing constituted a reason for war, and the ruler had a duty to try to correct wrongdoing in other ways. This warning against the use of force was reflected as well in Christian missionary activity, when, in the early medieval period, the Church abstained from converting Muslims. Instead of seeking martyrdom, Catholic missionaries – as well as Nestorians and Byzantines – were purposely sent out to preach to the pagans of the north, where the danger of conflict with Muslims was minimal and the chances of conversion high.[35]

Nevertheless, some Catholic figures did challenge the restrained position of the fathers of the early Church regarding warfare and the use of violence and sanctioned the death of martyrs. In 853, Pope Leo IV expressed the hope for a heavenly reward and eternal life for Christians who fell in the struggle against the Saracens.[36] This concept also emerged in Muslim Spain during the ninth century when Christians sought death as martyrs at the hands of the Muslim enemy as a way to publicly demonstrate their opposition to Islam. The city of Cordoba was prominent in this respect, experiencing a brief period of widespread public martyrdom and suicides on the part of the Christian community, which, additionally, elicited a wave of eschatological literature in Andalusia. Typically, a

---

[34] Kleinberg, *Prophets in Their Own Country*, chapter 1; Stephan Wilson, "Introduction," in idem (ed.), *Saints and Their Cults* (London: Cambridge University Press, 1985), p. 3; Michael Goodich, "The Politics of Canonization in the Thirteenth Century: Lay and Mendicant Saints," in Wilson (ed.), *Saints and Their Cults*, pp. 169–187; Pierre Delooz, "Towards a Sociological Study of Canonized Sainthood in the Catholic Church," in ibid., pp. 189–216.

[35] See Benjamin Z. Kedar, *Crusade and Mission: European Approaches toward the Muslims* (New Jersey: Princeton University Press, 1984), pp. 3–14.

[36] Ibid., pp. 14–18; Frederick H. Russell, *The Just War in the Middle Ages* (Cambridge: Cambridge University Press, 1975), pp. 32, 78.

Christian would convert to Islam and then publicly renounce his new religion, whereupon the qadi would try – unsuccessfully – to change the convert's mind, ending in the execution of the convert.[37]

A sociopsychological analysis shows that most of the martyrs in Cordoba in that period had divided identities – some as offspring of mixed Muslim-Christian marriages, and others as only partially integrated in the Muslim-dominated mainstream.[38] Some historians described the atmosphere as one of spiritual anxiety combined with spontaneous martyrdom. The Christian martyrs identified Islam with the secular world, which they rejected, and developed anxiety as to their personal salvation.[39] Responding to their defiant acts, the Muslim emir demanded that the local archbishop put an end to the martyrdom phenomenon in Cordoba and declare it to be false martyrdom. Indeed, some Christian priests viewed their executed coreligionists as suicides unworthy of salvation, and who, by their acts, exposed the community to suspicion and danger from the Muslims. These priests argued that the Muslims were monotheists, not pagans, and that there was no general persecution of Christianity in Cordoba that could justify acts of martyrdom.[40]

Similar events occurred in Palestine and Syria during that period, evoking a critical discourse in the Christian communities that led to an end to the martyrdom phenomenon. Ultimately, the Christian communities under Islamic rule realized that such rule would remain indefinitely, and many eventually converted to Islam.[41]

A more activist death in the name of faith emerged in Christianity during the Crusades in the eleventh century, when slain Crusaders began to be viewed as martyrs, because, as an incentive to join, a promise had been given by the Church that their sins would be forgiven. The First Crusade was thus an important episode in the history of martyrdom. It

---

[37] Kenneth B. Wolf, *Christian Martyrs in Muslim Spain* (New York: Cambridge University Press, 1988), mainly pp. 23–35; James Waltz, "The Significance of the Voluntary Martyrs of Ninth-Century Cordova," *Muslim World* 60 (1970), pp. 143–159, 226–236.

[38] Wolf, *Christian Martyrs in Muslim Spain*, pp. 107–119.

[39] Ibid., pp. 116–117; Waltz, "The Significance of the Voluntary Martyrs of Ninth-Century Cordova."

[40] Wolf, *Christian Martyrs in Muslim Spain*, pp. 63–66, 77–78.

[41] Bonner, *Jihad in Islamic History*, pp. 80–82. An earlier episode, in 639/44, involved the execution of sixty Byzantine soldiers for their refusal to convert to Islam shortly after the conquest of Gaza during the Muslim invasion of Palestine. See David Woods, "The 60 Martyrs of Gaza and the Martyrdom of Bishop Sophronius of Jerusalem," in Michael Bonner (ed.), *Arab-Byzantine Relations in Early Islamic Times* (Aldershot, Hants: Ashgate, 2004), pp. 429–450.

introduced the notion in Western Europe of a new path to martyrdom, namely death in the war against infidels and for Jesus and his community. However, the notion of martyrdom penetrated the consciousness of the Crusaders only gradually. The actual term martyr was not used, although the promise of a place with the saints and heavenly salvation was made to those who died in the Crusades. Chronicles and letters of the time reflected the beginning of the acceptance of the notion of fighting and dying for a holy cause, yet the first steps were still hesitant. There was no clear promise by the Church regarding the status of the martyr. Moreover, certain circles criticized the Crusaders as motivated essentially by crude material and commercial interests, or a desire for earthly glory.[42]

In the East, by comparison, the Orthodox Christians in the Byzantine Empire, who were in the forefront of the struggle against Islam, developed an activist perception of death, with the vigorous encouragement of the emperors, especially Nicephorus II Phocas (r. 963–969). The reality of defending the territory of the empire, side by side with the important role played by militarism in Byzantine culture, led to a rejection of Christ's injunction to turn the other cheek and an openness to the notion of a cult of warrior saints. Those who fell in battle were regarded as chosen by God in the struggle against the enemies of the faith and were commemorated by iconography and monuments in the public space.[43]

By the end of the Middle Ages, the early Christian perception of martyrdom in Europe had become outdated, although the phenomenon of martyrdom continued in various new forms, especially with growing schisms in the Church that generated religious wars and the torture and burning of martyrs. Catholics, Anabaptists, and Protestants all had their own martyrs, most of whom were executed by local authorities. These martyrs were memorialized in hagiographic anthologies published during the sixteenth and seventeenth centuries. Martyrologists such as the Anglican John Foxe of England, the Calvinist Jean Crespin of France, and the Lutheran Ludwig Rabus of Germany, who saved martyrs' documents and letters from the pit of oblivion, published these materials with alterations that emphasized the

---

[42] Colin Morris, "Martyrs on the Field of Battle Before and During the First Crusade," in Wood (ed.), *Martyrs and Martyrologies*, pp. 93–104; also see Thomas Sizgorich, *Violence and Belief in Late Antiquity: Militant Devotion in Christianity and Islam* (Philadelphia: University of Pennsylvania Press, 2009); Jonathan Riley-Smith, *The First Crusade and the Idea of Crusading* (Philadelphia: University of Pennsylvania Press, 1986).

[43] See Christopher Walter, *The Warrior Saints in Byzantine Art and Tradition* (Aldershot: Ashgate, 1988).

martyrs' extreme heroism, testifying to the righteousness of the church to which they had belonged.[44]

The large number of editions of martyrs' books that were published seems to indicate that Christian martyrdom was a popular aspect of the culture of this period. All streams of Christianity celebrated their heroes, creating martyrological traditions that became part of their collective identity. Martyrdom also evoked dissonance and separate identities even when Christians from different streams lived as good neighbors.[45]

Besides describing the martyr's execution, the martyrs' books included letters written from prison, poems, and declarations of faith. These materials were edited to improve their quality and heighten their universal appeal. A survey of the letters shows that they reflected not only personal feelings but also an opportunity for the prisoners to urge their colleagues and the readership at large to display loyalty to their faith and to sacrifice their lives joyously. Their preachings were phrased in scriptural terminology imbued with religious fervor to legitimize and promote their views and rise above their personal problems. They put their trust in God and Jesus, viewing them as the core of their being, so that their martyrdom was not a journey to the unknown.[46]

---

[44] Robert Klob, "Lutheran Martyrology in the Reformation Era," in Leemans (ed.), *More than a Memory*, pp. 295–313; idem, *For All the Saints: Changing Perceptions of Martyrdom and Sainthood in the Lutheran Reformation* (Macon, GA: Mercer University Press, 1987); Susan Wabuda, "Henry Bull, Miles Coverdale and the Making of Foxe's Book of Martyrs," in Diana Wood (ed.), *Martyrs and Martyrologies*, pp. 245–258.

[45] Gregory, *Salvation at Stake*, pp. 2–8.

[46] Ibid., pp. 23–29; Klob, "Lutheran Martyrology in the Reformation Era," pp. 295–300; Wabuda, "Henry Bull, Miles Coverdale and the Making of Foxe's Book of Martyrs," pp. 245–258; David Bagchi, "Luther and the Problem of Martyrdom," in Wood (ed.), *Martyrs and Martyrologies*, pp. 209–219.

2

Dying for God in Islam

The issue of martyrs is found in Islam as well. The Arabic term for martyr, *shahid* (pl. *shuhada'*), appears in the Qur'an primarily in the sense of "witness" – that is, Muslims should act as a living testimony for the rest of mankind. Later exegetical literature, however, broadened the meaning of *shahid* to martyr. This development was apparently influenced by the Syriac word *sahda*, as well as by the Christian tradition, which emphasized the pleasures of paradise that await those who die in the cause of faith.[1] Moreover, in contrast to Christianity and Judaism, Islam sanctified martyrdom in the battle against infidels. It had none of the tenacious passivism of early Christianity. Instead of metaphorical soldiers of God, it called for actual soldiers who bore arms and used them. As Michael Bonner observes, "If the Christian Church was built over the bones of its martyrs, the Islamic community admired its martyrs as models of physical courage, relentless striving (jihad), and the individual internalization of norms."[2] The chronicles of jihad battles in the formative period of Islam contain occasional accounts of military commanders who expressed complaints and frustration about volunteers under their command who sought paradise above all, with the result that the commanders sometimes favored

---

[1] On the Qur'anic discourse of *shahid* and its evolution in extra-Qur'anic literature, see Asma Afsaruddin, "Competing Perspectives on Jihad and Martyrdom in Early Islamic Sources," in Wicker (ed.), *Witnesses to Faith?* pp. 15–31.

[2] Bonner, *Jihad in Islamic History*, p. 76. See also Cook, *Martyrdom in Islam*, pp. 14–15; Keith Lewinstein, "The Revaluation of Martyrdom in Early Islam," in Margaret Cormack (ed.), *Sacrificing the Self: Perspectives on Martyrdom and Religion* (Oxford: Oxford University Press, 2002), pp. 78–80.

using soldiers who were more constrained regarding readiness for death and thus more effective in the battlefield.[3]

Martyrdom became a key ethos in the Islamic tradition. Broadly, it emanated from the perception of death as part of the natural, preordained order, linked directly to the acts of the living and marking the beginning of the journey into the next world. The conduct of human beings in this world determines the nature of their status in the hereafter.[4] Specifically, martyrdom (*shahada*) was directly associated with wartime jihad,[5] with its parameters defined in the context of war guided by a religious imperative: to make God's word supreme, or, alternatively, to block external aggression against His believers. In this context, the Arabic term *shahid* was defined by Muslim theologians as someone whose worthiness of a place in paradise was witnessed by God or his angels, or, in a slightly different interpretation, whose good and pure intentions were witnessed by God.

Writing about martyrdom in early Islam, Michael Berenbaum and Reuven Firestone show that martyrology became a means to glorify a certain behavior, such as fulfilling one's religious duties as a Muslim, and a way of guaranteeing that those who act appropriately will enter paradise,[6] with death in the battlefield recognized as a sublime way of leaving this world. Although this is not the place to expand on the centrality of the concept of jihad in the Islamic tradition, which is laden with tracts extolling it (*fada'il al-jihad*),[7] its legal status in the context of the fundamental injunctions of Islam merits exploration.

---

[3] Bonner, *Jihad in Islamic History*, p. 76.

[4] Larry A. Platt and V. Richard Persico, *Grief in Cross-Cultural Perspectives* (New York: Garland Publishers, 1992), pp. 236–237.

[5] Although jihad as armed combat, which is the main focus of this work, became prominent in judicial literature, it constitutes only one of multiple meanings of the term jihad, which literally means "struggle" or "striving" and includes a wide range of nonviolent activities to fulfill God's will and precepts. This also applies to the Qur'anic phrase *al-jihad fi sabil Allah* (striving in the path of God). The word jihad thus has a much wider semantic content than the word *qital* (fighting).

[6] Berenbaum and Firestone, "The Theology of Martyrdom," pp. 136–142.

[7] On the doctrine of jihad, see Peters, *Jihad in Classical and Modern Islam*, pp. 1–54; Majid Khadduri, *War and Peace in the Law of Islam* (Baltimore: Johns Hopkins Press, 1955), pp. 55–73; James T. Johnson and John Kelsay (eds.), *Cross, Crescent and Sword: The Justification and Limitation of War in Western and Islamic Traditions* (New York: Greenwood Press, 1990); John Kelsay, *Islam and War: A Study in Comparative Ethics* (Louisville, KY: John Knox Press, 1993).

An examination of the positions of the Islamic legal schools shows that collective jihad (*fard kifaya*) for the purpose of expanding the authority of Islam takes precedence over all the collective commandments. In the case of personal jihad (*fard 'ayn*), if unbelievers infiltrate into a Muslim land, the entire community is obligated to join the military campaign against them, which, according to the Hanafi, the Shafi'i, and the Maliki schools, takes precedence over prayer, fasting, or pilgrimage. The Hanbalis were a step behind, calling for prayer first, because neglecting this duty places the believer outside Islam, whereas abandoning jihad is not considered to be heresy. By contrast, the noted theologian Ibn Taymiyya (d. 1328) went even further than any of the four schools by pointing to the obligation of personal jihad as second in importance only to professing belief in God and His Prophet (*shahada*).[8]

The ultimate goal of jihad for God also led to a consolidation of the basic laws regarding the forbidden and the permitted in a jihad war (*adab al–harb*), namely the type of fighting and targets, including property, civilians, and enemy prisoners. Two Qur'anic verses are important in this context: "Fight in God's cause against those who fight you, but do not overstep the limits: God does not love those who overstep the limits" (Sura 2: 190); and "Fight them until there is no more persecution, and worship is devoted to God. If they cease hostilities, there can be no [further] hostility, except towards aggressors" (Sura 2: 193).

Still, as Rudolph Peters, and especially Ella Landau-Tasseron, have shown, the issue of harming noncombatants remained unclear in Islamic legal thought. The category of persons with full immunity (*'isma*) – that is, not to be harmed – includes only Muslims, their allies, and unbelievers who have a special legal contract, whether permanent, as *dhimmis*, or temporary, as foreign merchants in Muslim territory (*aman*). Harming them involves punitive sanctions. However, if a Muslim harms a civilian in the non-Muslim enemy population, he has committed a sin and must beg mercy from God, although he is exempt from punishment. In effect, Muslim law displayed forgiveness toward killing noncombatants if this was done mistakenly or if the

---

[8] *Ibn Taymiyya, al-Fatawa* (Beirut: Dar al-Ma'rifa, n.d.), Vol. 4, pp. 607–610; idem, *Majmu'at al-fatawa* (Cairo: Maktabat Ibn Taymiyya, n.d.), Vol. 28, pp. 7–12. A similar stance was adopted by modern scholars Yusuf al-Qaradawi in *al-Da'wa*, May 1977 and 'Abdallah 'azzam in his book *Fi'l-Jihad: fiqh wa-ijtihad* (Pashawar: Maktab Khidmat al-Mujahidin, n.d.), pp. 2–4, 51–54.

noncombatants were used as human shields when this served the interest of the Muslim side.[9]

In contrast to the issue of harming noncombatants, the legal discourse
was clear and precise regarding fighters who died for their faith: their
reward was the guarantee of paradise. As written in a hadith: "He whose
feet become covered with dust for the sake of God will not be touched by
the fire of hell."[10] Any other self-imposed death – as a result of disease,
imprisonment, torture, or despair – was perceived as forbidden and
punishable by hell.

SELF-IMMOLATION: THE CONDEMNED DEATH

The prohibition of self-immolation (*tahluka, intihar*) is ingrained in the
Islamic ethic, which, like Judaism and Christianity, preaches the duty to
bear suffering and pain, since life is a gift bestowed by God, with
continuity in the hereafter. Because God is the sole authority over
human affairs, self-immolation by His creatures constitutes a blatant
violation of that authority, punishable by excommunication from the
Muslim community.[11]

The prohibition of self-immolation is cited in the Qur'an, albeit ambig-
uously and in only a few verses. Two of them are most prominent. The first
is "Spend in God's cause: do not contribute to your own destruction with
your own hands" (Sura 2: 195). Early and medieval commentaries on this
verse, supported as well by radical commentators in the twentieth century,
interpreted it as referring to refraining from the duty of assisting jihad by
financial contributions, which is tantamount to self-destruction.[12] Another

---

[9] Peters, *Jihad in Classical and Modern Islam*, pp. 19–23; Ella Landau-Tasseron, *"Non-Combatants" in Muslim Legal Thought* (Washington, DC: Hudson Institute, December 2006), pp. 1–25; also Zafir al-Qasimi, *al-Jihad wa'l-huquq al-duwaliyya al'amma fi'l-Islam* (Beirut: Dar al-'Ilm li'l-Malayin, 1982), pp. 26–32, 314–338, 521–542.

[10] Abu 'Abdallah Muhammad ibn Isma'il al-Bukhari, *Sahih al-Bukhari* (3rd. ed., Beirut: Dar Ibn Kathir, 1987), Vol. 3, p. 1035. Still, not all commentators agree that this tradition refers to death in battle; for some it merely refers to participation in battle (even if the person concerned remains alive). See, e.g., ibn Hajar al-'Asqalani, *Fath al-bari fi sharh sahih al-Bukhari* (Beirut: Dar al-Ma'rifa, 1959), Vol. 6, p. 29.

[11] On the meaning of life and death in Islam, see Muhammad Mutawalli Sha'rawi, *al-Hayat wa'l-mawt* (Cairo: Akhbar al-Yawm, 1991).

[12] Franz Rosenthal, "On Suicide in Islam," in idem, *Muslim Intellectual and Social History* (London: Variorum, 1990), pp. 239–246. For modern commentaries, see, e.g., Muhammad Rashid Rida, *Tafsir al-Qur'an al-hakim* (2nd ed., Cairo: Matb'at al-Manar, 1931–1932), Vol. 2, pp. 213–214; Sayyid Qutb, *Fi Zilal al-Qur'an* (new ed., Beirut: Dar al-Shuruq, 1986), Vol. 1, pp. 191–192, Vol. 2, pp. 638–640; Sayyid Abul A'la Mawdudi, *Towards*

interpretation, by the renowned medieval scholar Abu Hamid al-Ghazali (d.1111), was that the prohibition of self-immolation does not apply to a person who attacks a group of unbelievers even though he knows he will be killed, thereby striking fear in the hearts of the unbelievers "in that they will see his courage and will believe that the rest of the Muslims care not for preserving their lives but seek death for God, and then their might will be broken." The prohibition, al-Ghazali argues, applies only to a person who knows that his attack will not cause severe damage to the enemy, for example, if it is mounted by someone who is blind or crippled.[13]

The second prominent verse contains the prohibition: "[D]o not kill each other, for God is merciful to you" (Sura 4: 29). Here, too, Islamic commentators (including modern ones) tended to interpret the meaning of the verse not only as murdering someone (a relative or a fellow Muslim) but also as taking the money of others fraudulently. For example, Muhammad Rashid Rida (d. 1935), the Syrian Islamic revivalist, viewed the meaning of the verse as prohibiting people to kill each other, as the nation must be united and maintain mutual responsibility for one another. A murderer's act is a form of suicide, in Rida's view, because he brings a verdict of death on himself, whether by legal decree or blood revenge. Another thinker, Sayyid Qutb (d. 1966), who had a key influence on Sunni revolutionary thought, held that the verse refers to financial fraud perpetrated against the public. The verse is a link in the chain of educational and judicial legislation that warns the population against coveting the possessions of others, which God has granted them, and instead turn to God with a request to grant them what they seek. In his view, illegal profits gained by cheating, bribery, gambling, monopolies of basic goods aimed at raising their price, or charging interest are tantamount to suicide and self-destruction, for which punishment is suffering in hell.[14]

Besides the paucity of verses regarding the prohibition against suicide, the verses themselves do not refer to the punishment of the transgressor. The twentieth-century jurist Mahmud Shaltut (Shaykh al-Azhar, 1958–1963) held that this absence stems not from a diminished gravity of the crime, or from a sense that it does not merit punishment, but rather from

Understanding the Qur'an (Leicester: The Islamic Foundation, 1990), Vol. 1, pp. 154–155, Vol. 2, pp. 31–32.

[13] Abu Hamid al-Ghazali, *Ihya' 'ulum al-din* (Cairo: Mu'assasat al-Halabi, 1967), Vol. 2, p. 408.

[14] Rida, *Tafsir al-Qur'an al-hakim*, Vol. 5, pp. 43–44; Qutb, *Fi zilal al-Qur'an*, Vol. 2, pp. 638–640.

the perception that a person who commits suicide does not deserve any mention or any special warning regarding this crime.[15]

The Qur'anic implicity regarding the prohibition of suicide or self-immolation was reversed and became explicit and absolute only in the hadith literature, which cited concrete situations and punishments.[16] It dealt with prohibitions against a wounded person killing himself, against strangling oneself, against jumping off a cliff, and against jumping into a river and drowning. More generally, it stipulated that a person cannot wish for death in the event that he has suffered tragedy in this world, because if he dies, his work for God will have been cut off, whereas life adds only goodness to the believer. Moreover, if a person has performed evil deeds, the act of suicide will deprive him of an opportunity to repent. Self-immolation due to personal distress is therefore absolutely forbidden in Islamic law. Tragedy or terminal illness is an expression of God's will to torment a person with suffering. Only those who possess endurance (*sabr*), which is considered to be a lofty virtue, will be granted entry into paradise. An absence of endurance in the face of suffering and pain is viewed as Satan's success in spreading despair and doubt regarding God's ability to grant mercy. Two well-known hadiths deal with the gravity of an act of suicide. The first states:

Whoever kills himself with an iron bar, is destined to continue holding his bar in his hand and piercing his belly with the fire of hell with it, remaining there for eternity. Whoever drinks poison and kills himself, will drink it in the fire of hell, remaining there for eternity. Whoever shall throw himself off a mountain and kill himself, will be thrown into the fire of hell, remaining there for eternity.

In the second hadith, referring to the battle of Khaybar (628) in which the Muslims fought the Jews living in the Khaybar oasis located near Medina, the Prophet said about a man who presented himself as a Muslim: "This person is destined for hell." During the battle the man proved to be an exceptional fighter until he was killed. The Prophet was asked how he could have said that the man deserved hell inasmuch as he fought with such bravery. The Prophet insisted: "To hell!" One or several Muslims were about to doubt the Prophet's ruling, when suddenly someone reported that the man was not dead but was critically wounded. That night, the man could not bear his pain any longer and killed himself. When the Prophet

---

[15] Mahmud Shaltut, *al-Fatawa* (Cairo: Dar al-Qalam, n.d.), pp. 420–421.
[16] Rosenthal, "On Suicide in Islam," pp. 239–259; also Shaltut, *al-Fatawa*, pp. 419–422.

was notified about this, he said: "God is great!" Afterward, he instructed his servant Bilal to announce to the people: "Only a Muslim soul will enter paradise." This hadith was the source of the rule decreed by jurists that bravery cannot whitewash suicide.[17]

Nevertheless, Muslim commentators hesitated to define suicide as total heresy, reflected in the fact that they permitted the recitation of prayers for someone who committed suicide. For example, Ahmad ibn ʿUmar al-Ansari al-Qurtubi (d. 1258) held that someone who kills himself because he assumes this act is permitted (*halal*) is an unbeliever (*kafir*) and will remain in hell for eternity. However, someone who does so while believing that the act is not permitted is not an unbeliever, for the possibility exists that God will forgive him. Al-Qurtubi also quoted a hadith as additional proof that a person who kills himself is not an unbeliever. One of the migrants to Medina in the wake of the Prophet's preaching was al-Tufayl ibn ʿAmr al-Dawsi, together with another person from his tribe. The other man took ill and cut the joints of his fingers and expired from loss of blood. Al-Tufayl saw the man in a dream and the man appeared to be well, although his hands were concealed. The man told al-Tufayl that God forgave him because he had migrated to join the Prophet, but his hands are covered because he was told: "What you have spoiled will never be repaired." Al-Tufayl recounted the dream to the Prophet, who then said: "O God! Please pardon him for his hands!" Al-Qurtubi viewed this hadith as proof that God can pardon even a grave sin, as the act that was perpetrated is not counted as polytheism (*shirk*).[18]

These interpretations, however, did not blur the strict prohibition against self-immolation. Its perpetrators were condemned to be among the last Muslims who would leave hell. In Rosenthal's view, religions that persuaded their loyal adherents regarding the destructive results of suicide managed to lessen its prevalence.[19]

---

[17] Ahmad ibn ʿUmar al-Ansari al-Qurtubi, *al-Mufhim* (Cairo: Dar al-Kitab al-Misri, 1992), Vol. 1, p. 310; Abu ʿAbdallah Ahmad ibn Hanbal, *Musnad Ahmad* (Beirut: Muʾassasat al-Risala, 2001), Vol. 12, p. 416, Vol. 13, pp. 453–454, Vol. 16, pp. 153, 224. The eleventh-century Hanafi scholar Shams al-Din al-Sarakhsi ruled that a fighter who is wounded is prohibited from asking his friend to release him from his suffering, as he will thereby violate the prohibition against suicide. At a later stage, suicide appears in the list of grave sins (*kabaʾir*). Scholars even debated whether it is graver than murder. Etan Kohlberg, "Martyrdom and Self-sacrifice in Classical Islam," *Peʿamim* 75 (Spring 1988), pp. 20–21 (in Hebrew).

[18] Al-Qurtubi, *al-Mufhim*, Vol. 1, pp. 322–324.

[19] Nevertheless, Rosenthal notes that at the start of the tenth century, which ushered in a growing climate of political insecurity in the Muslim world, the percentage of suicides rose.

MARTYRDOM: THE EXALTED DEATH

As for the other, sanctified type of sacrifice, early and medieval Islamic traditions distinguished between two types of fighters: one who was prepared to endanger his life for God and the faith but who also wished to emerge from the battle alive – that is, victorious – and the fighter who not only was prepared to sacrifice his life but actually sought an opportunity to do so. This behavior is known as seeking martyrdom (*talab al-shahada*). Everyone who joins the battle, Muslim theologians stressed, will be rewarded, but the greater reward will be the province of the fighter who seeks death and eventually finds it.[20] Such fighters are the best, according to one hadith, for they place themselves in the front line and do not retreat until they are killed.[21]

Their reward is great. It includes being purified from all sins with the first drop of blood that is shed, as "the sword cleanses sins"; being granted the absence of torment in the grave; being spared from judgment day; being wreathed in a crown of honor (*taj al-waqar*) whose every jewel is worth more than this world in its entirety; being married to seventy-two virgins with beautiful eyes (*hur 'in*); and lastly, having a seat of honor in paradise next to the prophets and the righteous. This last incentive is the pinnacle for the *shahid*s, as they are "knowers of God" (*al-'arifun*).[22] It is in this context that the verse, "Whoever obeys God and the Messenger will be among those He has blessed: the messengers, the truthful, those who bear witness to the truth, and the righteous – what excellent companions these are!" (Sura 4: 69), is to be understood. Indeed, the term *shahid* in this verse and others, as discussed at the start of the chapter, is understood to be "witness," as was also explained by the Qur'anic commentator Fakhr al-Din

---

Moreover, there are a large number of reported cases of suicide committed in the expectation of unavoidable death preceded by cruel torture. Blame, or any commentary at all, is hardly ever applied to this type of self-inflicted death. Apparently, Rosenthal argues, "old tradition of history and myth which offers many examples of self-inflicted death in the face of inescapable fate or the threat of dishonor has proved to be stronger than religious injunctions." Rosenthal, "On Suicide in Islam," pp. 251–259.

[20] Berenbaum and Firestone, "The Theology of Martyrdom," pp. 140–142.

[21] 'Ali ibn Abi Bakr al-Haythami, *Majmu' al-zawa'id* (Cairo: Dar al-Rayyan li'l-Turath, 1987), Vol. 5, p. 292.

[22] See Hasan Khalid, *al-Shahid fi'l-Islam* (Beirut: Dar al-'Ilm li'l-Malayin, 1971), pp. 37, 69–76; and the hadith on the six merits of the martyr in Muhammad ibn 'Isa al-Tirmidhi, *Sunan al-Tirmidhi* (Beirut: Dar Ihya' al-Turath al-'Arabi, 1991), Vol. 4, pp. 187–188; also Ibn Qayyim al-Jawziyya, *Zad al-ma'ad fi hady khayr al-'ibad* (Cairo: al-Matba'a al-Misriyya, 1959–1960), Vol. 2, pp. 62–64.

al-Razi (d. 1209). In his view, *shahada* is not necessarily the result of a violent death. A *shahid* is someone who bears witness that Islam is the true religion. Sometimes he bears witness by means of intellectual proofs and sometimes by means of the sword. The *shahid*s are those who play the role of witnesses that there is no God save Him (*al-qa'imuna bil-qist*).[23]

However, other Muslim commentators understood the term *shahid* as referring to martyr, an interpretation that became more important and widespread in later Islam. For example, in interpreting Sura (4: 69), cited earlier, Nasir al-Din al-Baydawi (d. 1316) observed that God divided the four groups mentioned (prophets, just men, witnesses, and righteous) into descending categories according to their status in knowledge and deeds: the prophets, who are endowed with knowledge and the most perfect deeds; just men, whose souls reached the apex of cognition through the observation of miracles and by taming and purifying the soul until they were able to see things as they were; martyrs (rather than witnesses), whose meticulous obedience and demonstration of truth led them to sacrifice themselves for the elevation of God's word; and the righteous, who dedicated their days to obeying God and their possessions to fulfilling His will.[24]

Two other Qur'anic verses are important in this context. The first is "There are men among the believers who honoured their pledge to God; some of them have fulfilled it by death, and some are still waiting. They have not changed in the least" (Sura 33: 23). According to al-Baydawi, the term "vow" may be defined as a commitment to fight for God until death, as demonstrated by the Prophet's relatives Hamza ibn 'Abd al-Muttalib and Mus'ab ibn 'Umayr in the Battle of Uhud (625).[25] The second verse is "God has purchased the persons and possessions of the believers in return

---

[23] Fakhr al-Din al-Razi, *Mafatih al-ghayb: al-tafsir al-kabir* (3rd ed., Beirut: Dar Ihya' al-Turath al-'Arabi, 2000), Vol. 10, p. 135.

[24] Nasir al-Din 'Abdallah ibn 'Umar al-Baydawi, *Tafsir al-Baydawi* (Beirut: Dar al-Fikr, 1996), Vol. 2, pp. 213–215; also al-Tirmidhi, *Sunan al-Tirmidhi*, Vol. 4, p. 187. On praise of the *shahid* in the hadith literature, see Abu Bakr 'Abd al-Razzaq ibn Hammam, *al-Musannaf* (Beirut: al-Majlis al-'Ilmi, 1970), Vol. 5, pp. 263–267; Abu Bakr Muhammad al-Sarakhsi, *al-Mabsut li'l-Sarakhsi* (Beirut: Dar al-Ma'rifa, 1985/1986), Vol. 2, pp. 49–56; Muhammad 'Abd al-Rahim, *Arba'un hadithan fi fadl al-shahid wa'l-shahada* (Damascus: al-Hikma, 1995); also Khalid, *al-Shahid fi'l-Islam*, pp. 103–104.

[25] A modern-day commentator, Muhammad Baqir Behbudi, argued that the verse refers explicitly to martyrs. In contrast, Behbudi's colleague, Muhammad Asad, defined the vow more broadly, namely all efforts involved in devotion to God's cause. M. B. Behbudi, *The Qur'an – A New Interpretation* (Richmond, UK: Curzon Press, 1997), p. 251; M. Asad, *The Message of the Qur'an* (Gibraltar: Dar al-Andalus, 1980), p. 594, n. 26.

for the Garden – they fight in God's way: they kill and are killed" (Sura 9: 111). Most of the Muslim commentators noted that this verse deals with holy war and sacrificing one's soul in return for going to heaven. Others ascribed a more general meaning to the verse as dealing with the striving of believers to follow all God's commands, including jihad. However, there was a consensus among earlier commentaries that this is an attractive transaction for the believer, albeit one-sided in that the believer is not allowed to bargain over it but to show total obeisance to God.[26] Clearly, the believer must be prepared to go to battle; signs of faintheartedness were viewed by Muslim scholars with disfavor.

Notably, a similar stance was adopted by Maimonides in Judaism. Maimonides ruled that anyone who begins to rethink or hesitate during a war, and thereby panics, violates a prohibition of omission. Moreover, if a person did not achieve victory and did not fight with all his heart, he is considered as responsible for the slaughter of all. However, in Maimonides' view, "anyone who fights with all his heart without fear and with the sole intent of sanctifying God's name is guaranteed to be safe from harm and untouched by trouble and will build a righteous house in Israel and he and his descendents will merit forever and will earn immortality in the next world." Gerald Blidstein points out that it is difficult to find support for these rulings – namely, a fearless ethos for fighters and the guarantee of security in this world and immortality in the next – in the Jewish tradition. Blidstein therefore argues that the Maimonidean rulings regarding war were influenced by the writer's Muslim environment, which attributed a highly significant status to holy war.[27]

Most Muslim sources, as Etan Kohlberg observes, do not even hint at the possibility that pride in the death of a loved one while fighting in a holy war can be accompanied by a sense of grief and loss.[28] For people to overcome the most primal human impulse – the dread of death – they must believe that the death was worthwhile. In essence, therefore, these martyrs become living martyrs. In referring to the Qur'anic verse – "[Prophet],

[26] Al-Baydawi, *Tafsir al-Baydawi*, Vol. 4, p. 370; Jalal al-Din al-Mahalli and Jalal al-Din al-Suyuti, *Tafsir al-Jalalayn* (Cairo: Maktabat Misr, n.d.), p. 127; Muqatil ibn Sulayman ibn Bashir al-Azdi al-Balkhi, *Tafsir Muqatil ibn Sulayman* (Beirut: Dar Ihya' al-Turath, 2003), Vol. 2, p. 198; also Cook, *Martyrdom in Islam*, pp. 18–19.

[27] Gerald J. Blidstein, *Political Concepts in Maimonidean Halakha* (Ramat-Gan: Bar-Ilan University, 1983), pp. 233–234, 261–263 (in Hebrew).

[28] Etan Kohlberg, "Martyrs and Martydom in Classical Islam," in A. Destro and M. Pesce (eds.), *Religions and Cultures* (Binghamton, NY: Global Publications, 2000), pp. 98–100.

do not think of those who have been killed in God's way as dead. They are alive with their Lord" (Sura 3: 169) – some commentators hold that the word "living" (*ahya*) in this verse applies to the body and that this approach is reflected in the traditions which assert that the martyrs will enjoy the company of black-eyed virgins in paradise even before the resurrection of the dead. According to another tradition, the Prophet said that even before the blood of the martyrs is dry, two maidens will approach him bringing fine clothing for him to wear. Yet another tradition holds that only the souls of martyrs remain alive. They rise directly to heaven, where they rest in the bodies of green birds near the throne of honor until the resurrection of the dead, when they are destined to return to the bodies of the martyrs. Clearly, then, the martyr's reward is great. He is situated at the pinnacle of the 100 levels, which the Prophet reserved for the fighters for God, and they populate the center of paradise and its loftiest portion (*firdaws*).[29]

The fighter who is killed in a jihad campaign acquires an exceptional status not only in the next world but in this world as well. He merits special burial ceremonies. Such martyrs are known as martyrs of this world and the next (*shuhada* al-dunya wa'l-*akhira*) and are thus differentiated from other types of martyrs – those of the next world only (*shuhada* al-*akhira*). To be considered fallen in battle, a fighter must fulfill certain conditions. The most important is the intent (*niyya*) of a fighter to show courage; however, if he lacks true belief, he will nevertheless be buried as a *shahid* – for no one can test a person's heart – but he will not earn redemption in the next world, and some say he will even be judged as destined for hell. At best he might be considered an apparent martyr. Another condition is that the death of the fighter must be directly and immediately caused by his wounds.

The intention to elevate the word of God was considered the ultimate test of authentic martyrdom, although jurists such as Ibn Hajar al-'Asqalani (d. 1449) did not reject the possibility of other motives so long as they were secondary, such as a desire for booty, status, the display of courage, anger, or the protection of wealth, family, or land.[30]

---

[29] Al-Bukhari, *Sahih al-Bukhari*, Vol. 6, p. 2700. See also the hadith cited in 'Abd al-Salam Harun, *al-Alf al-mukhtara min Sahih al-Bukhari* (Cairo: Dar al-Ma'arif, 1960), Vol. 4, pp. 62–63.

[30] Al-'Asqalani, *Fath al-bari*, Vol. 6, p. 28; quoted in Ayoub, "Martyrdom in Christianity and Islam," p. 70.

The hadith literature highlights many episodes of fighters who looked forward to death on the battlefield. A typical hadith relates to ʿAwf ibn al-Harith, one of the earliest Muslims, who, together with his two brothers, were among the first to obey the call of the Prophet and join the battle at Badr (624). Before the battle, al-Harith asked the Prophet, "What human deed will cause The Lord to laugh?" The Prophet replied, "Let him fight the enemy without any armor." On hearing these words, al-Harith cast aside his shield and fought against the infidels until he was killed.[31]

As in the case of early Christianity, these episodes evoked concern among jurists regarding blurring the line between self-sacrifice and suicide. However, the Islamic legal discourse did not disqualify the wish for a deliberate death from the incidence of martyrdom, as did early Christianity; rather, it set boundaries and rules.

The primary parameter was that the attributes of martyrdom were to be considered specifically in the context of holy war. This was reflected in rulings in various cases. Was a fighter permitted to attack a large enemy force? According to the learned Hanafi scholar Muhammad ibn al-Hasan al-Shaybani (d. 805), a lone person is permitted to attack even a thousand of the enemy's men if there is a reasonable chance that he will stay alive or will cause damage to the enemy before he is killed. If, however, there is a reasonable chance that he will be killed without causing damage to the enemy, then his act is deplorable, as he is exposing himself to death without the expectation of benefit to the Muslims.[32] Another renowned scholar, Muhyi al-Din Ibn al-ʿArabi (d. 1148), compiled several opinions reflecting the influence of the Maliki school, to which he belonged, ruling that there is nothing wrong in a lone fighter attacking a large enemy force on the condition that the fighter is devoted to God, bears arms, and has physical or internal strength. In the absence of these conditions, his act is considered self-destruction and thus prohibited. Other Maliki scholars demanded only that the fighter be sincere in intent even when it is clear to him that he will not overcome a whole army. His goal must be to harm an enemy soldier. Ibn ʿArabi also contended that a fighter who joins the campaign with the intention of becoming a martyr might thereby have a positive influence in that not only will he harm one of the enemy soldiers but also he will reinforce the Muslims' determination, while weakening the

---

[31] Abu Bakr ʿAbdallah ibn Muhammad ibn Abi Shayba, *Musannaf ibn Abi Shayba* (Riyadh: Maktabat al-Rushd, 1989), Vol. 4, p. 223; Abu Jaʿfar Muhammad ibn Jarir al-Tabari, *Taʾrikh al-rusul waʾl-muluk* (Cairo: Dar al-Maʿarif, 1968), Vol. 2, p. 33.

[32] Kohlberg, "Martyrdom and Self-sacrifice in Classical Islam," p. 22.

spirit of their rivals. Once the enemy soldiers realize what a single Muslim can do, they might fear the outcome of a coordinated Muslim attack all the more.[33]

The motif of the usefulness of harming enemy forces is also cited in Ibn Taymiyya's (d. 1328) perception of *inghimas* (plunging into the enemy) – namely an individual or group who plunges into unbelievers' forces that outnumber their own. In Ibn Taymiyya's view, this is permitted when it benefits Islam, even if the fighter or fighters assume they will be killed. To remove any doubt that such an act is martyrdom and not suicide, the author describes three possible situations in which *inghimas* is permitted based on a consensus of all the legal schools and supported as well in the Qur'an and the Sunna: The first situation is when a believer charges alone into a group of infidels and "disappears in their midst like an object that sinks into something flooding over him." The second is when a believer kills one of the commanders of the infidels, and he is certain that he himself will be killed. In the third situation the believer, whose comrades have been defeated and have retreated, remains to fight the enemy alone or with a few people. They believe they will be killed, but they also know that they will cause severe damage.[34]

To reinforce the principle of *inghimas*, Ibn Taymiyya emphasizes that God ordered the Muslims to carry out jihad in life and in property even if this endangers the fighters. On the contrary, death in the battlefield is an inseparable part of jihad. The Qur'an says that fleeing from death is prohibited and ineffective, because "you will be permitted to enjoy [life] for a short while" (Sura 33: 16). Those who do so commit a severe sin, and "Hell will be his home, a wretched destination" (Sura 8: 15–16).[35]

Ibn Taymiyya also cites important battles, such as the Battle in Badr, in which the unbelievers were at least three times as numerous as the Muslims, yet the battle became one of the most glorious in the history of Islam. This was also the case with the battle of the Pit (*al-Khandaq*) in 627 against Quraysh and their allies, as well as against the Jewish of Qurayza who violated the treaty with the Muslims. As a rule, Ibn Taymiyya concluded, the act of *inghimas* was a known norm during the time of the Prophet and of the caliphs who came after him.[36] Clearly, Ibn Taymiyya,

---

[33] Ibid. Also Bonner, *Jihad in Islamic History*, pp. 77–78.

[34] Ibn Taymiyya, *Qaʿida fiʾl-inghimas fiʾl-ʿaduww hal yubah?* (Riyad: Maktabat al-Salaf, 2002), pp. 23–31. See also Rebecca Molloy, "Deconstructing Ibn Taymiyya's Views on Suicidal Missions," *CTC Sentinel* 2/3 (2009), pp. 16–19.

[35] Ibn Taymiyya, *Qaʿida fiʾl-inghimas*, pp. 39–41.

[36] Ibid., pp. 45–47.

as Ibn al-ʿArabi and other jurists, approved of *inghimas* only in the battle-field, only in situations of numerical inferiority, and only when Islam would benefit from it.

Beyond its operative importance in the battlefield, the ethos of martyr-dom also served as "cultural capital" and had a recruitment function in heightening morale, reinforcing collective solidarity, and sharpening the division between the "us" (the good) and the "them" (the evil). Moreover, martyrdom was bound up with another moral duty that was no less central: to command right and forbid wrongdoing, defined by al-Ghazali as "the most important pillar of religion." This imperative implies self-sacrifice, for a person who gives up his life to fulfill it is considered a martyr. By contrast, a person who fears death and does not try to dissuade evildoers violates a prohibition (*haram*). Al-Ghazali, relying on hadith literature, inferred that the Prophet defined those who rise up against a despotic ruler with the demand to forbid wrongdoing as "the noblest martyrs of all in the eyes of God." Their status in paradise will be as follows:

Each one of them is to be found in a room that is above the rest of the rooms, above the rooms of the martyrs, with each room having 300,000 doors made of hard, transparent, colored precious stones and green emeralds, with a light above each door. Each one of them marries three hundred young virgins with dark eyes, who each say to him each time he looks at them: Do you remember the day when you commanded right and forbade wrongdoing?[37]

In this context, the Qur'an states: "[Believers], you are the best community singled out for people: you order what is right, forbid what is wrong, and believe in God. If the People of the Book had also believed, it would have been better for them. For although some of them do believe, most of them are lawbreakers" (Sura 3:110).[38] This verse embodies all the necessary justifications for martyrdom: the moral superiority of the Muslims over

[37] Al-Ghazali, *Ihya' ʿulum al-din*, Vol. 2, p. 396. Notably, the subject of *hur ʿin* (fair black-eyed women) is presented in the Qur'an as part of a series of pleasures that await the believer in paradise and is not necessarily connected to martyrs only. The connection with martyrs was developed in the Islamic context through the hadith, as represented earlier and elsewhere, and was adopted by modern Islamic movements as part of the projection of a masculine, courageous image of the fighter.

[38] Al-Ghazali, *Ihya' ʿulum al-din*, Vol. 2, pp. 393–453. For the relevant hadiths, see ibid., pp. 396–397. For a detailed treatment of the imperative of "forbidding wrong," see Michael Cook, *Commanding Right and Forbidding Wrong in Islamic Thought* (Cambridge: Cambridge University Press, 2000); also R. C. Martin, "The Religious Foundation of War, Peace, and Statecraft in Islam," in Kelsay and Johnson (eds.), *Just War and Jihad*, pp. 92–93, 97.

other people, the explicit command to uproot all indecent behavior, and the deviation of many "people of the book" from God's path.[39]

IDEOLOGY AND HISTORY

Retrospectively, the twin ideals of jihad and martyrdom did not necessarily determine the course of Muslim history. The term martyr acquired other attributes besides dying on the battlefield in wars against unbelievers, for example, by the Kharijites, the Sufis, and the Shi'is. The Kharijites were an early militant puritanical sect that sanctioned the right of the believers to depose a caliph who had deviated from the right path and also branded Muslims who committed a mortal sin as apostates (s. *murtadd*, pl. *murtaddun*). They advocated an activist conception of death stemming from a scornful view of life in this world and a desire to exchange it for eternal life in paradise. As such they were referred to as *shurat* (vendors).[40]

Sufism introduced a new concept of martyrs – "living martyrs," a term applied in particular to ascetic and mystic circles to describe people who battled their baser instincts. In the Sufi view, the wayfarer's progress along the various stages of the mystical path involves restraining the *nafs* (soul; baser self), which is perceived as a powerful, lustful, and impulsive entity. This struggle constitutes the great meritorious war (*al-jihad al-akbar*), which is more difficult and more obscure than the small meritorious war (*al-jihad al-asghar*). The taming of the soul is reflected in prolonged fasts, abstinence from pleasurable foods, reclusiveness, standing in prayer for hours, and so forth, which are the primary means for removing the barriers between man and his creator. If these measures should lead to death, it will be a martyr's death. In the view of Sahl al-Tustari (d. 896), all good deeds performed for God involve a battle with the soul. No battle is easier than a battle by the sword, and no battle is more difficult than the struggle with one's soul.[41]

Shi'ism, for its part, bestowed the term martyr on believers who were killed in confrontations between Muslim factions and nurtured the

[39] See, e.g., Hasan Ayyub, *al-Jihad wa'l-fida'iyya fi'l-Islam* (2nd ed., Beirut: Dar al-Nadwa al-Jadida, 1983), p. 162; *The Hamas Covenant* (n.p., August 1988), introductory section.

[40] G. Levi Della Vida, "Khāridjites," in *The Encyclopaedia of Islam* 4 (1997), pp. 1074–1077; Lewinstein, "The Revaluation of Martyrdom in Early Islam," pp. 84–86.

[41] Abu Muhammad Sahl ibn 'Abdallah al-Tustari, *Tafsir al-Qur'an al-'Azim* (Cairo: Dar al-Kutub al-'Arabiyya al-Kubra, 1911), p. 43. On *jihad al-nafs* in the Sufi tradition, see Sara Sviri, *The Sufis: An Anthology* (Tel Aviv: Tel Aviv University, 2008), pp. 295–306 (in Hebrew).

paradigmatic martyrdom of the disempowered and tyrannized. Self-sacrifice and martyrdom served as the backbone of the Shiʻi stream practically from its beginnings with the assassination in 661 of ʻAli ibn Abi Talib, son-in-law and cousin of the Prophet. Shiʻi opposition to the Umayyad and Abbasid dynasties resulted in a long, pedigreed list of martyrs of ʻAli's descendants, honored with devotion to this day. This pedigree enhanced the holiness of ʻAli's dynasty, which was essentially derived from upholding divine knowledge and providing continuity and legitimation throughout the centuries. The most glorified martyr was Imam Husayn, son of ʻAli and grandson of the Prophet, who fought the Umayyad tyranny and was killed in the battle of Karbala in 680, known thereafter as the "prince of martyrs."[42]

The Karbala paradigm, or "complex," in Hamid Dabashi's terminology,[43] marked the split of the Shiʻa from the Sunna and the greater spread of the practice of self-sacrifice among the Shiʻis. Husayn's death was commemorated as a tragedy, codifed and memorialized by the ʻashura symbols and rituals of mourning, weeping, and self-flagellation. Whereas the Sunna perception of the martyr was as a victorious figure whose death was to be celebrated joyously, the dominant Shiʻa perception in premodern history was one of redemptive sorrow and mourning.

Despite the revolutionary potential of Shiʻi martyrdom, the Twelvers, or Imamis (the largest Shiʻi group)[44] adopted a policy of noninterference in politics, showing a preference for compromise and a low profile in its historical relationships with the Abbasids. Its priority was the practice of the Shiʻi creed and group survival. In tandem, a perception of martyrdom developed in Shiʻi discourse, which held that adherence to the Shiʻa faith during one's lifetime is of equal value to jihad in the battlefield and endows the believer with the title of *shahid*, or martyr, whose status is exalted and equal to that of the fighters alongside the Prophet at the beginning of Islam. Shiʻa thereby offered the believer an alternative, convenient, and safe path of spiritual rather than physical jihad by which to attain the status of martyr. This approach complemented its quietist (*quʻud*) policy. By contrast, and as part of the reinforcement of the Shiʻa identity, and hence the

[42] Cook, *Martyrdom in Islam*, pp. 53–58.
[43] Hamid Dabashi, *Shiʻism: A Religion of Protest* (Cambridge, MA: The Belknap Press of Harvard University Press, 2011), pp. 79–90.
[44] The Twelvers are named after the twelfth Imam, Muhammad al-Mahdi, who was believed to have gone into a state of occultation (*ghayba*) in 874 and is expected to return at the end of time as a messianic imam who will restore justice and equality on earth.

"true faith," the ineligibility of a non-Shi'i Muslim to attain martyr status – even through jihad – was emphasized.[45]

The appearance of various types of martyrs – ascetics, or those who died as a result of internal wars among Muslims – resulted in a more flexible perception of martyrdom. Even the type of death on the battlefield became less of an issue in light of historical circumstances. The ongoing war against unbelievers proved to be impractical and was frequently neglected in favor of armistices and peace agreements.

The historical reality also influenced the legal discourse. As early as the end of the eighth century, a quietist tendency appeared, questioning the status of jihad. As Jacqueline Chabbi (1995), and thereafter Roy Mottahedeh and Ridwan al-Sayyid (2001) pointed out, religious jurists in the Hijaz (primarily in Medina) and in the widespread Maliki school asserted that the worthiest form of piety is purification, prayer, and one's presence in the mosque, and not necessarily warfare on the frontier.

They also challenged the demanding character of jihad, narrowing its parameters to defensive warfare only. The backdrop to this development was the jurists' reservations regarding the legitimacy of the Umayyad regime, including the transfer of the seat of the capital from Medina to Damascus. The Hijazi scholars criticized the increasingly dominant line adopted by their colleagues in Syria – namely their desire to intensify the fighting along the front against the Byzantines in the belief that aggressive warfare was essential – whereas the Hijazi view of jihad was as an ascetic practice. Moreover, the growing focus on the management of the Islamic state and its fiscal affairs, rather than military campaigns, and the coalescence of the perception regarding the "realm of Islam" (in which the law of Islam prevailed) and the "realm of war" (the territories inhabited by infidels) also reflected the weakening perception of an ongoing war against unbelievers and the aim to place the entire universe under Islamic

---

[45] Roy Vilozny, "A Ši'i Life Cycle According to al-Barqi's Kitab al-Mahasin," *Arabica* 54/3 (2007), pp. 385–390; Maria Massi Dakake, *The Charismatic Community: Shi'ite Identity in Early Islam* (New York: State University of New York Press, 2007), pp. 177–189. With the advance of European imperialism in the early nineteenth century, however, the quietist orientation, which was adopted by the Shi'i 'ulama' in light of the doctrine of the Hidden Imam, began to change, and the 'ulama' became increasingly involved politically. The change was reflected in particular during the Qajar period (1796–1925), although it was not sustained consistently. Most of the 'ulama' resumed a quietist policy when possible and avoided politics until the 1960s, with the appearance of Ayatollah Khomeini. See Vanessa Martin, *Islam and Modernism* (London: Tauris, 1989), pp. 11–35; chapter 3 in this book.

rule. Other contributing factors included the halt of new conquests, military setbacks (on the Byzantine frontier, in Western Europe, and in Central Asia), and the disbanding of Arab tribal armies, mainly in the ninth and tenth centuries.[46]

Battlefield martyrdom reappeared periodically, led mainly by subversive and dissident groups on the margins of the Islamic spectrum for whom martyrdom was a powerful lever in cementing loyalty and internal cohesion. The most prominent example in the late eleventh and twelfth centuries was the Assassins (Nizaris), a radical offshoot of the Ismaʿili (Sevener) Shiʿi sect in northern Persia. The Assassins mounted murderous attacks against political leaders who were perceived as infidels and tyrants in the certain knowledge that the attacks would result in the perpetrators' death. Such self-sacrifice placed the Assassins out of reach. They could not be stopped, only feared. Personal survival, or the failure of an attack, was viewed by this radical sect as a disgrace. Ultimately, the Assassins failed to undermine Sunni hegemony and were perceived as a fanatical cult in Islamic history. They were destroyed almost entirely in Persia by the Mongols during the second half of the thirteenth century and in Syria by the Mamluks in the final third of that century.

Meanwhile, the de facto waning of the ethos of jihad and martyrdom in the battlefield continued.[47] The religious compensation for believers was provided by elevating the status of the "greater jihad," namely the struggle of the believer with his baser instincts. Moreover, the parameters of martyrdom were expanded to include not only military martyrdom but also death while carrying out the duties of worship, such as praying, fasting, and the pursuit of learning (*talab al-ʿilm*), or as a result of disaster or disease such as drowning, fire, childbirth, accident, or plague.[48] Some of these, and other types, of death assigned to *shahada* were to be found in early hadith literature, for example, in the compilations of Malik ibn Ans (d. 796), ʿAbd al-Razzaq al-Sanʿani (d. 827), Ibn Abi Shayba (d. 850), and

[46] J. Chabbi, "Ribat," in *The Encyclopaedia of Islam* 8 (1995), mainly pp. 495–496; Roy P. Mottahedeh and Ridwan al-Sayyid, "The Idea of the Jihad in Islam before the Crusade," in Angeliki E. Laiou and Roy P. Mottahedeh (eds.), *The Crusades from the Perspective of Byzantium and the Muslim World* (Washington, DC: Dumbarton Oaks, 2001), pp. 23–29. See also Lewinstein, "The Revaluation of Martyrdom in Early Islam," pp. 80–84.

[47] Bernard Lewis, *The Assassins: A Radical Sect in Islam* (New York: Basic Books, 1976); Karin Andriolo, "Murder by Suicide: Episodes from Muslim History," *American Anthropologist* 104/3 (September 2002), pp. 737–738.

[48] Lewinstein, "The Revaluation of Martyrdom in Early Islam," p. 81.

Isma'il ibn Muhammad al-Isbahani (d. 1141).[49] Several jurists, exemplified by Taqi al-Din al-Subki (d. 1370), went so far as to delegitimize self-sacrifice as a lofty value, holding that persuading a person to convert to Islam by peaceful means is preferable to self-sacrifice, based on the hadith: "The ink of scholars is better than the ink of martyrs."[50] The varied types of *shahada* were compiled in an orderly fashion by Jalal al-Din al-Suyuti (d. 1505) in his book *Abwab al-sa'ada fi asbab al-shahada* (The Gates of Happiness Concerning the Circumstances of Martyrdom), which cites some sixty categories of *shahid*.[51]

However, the ethos of jihad and self-sacrifice in confronting the infidels in the battlefield continued to hold an elevated status in the hadith and in judicial literature, as distinct from various categories of noncombatant martyrs. It gained new momentum during the Crusader and Mongol invasions of the medieval period and later in the Ottoman drive to regain and expand territory from the fourteenth to seventeenth centuries. With the rise of European imperialism, followed by the thrust toward nationalism during the nineteenth century, it lost ground again. By then, episodes of jihad and self-sacrifice were mainly the province of revivalist and anti-colonial movements, especially on the fringes of the Islamic world, as in Africa, South and Central Asia, and the Far East.[52]

Of special interest in this context is the Mahdiyya movement in Sudan. The Mahdiyya was a messianic movement founded in the late nineteenth century by Muhammad Ahmad ibn 'Abdallah, who proclaimed himself Mahdi (divinely appointed guide).[53] The movement had an apocalyptic character in its vision of the end of days and the creation of a kingdom of

[49] Malik ibn Anas, *Muwatta' al-Imam Malik* (Beirut: Mu'assasat al-Risala, 1992), Vol. 1, p. 393; al-San'ani, *Musannaf*, Vol. 5, pp. 268–270; Ibn Abi Shayba, *Musannaf*, Vol. 1, p. 161; Isma'il ibn Muhammad al-Isbahani, *al-Targhib wa'l-tarhib* (Cairo: Dar al-Hadith, 1993), Vol. 1, p. 192.

[50] Al-Subki quoted in Etan Kohlberg, *Suicide and Self-sacrifice in Islamic Tradition* (Jerusalem: Institute for Asian and African Studies, 1987), p. 74 (in Hebrew).

[51] Jalal al-Din al-Suyuti, *Abwab al-sa'ada fi asbab al-shahada* (Cairo: al-Maktaba al-Qayyima, 1987).

[52] On these jihadi episodes and movements, see Peter Von Sivers, "The Realm of Justice: Apocalyptic Revolts in Algeria (1849–1879)," *Humaniora Islamica* 1 (1973), pp. 47–60; Julia Clancy-Smith, "Saints, Mahdis, and Arms: Religion and Resistance in Nineteenth-Century North Africa," in Ira M. Lapidus and Edmund Burke, III (eds.), *Islam, Politics and Social Movements* (Berkeley: University of California Press, 1988), pp. 60–80; David Cook, *Understanding Jihad* (Berkeley: University of California Press, 2005), pp. 73–92.

[53] On the Mahdiyya, see, e.g., P. M. Holt, *A Modern History of Sudan* (2nd ed., London: Weidenfeld and Nicolson, 1967), pp. 77–108.

justice with a fitting reward in paradise for the fighters, thereby acquiring added motivation by its supporters. The Sudanese Mahdi declared that "Muslims must think about the next world, as this world is coming to an end, for the very appearance of the Mahdi is one of the most pronounced signs of the day of judgment."[54] Whoever fails to allocate a portion of his possessions to equip the fighting forces – a failure that testifies to a weak faith in God – does harm to himself in the next world. An even graver judgment is the province of anyone who shirks jihad and self-sacrifice without justification, as he is considered to have committed a grave sin. He is in the same category as an idol worshipper or a hypocrite. He is obliged to repent and ask for mercy. Martyrdom is the greatest act in the world, and the encounter with God is the greatest favor of all. Charging at the enemy does not reduce the life-span of the attackers, just as fear of attacking does not add to the life-span of the cowards. "While in fear there is disgrace, in attack there is honor," the Mahdi wrote,[55] quoting the following hadith:

God summons the dwellers in paradise on the day of the resurrection of the dead, and the latter come with all their decorations and God will then say: "Where are all my slaves, who were killed for me, were harmed for me and carried out jihad for me? Did they enter paradise?" Then they enter, coming to him without giving an account of their deeds and without suffering in a grave. Afterwards, the angels come and say: "O our lord, we praise them day and night, and sanctify you. Who are these, whom you have favored over us?" God says: "These fought for me and were harmed for me." Then the angels come to the martyrs from every gate and say: "Peace be with you by the grace of the suffering you bore, how good is the reward of the next world."[56]

The afterlife was also the concept by which the Mahdi sought to motivate his soldiers in a determined struggle against the Egyptian and British forces in Sudan. Those who fell were defined by the Mahdi as heirs of the Prophet's companions (*sahaba*), who, by discarding everything that invalidates the worship of God, displayed a disdain for life in the present world and a longing for God and the company of the Prophet. The swords were undecorated, reflecting the Mahdi's puritan attitude toward the act of sacrifice, which must be for God only and not for self-enhancement in this world;

---

[54] Al-Mahdi, *Manshurat al-Imam al-Mahdi al-ahkam wa'l-adab* (Khartum: Wizarat al-Dakhiliyya, 1964), Vol. 3, p. 65.

[55] Al-Mahdi, *Manshurat*, Vol. 3, pp. 13–14, 64–65, 234–236.

[56] Ibid., p. 111. The hadith appears in Abu 'Abadallah Muhmmad Hakim al-Naysaburi, *al-Mustadrak 'ala al-sahihayn* (Beirut: Dar al-Kutub al-'Ilamiyya, 1990), Vol. 2, p. 81.

otherwise, there is no certainty of the *shahid* entering paradise, and even if so, whether his level might be lower than that of God's chosen few.[57]

In the Indian subcontinent, two leaders of jihad, Sayyid Ahmad and Shah Ismail, became icons of self-sacrifice in southern Asia when they fell in a battle against the Sikhs in May 1831 and were commemorated as the martyrs of Balakot in northwest Pakistan. The jihad movement, which sought to establish Islam there, ultimately failed. However, legends about the bravery of the Muslim fighters against a superior army of infidels became engraved in local memory and were perceived as a preliminary stage to the Indian Revolt of 1857–1858,[58] and, more significantly, as an anti-colonialist resistance to the British at the start of the twentieth century. The graves of the two martyrs became holy places.[59]

A somewhat different version of martyrdom for Islam was adopted in the Philippines. The Muslim Philippinos, or Moros, as they called themselves, mounted two types of attacks against Europeans and native Christians in the wake of losing wars against the Spanish army in the sixteenth century. Small groups of Moros volunteered to burst into the enemy forces and attack until they were killed. Another, more personal type of attack involved a single person entering a Christian enclave armed with a dagger, called a *kris*, and sometimes a small arrow, and attacked anyone he encountered. Non-Christians, women, and children were sometimes spared by the attacker, but the element of surprise and frenzy caused loss of life before the perpetrator was killed.

These types of "suicide" attacks constituted the last step of an established practice, which the Spanish identified as *juramentado* (having sworn an oath), a reasonable translation of what the Muslims in the Philippines called *fi sabil Allah* (fighting in the way of God). The person who intended to swear an oath first requested permission from his parents and then from a local or a higher authority. Thereafter, he performed religious rituals intended to purify body and soul, recited prayers, and prepared his body for burial. Other activities devoted to strengthening his body involved shaving his head, plucking his eyebrows, and binding his

---

[57] Al-Mahdi, *Manshurat*, pp. 64–65, 110–111.

[58] The leaders of the mutiny praised the virtues of martyrdom, but only in generalities, as there was opposition within the Indian Muslim discourse community regarding the legitimacy of a declaration of jihad against the British, especially in light of the obvious asymmetry between the two forces. Instead of confrontation, the Muslim leadership preached accommodation to the colonial regime. Ayesha Jalal, *Partisans of Allah* (Cambridge, MA: Harvard University Press, 2008), pp. 117–148.

[59] On the martyrs of Balakot, see Jalal, *Partisans of Allah*, chapter 4.

penis in an upright position. Although Islamic tradition forbade suicide, the Philippinos did not obey this prohibition, holding that even if a person performs suicide, by murdering others he can reach paradise.[60]

Viewed in a historic perspective, militant jihad aimed against Christian European penetration – and sometimes against Muslim forces as well – during the nineteenth and early twentieth centuries was carried out primarily by revivalist movements in peripheral and tribal regions of the Islamic world. These movements represented, in James Scott's terminology, the "little tradition," which struggled for identity, purity, resources, and political power and attacked the more restrained and reformist orientation of the "great tradition" embodied by the hegemonic political culture in the metropolitan centers of Islam.[61]

[60] J. Franklin Ewing, "Juramentado: Institutionalized Suicide among the Moros of the Philippines," *Anthropological Quarterly* 28/4 (October 1955), pp. 148–155; Thomas Kiefer, *The Tausug: Violence and Law in a Philippine Moslem Society* (New York: Holt, Rinehart and Winston, 1972), pp. 132–133; Morris Frellich, "In the Relevance of Culture," in idem (ed.), *Masked Suicide and Culture* (New York: Bergin and Garvey, 1993), pp. 165–186; Cesar Adib Majul, *Muslims in the Philippines* (Quezon City: University of the Philippines Press, 1973), pp. 352–360. For a broader discussion on martyrdom in the Indian Ocean region, see Stephen Frederic Dale, "Religious Suicide in Islamic Asia," *Journal of Conflict Resolution* 32/1 (March 1988), pp. 37–59.
[61] James C. Scott, "Protest and Profanation: Agrarian Revolt and the Little Tradition," *Theory and Society* 4 (1977), Parts 1–2, pp. 1–38, 211–245.

3

Modern Islamist Perceptions

The Arab states that were established on the ruins of the Ottoman Empire in the post–World War I period nationalized Islam to promote their own agendas. This development encompassed the concept of jihad as well, but with important alterations. The combative meaning of jihad was marginalized in favor of its spiritual and social aspect of good works for the benefit of the community (*jihad al-nafs*), albeit with the exception of regions in which violent struggles were conducted against a foreign presence, such as in Algeria against the French and in Palestine against the British and the Zionists.

The strategy of restraining the warlike jihad ethos was well illustrated in the case of the Ikhwan (Brethren) movement in Saudi Arabia in the late 1920s, which functioned as the ideological springboard for the spread of Wahhabi Islam in the Arabian Peninsula and the establishment of the Saudi kingdom. However, when the Ikhwan mounted incursions in the name of jihad into the neighboring countries of Jordan and Iraq, King 'Abd al-'Aziz ibn Sa'ud moved to suppress the zealot warriors so as to stabilize the kingdom's borders and reinforce relations with its ally, Britain.[1]

Later, in Egypt during Nasser's regime, Shaykh al-Azhar Mahmud Shaltut (1958–1963) argued, typically, that Islam has a strong aversion to the use of force as a means of spreading the faith and that the obligation of military jihad is enforceable only in times of self-defense against external aggression.[2] A similar position was adopted by 'Abd al-Halim Mahmud,

---

[1] Joseph Kostiner, *The Making of Saudi Arabia 1916–1936* (New York: Oxford University Press, 1993), pp. 71–140.

[2] Peters, *Jihad in Classical and Modern Islam*, pp. 59–101.

Shaykh al-Azhar (1973–1978) under Sadat, who, reflecting the influence of his Sufi background, emphasized that only through the spiritual, or greater, jihad can man attain moral wholeness and improve the condition of his community. In interpreting the hadith, "We have returned from the little jihad to the greater jihad," Mahmud explained that the little jihad against enemies is termed little because the burden it imposes begins and ends with killing, capturing, or subduing an enemy, which takes a limited amount of time. By comparison, he argued, the greater jihad, which is a spiritual struggle, is described thus because the soul makes ongoing demands and always longs for the pleasures of this world. That struggle does not end until the soul is returned to the Creator. It is no surprise, therefore, that in the eyes of God the status of the righteous is greater than that of the *shahid*s. Moreover, although the little jihad constitutes a vital basis for attaining victory over external enemies, the attainment of such a victory does not mean that every Muslim must leave his place of work, bear arms, and join the battlefield. Rather, every state and every individual must be oriented to support victory in various ways: workers through their labor, industrialists through industry, scholars through their knowledge, and soldiers through their arms.[3]

Thus, in adjusting themselves to new realities in the twentieth century, Arab-Muslim political elites, with the backing of establishment 'ulama', adopted three aims: stabilizing the state system, neutralizing the Islamists' challenge and diffusing the traditional dichotomy between the "realm of Islam" and the "realm of war," thereby facilitating integration in the international community.[4]

Whereas historically jihad was identified both as defensive and offensive or expansionist, modern 'ulama' emphasized its defensive nature, aimed at removing external aggression embodied most prominently by Israel. The call to mount a jihad against Israel was defined as a personal duty, given the perception of Israel as an aggressor against Muslims and as removing them from their habitations unjustly. Shaykh al-Azhar Mahmud cited the Qur'an verses: "Those who have been attacked are permitted to take up

---

[3] 'Abd al-Halim Mahmud, *Fatawa* (4th ed., Cairo: Dar al-Ma'arif, 1996), Vol. 1, pp. 106–107, 320–321; Vol. 2, pp. 105, 116–117.

[4] See, e.g., H. R. Rahman, "The Concept of Jihad in Egypt – A Study of Majallat al-Azhar 1936–1982," in Gabriel R. Warburg and U. M. Kupferschmidt (eds.), *Islam, Nationalism and Radicalism in Egypt and the Sudan* (New York: Praeger, 1983), pp. 249–261; Peters, *Jihad in Classical and Modern Islam*, pp. 59–101. See also 'Ali 'Abd al-Halim Mahumd, *Wasa'il al-tarbiya 'inda al-Ikhwan al-Muslimin* (4th ed., Mansura: Dar al-Wafa', 1990), pp. 104–105.

arms because they have been wronged – God has the power to help them –
those who have been driven unjustly from their homes only for saying,
'Our Lord is God'" (Sura 22: 39–40). Whoever bears arms against Israel,
Shaykh al-Azhar Mahmud ruled, will ultimately reach paradise, whether
he is victorious and returns home or falls as a martyr for God. Significantly,
the longed-for goal – paradise – was depicted by Mahmud as "dwelling
under the shade of the swords."[5] Jihad against Israel was a recurring theme
in the legal rulings at al-Azhar between 1947 and 1979, when the Camp
David agreements were signed. Martyrdom and its rewards in the next
world were given a place of honor in these rulings, implying the fulfillment
of the injunction, "hasten your steps to paradise," alongside a threat of
sanctions against anyone who did not contribute his body and soul to the
campaign in Palestine, namely being judged a sinner.[6]

However, for Islamists during most of the twentieth century, educated
in nationalist school systems and motivated by social and political grievances, Palestine was a secondary arena of activity. The primary need was
for an internal refashioning of the polity, and in this context the ethos of
jihad and martyrdom gained relevance as sources of inspiration. In the
view of some Islamists, these elements provided order and meaning and
created the essence of the difference between Islamic society and an ordinary society.

THE MUSLIM BRETHREN: PATHOS AND PRAGMATISM

Indeed, key molders of Islamist activism ascribed an important role to
the concept of martyrdom, although with varied interpretations and
emphases, reflecting the historical context in which Islamist movements
were active and thereby providing another indication of the multifaceted
nature of modern Islam. Hasan al-Banna (d. 1949), the charismatic
founder of the Muslim Brethren in Egypt and a major inspiration for
most of the contemporary Islamist movements, wrote in the 1930s that
Islam sanctifies the basic principle of tranquility, peace, and stability, but
so long as base instincts and struggles for survival exist, it is only natural

---

[5] Mahmud, *Fatawa*, Vol. 2, p. 106; idem, *Kitab al-jihad* (Cairo: Dar al-Ma'arif, 1983), pp. 5–6.
[6] Mahmud, *Fatawa*, Vol. 2, pp. 111, 113; Jawad Muhammad Ahmad (ed.), *Fatawa al-Azhar fi wujub al-jihad wa-tahrim al-ta'amul ma'a al-kiyan al-Sahyuni* (Cairo: Marakz Yafa, 1998), pp. 11–14, 25–38; also *Majallat al-Azhar*, 19 (1947/1948), pp. 145–151; Yitzhak Reiter, *War, Peace and International Relations in Islam* (Brighton: Sussex Academic Press, 2011), pp. 79–93.

that there will also be wars. The war for Islam is a social imperative and a necessary evil. It seeks to protect the exploited and rout the exploiters. Moreover, it has a religious sanction and is viewed as one of the pillars of Islam alongside prayer and fasting, with a close affinity to the Qur'anic command to "forbid wrong"[7] and to the hadith, "One of the lofty types of jihad is to speak truth before a tyrannical ruler."[8] Al-Banna also pointed out that jihad must be interpreted in modern times as defensive, in view of the widespread attack on Muslims who find themselves under subordination by nonbelievers, with the commands of their religion unimplemented. Jihad thus becomes a duty for every individual.

In al-Banna's view, the fear is the unbelievers' values, not death, that believers must accept with open arms.[9] This was also reflected in the movement's motto: "God is our goal. The Prophet [Muhammad] is our leader. The Qur'an is our constitution. Struggle is our way. Death in the service of God is the loftiest of our wishes. God is Great, God is great."[10] In an essay titled "The Message of Jihad" (*Risalat al-jihad*) al-Banna wrote:

A nation familiar with the profession of death and that knows how to die an honorable death, will be bestowed by God a glorified life on earth and eternal pleasures in the hereafter. We have been stricken by tragedies only because of a love of this world and a hatred of death. Restore yourselves to perform great and blessed acts, and adhere to death. You should know that there is no escape from death, which occurs only once. If you dedicate it to God, you will earn the blessings of this world and be rewarded in the hereafter, and you will experience no evil except that which is decreed by God.[11]

In another essay, published in 1938, al-Banna referred to self-sacrifice as the profession of death (*sina'at al-mawt*).[12] This expression was originally coined by the Iraqi educator Sami Shawkat in the early 1930s, reflecting

---

[7] See, e.g., Sura 3: 104.

[8] See, e.g., al-ʿAsqalani, *Fath al-bari*, Vol. 13, p. 53.

[9] Al-Banna, "Risalat al-jihad," in idem, *Majmuʿat rasaʾil al-imam al-shahid* (Beirut: al-Muʾassasa al-Islamiyya, n.d.), pp. 246–264. For an English translation of the essay, see Charles Wendell, *Five Tracts of Hasan al-Banna* (Berkeley: University of California Press, 1978), pp. 133–161. Also al-Banna, *al-Salam fi'l-Islam* (2nd ed., Cairo: Manshurat al-ʿAsr al-Hadith, 1971), pp. 50–56, 71; idem, "al-Jihad fi sabil Allah wa-manzilatuhu min al-Islam," article dated 24 January 1929, republished in *al-Taliʿa al-Islamiyya* (London), January 1, 1981, pp. 16–21.

[10] Mitchell, *The Society of the Muslim Brothers*, pp. 193–194.

[11] Al-Banna, "Risalat al-jihad," p. 264.

[12] Hasan al-Banna, "Sinaʿat al-mawt," *al-Nadhir*, no. 18 (September 26, 1938), pp. 3–5; reprinted in (no author), *al-Imam al-shahid yatahaddathu ila shabab al-ʿalam al-Islami* (Beirut: Dar al-Qalam, 1974), pp. 129–132.

the influence of the military training program in Nazi Germany.[13] Shawkat
held that the honor and independence of a nation are built not only on the
foundations of a developed economy, the wealth of natural resources, or
progressive education for its subjects but also, first and foremost, on
strength and self-sacrifice, as follows:

Strength is the soil on which the seed of justice burgeons; the nation which has no
strength is destined to humiliation and enslavement. ... Strength, as I use the word
here, means to excel in the profession of death. The nation which does not excel in
the profession of death with iron and fire will be forced to die under the hooves of
the horses and under the boots of a foreign soldiery. If to live is just, then killing in
self-defense is also just.[14]

Whereas Shawkat placed the perception of self-sacrifice in a secular nationalist context, citing examples of the achievements of Mussolini in Italy,
Ataturk in Turkey, and Reza Shah in Iran, al-Banna lauded self-sacrifice in
an Islamic religious context, citing examples from the generation of the
Prophet and his companions. However, both viewed self-sacrifice as a for-
mula for strength, and both viewed its ideal realization as dependent on
young people and on their careful training. The notion of self-sacrifice was
perceived by both at a form of warfare, which demanded study and excellence, and included nurturing military strength, discipline, altruism, total
devotion to the ideal, and obedience to the hierarchical order.

     According to al-Banna, an adherence to martyrdom elevates the believers
and casts fear on their enemies, whereas the neglect of this adherence
degrades them and turns them into easy prey for enemies. He wrote, in 1938:

Indeed, the profession of death, for death is a profession like all other labor. Some
people do it well, and know how to die an honorable death and how to choose an
honorable venue and the appropriate time for their death, and then sell their drop
of blood at the highest price and profit greatly by all that is imaginable – they profit
by the happiness of the present world and the reward of the world to come. All this
without hastening the end that God has determined for them. There are also
frightened and wretched people, who do not know the secret of this labor, and
are not aware of its attributes, and thus each one of them dies a thousand despicable
deaths every single day, remaining with these deaths until the great death comes,

13 The essay was based on a speech delivered by Shawkat to students of the Central Secondary
    School, Baghdad, in 1933, and was printed in his *Hadhihi ahdafuna* (Baghdad:
    Matba'at al-Tafid al-Ahliyya, 1939), pp. 1–3; for an English translation, see Sylvia
    G. Haim, *Arab Nationalism: An Anthology* (Berkeley: University of California Press,
    1962), pp. 97–99. On Shawkat's life and views, see Peter Wein, *Iraqi Arab Nationalism:
    Authoritarian, Totalitarian, and Pro-fascist Inclinations 1932–1941* (London: Routledge,
    2006), pp. 83–88, 101–105.
14 Haim, *Arab Nationalism*, p. 98.

despicable as well – without honor or elevation, in a wretched field of nothingness – and dying without honor, their blood spilled without resurrection.

The Qur'an taught Muslims the secret of this profession, guiding them toward its virtues and benefits and conveying them in many verses.... After them generations of Muslims came into the world who clung to trivial things and pleasures in this world, and neglected the materials of strength, were unfamiliar with the profession of death, were in love with life, and competed amongst themselves for false titles, fleeting greatness, transient possessions and a false outward appearance. How pathetic were the worshippers of money and of velvet until they were plundered and the enemies overcame them and they lost their supremacy in this world. And how bad was their end in the next world. Indeed, the words of the Prophet apply to them, for all the nations of the world gathered against the Muslims, and God tore away their enemies' awe of them, and left weakness in their hearts, which is the love of this world and the revulsion against death.[15]

In his memoirs, Shaykh Yusuf al-Qaradawi, who was a former member of the Muslim Brethren, recalled that at an event which he attended in his youth al-Banna discussed the concept of an "appropriate death" and said that the Muslim Brethren are prepared to sacrifice thousands of young boys as an offering to their homeland. "What is an appropriate death?" al-Banna asked. "Is it that you should die beside your wife, your children and your relatives? The appropriate death, as I imagine it, is that this head should be severed – pointing to his head – from this body, for God."[16]

The heroic pathos in al-Banna's essay previously quoted was aimed at the struggle in Palestine, namely to arouse Muslims to support their brothers' campaign there. A short time before he was assassinated, al-Banna lauded the participation of the Brethren in the 1948 War out of love of jihad and sacrifice, adding that had the campaign been managed from the start by his movement, matters would have turned out differently.[17] Indeed, the sweeping rhetoric of martyrdom employed by the leader of the Egyptian Brethren in the 1930s and 1940s was aimed at British imperialism and the Zionist presence in Palestine. This rhetoric served as a central theme of the hagiographic literature published by the Brethren over the years extolling the image of the fallen in battle. For example, the fighters from the Muslim Brethren in Palestine were described as competing with each other for the honor of carrying out jihad in the holy land so as to merit one of two attainments: victory over the Jews or martyrdom for God. They would purify themselves before joining the campaign "with faith in their hearts, Qur'anic texts in their pockets, and machine guns in their hands." When one

[15] Al-Banna, "Sina'at al-Mawt," pp. 129–132.
[16] Al-Qaradawi quoted in *al-Hayat*, February 19, 2005.
[17] Al-Banna quoted in *al-Mukhtar al-Islami*, October 24, 2006, p. 70.

of them was struck by a bullet, he would call out, "Allah akbar," declare his faith in God and the Prophet, and say, "Here, I have hurried to you, my lord, so that you might be satisfied." Clearly, the martyrs internalized the motto: "Freedom is not granted by the oppressors, it is taken by the fighters with their blood."[18]

By contrast, the mainstream struggle over the image of the Egyptian polity during the same period was mainly waged through intensive cultural and communal activity (often termed *da'wa*), with the declared aim of blocking the dangerous waves of Western hedonistic culture that swept over society and rejuvenating society's Islamic morals.[19] Jihad in this milieu was essentially social and not military, reflecting the notion of *jihad al-tarbiyya* (educational-cultural jihad). Al-Banna, too, included social aspects in the term martyr, such as the individual's protection of his family or his possessions. In the same vein, al-Qaradawi pointed out that for the Brethren, jihad was more than discipline, training, and warfare; it also – and primarily – encompassed faith and morality and the imperative of combating injustice on the part of Muslim rulers through preaching and chastisement.[20]

The communal and educational aspects of the Brethren's religious credo were even more pronounced in Syria and Jordan during the mid-twentieth century, where the Brethren movements were led mainly by 'ulama' and notables who adopted a more pragmatic orientation than their urban middle class and lay colleagues in Egypt. Their general strategy was to integrate into the existing political order through political alliances and communal activity, the latter gradually elevated to the status of a sanctified social ritual (*'ibada ijtima'iyya*).[21]

---

[18] See, e.g., Kamil al-Sharif and Mustafa al-Siba'i, *al-Ikhwan al-Muslimun fi harb Filastin* (3rd ed., Cairo: Maktabat Wahaba, n.d.); Husayn ibn 'Ali Jabir, *al-Tariq ila jama'at al-Muslimin* (Kuwait: Dar al-Da'wa, 1969); also Yusuf al-Qaradawi, *al-Tarbiya al-Islamiyya wa-madrasat Hasan al-Banna* (Cairo: Maktabat Wahaba, 1979), pp. 39–49.

[19] On the Brethren's communal orientation, see Lia Brynjar, *The Muslim Brotherhood: The Rise of a Mass Movement* (London: Ithaca Press, 1991); Meir Hatina, "Restoring a Lost Identity: Models of Education in Modern Islamic Thought," *British Journal of Middle Eastern Studies* 33 (November 2006), pp. 180–184.

[20] Al-Banna, *al-Salam fi'l-Islam*, pp. 52–53; al-Qaradawi, *al-Tarbiya al-Islamiyya*, pp. 39–40, 46.

[21] A phrase coined by Muhammad al-Ghazali, initially one of the ideologists of the Muslim Brethren in Egypt in the 1940s and 1950s, in his book, *Ma'a Allah: dirasat fi'l-da'wa wa'l-du'at* (3rd ed., Cairo: Dar al-Hadith, 1965), p. 175. See also Bayly Winder, "Islam as the State Religion – A Muslim Brotherhood View in Syria," *The Muslim World* 44 (1954), pp. 215–226; J. Salt, "An Islamic Scholar-Activist: Mustafa al-Siba'i and the Islamic Movement in Syria 1945–1954," *Journal of Arabic, Islamic and Near Eastern Studies* 3

Other Islamist groups, however, adopted a radical strategy of violence which highlighted the more militant aspects of jihad and self-sacrifice. In their political vocabulary, extremism in achieving godly justice was a merit, whereas moderation was a disadvantage.

THE RISE OF MILITANT GROUPS: CALCULATED FERVOR

If the state continued to emphasize the pacifistic nature of Islam, with the aim of neutralizing religious militancy, radical Islamists sought to release the potential energy of the jihad imperative to overturn the political order. The use of force, which was perceived in Islamist discourse until then as the privilege of the state (*siyasa sharʿiyya*), underwent "privatization" by radicals and became the prerogative of the Muslim public at large, with the Islamists in its vanguard. Inter alia, this prerogative relied on the important Qurʾanic commandment to "forbid wrong," supported as well by radical interpretations given by several jurists in the Middle Ages, most prominently Abu Hamid al-Ghazali, who sided with the formation of armed bands to enforce this injunction even without permission from the sovereign or the state.[22] In the event, the modern radicals went a step further by turning such "legal" violence against the state itself, which in their view embodied two main evils – political tyranny and hedonistic secularism – thereby bearing primary responsibility for the material and moral bankruptcy of Muslim societies.

One writer argued that the Crusades had never passed from the world, and had even expanded, so that the Arab-Muslim orbit had become a space conquered palpably by Crusader agents, as exemplified by the Zionist presence in Palestine or culturally through the media, books, academic campuses, and school curricula.[23] Jihad was perceived as a "pedagogic" tool no less than it was an operational tool, living proof of the moral validity of Islam and its uncompromising stance against the forces of heresy.[24]

(1996), pp. 103–115; Amnon Cohen, *Political Parties in the West Bank under the Jordanian Regime, 1949–1967* (Ithaca: Yale University Press, 1982), pp. 144–208; Hatina, "Restoring a Lost Identity," pp. 184–185. On daʿwa and martyrdom, see Abu al-Fazl Ezzati, *The Spread of Islam: The Contributing Factors* (4th ed., London: Islamic College for Advanced Studies Press, 2002), pp. 72–90. Ezzati, a professor of Islamic studies who studied in Teheran and London, claimed that daʿwa involves the concept of martyrdom and explains the interrelationships between "forbidden wrong," daʿwa, jihad, *shahada*, and *shahid*.

[22] Al-Ghazali, *Ihyaʾ ʿulum al-din*, Vol. 2, pp. 393–453; Michael Cook, *Commanding Right and Forbidding Wrong*.
[23] Al-Qasimi, *al-Jihad waʾl-huquq al-dawaliyya al-ʿamma fiʾl-Islam*, pp. 5–6.
[24] *Hatina*, "Restoring a Lost Identity," pp. 185–190.

The radicals were driven by a strong sense of injustice (*zulm*) and a desire for revenge against the ruling elites, whom they perceived as responsible for social inequity and ethical and political perversion. Describing these manifestations as obsolete, barbarous, and odious, the radicals dedicated their lives to destroying the regimes. In this respect, a parallel may be drawn between the Muslim radicals of the late twentieth century and the Russian revolutionaries of the late nineteenth century, represented primarily by the Narodnaya Vola (The People's Will) movement. This movement defined the Czarist state a priori as the embodiment of evil and as a "usurping band," so that the salvation of the exploited peasants could never emanate from political parties or from education and preaching, but only through sweeping nihilistic violence. This demanded that the members of the group show total commitment, altruism, and a readiness for self-sacrifice. Like the radical Islamists a century later, they did not seek to destroy the institutions of the state but rather to use them to entrench a revolution that would produce a system of harmony and justice that would preclude the need for repressive measures.[25]

Describing the movement's goal and how it would be implemented, one of its leaders, Alexander Mikhaliov, wrote a letter to his comrades just before his trial in 1882, in which he stated: "Do not let yourselves be carried away by the desire to avenge or free your comrades.... Do not be carried away by fine theories. There is only one theory in Russia: to acquire freedom to own the land ... and there is only one way to do it: fire at the centre."[26] This was the vision and strategy of the radical Islamists as well, as formulated by their ideological mentors.

One such influential ideologist, Abu al-Aʿla Mawdudi (d. 1979), of Indo-Pakistani origin, viewed the modern era as "neo-pagan" (*jahiliyya*) and preached aggressive jihad for God's cause. Mawdudi emphasized that Islam is a revolutionary concept that seeks to destroy the world's social order from its foundations and rebuild it according to Islam. Jihad is the embodiment of this revolutionary notion, which does not seek conquest and territory for its own sake but only for God and the complete restoration of His sovereignty (*hakimiyya*). This is the sole parameter of the legitimacy of Islamic warfare, differentiating its believers from the rest of

---

[25] On the Narodnaya Vola, see Franco Venturi, *Roots of Revolution: A History of the Populist and Socialist Movements in Nineteenth Century Russia* (London: Weidenfeld and Nicolson, 1960), pp. 316–708; Boris Savinkov, *Memoirs of a Terrorist* (New York: Kraus Reprint Co., 1972). On the theme of revenge, see Susan Jacoby, *Wild Justice: The Evolution of Revenge* (New York: Harper & Row, 1983).

[26] Venturi, *Roots of Revolution*, p. 708.

the nations of the world. The acute reality of heresy does not permit a distinction between defensive and aggressive jihad, for the Islamic stream is simultaneously attacked by, and responds to, regimes that oppose Islam. Whoever does not dedicate himself to this course both bodily and with his possessions, Mawdudi warns, is viewed as an apostate (*murtadd*) who has no place in the next world.[27]

Interpreting the Qur'anic verse, "God has purchased the persons and possessions of the believers in return for the Garden – they fight in God's way: they kill and are killed" (Sura 9: 111), Mawdudi stated:

When a man has true faith it involves a commitment to devote himself sincerely to God and God's promise of reward in return for that commitment. This two-way commitment has been described as a "transaction." What this means is that faith is not just the affirmation of a set of metaphysical propositions. It is in fact a contract according to which man places all that he has – his life, his wealth – at the disposal of God; he "sells" them to God. In return, he accepts God's promise of Paradise in the Next Life ... when someone refuses to make this transaction ... then this person is an unbeliever.[28]

Nevertheless, in the same breath Mawdudi asserted that in contrast to what has been attributed to him in the West, Islam is not a religion of the sword, and modern Islamists are essentially preachers (*du'at*). Jihad for God has a broader significance than violent struggle, and the recourse to war (*qital*) is undertaken only in a time of palpable need for self-protection against external, non-Muslim attackers.

Putting this more moderate view into practice, Mawdudi later relegated the notion of jihad and martyrdom to an intellectual exercise when his movement, *Jama'at-i Islami* (Islamic Group), made a decision to promote the reformation of society by education and entering establishment politics, rather than by coercion, on the formation of Pakistan in 1947.[29] His most outstanding student, Abul Hasan 'Ali Nadwi (d. 2000), preached the importance of preserving the memory of jihad for God and the yearning for martyrdom as a repository of faith (*thawra imaniyya*) and energy (*taqa*) that distinguishes the Muslim nation from others both in the past and the present. Relinquishing this wealth and energy would lead to an

[27] Mawdudi, "Al-Jihad fi sabil Allah," in *Thalath rasa'il fi'l-jihad* (Amman: Dar al-'Umr, 1992), pp. 5–65.

[28] Mawdudi, *Towards Understanding the Qur'an*, Vol. 3, pp. 254–257.

[29] Mawdudi, "al-Jihad fi'l-sabil Allah," pp. 5–10; idem, *Towards Understanding the Qur'an*, Vol. 1, p. 169; also, Seyyed Vali Reza Nasr, *The Vanguard of the Islamic Revolution: The Jama'at-i Islami of Pakistan* (Berkeley: University of California Press, 1994); idem, *Mawdudi and the Making of Islamic Revivalism*, p. 74.

irretrievable loss and a vacuum, whether in expanded knowledge or cultural development, which could never be restored. Nadwi published a book about the history of jihad and self-sacrifice during the struggle against the British in India during the nineteenth century. In it he describes the martyrs of the so-called Indian Mutiny of 1857–1858 as the most faithful and moral pure souls, who shunned materialism and displayed willingness for self-sacrifice for Islam and God to an extent not seen for a long time in Muslim history. Nadwi held up those martyrs as an example to contemporary Muslims to act with determination and devotion for the restoration of the pure community of believers.[30]

Despite his ideological fervor, however, Nadwi, as his mentor Mawdudi, focused on preaching and on combating the secularization that had spread through society. This task was reflected as well in his work as director of the *Nadwat al-ʿUlamaʾ* (Council of Religious Scholars) in Lucknow, India. His credo was that removing the causes of the people's moral laxity – namely love of the present world, permissiveness, and so forth – is more important than, and takes precedence over, the removal of traces of foreign domination.[31]

Only from the 1960s onward did political violence, and with it the readiness to die, become an uncompromising norm put into practice by Sayyid Qutb, Saʿid Hawwa, ʿAbd al-Salam Faraj, and other Sunni radicals in response to the repressive regimes of Nasser in Egypt and the Baʿth in Syria.[32] The ideological blueprint was provided by Qutb, who, like his colleague Mawdudi, opposed categorizing jihad in modern times as defensive only, searching for justifications for its implementation, and thereby diminishing the essence of Islam as an emancipating religion that seeks to free man from enslavement to his fellow man and restore him to the worship of God only.

The duty of all Muslims, Qutb asserted, is to "smash every force" that stands between the thrust to return people to the Islamic creed freely or that compels people to leave Islam. Put another way, jihad is essential to advance daʿwa; without it, the faith remains a philosophy only. Those who implement jihad have already triumphed in the mighty war against

---

[30] Abul Hasan ʿAli Nadwi, *Tarshid al-sahwa al-Islamiyya*, lecture delivered in Abu Dabi in November 1988, quoted in http://wadelhilew.ahlamontada.com/t111-topic (accessed January 4, 2012); idem, *Idha habbat rih al-iman* (new ed., Beirut: Muʾassat al-Risala, 1985), mainly pp. 11–12, 135–136, 201–206.

[31] Nadwi, *Tasaʾulat wa tahadiyyat ʿala tariq al-daʿwa* (Cairo: Dar al-Kalima, 1998), mainly pp. 27–32, 37–40; idem, *Izalat asbab al-khudhlan ahamm wa-aqdam min izalat ʿathar al-ʿudwan* (India: Dar al-ʿArafat, n.d.).

[32] On the Sunni revolution, see Sivan, *Radical Islam*, mainly pp. 1–129.

inner lusts and have no fear of death, for death is predestined and cannot be altered. Their deep understanding that all is in God's hands leads them to deal with something truly important – to earn the love of God and the exalted joy of the next world by fulfilling the goal of dying in the battlefield.[33]

Such Muslims were described by Qutb as counted among the army of the faithful, noble, and pure of heart, with a soul that is blessed.[34] By contrast, those who remain behind, who only testify to their faith in God and His Prophet but do not go out to implement jihad, are portrayed by Qutb as resembling ants who cannot see beyond the ground beneath them. They are not believers, for jihad and death for God are a great favor from God, which He grants to selected people to release them from the shackles of this world so that they may enjoy the sublime life in paradise.[35] Qutb writes:

The chosen martyrs are those whom God selects from among the *mujahidun* and takes them for himself. Therefore, there is no tragedy or loss when someone falls in sanctifying the name of God. On the contrary, the fallen person has been carefully chosen by God and is thus honored. Indeed, God has granted martyrdom especially to them when He has chosen them for himself and grants his proximity especially to them.[36]

Qutb highlights the martyr's close affinity to God, as written in the Qur'an ("God has purchased the persons and possessions of the believers in return for the Garden" (Sura 9: 111)). Similarly to Mawdudi, Qutb defined this verse as "powerful" (*nass rahib*) because it symbolizes the essence of the relationship between man and his Creator and the core of allegiance to Islam. Fulfilling this allegiance in worship, but mainly in jihad, grants man the title of "believer." Refusal turns him into an infidel. In any event, Qutb points to a one-sided agreement in which "the buyer [God] is permitted to do whatever he wishes in accordance with the rules he has specified. The seller cannot do anything … he can only say: 'We will do and listen,' and submit. The price is Paradise."[37]

Elsewhere, Qutb stated: "If you live for an idea, life will appear to you to be a long-term process that began with the dawn of humanity and

---

[33] Qutb, *Fi zilal al-Qur'an*, Vol. 1, p. 187.
[34] Sayyid Qutb, "al-Jihad fi sabil Allah," in (no author), *Thalath rasa'il fi'l-jihad*, pp. 107–148; also Qutb's commentary on Sura 3: 140–147, in his *Fi zilal al-Qur'an*, Vol. 1, pp. 479–489; Vol. 3, pp. 1712–1717.
[35] Qutb quoted in *al-Tali'a al-Islamiyya*, January 1981, pp. 2–3.
[36] Qutb, *Fi zilal al-Qur'an*, Vol. 1, p. 481; also Vol. 2, pp. 700–701.
[37] Ibid., Vol. 3, pp. 1712–1717; also Vol. 6, pp. 3559–3560.

continues much beyond the moment you leave your earthly life."[38] This comment also formed the basis of Qutb's interpretation of the motif of the "living martyr," cited in the following verses: "Do not say that those who are killed in God's cause are dead; they are alive, though you do not realize it" (Sura 2: 154); and "[Prophet], do not think of those who have been killed in God's way as dead. They are alive with their Lord, well provided for, happy with what God has given them of His favour" (Sura 3: 169). In Qutb's view, the purpose of the verses is to instill tranquility in the believers and to stress that the martyrs must not be considered as dead, and should not be spoken of as dead, nor should sorrow be shown over parting from them, for God himself testifies that they are alive. He grants them a status of honor next to His seat and on the same level as the prophets, the righteous, and the pure of heart. They were only apparently killed, but one must not be misled by appearances.

Death, Qutb points out, is not the end of the road, and there is no separation between the world of the living and the world beyond life. Thus, martyrs can live in a different type of existence – a type that we are unable to see or understand. Their burial is also unconventional: their body is not washed, and they are buried in their clothing, proof that they are clean, pure, and free of all appetites or material interests except their desire to please and give joy to their Creator. Moreover, they alone can request God to allow them to return to life and be killed again for him.

In this context Qutb relies on the hadith, which says that the souls of martyrs are carried in the stomachs of green birds that fly in paradise and position themselves near the chair of God. When God sees them and asks them what they wish, they reply that they cannot request anything, as they have already received that which is longed for, which no one else but they have received – the status of martyr. This dialogue is repeated again and again, until the souls understand that they must request something, and they decide to request that God return them to earth so that they can fight for Him again and die again. The fact that martyrs are not truly dead, Qutb adds, causes the family's sense of parting to be lightened as well.[39] He explains:

The main attribute of life is activism, development and expansion, and the main attribute of death is passivity, extinguishment and cessation. The activism of those

---

[38] Qutb quoted in Emmanuel Sivan, *The Clash within Islam* (Te Aviv: Am Oved, 2000), p. 60 (in Hebrew).

[39] Qutb, *Fi zilal al-Qur'an*, Vol. 1, pp. 143–144, 517–518. The hadith is cited in Abu Muhammad 'Abd Allah ibn 'Abd al-Rahman al-Darimi, *Sunan al-Darimi* (Beirut: Dar al-Kitab al-'Arabi, 1987), Vol. 2, pp. 271–272.

who are killed for the sake of God provided the victory of truth, for which they were killed, and such activism is effective. The idea for which they were killed is nourished by their blood and expands, and their influence on those left behind is strengthened and expands. They continue to constitute an active and influential element in molding and guiding the life of their community. This is their main life attribute, and thus their existence as living martyrs as well.[40]

The violence sanctified by Qutb was directed against the modern state and its systems but did not challenge its geographic boundaries or seek to reinstate the caliphate. That goal, by contrast, was espoused by Shaykh Taqi al-Din al-Nabhani (d. 1977) and his movement, the Islamic Liberation Party, which emerged in Jordan during the 1950s. It assigned a key role to jihad in routing infidel regimes and restoring the dichotomous division of power between the "realm of Islam" and the "realm of war."

Al-Nabhani asserted in his writings that jihad is a war to remove every obstacle blocking the elevation of the word of God and the spread of Islam, meaning a concrete activity that yields a spiritual value and elevates man above his life in the present world. To enhance the status of jihad, al-Nabhani emphasized that only acts related directly to the battlefield, including preaching and writing, may be viewed as jihad, in contrast to political struggle or social protest. He reserved the highest praise for those who come forward to fulfill the duty of jihad, especially those who fell while carrying out this duty, distinguishing them from other categories of martyrs – namely those who enter the next world after death from illness or plague, or those who remain in this world and fight for prestige or possessions. Al-Nabhani also removed any doubt regarding their life in the eternal world, enjoying the favors of God. He not only relied on the familiar Qur'anic verse, "[Prophet], do not think of those who have been killed in God's way as dead. They are alive with their Lord, well provided for" (Sura 3: 169), but also categorized the fallen martyrs as among those belonging to the hidden world that cannot be understood but only believed in completely.[41]

The radical discourse of the 1960s and 1970s depicted the faithful, or *mujahidun*, as "Islam's capital" and the "spirit of the nation" who truly

---

[40] Qutb, *Fi zilal al-Qur'an*, Vol. 1, p. 143. A compilation of Sayyid Qutb's notions of martyrdom and martyrs, based on his book, *fi zilal al-Qur'an*, can be found in 'Ukasha 'Abd al-Mannan al-Tibi (ed.), *Shahada wa'l-istishhad fi zilal al-Qur'an li'l-Shaykh Sayyid Qutb* (new ed., Cairo: Maktabat al-Turath al-Islami, 1994).

[41] Taqi al-Din al-Nabhani, *Nizam al-hukm fi'l-Islam mafahim Hizb al-Tahrir* (2nd ed., Jerusalem: Manshurat Hizb al-Tahrir, 1953), pp. 57–58; idem, *al-Shakhsiyya al-Islamiyya* (5th ed., Beirut: Dar al-Umma, 2003–2005), Vol. 2, pp. 146–150, 165–172; Vol. 3, pp. 5–15, 15–16, 29.

revered God and were committed to defending justice by force. They constituted the backbone of society, the first to resist and the last to surrender, exhorted to fight to the death. This desired ambition marked the dividing line between those who truly aspired to jihad and those who sought to avoid it. As written in a hadith: "The faith of he who died and did not fight or express willingness to die [for God] is tantamount to one who dies as a hypocrite."[42] Nevertheless, this revolutionary perception of self-sacrifice did not become a pure cult of death. On the contrary, it had restraining parameters in two respects. First, the fighter's declared mission was to strike and kill without exposing himself to intentional death. If, however, he was killed, and by enemy forces, this would be an act of jihad. Underlying this premise was the theological prohibition of self-immolation, which condemns a person to the torments of hell. Secondly, the targets of the attack were the symbols of the state, not civilians, who were perceived as Muslims even if they had strayed from the authentic faith.

In this respect Sunni radicals broke the Muslim taboo against opposing local rulers, in that they readily adopted literature praising (*fada'il*) jihad and self-sacrifice promoted by 'ulama' of the past and present. However, as their predecessors, they continued to be cautious regarding the type of death of the fighter, which had to be circumstantial during warfare and not pre-planned, lest it be pronounced a suicide, which constitutes weakness and submission to Satan; and it could not cause harm to Muslim civilians, whose lives are sanctified by Islam.

'ABD AL-SALAM FARAJ'S "ABSENT IMPERATIVE"

In Egypt, the religious resurgence that swept over the Middle East in the early 1970s was reflected in ideological extremism fueled by the broader latitude granted to Islamic activity by President Sadat in an effort to reinforce his status vis-à-vis his Nasserist and leftist rivals. Sadat's initial

---

[42] Al-Qasimi, *al-Jihad wa'l-huquq al-dawaliyya*, p. 339; Sa'id Hawwa, *Fi 'Afaq al-ta'lim* (Cairo: Maktabat Wahaba, 1980), pp. 167–168, 170–171; Fathi Yakan's writings, *Nahwa haraka Islamiyya 'alamiyya wahida* (3rd ed., Beirut: Dar al-Imam, 1977), pp. 33–34; *Abjadiyyat al-tasawwur al-haraki li'l-'amal al-Islami* (Beirut: Mu'assasat al-Risala, 1987), pp. 55–64; *Mushkilat al-da'wa wa'l-da'iya* (Beirut: Mu'assasat al-Risala, 1987), pp. 48–61, 66–71, 90–93, 163–167; *Madha ya'ni intima'i li'l-Islam* (Beirut: Mu'assasat al-Risala, 1977), pp. 127–128, 171. The quoted hadith is taken from ibn al-Hajjaj al-Qushayri Muslim, *Sahih Muslim* (Beirut: Dar Ihya' al-Turath, n.d.), Vol. 3, p. 1517; also Abu al-Fida' Isma'il ibn 'Umar ibn Kathir, *Tafsir Ibn Kathir* (Beirut: Dar al-Fikr, 1980–1981), Vol. 1, p. 253.

emphasis on his commitment to implement the shariʿa and expand religious content in the educational curriculum and the media fostered expectations for the creation of a new political order based on Islam. Later, his retreat from this religious line, and the limitations he imposed on the Islamists' activity, antagonized them, leading some Islamists to resort to violence and the formation of radical organizations.

The most prominent of these was the Egyptian Jihad movement, founded in 1977, centered primarily in Alexandria, Cairo, and Asyut. Its membership consisted mainly of students from marginalized urban sectors of society, along with a number of noncommissioned army officers. Its ideological platform was inspired at first by Shaykh ʿUmar ʿAbd al-Rahman and, after he left for a rival group in 1978, by Muhammad ʿAbd al-Salam Faraj, largely based on the principles in the "Absent Imperative" (*al-Farida al-ghaʾiba*, 1981).[43]

An engineer by profession, Faraj belonged to the second generation of Sunni radicals who followed Sayyid Qutb, Saʿid Hawwa, Fathi Yakan, and other founders of radical Islam in the 1960s. His booklet focuses on the obligation of jihad and the fact that it is ignored in modern times, a development that, in his view, resulted in the decline of Islam. Reaffirming the classical concept of jihad as a war against infidels, Faraj took a revolutionary step by linking the notion of jihad against an external enemy to domestic jihad against hypocritical Muslim rulers who demonstrate only nominal loyalty to Islam while enforcing corrupted Western laws. Applying history to the contemporary reality, Faraj perceived a common link between the Mongols of the thirteenth century and contemporary Arab rulers in their deviation from Islam, thereby meriting merciless punishment by armed jihad. The neglect of this duty, Faraj asserted, is tantamount to self-immolation.[44]

Moreover, Faraj was not satisfied with defying the Sunni taboo against forbidding revolt against a Muslim ruler, even an unjust one, for fear of civil strife. He also criticized the modus operandi of various Islamist movements

---

[43] See, e.g., Gilles Kepel, *Muslim Extremism in Egypt: The Prophet and the Pharaoh* (new ed., Berkeley: University of California Press, 2003), pp. 191–222. Faraj's booklet was edited by Muhammad ʿImara, *al-Farida al-ghaʾiba: judhur wa-hiwarart, dirasat wa-nusus* (new ed., Cairo: Nahadat Misr, n.d.), pp. 79–138. All references, unless otherwise stated, are from this version.

[44] The condemnation of the Mongols, which relies on a ruling by the medieval scholar Ibn Taymiyya, was based on their retention of a pagan law (the Yasa code) even though they had converted to Islam and their vulgar and licentious behavior in public. ʿImara (ed.), *al-Farida al-ghaʾiba*, pp. 85–94, 107–113.

to establish the aspired theocratic state – mainly the emphasis on communal activity by the Muslim Brethren and, by contrast, the disengagement from society demonstrated by the *al-Takfir wa'l-Hijra* (Excommunication and Holy Flight) movement. In Faraj's view, an emphasis on communal activity reinforces the legitimacy of a deviated regime, whereas withdrawal from society results in the extinction of its adherents. The correct strategy is a relentless war from within against the existing order of the state, for example, by penetrating the army (which, in the event, led to Sadat's murder).[45]

In Faraj's view, jihad for God allows the use of a variety of means, to be determined by the judgment and needs of the believers, to ensure the distraction of the enemy and its defeat but with as little human loss as possible. The violence involved must not be sweeping violence but rather focused and subject to moral restrictions. Clearly, Faraj perceived no dilemma regarding violence against infidels, whom he described first and foremost as the "near enemy" – that is, local rulers who strayed from the path of Islam. He did, however, display caution in his detailed position on violence toward Muslim believers who are in proximity to infidels in three types of situations.

The first concerns Muslim fighters serving in the army together with infidels, who find themselves in a confrontation with Muslims faithful to Islam. In Faraj's view, the fighters are obliged to fight in this army even if some soldiers are fighting against their will, because there is no way to discern who has been forced to fight and who has volunteered. Therefore, "We [the Muslim worriers] will fight them by God's command, we will be rewarded for this, and we will be exempt from punishment, while they [the soldiers] will earn their just reward on the day of resurrection according to their intentions."[46]

The second situation regarding Muslim believers in proximity to infidels concerns the use made by the enemy of Muslim prisoners of war as human shields. Faraj argues that if there is any chance that the Muslim army will be harmed if it does not fight, then it must fight even if this will lead to the killing of Muslims used as human shields. Even in the absence of this

---

[45] Ibid., pp. 101–106.

[46] Faraj was thus quoting from the hadith in which the Prophet, when asked what the rule is for a Muslim who takes part against his will in a military campaign mounted by unbelievers against Mecca, replies that the earth will swallow him up together with the army of unbelievers, but on the day of judgment he will be resurrected according to his intentions. Ibid., pp. 121–122. The hadith is quoted in al-Naysaburi, *al-Musdatrak 'ala al-sahihayn*, Vol. 4, p. 475.

likelihood, the religious scholars permitted harming Muslim prisoners, explaining that if they were killed, they would become martyrs, and the duty of jihad must not be neglected for the sake of someone who is killed as a martyr.

The third situation regarding Muslim believers in proximity to infidels concerns special circumstances, such as night attacks, when jihad allows for the possibility that persons related to a targeted victim (as part of his entourage) might be injured or killed. Faraj's ruling is based on a hadith of the Prophet, who, when asked about children of idol worshippers who were killed during a Muslim night raid, replied: "They are from them," – that is, he allowed it.[47] However, innocent civilians who have no connection to the targeted victim, Faraj stipulated, must not be attacked under any circumstances, especially women, children, and the aged.[48]

Support for refraining from harming civilians was provided by Faraj's follower, Ayman al-Zawahiri, who, in his memoirs in 2001, stated that the Jihad movement always made sure to warn people close to those in power who were targeted for assassination. In cases in which civilians were harmed, he pointed out, the Jihad movement offered the payment of blood money (*diya*) to their families.[49]

The perpetrator, Faraj argued, is committed to fight to the death, although his primary mission is to attack and kill without exposing himself to deliberate death. If he dies, his death is considered to be the result of an act of jihad. If he has the choice of surrendering or fighting to the end, he must choose the latter option.[50] Based on Ibn Taymiyya, Faraj sanctioned a situation in which a believer penetrates the infidel ranks in the knowledge that he may die (*inghimas*), yet that act will benefit Muslims even if

---

[47] 'Imara (ed.), *al-Farida al-gha'iba*, pp. 121, 128; Abu 'Abdallah Muhammad ibn Isma'il al-Bukhari, *al-Jami' al-sahih* (Beirut: Mu'assasat al-Halabi, 1960), Vol. 5, p. 144; Muslim, *Sahih Muslim*, Vol. 3, p. 1365.

[48] 'Imara (ed.), *al-Farida al-gha'iba*, p. 129. Here, too, Faraj quotes a hadith in which the Prophet was informed that a woman had been found killed in one of the battles. He denounced the act and forbade the killing of women and children. Al-Bukhari, *al-Jami' al-sahih*, Vol. 5, p. 144; Muslim, *Sahih Muslim*, Vol. 3, p. 1365.

[49] Al-Zawahiri's memoirs were compiled in a book, *Fursan tahta rayat al-nabi* (*Knights under the Banner of the Prophet*, 2001): http://azelin.files.wordpress.com/2010/11/ayman-al-zawahiri-knights-under-the-prophets-banner-first-edition.pdf (accessed date November 6, 2013). For an English version, see Laura Mansfield, *His Own Words: Translation and Analysis of the Writings of Dr. Ayman al-Zawahiri* (Old Tappan, NJ: TLG Publications, 2006), pp. 17–225.

[50] 'Imara (ed.), *al-Farida al-gha'iba*, pp. 118–119, 127, 131–132.

he himself will not have the opportunity to see the positive results of his attack.[51] Clearly, however, Faraj did not refer to the type of "human bomb" who deliberately kills himself first, thereby causing death to others. This relatively restrained position reveals moral reservations regarding self-immolation and the killing of innocent people in Muslim society. It largely conforms to the religious principle that a sinful Muslim is still a Muslim: he has reneged on his duty to fulfill God's instructions and has failed to resist temptation (*mu'min 'asi*), yet his sin is less severe than that of an aposted who a priori, and publicly, rejects God's path. A similar approach can be found in Judaism in the Babylonian Talmud, Tractate Sanhedrin: "Even though it [Israel] has sinned, it remains Israel."[52]

The theological restraint regarding attacking innocent civilians was also imbued with a pragmatic consideration. The external environment was perceived by the radicals less as beyond the pale, or alien, than as a human reservoir for political recruitment by which the small enclave could be expanded to a larger and more effective enclave in combating local regimes.[53]

A revealing glimpse of Faraj's and his followers' relatively restrained conception of martyrdom is provided in the record of the interrogation of Sadat's assassins in 1981. The perpetrators emphasized the importance of jihad against heretic rulers but did not refer at all to the question of their imminent death or self-sacrifice, with the exception of their leader, Faraj. He mentioned laconically that he is aware that he will be killed and that he longed for this, as he had done what was required of him. Moreover, most of those involved stressed that the attack was aimed solely against Sadat. If anyone else was harmed, "each would be resurrected according to his intention," asserted Khalid al-Islambuli, an army officer who commanded the attack.[54]

Similarly, the discourse of the Muslim Brethren in Syria, who began mounting confrontations against the Allawite regime in the 1970s, culminating in the Hama massacres in 1982, advocated self-sacrifice and

---

[51] Ibid., p. 127; also Ibn Taymiyya, *Qa'ida fi'l-inghimas.*

[52] J. Neusner, *The Talmud of Babylonia* (Atlanta, GA: American Scholars Press, 1996), pp. 23, 223.

[53] On "enclave culture" and its relationship with the external environment, see Gabriel A. Almond, R. Scott Appleby, and Emmanuel Sivan, *Strong Religion: The Rise of Fundamentalisms around the World* (Chicago: Chicago University Press, 2003), chapter 2.

[54] Mahmud Salah, *Hakadha qatalna al-Sadat: 'i'tirafat Khalid al-Islambuli wa-zumalaihi fi hadith al-minassa* (Cairo: Maktabat Madbuli al-Saghir, 1995), mainly pp. 15, 40, 56–57, 88–89, 132.

commemorated the fallen martyrs in varied types of hagiographic literature. The experience of repression, imprisonment, execution, and exile by the regime, which was perceived both as secular and as ethnic heterodoxy, molded the Brethrens' historical memory and turned the motif of self-sacrifice into a key concept in their discourse.

A central figure and source of inspiration was Marwan Hadid, a Brethren leader who incited the armed revolt against the Syrian regime in 1964 and died in prison in 1976.[55] In the wake of his death, Hadid became a stellar martyr in the movement's narrative, parallel to Sayyid Qutb in the Egyptian context, who also died in prison. Hadid's image was fortified by his close friends and leaders of the movement, who described him as a legend (*ustura*) whose words and deeds were invaluable to the determined struggle against tyranny and heresy and who ignited the fire of passion to die as a holy martyr. Hadid described the moment of his capture as the happiest in his life, and his time in prison, struggling between life and death, as the test of the believer's strength and capacity to endure distress. Hadid's mythicization was not only limited to his bravery and leadership in the jihad field from a position of inferiority and persecution (*mihna*) but also incorporated praise for his modesty, piety, and impartiality toward comrades and followers.[56]

Martyrological literature about Hadid made use of a compilation of his short poems selected and edited to posit an obligatory ethical code for the members of the movement and published in 1982. The core of this compilation consisted of poems praising jihad and self-sacrifice as a ritual act and as the implementation of God's will, which alone can route the forces of tyranny that have overpowered the homeland. He describes himself and those who uphold his code as knights of truth and justice (*fursan al-haqq*) for whom life in this world is temporary in comparison to the eternity and the pleasures of the next world. By contrast, those who display hesitation, weakness, and submission, including the 'ulama', are described as active accomplices in tyranny and corruption.[57]

This code of behavior was clearly articulated in one of Hadid's poems, titled "We Were Born to Worship God":

---

[55] On Hadid see Abd-Allah, *The Islamic Struggle*, pp. 103–107.

[56] *Diwan al-qa'id al-shahid Marwan Hadid* (n.p., 1983), pp. 1–8. The full text appears in minbar al-tawhid wa'l-jihad at http://www.tawhed.ws/a?a=zodhchjh (accessed February 28, 2012). Literally, the term *mihna* means test. It appears in Muslim history as a type of inquisition: The caliph al-Ma'mun (r. 813–833) imposed a *mihna* against the Muslim sages to force his theological views on them.

[57] Ibid., mainly pp. 16, 17, 19, 23–25, 36, 44–45,47–48, 53, 58, 67, 79, 81, 88, 90–91.

We were born to worship God, and God's will has tested us.
If we obey God, we will live in pleasure and happiness.
All of us want a life that is pleasant, all of us want more and more.
We all wish for a life of warfare to attain martyrdom.
We all long for God, and yearn for a good welcome in Paradise.
Victory or a war to the death is all the same to us...
God's satisfaction is always realized in jihad without compromises, in true jihad
against heresy, without fear or laziness.
Others are happy with heresy, and even grant it the reins of leadership.
Others live in baseness, and claim that life is to be lived in mortification.
Others wish for a life in which acts of abasement proliferate.
They do not hold up the life of the next world; the present world has become
their aim.
And they fear death to the extent that their constant prayer is that it be far off.
They fear everything, to the extent that they always claim neutrality.[58]

This sharp dichotomy between purity and defilement, and between passivity in the face of martyrdom, as outlined by Hadid, became a central tenet in his movement's nurturing of martyrdom, especially in the wake of the traumatic events of Hama in 1982.

The masthead of the Brethren official journal, *al-Nadhir* (The Herald), contained the Qur'anic verse: "So go out, no matter whether you are lightly or heavily armed, and struggle in God's way with your possessions and your persons: this is better for you, if you only knew" (Sura 9: 41). The journal devoted a column, titled "*al-Shahid*," to heroic personal stories about the fighters, highlighting their religious piety, moral attributes, acts of bravery, and the circumstances of their death.[59] Photographs of them were also circulated widely.

A representative example of such hagiography is the story of 'Abd al-Sattar al-Za'im, a thirty-year-old martyr who is depicted to be wise, brave, broad-minded and a genius in carrying out political and military planning; to have the heart of a lion and the eyes of an eagle; and to be pure as clear water, an ascetic, and a God-fearing man. When the Muslim nation conducts an evaluation of these martyrs, *al-Nadhir* stated, it will find that al-Za'im was the jewel in the crown of the martyrs of the twentieth century. He grew up under the wings of obedience to God, succeeded in breaking through the complex of fear of that day which people dread, succeeded in reviving the spirit of sacrifice in the name of

---

[58] Ibid., p. 23.
[59] *Al-Nadhir* (January 8, 1980), pp. 20–21; no. 10 (February 1, 1980), p. 1; no. 11 (February 1980), pp. 13, 28; no. 58 (August 1, 1983), pp. 48–51; no. 60 (September 1983), pp. 30–34; no. 61 (October 1983), p. 26; *al-Bayan*, no. 9 (March 1988), p. 5; no. 15 (October 1989), p. 9.

God after it had dwindled in many, and succeeded in causing the most traitorous and terrorist [Hafiz al-Asad] regime in the world to tremble under divine thundering blows.[60]

The Syrian Brethren's discourse of self-sacrifice depicted columns of martyrs "raising the flag of jihad," their pure blood bringing the day of victory closer. One of their defiant messages to Assad warned: "Know, hangman of Syria, that we have brought you people who love death just as you love life. We have long yearned to join the Prophet Muhammad and his companions in the eternal gardens of the seat of truth near the omnipotent king."[61] Nevertheless, as in the Egyptian case, the theology of self-sacrifice was measured and did not embrace pre-planned death but rather stipulated death in the battlefield without harming civilians and aimed solely at the soldiers of a heretical regime. Typically, *al-Nadhir* reported in June 1980 that in the city of Homs "a group of holy fighters attacked an army bus carrying a large number of ethnic [i.e., Allawite] officers and shot at them with rifles and bombs. As a result, approximately 17 of them were killed and the rest were wounded.... The holy fighters withdrew without casualties, praise God."[62] However, several leaders of the Syrian Brethren, including Sa'id Hawwa (d. 1989), pointed to the complexity of the jihad concept, which could range from unspoken or spoken censure all the way to fighting for God, whereas the concept of sacrifice includes sacrificing time and possessions, and not necessarily life, depending on the circumstances.[63]

In translating revolutionary ideas into action, religious violence in such countries as Egypt and Syria in the 1970s and 1980s took the form of conventional armed attacks aimed at symbols of the state – the army, the offices of political parties, and at times the religious establishment. The conventional nature of Sunni violence was also reflected in a detailed list of modern weapons recommended for possession by the Muslim fighter, as cited by the Lebanese Islamist Fathi Yakan in an essay in 1981. No mention is made of an explosive belt or "human bomb."[64]

---

[60] *Al-Nadhir*, no. 4 (October 22, 1979), p. 15.
[61] Ibid., no. 10 (February 1, 1980), pp. 23–26.
[62] Ibid., no. 19 (June 1980), p. 7; no. 59 (August 1, 1983), pp. 41–42.
[63] Hawwa, *Fi 'afaq al-ta'lim*, pp. 112–114.
[64] Yakan, *Abjadiyyat al-tasawwur al-haraki*, pp. 97–100. See also Muhammad Na'im Yasin, *Athar al-Islam fi takwin al-shakhsiyya al-jihadiyya li'l-fard wa'l-jama'a* (Kuwait: Dar al-Arqam, 1984), pp. 97–107; Sa'id Hawwa, *Jund Allah* (2nd ed., n.p., 1991), p. 251. However, mention was made of weapons of "mass destruction," which some radical writers urged Muslims to adopt on the basis of its effectiveness in the struggle against

Underlying this concept of violence was the inherent assumption that taking power begins from above in a political coup d'état. Civilians were excluded from the range of harm. However, scattered episodes of violence against non-Muslim minorities in Egypt and Sudan, and against fellow Muslims in Algeria,[65] revealed that domestic jihad had become a religious ritual, akin to prayer and fasting, although it was not death worship or indiscriminate killing.

THE AWAKENING SHI'A

The projection of violence as a sacred act and as an essential condition for the correct and ultimate understanding of God's will transformed the ordinary believer from a mute voice to the bearer of a mission, capable of fomenting a revolution and bringing about salvation. This was evident most explicitly in modern Shi'i discourse.

Ayatollah Ruhullah Khomeini argued that "[t]he Qur'an is a book designed to produce true human beings; it is a book intended to create active human beings." Ayatollah Mahmud Taleqani asserted that there is no government or ruler in Shi'i Islam, because the twelfth imam is absent; rather, the masses themselves, under the guidance of the _mujtahid_, conduct their own affairs.[66] 'Ali Shari'ati, a lay colleague of Khomeini and Taleqani, went further, employing the image of the "God-like" man who has divine attributes and is the master of his own fate. In Shari'ati's words, "man is the only creature who is responsible not only for his own fate but also has a mission to fulfill the Divine Purpose in the world. Thus he is a trustee in the universe."[67] Defying predestination and assigning man

their enemies. They also sanctioned directing such weapons against civilians if this benefited the Muslims' cause. See, e.g., al-Qasimi, _al-Jihad wa'l-huquq al-duwaliyya_, pp. 545–546; Muhammad Khayr Haykal, _al-Jihad wa'l qital fi'l-siyasa al-shari'iyya_ (Beirut: Dar al-Bayariq, 1993), Vol. 2, pp. 1343–1361.

[65] In Algeria, there was also religious violence aimed at the entire Muslim population, including women and children, carried out by the Groupe Islamique Armè (GIA) during the 1990s. Some of the GIA's car bombings were perpetrated in the form of "suicide" attacks.

[66] Hamid Algar, _Islam and Revolution: Writings and Declarations of Imam Khomeini_ (Berkeley: Mizan Press, 1981), p. 226; idem, _Society and Economics in Islam: Writings and Declarations of Ayatullah Sayyid Mahmud Taleghani_ (Berkeley, CA: Mizan Press, 1982), pp. 209–217; Mahmud Taleqani, "Jihad and Shahadat," in M. Abedi and G. Legenhausen (eds.), _Jihad and Shahadat: Struggle and Martyrdom in Islam_ (Houston: Institute for Research and Islamic Studies, 1986), pp. 47–80.

[67] Ali Shariati, _Man and Islam_, trans. Fatollah Marjani (Houston: Free Islamic Lit, 1982), mainly pp. 1–9; also Hamid Dabashi, _Theology of Discontent_ (New York: New York University Press, 1993), pp. 120–121. For Shari'ati's biography, see Ali Rahnema, _An Islamic Utopian: A Political Biography of Ali Shari'ati_ (London: I.B. Tauris, 1998).

with political responsibility constituted a distinctly modern perception – a by-product of the rise of mass politics. It was a functional type of individualism, with the faithful drafted for the collective goal of creating an exemplary community of believers.

Led by Ayatollah Khomeini and the clerical regime in Tehran, the Shi'a creed, fueled by a sense of humiliation over Sunni hegemony, and nurturing an eschatological expectation of salvation, became a culture of rage and active confrontation with perceived global forces of injustice and tyranny. The world was divided into oppressed and oppressors, with jihad depicted as purely defensive.

Jihad and self-sacrifice became key concepts in the Shi'a awakening and in the entrenchment of the Islamic Revolution,[68] shunting aside the older religio-historic tradition of *taqiyya*, namely, sanctifying the preservation of life and preaching caution and accommodation in times of persecution, mainly by Sunni rulers. The new concepts also severed the strong identification in the Shi'i tradition between martyrdom and the venerated imams of the House of 'Ali, shifting it from an elitist to a mass perception. Just as revolutionary Shi'ism expropriated the Pahlavi State monopoly over violence, it also expropriated the imamate's monopoly over martyrdom, which became "democratized." In its wake, Shi'i rage was shifted from the ritualistic and ceremonial sphere (the *'ashura* and the *ta'ziya*)[69] to the political sphere, metamorphosing into revolutionary fervor. The holy time periods (e.g., the month of *Muharram*) were also appropriated, becoming the province of the whole year.[70]

Notably, Marxist guerilla movements that emerged in the 1960s to combat the Shah's regime, such as the Fedayin, and especially the Mujahidin Khalq, recognized the revolutionary potential of the Shi'a, based on the story of the life and death of Imam Husayn. In promoting their political agenda they made extensive use of the notions of struggle and self-sacrifice as the ultimate representation of the Muslim revolutionary.

---

[68] On the indoctrination of jihad and martyrdom in revolutionary Iran, see Algar, *Islam and Revolution*, pp. 239–245, 249–251, 265–274; Ram, *Myth and Mobilization in Revolutionary Iran*, pp. 61–87; M. Abedi and G. Legenhausen (eds.), *Jihad and Shahadat*; Dabashi, *Theology of Discontent*, pp. 175–179; Amir Taheri, *Holy Terror: The Inside Story of Islamic Terrorism* (London: Hutchinson Ltd., 1987), pp. 80–85, 228–243.

[69] Peter Chelkowski (ed.), *Ta'ziyeh: Ritual and Drama in Iran* (New York: University Press, 1979); Hamid Anyat, *Modern Islamic Political Thought* (Austin: University of Texas Press, 1982), pp. 181–194.

[70] Algar, *Islam and Revolution*, pp. 242–245; idem, *Society and Economics in Islam*, pp. 113–126, 130–132; also Farhad Khosrokhavar, "Toward an Anthropology of Democratization in Iran," *Critique: Critical Middle Eastern Studies* 9/16 (2000), pp. 6–8.

Those among their activists who were killed or executed became *shahid*s in these movements' official commemorative pantheon.[71]

The shift of the narrative of salvation through grief to a heroic narrative of national redemption was enabled significantly by the charisma and rhetorical skills of the Shi'i religious scholars, led by Khomeini, as well as by their ability to rework past traditions, or, as described by historian Haggai Ram, to bring about an "ideological rejuvenation of tradition." As a result, Shi'i history was transformed into one long march of defiance and a longing for death as martyrs.[72]

In the revolutionary narrative, self-sacrifice – in contrast to other kinds of death, such as death because of illness or death by accident, which are natural events, or death as a result of grief, murder, or suicide, which have no value or honor – is a heroic death and the object of esteem, inasmuch as it stems from a voluntary, conscious, non-egoistic act. This is the only type of death that is lofty, uplifting, and holier than life itself. The martyr was depicted as infusing society with new blood and a new light. It is no wonder, Ayatollah Murtada Mutahhari (d. 1979) claimed, that the martyr's true status is far superior to that of other social agents, such as scholars, philosophers, inventors, or teachers: it is he who creates the atmosphere that is conducive to their productive work on behalf of humanity.[73] According to Mutahhari, who was known for his poetic oratory, "The *shuhada* are the candles of society. They burn themselves out and illuminate society. If they do not shed their light, no organization can shine. ... Had they not shed their light on the darkness of despotism and suppression, humanity would have made no progress."[74]

A prominent Iranian architect of the revolution, 'Ali Shari'ati went even further in his activist conception of martyrdom, viewing the essence of life and the aspiration for death as intertwined. Every revolution, he argued, contains elements of self-sacrifice. The first element is blood, the second is the message. The red blood of the martyr is the antithesis of the black blood of

---

[71] See, e.g., Ervand Abrahamian, *The Iranian Mojahedin* (New Haven: Yale University Press, 1989).

[72] Jill D. Swenson, "Martyrdom: Mytho-Cathexis and Mobilization of the Masses in the Iranian Revolution," *Ethos* 13/2 (Summer 1985), pp. 121–149; Haggai Ram, *Iranophobia: The Logic of an Israeli Obsession* (Stanford, CA: Stanford University Press, 2009), chapter 4.

[73] Murtada Mutahhari, "Shahid," in Abedi and Legenhausen (eds.), *Jihad and Shahadat*, pp. 125–128; idem, *Jihad: The Holy War of Islam and Its Legitimacy in the Qur'an*, trans. by Mohammad S. Tawhidi (Tehran: Department of Translation and Publication, 1998); also Muhammad Husayn Tabataba'i, *Shi'ite Islam* (2nd ed., Albany: State University of New York Press, 1977), pp. 197–200.

[74] Mutahhari, "Shahid," p. 126.

the coward and the faint-hearted, who are historically numerous. In identifying the martyr as the beating heart of history, Shari'ati sought to link the struggles of the past to those of the present.[75] The ultimate link, in his view, was Imam Husayn, grandson of 'Ali, and his role in the Karbala episode.

The centrality of the Karbala myth in Shi'i consciousness over the generations allowed Shari'ati, through creative interpretation and rhetorical finesse, to develop and define a separate, ultimate category of martyrdom that was not an extension of jihad but was detached from it and even loftier than it. In his words, "a shahid is a person who from the beginning of his decision chooses his own *shahadat*, even though, between his decision-making and his death, months or even years may pass."[76] This deviation from the Shi'i narrative, and from the Islamic narrative generally, may be perceived as a reflection of Shari'ati's revolutionary extremism but also as a reflection of his self-educated background, which allowed for a freer mindset regarding the issue of self-sacrifice than that of his 'ulama' colleagues.

In Shari'ati's innovative notion, the believer walks toward death consciously and deliberately to convey the message of sacrifice for the faith in the most effective way possible.[77] The historic model, in his view, was the acquiescent death of Imam Husayn at the hands of the Umayyid army in Karbala (680), rather than the death in battle of Hamza, the Prophet's uncle, at Uhud (625). Hamza was a fighter and a hero who went into the battlefield to attain victory over the enemy – the people of Mecca. Instead, he was defeated, killed, and made a martyr. By contrast, Husayn did not enter the campaign with the intention of killing the enemy and attaining victory. Rather than aspiring to emerge alive, he welcomed his death, so as to ratify and reinstate the sanctity of the religious ideal that had been eroded under the tyrannical and materialistic rule of the Umayyads. "In the case of Hamza, shahada is a negative incident; in Husayn's case it is a decisive goal, chosen consciously."[78]

Shari'ati wanted to re-illuminate the episode of Husayn's death not only as a fighter who fell in the battlefield (*shahid al-ma'raka*) but as a loftier

---

[75] Ali Shari'ati, "A Discussion of Shahid," in Abedi and Legenhausen (eds.), *Jihad and Shahadat*, pp. 230–241; also Cook, *Martyrdom in Islam*, pp. 314–315.

[76] Shari'ati, "A Discussion of Shahid," p. 239; also idem, "Shahadat," in Abedi and Legenhausen (eds.), *Jihad and Shahadat*, pp. 201–202.

[77] Shari'ati, "A Discussion of Shahid," pp. 237–238.

[78] Ibid., pp. 230–241; Shari'ati, "Shahadat," pp. 181–182; also idem, *Martyrdom: Arise and Bear Witness*, trans. by Ali Asghar Ghassemy (Tehran: Ministry of Islamic Guidance, 1981).

model: to turn the episode from a tragedy forced by the enemy, which generated lamentation and grief, into an exalted act of initiated and desired death prompted by clear and intelligent thought, without any consideration of the asymmetry of the military forces.

Shari'ati also refashioned the background setting of the drama at Karbala by painting Husayn in heroic terms as a lone figure in the shadow of a Shi'i community whose thinking was paralyzed and whose ranks were sparse, lacking recruits and weapons. Husayn had the prerogative of keeping silent, or of migrating to a more secure place, but he was aware of the extent of the responsibility placed on him in standing against the intention to defeat the truth and destroy the people's rights. For him, the question of capability, whether present or absent, was unimportant. What was important was the opposition to injustice and the public expression of it, so that others would understand the need to engage in a jihad to end injustice.[79] Equipped with this insight, Husayn arrived at Karbala and, by his self-sacrifice, sought first to expose the illegitimate and traitorous nature of the regime; secondly, to atone for the evil deeds of his community on the day of judgment, thus functioning as a later reincarnation of Jesus who sacrificed himself for humankind to restore them to paradise; and thirdly, to separate the exalted spirit from the material and the corporeal and turn it into celestial light.[80]

Indeed, the Karbala paradigm became part of the revolutionary pantheon as an active episode of self-sacrifice. Its hero, Husayn, was pronounced a lord of martyrs (*sayyid al-shuhada*') who gave his life for the righteous struggle for truth, justice, and faith. His altruistic death became a symbol of the triumph of blood over the sword and the victory of sacrifice over evil and tyranny.

Husayn's martyrdom was fortified by his family genealogy, thereby creating a continuum of purity of faith and the struggle for justice. His persona was largely bound up with that of both his parents – 'Ali, the Prophet's cousin, and Fatima, daughter of the Prophet and the figure who prepared him for heroism and self-sacrifice. 'Ali was described as experiencing suffering and persecution, yet displayed bravery and died for a divine cause. Fatima was depicted as committed not only to home but also to community, thus symbolizing the ideal Muslim woman. The foundations underlying the description of Fatima's activist image had been laid in the 1950s by the Iraqi scholar Muhammad Baqir al-Sadr, who led the

---

[79] Shari'ati, "Shahadat," pp. 173–190.
[80] Ibid., pp. 194, 200, 208–214; also, idem, *Martyrdom: Arise and Bear Witness*.

oppositionist al-Daʿwa Party against Saddam Husayn's regime and was executed in 1980. Al-Sadr emphasized Fatima's involvement in the public domain, the fiery sermons she preached to the believers, and her resolute stance in the face of those in power, especially the first caliph Abu Bakr, demanding her rights to her father's inheritance and challenging the deviant conduct of the caliphate regime. In al-Sadr's view, Fatima ultimately failed in her struggle at the time, but her claim for justice was engraved forever in the Shiʿi memory in the generations to come.[81]

A more systematic analysis of Fatima's revolutionary image was provided by ʿAli Shariʿati in Iran in the early 1970s. Shariʿati positioned Fatima as the highest manifestation of motherhood in Islamic history and as a role model for the contemporary Muslim woman, whereas the Western cultural invasion aimed at divesting women of any moral attribute in the name of individual and sexual freedom. He depicted Fatima as a warrior who, throughout her life, from childhood to death,

felt herself to be a responsible, committed person, a part of the destiny of the community, defending what was right, supporting justice in thought, idea and deed and confronting the usurpation, oppression and deviation, which existed in her society. She did not remain silent until here death even though she knew that she would not succeed in this fight. This is the meaning of social commitment and responsibility. This is the lesson that can be learned from Fatima's life.[82]

A direct historical line was thus drawn between Fatima's activist legacy and Husayn's sacrifice in Karbala. Karbala represented an alternative reading of Islam and provided the clerical regime in Iran with a discourse of opposition and a more acute Shiʿi identity.[83] It presented death as "no more than a hyphen between the two parts of man's existence" – this world and the hereafter – and its rationale as striving to eliminate oppression and

[81] Muhammad Baqir al-Sadr, *Fadak fi'l-ta'rikh* (Beirut: Dar al-Taʿaruf al-Islami, 1990), mainly pp. 14–22, 87–100. On al-Baqir's political biography see T. M. Aziz, "The Role of Muhammad Baqir al-Sadr in Shiʿi Political Activism in Iraq from 1958 to 1980," *International Journal of Middle East Studies* 25/2 (1993), pp. 207–222.
[82] ʿAli Shariʿati, "Expectations from the Muslim Women," in Laleh Bakhtiar, *Shariati on Shariati and the Muslim Women* (Chicago: ABC International Group, 1996), p. 68; for a broader discussion, see Shariʿati's "Fatima is Fatima," ibid., chapter 9.
[83] Khomeini quoted in Algar, *Islam and Revolution*, pp. 242–245; Ram, *Myth and Mobilization in Revolutionary Iran*, pp. 61–87; Juan R. Cole, *Sacred Space and Holy War: The Politics, Culture and History of Shi'ite Islam* (London: I.B. Tauris, 2002), p. 21; also, Aghaie, *The Martyrs of Karbala*, mainly chapter 8. Notably, the Karbala episode was also expropriated from its Shiʿi context by non-Muslim politicians and reformers who gave it a more trans-sectarian and transnational context embodying the ideas of universal justice, resistance to colonialism, and global solidarity. See Syed Akbar Hyder, *Reliving Karbala: Martyrdom in South Asian Memory* (Oxford: Oxford University Press, 2006).

injustice, thereby preventing Muslims who experience oppression from abandoning their faith.[84]

In modern Shi'i martyrology (and in its Sunni counterpart, discussed in Chapter 6), the perpetrator was seen as a candle illuminating the darkness of tyranny, thereby serving as a pedagogic model parallel to Christian saints in the medieval period whose elevated moral status provided an example for the living. In both historical contexts, Christian and Islamic, self-sacrifice was perceived not as a tragedy but as an exalted ideal by which the martyr demonstrates his community's unshakable faith and challenges the superior power of the enemy. However, whereas the Christian martyr is a hero by virtue of a passive act – death by persecutors and torturers – the Muslim martyr is a hero by virtue of an active, self-initiated act as befitting a victorious religion such as Islam in its formative stage.[85]

Elevating martyrdom, the Iranian revolutionary regime dispatched teenage boys to be exploded in the Iraqi minefields during the Iran-Iraq War (1980–1988) to clear the way for the troops in the cause of Islam. These boys were depicted as "new and purer generations" whose religious devotion was unquestionable and who were pronounced *basijis* (volunteers in the paramilitary militia called *basij*). As far back as the early 1970s Khomeini lauded the stage of youth, writing in 1972:

As man's age advances, the obstacles to his happiness increase, and his strength to resist them decreases. So when you reach old age, your chances for success in purifying and reforming yourselves and attaining virtue and piety are small.... While you are still young you can accomplish something. While you still have the energy and willpower of youth, you can ward off ... passionate desires, worldly longings and animal wants. But if you do not begin to reform yourselves in youth it will be too late in old age.... If you devote your precious time and the spring of your youth to the cause of God and a sacred, precise aim, you will not lose anything. On the country, your welfare in this world and the hereafter will be assured.[86]

A religious ruling issued by Khomeini in 1979 permitted boys more than twelve years of age to volunteer for the front without parental permission. These youngsters thereby became "children of the Imam" and were promised a place in paradise if they fell in battle. Tens of thousands were given "keys to paradise" and purple headbands inscribed with the slogan "Long live Khomeini." Here too the figure of Imam Husayn played a central role,

---

[84] Taheri, *Holy Terror*, pp. 230, 233; also Taleqani, "Jihad and Shahdat," pp. 47–80.

[85] Ayoub, "Martyrdom in Christianity and Islam," pp. 67–77.

[86] Algar, *Islam and Revolution*, pp. 359–360.

as can be learned from official posters circulated during the war. Aimed at the fighters and their families, the posters featured Husayn's likeness as a fearless fighter worthy of emulation and as a hero and savior. His presence in the battlefield was emphasized as watching over the fighters and providing them with spiritual backing for their sacrifice. Some of the battles were named Karbala 1, Karbala 2, and so forth.[87] Posters depicting those battles show Husayn as the savior of war fatalities, gathering them up and bringing them with him to paradise, or awaiting with them at the gate to paradise.

Speeches by religious figures emphasized that families should be proud of their *shahid* sons, be happy in their death, and send additional sons to battle.[88] This was also reflected in wills or testaments (Persian *vasiyyat/* Arabic *wasaya*) left by the fallen, published in the official press, and anthologized thereafter in printed volumes. In these wills, many of the young soldiers address their mother with the request to accept their death, as it was their wish to follow the path of Husayn. In one will, the would-be martyr wrote: "How pathetic, how unfortunate, how ignorant I was during the 14 miserable years of my life when I did not know God. The Imam opened my eyes ... how sweet, sweet, sweet is death, like a blessing that God imparts to those he loves."[89] The wills nurtured the notion of the ultimate union of citizen and nation, of the faithful and his Creator. In engendering religious excitement and the mobilization of young people, concepts and metaphors from classical Persian mysticism, such as moths and candles, which represent the annihilation of the ego and the union with the Beloved, were also used, emphasizing the longing for transcendence. According to Ashar Seyed-Gohrab, mystic motives that advocated non-violence, love, piety, and an ascetic way of life "were transformed during the Iran-Iraq War into the violent and bloody reality of war."[90]

---

[87] Taheri, *Holy Terror*, pp. 81–83; Shahram Chubin and Cahrles Tripp, *Iran and Iraq at War* (Boulders: Westview Press, 1991), pp. 41–52; Joyce M. Davis, *Martyrs: Innocence, Vengeance and Despair in the Middle East* (New York: Palgrave Macmillan, 2003), pp. 49–52.

[88] Efrat Harel, *Mobilizing Iranian Society during the War with Iraq, 1980–1988* (PhD dissertation; Tel Aviv: Tel Aviv University, 2003), pp. 119–159 (in Hebrew).

[89] Menashri, *Iran in Revolution*, pp. 237–238; Nazemi, "Sacrifice and Authorship," pp. 263–271; Werner Schmucker, "Iranische Märtyretestamente," *Die Welt des Islams* 27 (1987), pp. 185–249; also Mateo Mohammad Farzaneh, "Shiʿi Ideology, Iranian Secular Nationalism and the Iran-Iraq War," *Studies in Ethnicity and Nationalism* 7/1 (2007), pp. 96–99.

[90] Varzi, *Warring Souls*, pp. 44–75; Asghar Seyed-Goharb, "Martyrdom as Piety: Mysticism and National Identity in Iran-Iraq War Poetry," *Der Islam* Bd. 87 (2010), pp. 248–273 (the quote is on p. 249).

Visual manifestations of martyrdom in the public sphere were also employed. *Ta'ziya* ceremonies held in the streets, reenacting the battle at Karbala, presented the image of the ideal hero who faces the ultimate test of heroism, while the enemy is depicted as a murderous figure who kills the faithful. Streets were named for young war martyrs, their images were posted on walls, and documentary films kept their memory alive.[91] The religious reward for a son's metamorphosis to a *shahid* was also embodied in material support – namely monetary grants, loans, and other incentives to the families, although these were reduced when the regime faced financial difficulties.[92]

Iranian martyrdom thus became state policy, entrusted mainly to the Ministry of Islamic Guidance. Martyrdom was closely linked to Khomeini by means of the continuous reinforcement of his image and the delegitimation of his rivals, thereby providing an additional impetus to the entrenchment of the Islamic revolution, which was still in a nascent stage. Khomeini was portrayed in posters and wills as following in the footsteps of the Prophet and the imams, with an emphasis on the Third Imam – Husayn – and as a leader of the Muslims toward redemption and a decisive victory.[93]

The visible commemoration of martyrs and martyrdom continued well after Khomeini's death in 1989. A martyrs' museum was built in Tehran displaying the names, birth and death dates, and clothing and personal effects of the martyrs of the Islamic Revolution and the war with Iraq. "The purpose of this museum," as described by its director, "is to keep alive the stories of the brave people who sacrificed their souls for the goals of the Islamic revolution and the war with Iraq."[94] Islamic Republic Internet sites also played a role in commemoration. An official blog by a student, Basij, cited the memorial days of all the martyrs of the war with Iraq. One martyr, Muhammad Husayn Fahmida, was identified as "one of the thousands of children who, in sacrificing their blood, contributed to the freshness and redness of the blood of the martyrs in the imposed war."[95] The illustration attached to this blog text, and also posted in a major road of

[91] Varzi, *Warring Souls*, chapters 3 and 4; William O. Beeman, *Iranian Performance Traditions* (Los Angeles: Mazda Press, 2010), mainly chapters 5, 6, and 8.

[92] Taheri, *Holy Terror*, p. 83.

[93] Nazemi, "Sacrifice and Authorship."

[94] Davis, *Martyrs*, pp. 45–49.

[95] Basij's official blog: http://basijpqm.persianblog.ir/tag/%D8%AD%D8%B3%DB%8C% D9%86_%D9%81%D9%87%D9%85%DB%8C%D8%AF%D9%87 (accessed April 10, 2011).

Tehran, shows Fahmida in a battlefield surrounded by tanks, while over-head the image of Ayatollah Khomeini is looking down at him in his act of martyrdom.[96]

The Iranian model of initiated or offensive death, as reflected in the military practice of sending boys to clear minefields, served as a source of inspiration in other regions of the Middle East and the Muslim world. It became integral in the dissident discourse of religio-national liberation movements, presenting self-sacrifice as a basis for the survival of the community. This discourse also harbored the phenomenon of "martyrdom operations" (*'amaliyyat istishhadiyya*), commonly known in Western discourse as "suicide" attacks or "suicide" missions, discussed in the next chapter.

---

[96] Ibid. See also http://media/npr.org/news/images/2009/feb/04/mural_540-8fa5beeb90c9fd 93e1ffd31333315e3eae230ade-s51.jpg (accessed August 15, 2013).

4

The "Army of Shrouds": "Suicide" Attacks in Ethno-national Conflicts

"Suicide" attack is defined as an operational method in which the act of the attack itself is dependent on the death of the perpetrator.[1] The term *istishhad*, which was rare in Arab Muslim discourse – in contrast to the prevailing term *shahada* – became widespread, denoting the active seeking of martyrdom. "Suicide" attacks constituted an updated format in the evolution of the tactics and techniques used by Islamist groups in response to rapid changes in the local, regional, and global environment. The first systematic use of "suicide" as a weapon occurred in Lebanon in the early 1980s, although, as shown in Chapter 3, its theological, political, and operational underpinnings were largely lain down by Iran in the 1970s and during the early years of the Islamic Revolution.

HIZBALLAH MARTYRDOM: THE WEAPON OF THE OPPRESSED

In Lebanon, followers of Khomeini – namely, the Hizballah movement – mounted a series of successful "suicide" attacks against Western and Israeli military targets during 1983–1985. These attacks should be viewed in the wider perspective of the Shiʿa awakening in Lebanon in the 1970s, which was multifaceted: it was not only militarily but also socially demanding, under the charismatic leadership of Musa al-Sadr (d. 1978),

---

[1] See, e.g., Boaz Ganor, "Suicide's Terrorism: An Overview," *Countering Suicide Terrorism*, 2000, available at http://www.ict.org (accessed July 15, 2010); Gambetta (ed.), *Making Sense of Suicide Missions*.

for equal share in the country's resources to reflect the demographic growth of the Shi'a sector.[2]

Until the 1970s, protest and martyrology in the Lebanese discourse, as in Iran, were largely limited to the realm of ritual and rhetoric. A typical example was the sermon delivered by al-Sayyid Muhammad Sharaf al-Din in the Burj Hammud Mosque during the *'ashura* ceremonies in October 1955, summarized in the periodical *al-'Irfan*. The essence of the sermon was devoted to the image of the martyr Imam Husayn and his struggle against the army of oppression and for the rescue of the faith, which became a source of pride and a symbol for martyrs who came after him. The preacher appealed to contemporary Shi'is to sacrifice their soul and their possessions for the lofty values for which Husayn fought until his last breath, even though the power balance between the people of justice and the people of falsehood remained as it had been – the few against the many.[3]

Only in the early 1980s did ceremonial martyrdom metamorphose into an operational mode, riding the waves of success of the Iranian Revolution and nurtured by the fallout from the Israeli invasion of Lebanon. Some researchers, such as Martin Kramer, attributed these acts of self-sacrifice to internal rivalries in the Shi'a community, especially between Hizballah and the older established Amal movement, and the desire by both movements to avert domestic bloodshed by channeling violence toward the foreign invader.[4]

The "suicide" attacks that were carried out by Hizballah against Western and Israeli military targets, especially by means of car bombs, were lauded as "illuminating the Lebanese horizon after the heavy darkness that had enveloped it."[5] Its perpetrators were commemorated in extensive hagiographical literature, which, like the Iranian version, glorified their martyrdom and linked them closely to the death of Imam Husayn, with the mourners in the *ta'ziya* ceremonies urged to direct their self-flagellation at the enemy.[6]

---

[2] Fouad Ajami, *The Vanished Imam: Musa al-Sadr and the Shia of Lebanon* (London: I.B. Tauris, 1986); Augustus R. Norton, *Amal and the Shi'a: Struggle for the Soul of Lebanon* (Austin: University of Texas Press, 1988), pp. 13–58.

[3] Al-Sayyid Muhammad Sharaf al-Din, "Ayyuha al-batal al-shahid," *al-'Irfan* (October 1955), pp. 77–78.

[4] Martin Kramer, "Sacrifice and Fratricide in Shiite Lebanon," in Mark Jurgensmeyer (ed.), *Violence and the Sacred in the Modern World* (London: Frank Cass, 1992), pp. 30–47.

[5] Sa'd Abu Diya, *Dirasa tahliliyya fi'l-'amaliyyat al-istishhadiyya fi Janub Lubnan* (Amman: Jam'iyyat 'Ummal al-Matabi' al-Ta'awuniyya, 1986), pp. 13–14.

[6] Salwa al-'Imad, *al-Imam al-shahid fi'l-ta'rikh wa'l-idiolojiyya: shahid al-Shi'a muqabil batal al-Sunna* (Beirut: al-Mu'assasa al-'Arabiyya, 2000); *al-'Ahd*, May 24, 1985, and

Lebanese Shi'ism largely adopted the Iranian narrative of Karbala and its related *'ashura* ceremonies. Hizballah's ideological leader, Shaykh Muhammad Husayn Fadlallah (d. 2010), ruled that the perception of the *'ashura* as a tragic event involving grief, suffering, and self-flagellation blurs the nature of the struggle and turns the *'ashura* into rivers of tears, with the believer commemorating this aspect instead of responding to a revolutionary impulse.

Fadlallah did not dismiss the importance of the passion for the *'ashura* ceremonies. On the contrary, he viewed it as an important commemorative stimulus. However, he wished to heighten its effectiveness in stimulating the spirit of the "Husayni revolution," lest it distort the essence of Shi'ism, foment disorder, and serve the enemies of Islam. The true value of the *'ashura* is not to be found in the annual ceremonies and commemorations, he wrote, but in its constant presence in the life of the nation, providing it with energy and protection. The story of Husayn and his exalted self-sacrifice, Fadlallah explained, is to a great extent the story of Islam and, thus, inherent in the life of every Muslim wherever there is arrogance, injustice, and tyranny – whether in Iran, Iraq, Afghanistan, Lebanon, or Palestine. Fadlallah thereby sought to downplay the narrowed Shi'i character of the *'ashura* and portray it as a symbol of Islamic justice generally. In the perception of this leading Hizballah ideologue, the *'ashura* served as a window of opportunity for the Islamic movement – the gate through which Islam would penetrate a dormant society and galvanize the struggle against arrogance and repression.[7]

Even the battle zone in southern Lebanon aimed at Israel was equated with the battle of Karbala, reinforced by recruited media that heightened the drama by means of written and photographed testimonies of martyrs. Framing "suicide" attacks in eschatological contexts also served domestic political ends to repel demands to disarm Hizballah. As the secretary general of the movement, Hasan Nasrallah, stated, "Whoever considers disarming Hizballah will be attacked by the organization as did the martyr in the battle of Karbala."[8]

Other incentives, besides the close identification with the heritage of the sanctified Imam, were also put forward, including imminent marriage to dark-eyed virgins in paradise. A compilation of Hizballah songs included

November 14, 1986; also Hala Jaber, *Hizballah: Born with a Vengeance* (New York: Columbia University Press, 1997), pp. 75–88.

[7] Muhammad Husayn Fadlallah, *'Ala tariq Karbala'* (Beirut: Dar al-Tayyar al-Jadid, 1984). On the *'ashura* in Lebanese Shi'i rituals, see Augustus R. Norton, *Hezbollah: A Short History* (Princeton, NJ: Princeton University Press, 2007), pp. 47–68.

[8] *Al-Nahar*, March 11, 1985; *al-'Ahd*, November 14, 1986; *al-Manar*, April 20, 2005.

one titled "The Blood Wedding," with the lyrics: "My only mother. I married in this world, the day of sacrifice, the day I will meet the fair black-eyed virgin, the day my congealed blood will be as a decoration for the day I welcome the Prophet, and Husayn will bless me with great light."[9] The martyr's mother became an object of esteem, as did the rest of the family, with Hizballah reaching out to them with an organized support system. Financed by Iran, this network, called the Institution of the Martyr (*mu'assasat al-shahid*), had several branches throughout Lebanon, thereby playing a key role in sustaining self-sacrifice. Children of married martyrs were granted educational sponsorships by the Hizballah movement, which included the costs of enrollment in school, the purchase of school books and notebooks, and special summer camps. Trips and tours connected with resistance sites and related religious topics were organized to reinforce their tie with the heritage of self-sacrifice. This support extended to university studies as well.[10]

The moral imperative of the "suicide" attacks, and especially the use of car bombs, as discussed by the Lebanese historian Sa'd Abu Diya in a book published in 1986,[11] was twofold: the necessity to oust an alien and infidel occupier without delay and the effectiveness of using an unconventional weapon. This strategy indeed proved itself, first in the withdrawal of the American and French troops from Lebanon in 1983 and later in the retreat of the Israeli forces to a narrow strip along the Lebanese-Israeli border in 1985. It was the first time in the history of the Arab-Israeli dispute, Abu Diya emphasized, that Israel was forced to withdraw from territory under its control not because of international pressure or Arab military superiority but because of acts of self-sacrifice. This phenomenon reflected the determination of the residents of the region, who recognized self-sacrifice as an effective force for change in the balance of power. A key role in this process was played by religious scholars in their preaching and rulings, thereby creating a congenial spiritual and psychological climate.[12]

The historical roots of this type of martyrdom, Abu Diya pointed out, lie in the resolute resistance and moral immutability of the peoples of the East in the face of their enemies. He referred especially to the residents of the Fertile Crescent, as well as to populations in the Far East, as exemplified by the Japanese kamikaze pilots during the confrontation with the United

---

[9] Quoted in Abu Husayn, *Ya thar Allah: latamat Husayniyya* (Terhan: n.p., 1984), pp. 106–107.

[10] See, e.g., *al-'Ahd*, February 14, 1987, p. 2.

[11] Abu Diya, *Dirasa tahliliyya fi'l-'amaliyyat al-istishhadiyya*.

[12] Ibid., pp. 13–14, 23–26, 92–102.

States in World War II.[13] Another theme emphasized by Abu Diya was the abiding readiness to die for the group, which sprang from Islamic doctrine and from group-oriented lifestyle patterns based on solidarity and cooperation embedded in Lebanese society. With this, Abu Diya also quoted Lebanese 'ulama' who emphasized that "suicide" attacks did not constitute a systematic or mass modus operandi but were implemented in emergency situations only and within specific Islamic parameters.[14]

Not all members of the Shi'i learned community were satisfied with the systematic use of the "suicide" weapon. Prominent in this respect was Muhammad Mahdi Shams al-Din (d. 2001), head of the Supreme Islamic Shi'i Council, who represented a more moderate position in the Shi'i legal discourse in Lebanon. In a speech delivered in 1983 during the *'ashura* celebrations in the village of Betuniya, he praised Islam as an abiding revolution and extolled the self-sacrifice of Husayn at Karbala for the preservation of the values of the faith – the loftiest level of sacrifice – yet he also pointed out that Husayn and his friends did not become martyrs only on their death. They were already martyrs during their lives. Martyrdom is not acquired solely in death; it is applicable as well through adherence to a just cause. It is a concern not for an individual or a group, but for the nation as a whole. Moreover, the struggle against Israel must not be the province of a particular group but must be managed along a broad front that includes all of Lebanese society. Additionally, the emphases of the struggle must be no less popular and civilian (*madaniyya*) than military, and perhaps even more so. Shams al-Din thereby conveyed an indirect criticism of Hizballah, both for underscoring the exclusively Shi'i nature of the struggle against Israel and for its military emphases.[15]

Known as being moderate, Shams al-Din believed in religious tolerance regarding the other sectors of the population and favored a free and sovereign Lebanon over the adoption of a pan-Islamic ideology. He continued to adhere to his critical position vis-à-vis Hizballah and later expanded it. In his book, *Fiqh al-'unf al-musallah fi'l-Islam* (The Jurisprudence of Armed Struggle in Islam), written in 2001, he sought to trace the roots of the legitimacy of armed struggle in Muslim law. Positing a broad analysis of the martyrdom of Imam Husayn, he described Husayn's acts as a "suicidal revolution" (*thawra intihariyya*) and criticized Shi'i scholars who use that revolution to justify armed struggle against

---

[13] Ibid., pp. 92–102.
[14] Ibid., p. 93.
[15] Shams al-Din's sermon quoted in *al-Irafan* (October 1983), pp. 104–112.

domestic regimes – even despotic regimes – to sanctify unrestricted martyrdom.

Shams al-Din pointed out that the compromise and acceptance shown by Imam Hasan, Husayn's brother, toward Mu'awiya's political despotism should serve as a guide in situations in which Islam is not threatened so that the unity of the nation is preserved. In the case of Husayn, armed resistance against Yazid, son of Mu'awiya, was justified and worthy, as Islamic faith as a whole was endangered. Husayn's greatest accomplishment, in Shams al-Din's view, was the successful separation of the caliphate's religious authority from its political authority, a position that he believed should lead contemporary Shi'i 'ulama' to distance themselves from politics. This point revealed Shams al-Din's dissatisfaction with the notion of Khomeini's "rule of the jurist" and its supporters in Hizballah, which he also perceived as infringing on the independence and sovereignty of Lebanon itself. Moreover, his description of Husayn's acts as "suicide" hinted at his rejection of the ideology of "suicide" attacks as a means of carrying out jihad.[16]

Hizballah was not indifferent to the criticism directed against some of the "suicide" acts. The movement's spiritual leader, Fadlallah, made a point of emphasizing that death is not a tragic event for the Muslim fighters, nor does it represent a state of despair or sentimentality. On the contrary, it is thought out in advance to serve specific goals. "A person feels spiritual happiness when he is about to die," he asserted. He approaches the battle from a consciousness of faith and with the strength of confidence in God. Consequently, he accepts death with indifference and confronts the infidels with all his might, even in a situation of Muslim numerical inferiority against their enemies by half or worse. Faith is a noble human trait, like courage, righteousness, and confidence in God, so that the fighter is about to merit one of two favors: *shahada* or victory.[17] "By means of *shahada* he will pave his way to paradise, while by means of victory he will fulfill the will of God."[18]

Essentially, Fadlallah argued, faith endows the fighter with moral strength, a sense of mission, and loyalty to the goal. Thus, there is no essential difference between the death of a Muslim on the battlefield with a weapon in his hand and a fighter who explodes himself in the proximity of enemy soldiers. What is important is the presence of injustice and tyranny

---

[16] Muhammad Mahdi Shams al-Din, *Fiqh al-'unf al-musallah fi'l-Islam* (Baghdad: Markaz Dirasat Falsafat al-Din, 2004), mainly pp. 124–130.

[17] Fadlallah's book, *Kitab al-jihad* (Beirut: Dar al-Malak, 1996), pp. 185–201; also idem, *al-Islam wa-mantiq al-quwwa* (4th ed., Beirut: Dar al-Malak, 2003), mainly chapter 9.

[18] Fadlallah, *al-Islam wa-mantiq al-quwwa*, pp. 201–202.

and the true intention of the perpetrator to fight them. Fadlallah also widened out the parameters of self-sacrifice to include any act aimed at weakening the morale of the enemy or undermining its stability. However, he added, each act must be evaluated in the context in which it is carried out, as only in certain circumstances is it desirable.[19]

Another Hizballah religious leader, Shaykh Yusuf Da'mush, pointed out that carrying out an act of self-sacrifice requires (as indeed was the practice) a fatwa from a religious authority, for "a believer may not perform any act without considering the principles of religious law."[20] Similarly, the deputy director of Hizballah, Na'im Qasim, posited boundaries for the phenomenon of self-sacrifice. A person who wishes to sacrifice himself must first request permission from a religious expert, for the soul is precious and may be sacrificed for a religious purpose only, and, furthermore, only after the political movement has examined the political and military advantages of such an act. Additionally, the person who is recruited for a "suicide" mission must be of stable character, between the ages of seventeen and twenty years and thus responsible for his actions, and unmarried, thereby enabling the organization to avoid accusations that the perpetrators had suicidal tendencies, were too young, or were burdened with the responsibility of supporting a family.[21] In Qasim's view, as reflected in a book he published in 2002:

Martyrdom is a voluntary act undertaken by a person who has every reason to live, love life and cling to it. It is thus an act of one who does not suffer from any reasons compelling him to commit suicide. It is an accomplishment by men at the early stages of their lives, young and full of vitality and hopes for the future. But it is also an act of those who are attached to a religious and spiritual conception based on altruism and manifested through a preference for the hereafter over life, the nation over the individual, and sacrifice over small, contemptible gains.[22]

Qasim also pointed out that martyrdom filled the legal criterion of attacking the enemy with a minimum of losses on the Muslim side, while emphasizing its proven accomplishments in closing the significant gap in the ratio of military forces between Hizballah and Israel, forcing the Israeli enemy to reexamine its military policy in Lebanon, nurturing patriotic

---

[19] Fadlallah, *Kitab al-jihad*, pp. 185–210; Freamon, "Martyrdom, Suicide and the Islamic Law of War," pp. 355–356; *al-'Ahd*, April 5, 1996; Martin Kramer, "The Moral Logic of Hizballah," in Reich (ed.), *Origins of Terrorism*, pp. 143–147; Magnus Ranstorp, "Terrorism in the Name of Religion," *Journal of International Affairs* 50/1 (Summer 1996), p. 55, cited originally by George Nader in *Middle East Insight* (July 1985).

[20] Da'mush in an interview with *al-Safir*, August 14, 1986.

[21] Qasim quoted in *Ha'aretz*, December 6, 1995; also his book, *Hizbullah: The Story from Within* (London: Dar al-Saqi, 2005), pp. 34–69, originally published in Arabic, *Hizbullah al-minhaj, al-tajriba al-mustaqbal* (Beirut: Dar al-Hadi, 2002).

[22] Qasim, *Hizbullah*, p. 47.

fervor in the region, and igniting the First Palestinian Intifada. In any event, Qasim stressed, this was only one means among a variety of others to advance the struggle against Israel.[23]

This measured position reflected caution regarding a sweeping adoption of the new tactic despite its proven effectiveness. Nevertheless, "suicide" attacks constituted one of the formative elements in the development of the Hizballah movement and helped upgrade it in Lebanese politics.

This development also led other secular-oriented organizations in Lebanon to adopt and widen the parameters of the new tactic so as to enhance their influence. For them, the question of whether the perpetrator caused damage to the enemy forces was marginal; the act itself was what was important.[24] Examples were the Amal organization[25] and, especially, the Syrian Social Nationalist Party (SSNP), which defined the history of its struggle against the French and the Zionists in the 1930s and 1940s as an ongoing sacrifice and its fatalities as *shahid*s. In the SSNP's narrative, "suicide" missions, which included a significant number of women, inscribed a new page in the history of the "national and social struggle."[26] Accounts of

FIGURE 4.1 SSNP commemorating its martyr, Hamida Mustafa al-Tahir. *Source: Al-Safir*, November 27, 1985.

---

[23] Ibid., pp. 49–50.
[24] Merari, "The Readiness to Kill and Die," pp. 204–205; Kramer, "Sacrifice and Fratricide in Shiite Lebanon," pp. 30–47. According to Merari, these secular organizations perpetrated most of the "suicide" attacks in Lebanon during the 1980s: thirty-seven attacks, compared to fourteen perpetrated by Hizballah. Merari, *Driven to Death*, p. 243.
[25] See, e.g., *al-Safir*, February 7, 1985.
[26] Norton, *Hezbollah*, p. 80; Ahmad Hamzeh, *In the Path of Hizbullah* (Syracuse: Syracuse University Press, 2004), pp. 83–84; *al-Nahar*, November 27, 1985, available at http://ssnp.net/content/view/10077/138; http://www.ssnp.info/index.php?article=25314 (accessed June

the life and death of these martyrs were commemorated in a special section in the official SSNP Web site, along with photographs and wills, thereby preserving and memorializing their self-sacrifice long after it occurred and reinforcing the party's ideological and group solidarity.

A comprehensive example is to be found in the account of seventeen-year-old Sana' Muhaydli, who exploded a car bomb in the vicinity of Israeli forces in Jezin in 1985 and whose remains were returned to Lebanon in the context of an exchange of prisoners and the remains of prisoners between Israel and Hizballah in 2008. The return of her remains enabled the SSNP to resurrect her memory in Lebanon, alongside additional martyrs, thereby fortifying the party's significant record in the resistance to the Israeli occupation of Lebanon.

Muhaydli's martyrology encompassed her life story and the atmosphere of occupation in which she lived and which she opposed, a detailed description of her act of self-sacrifice including technical details about the type of car and the weight of the explosive, media coverage, eulogies in the wake of the act, memorialization in naming streets and schools after her, and her recorded will before she set out on the mission. A review of the will reveals several noteworthy aspects: the intertwined secular and religious semantics of martyrdom, namely, *fida'*, *istishhad*, and *shahid*; the altruistic character of the act, aimed at liberating conquered land; the creation of a genealogy of martyrs emanating from the movement, ending with Muhaydli; and an emphasis on the transience of life vis-à-vis the joy of self-sacrifice and, thus, a request of family and friends to be glad and eschew tears. All this reflects the obvious influence of Islamist martyrdom on the SSNP narrative of resistance and self-sacrifice.[27] Nevertheless, the narrative remains essentially nationalistic and secular, a reflection of declarations by party leader ʿAli Qansu, who in 2007 ratified the ideological legacy of its founder, Antun Saʿada (d. 1949), in the struggle against sectarianism and for the separation of religion and state.[28]

15, 2010). For general literature on the role of females in "suicide" missions, see, e.g., Mia Bloom, *Dying to Kill* (New York: Columbia University Press, 2005), pp. 142–165.

[27] http://www.islamonline.net/servlet/Satellite?c=ArticleA_C&pagename=Zone-ArabicArt
Culture%FACALayout&cid=1218614731876 (accessed June 15, 2010); also see *al-Nahar*, November 27, 1985; *al-Safir*, November 27, 1985, and May 24, 2001; http://www.youtube.com/watch?v=mEoYm-35ZOY (accessed June 15, 2011).

[28] Qanasu quoted in http://www.ssnp.info/index.php?article=25314 (accessed July 3, 2010). On Saʿada's stance toward sectarianism and religion, see his published work, *al-Islam fi risaltihi al-Masihiyya waʾl-Muhamadiyya* (4th ed., Beirut: n.p., 1980), pp. 204–214; *al-Muhadharat al-ʿashr* (n.p., 1948), pp. 111–129; *Fiʾl-Masʾala al-Lubnaniyya* (2nd ed.,

Although "suicide" bombings in Lebanon came to a near halt in 1985, replaced by a more conventional style of guerrilla warfare, they were mythologized in the Muslim world and were reinforced in such arenas of national liberation struggles as Palestine, Chechnya, and Afghanistan (following the American occupation in 2001).[29] Resistance fighters in those contentious regions were aware of their military inferiority but were convinced of their ability to overcome the enemy's military and technological advantage and exhaust its strength systematically through ideological willpower and especially through endurance and self-sacrifice. This was also the role they assigned to "suicide" attacks.

The shift of "suicide" acts from the Shi'a to the Sunni milieu reflected a decisive influence by revolutionary Iran on Islamist thought. Many Western observers tended to dismiss Khomeini's pan-Islamism in the early 1980s, depicted as failing to bring about a substantial rapprochement between Shi'i and Sunni radicals as a result of historical animosity and theological disputes. However, the ethos of self-sacrifice, intensively nurtured in Shi'i rhetoric and practice in Iran and Lebanon, penetrated the Sunni discourse, which until then had displayed restraint on this issue by emphasizing the goal of survival and victory over deliberate death, which was viewed as tantamount to self-immolation. Eventually, Sunni martyrdom went even a step further and targeted not only military forces but also, and mainly, civilians.

Moreover, the legitimation of "suicide" attacks came about in the context of classic Sunni traditions through creative interpretation to suit a contemporary framework. "Suicide" attacks were depicted as the weapon of the weak in their struggle for liberation from the yoke of foreigners. This was aptly summarized by Ramadan Shalah, leader of the Palestinian Islamic Jihad: "We have nothing with which to repel the killing and thuggery against us except the weapon of martyrdom. It is easy and costs us only our lives ... human bombs cannot be defeated, not even by nuclear bombs."[30] Defining the campaign for national viability as defensive jihad, whose goal was to

---

Beirut: Dar al-Fikr, 1991). Sa'ada's appeal to separate religion and state did not preclude him at times from making use of the notion of jihad in depicting the secular struggle of the party. See, e.g., *Antun Sa'ada fi mughtarabihi al-qasri al-a'mal al-kamila* (n.p., 1942), pp. 71–74.

[29] For data on this phenomenon in these areas, see, e.g., Shai, *The Shahids*, pp. 52–80, 108–114.

[30] Shalah quoted in Sprinzak, "Rational Fanatics," p. 68. Shalah later acknowledged that Hizballah's "suicide" attacks in 1983 served as a source of inspiration for the Islamic Jihad. *Al-Hayat*, January 7, 2003.

restore Muslim land to its legal owners, allowed for greater flexibility in utilizing different types of warfare and an effective way of striking at not only the enemy's army but also its civilian population.

The ethos of martyrdom was particularly prominent in Palestine. With the passage of time, Palestinian "suicide" attacks were ideologically systematized and became prominent in scale, as compared to similar phenomena in other conflict areas.

PALESTINIAN MARTYRDOM: THE PATH TO SALVATION

Self-sacrifice constituted a formative ethos for Palestinian Islam in its struggle against Israel from the early 1990s onward and became an important component of identity politics, merging theological elements with a political agenda. The very act of killing as a moral imperative was a political statement, delivering a dramatic and effective message that the conflict in Palestine was as much cultural as territorial. Islamic violence against Israel aimed to infuse metaphysical values into Palestinian life, while also serving as an effective mode of resistance in a period of a search for peace, thereby positing a political alternative to the Palestine Liberation Organization (PLO) and the Palestinian Authority (PA). It aimed to reinforce the exclusivity of the Palestinian identity and block political compromise.

The intertwining of religion and politics impelling Islamic violence was aptly articulated by the leader of Islamic Jihad, Fathi al-Shiqaqi, in November 1994, shortly after the establishment of the PA: "Without the martyrs we have no life or history, no past, no glory or value. It is they who pave the way for us for the future, and not the cowards who keep silent, defeatists who trade the homeland and sell off Jerusalem."[31]

Supported by two religious imperatives – death for the sake of God and the duty to "forbid wrongdoing" (*al-nahy 'an al-munkar*) – self-sacrifice became a moral code justifying "suicide" attacks against Israel. A contributing factor was the strong presence of an ethos of self-sacrifice in Palestinian historiography and terminology, including in the secular-leftist factions of the PLO. The Islamic notions of *jihad* (holy war), *mujahid* (God's warrior), and *shahid* (martyr) were closely connected to such

---

[31] Al-Shiqaqi quoted in Rif'at Sayyid Ahmad (ed.), *Rihlat al-dam al-ladhi hazama al-sayf* (Cairo: Markaz Yafa, 1997), Vol. 2, pp. 1357–1361.

modern secular symbols of struggle as *thawra* (revolution) and *fidaʾ* (sacrifice), forming a broad semantic reservoir of resistance (*muqawama*) familiar to all Palestinians regardless of ideological inclination.[32]

Key roles in the creation of this semantic reservoir were played by the Supreme Muslim Council and the ʿIzz al-Din al-Qassam movement in the 1920s and 1930s and by the Fatah in the 1950s and 1960s. The approach of the former bodies to Islam was more authentic, whereas that of Fatah, and later the PLO, was more pragmatic, blurring the boundaries between national and religious symbols to enable the organization to function in various discourse circles simultaneously and to gain legitimation.[33] Noteworthy in this context is Palestinian Martyr Day, established by Fatah in 1974 and commemorated officially on January 7 ever since by mass assemblies and speeches with the participation of the bereaved families.[34]

Viewed historically, as pointed out by Tariq Tahabub, the "suicide" attack phenomenon aimed at Israel did not emerge in a vacuum, but rather reflected the "rationale of sacrifice" (*al-ʿaqliyya al-istishhadiyya*) that developed in the Palestinian nation during a hundred years of dispute and constitutes the epitome of the struggle (*al-qima al-nidaliyya*).[35]

According to Durkheim, suicide, although having a distinct personal dimension, cannot be disconnected from the social and historical ethos of the community in which it occurs.[36] In the Palestinian case, the Islamic umbrella of judicial, moral, and political legitimation of "suicide" acts blurred the personal motives of the perpetrators – whether socioeconomic distress or personal and familial trauma under the Israeli occupation. The exalted cause of death for God was positioned at the fore, with the perpetrator attaining the highest level of sanctity as a martyr in this and the next world.

---

[32] Uri M. Kupferschmidt, *The Supreme Islamic Council: Islam under the British Mandate for Palestine* (Leiden: Brill, 1987), pp. 221–254; N. Johnson, *Islam and the Politics of Meaning in Palestinian Nationalism* (London: Kegan Paul International, 1982), pp. 65–87; also, Yezid Sayigh, *Armed Struggle and the Search for State: The Palestinian National Movement 1949–1993* (Oxford: Clarendon Press, 1997), pp. 195–196; Michael Milstein, *Mukawama: The Challenge of Resistance to Israel's National Security Concept* (Tel Aviv: The Institute for National Security Studies, December 2007), pp. 34–38 (in Hebrew).

[33] Salah Masʿud Abu Basir, *Jihad shaʿb Filastin khilala nisf qarn* (Beirut: Dar al-Fatah, 1968), mainly pp. 175–177, 194–201, 385–386, 569–571.

[34] See, e.g., *Filastin al-Thawra*, January 9, 1974, and January 12, 1975.

[35] Tahabub quoted in http://www.assabeel.net/previous3/1stpage-6.html (accessed August 6, 2010).

[36] Durkheim, *On Suicide*, pp. 297–300.

FIGURE 4.2 The Palestinian Martyr Day. Designer: Burhan Karkoutly.
Source: The Palestinian Poster Project Archives, available at http://www.palestinian
posterproject.org.

The prolonged reality of foreign occupation was the main factor nurturing the theological entrenchment of self-sacrifice in the Palestinian and
Arab discourse, while distancing it from an association with prohibited
suicide. Two other factors supported this process as well: the historio-
graphic factor relating to the demonization of the Jews in modern Islamic
literature[37] and the sociological factor of a low suicide rate in the population, which pointed to sustained religio-ethical restrictions and a strong
social safety net that included patriarchalism, family solidarity, and
mutual responsibility.[38] Although taking one's life out of despair was
condemned as unlawful, the death of martyrs became a cultural icon.

---

[37] Meir Litvak and Esther Webman, *From Empathy to Denial: Arab Responses to the
Holocaust* (New York: Columbia University Press, 2009).
[38] *Al-Ayyam*, June 2, 1997; *Ha'aretz*, May 31, 2002; also As'ad Yusuf Abu Ghalyun in
Hadyu'l-Islam, no. 158 (January–February 2003), pp. 91–97.

Ideological Foundation: The Islamic Jihad
Manifesto of 1988

A formative text in this process, largely unexplored in the research literature, is a manifesto titled "Readings in the Laws of Martyrdom" (*Qira'a fi
fiqh al-shahada*). It appeared as a supplement in a journal published in
Nicosia identified with the Islamic Jihad, *al-Islam wa-Filastin*, in June
1988.[39] Disseminated by Islamic Jihad, the manifesto laid down the ideological foundations of martyrdom in Palestine. Islamic Jihad, founded in
the late 1970s, was the first movement in the Palestinian arena to turn
Islam into a theology of liberation against Israel, as well as the first to
legitimize the ethos of self-sacrifice.[40]

According to Abdulaziz Zamel, an Arabic scholar at Tampa University,
Florida, who was associated with Palestinian Jihad circles, Misbah al-Suri
was the author of the unsigned manifesto, and the content was based on
lectures he had delivered to fellow detainees in an Israeli prison.[41] Al-Suri,
a former leftist, became a strict Muslim and thereafter was a key activist in
the military arm of Islamic Jihad in the Gaza Strip. He was killed in a clash
with Israeli forces in October 1987. Another possibility regarding the
source of the essay, no less plausible, is that it was written by one of the
two leaders of the movement, Fathi al-Shiqaqi or Shaykh 'Abd al-'Aziz
'Awda.

The manifesto was distributed during the early stages of the 1987
intifada ("uprising") with the aim of heightening the momentum of the
Palestinian revolt against the Israeli occupation from a civil protest to a
military operation. Although the extent of the manifesto's circulation is
unclear, the timing of its publication overlapped with the forging of a close
link between the Islamic Jihad and Iran and its protégé in Lebanon,
Hizballah, in the wake of Israel's expulsion of the senior Islamic Jihad
leadership to Lebanon at that time. The revolutionary Shi'a in Iran and

---

[39] *Qira'a fi fiqh al-shahada*, published as a supplement in *al-Islam wa-Filastin*, June 5, 1988,
pp. 1–15. Excerpts from the essay were republished in the Islamic Jihad's organ, the Beirut-
based *al-Mujahid*, December 13 and 15, 1993.

[40] Preliminary indications of the legitimation of self-sacrifice appeared in articles written by
movement founders Fathi al-Shiqaqi and Bashir Nafi' during 1979–1983 in the monthly
organs *al-Mukhtar al-Islami* (Cairo) and *al-Tali'a al-Islamiyya* (London), and especially in
the book, *al-Jihad fi Filastin farida shar'iyya wa-darura harakiyya* (n.p., 1983). For a
historical and ideological profile of the movement, see Meir Hatina, *Islam and Salvation in
Palestine* (Tel Aviv: The Moshe Dayan Center, 2001), pp. 17–62.

[41] A. I. Zamel, *The Rise of Palestinian Islamist Groups* (MA thesis; Tampa: University of
South Florida, 1991), p. 195.

Lebanon, besides serving as a source of ideological inspiration, evolved at that point into a logistic arm of Islamic Jihad.[42] This close affinity also engendered new emphases in the rhetoric of the struggle in Palestine, focusing especially on self-sacrifice – emphases that figure prominently in the manifesto.[43]

Alternating between defiance and apologetics, the manifesto aims to mold a new type of believer imbued with determination and a sense of mission going beyond ritual to an embrace of revolutionary activism. It also seeks to formulate a new agenda for Islamist politics in Palestine and beyond, based on a carefully constructed ethos of death that relies both on judicial arguments and on the critical nature of the conflict in Palestine. The text opens, pointedly, with a discussion of the differences between self-immolation, which lacks any religious purpose and is motivated solely by a desire for relief from personal distress, and martyrdom, which takes place in the battlefield and represents the pinnacle of faith. Self-immolation condemns the perpetrator to endless torment in hell, whereas martyrdom grants him the pleasures of heaven.[44]

The need to sharpen the divide between these two types of death, reiterated in the text several times, relies heavily on verses from the Qur'an and the hadith. The focus on this issue reflected the awareness by Islamic Jihad of the sensitivity of the notion of suicide in Islam and the fear that martyrdom acts would be interpreted as acts of desperation purely as a result of the ongoing occupation. Such an interpretation would detract from the attractiveness of Islam as a theology of liberation and as the sole vehicle for the final victory. To neutralize such a danger, and to keep "suicide" attacks within the confines of sanctity, the manifesto highlighted two basic elements: the duty of jihad and the acute nature of the struggle in Palestine.

The manifesto's reference to the doctrine of jihad is pointed and insistent, on the basis of the central position of holy war in Islamic law. Jihad, as depicted in the text, is linked to the ultimate goal of reaffirming the moral superiority of Islam over other cultures and sharpening the divisions between Muslims and infidels. Any neglect of military jihad is tantamount to a grave sin and to *nifaq* (a form of hypocrisy) – that is, showing

---

[42] Hatina, *Islam and Salvation*, pp. 38–42, 53–57.

[43] A fuller discussion of the manifesto may be found in my article, "Theology and Power in the Middle East: Palestinian Martyrdom in a Comparative Perspective," *Journal of Political Ideologies* 10 (October 2005), pp. 242–254.

[44] *Qira'a*, pp. 3–4; also Raphael Israeli, "A Manual of Islamic Fundamentalist Terrorism," *Terrorism and Political Violence* 14 (Winter 2002), pp. 31–33.

weakness of faith or even undermining the faith of others.[45] Positioning jihad as an inspirational model, the 1988 manifesto thereby paved the way to the link between jihad and self-sacrifice.

The doctrine of jihad, the manifesto argues, also defines the essence of life on earth, which is not limited to self-preservation and satisfying man's physical needs but includes dedication to spreading the word of God, thereby signifying the victory of truth and justice. The notion of the negligibility of life as compared to complete devotion to God is aptly expressed in the manifesto by quoting Khalid ibn al-Walid (d. 642), the commander of the Muslim armies who brought an end to Byzantine rule in Syria and Palestine.[46] He observed that the mission to encounter God's enemies after a freezing night on the battlefront is far stronger than the passion for the embrace of a young bride on a warm night.[47] Total commitment to an exalted act beyond the mundane realm leads the Muslim martyr to cease caring about his personal fate and to focus on the meaning of life in relation to a welcome death. In this sense, jihad for God does not contradict the value of preserving life.[48]

Moreover, the manifesto emphasizes that killing others is proscribed by certain restrictions, quoting the Qur'an: "[D]o not take the life God has made scared, except by right" (Sura 6: 151). Jihad against unbelievers, however, is an exception, because it is killing for the purpose of promoting "a just cause" (*haqq*, which is also a synonym for God).[49]

---

[45] The term *nifaq* in the Qur'an applies to a specific group, headed by 'Abdallah ibn Ubayy, which failed to fully support Muhammad's Islamic cause in critical military campaigns against the pagans.

[46] On Khalid ibn al-Walid proclaimed "the Sword of Islam," see Khayr al-Din al-Zirkili, *al-A'lam: qamus wa-tarajim* (15th ed., Beirut: Dar al-'Ilm li'l-Malayyin, 2002), Vol. 2, p. 300.

[47] *Qira'a*, p. 8. See also Shaykh Yusuf al-Qaradawi, the Egyptian Islamist whose influence on Palestinian Islam was (and still is) well known, in *al-Da'wa* (Cairo), May 1977.

[48] *Qira'a*, pp. 3–4; also see an earlier essay published in 1983, *al-Jihad fi Filastin*, pp. 95–99. Preserving life is also embodied in the duty of *taqiyya*, i.e., concealing one's beliefs when faced with oppression. The concept of *taqiyya* had the effect of restraining the religious fervor of the believer, cautioning him to conceal his faith whenever it endangered his life or threatened the survival of his community. *Taqiyya* was stressed particularly by the Shi'a sect, which had been subjected to periodic persecution under Sunni rulers. E. Kohlberg, "Taqiyya in Shi'i Theology and Religion," in H. G. Kippenberg and G. G. Stroumsa (eds.), *Secrecy and Concealment: Studies in the History of Mediterranean and Near Eastern Religions* (Leiden: Brill, 1995), pp. 345–380.

[49] *Qira'a*, pp. 3–4. Other exceptions are killing a murderer, an apostate (*murtadd*), or a married adulterer (for not resisting sexual temptation even though he experiences sex because he is married, in contrast to a bachelor adulterer, whose punishment is only

The definitive test for pleasing God is the intention (*niyya*) to become a martyr, according to the manifesto. This elevates Islam to a higher moral plane than Western philosophies, which justify death and bloodshed only for the purpose of gaining material assets such as imperial expansion or, alternatively, sanctify the value of life over the worship of God. The result is tyranny, exploitation, and selfishness, which are avoided in Islam precisely because of the balance dictated by Islam between preserving life and martyrdom.[50]

Clearly, Islamic Jihad, as a quasi-military movement that promoted assertive martyrdom in Palestine, was not interested simply in maintaining this balance in Islam but in altering it in favor of the martyrdom dimension. Martyrdom is exalted in the manifesto as an act of worship, parallel to a vow or an obligation that must be fulfilled as part of the belief in God.[51] It is placed in the same category as refusing to submit to pressure to speak heresy, or taking a firm stand in the name of holy truth against tyrannical rules, in situations in which the believer knows that such behavior will lead to his death. As an act of worship, martyrdom exchanges transient life for eternal life. It bestows ample rewards in paradise, such as purifying the martyr's soul from all sins; bringing him into the company of the prophets, the just, martyrs, and the righteous; and ensuring a place in heaven for seventy of his relatives.[52] Notably, the sexual motivation of marrying seventy-two black-eyed virgins, which captured Western attention, does not appear in the manifesto, but only in later documents, mainly wills left by "suicide" bombers.[53] Conceivably, this issue was avoided in the interest of presenting arguments that were weightier and more sober.

---

flogging). Al-Mahalli and al-Suyuti, *Tafsir al-Jalalayn*, p. 125; Ahmad Fathi Bahansi, *al-Siyasa al-jina'iyya fi'l-shari'a al-Islamiyya* (Cairo: Dar al-Shuruq, 1988), pp. 262–263.

[50] *Qira'a*, pp. 3–4.

[51] *Qira'a*, pp. 4, 7; also *al-Jihad fi Filastin*, pp. 68–84, 90–91, 95. Here the essay cites verse 33:23, which highlights the commitment to fight for Allah until death, and verse 9:111, which deals with holy war and sacrificing one's soul in return for going to heaven. See also Chapter 2 in this book, notes 24–25.

[52] *Qira'a*, pp. 10–11. The various rewards of the *shahid* in heaven are listed in al-San'ani, *Musannaf*, Vol. 5, pp. 263–266. Regarding closeness to the venerable figures of Islam (Sura 4: 69), not all Muslim commentators interpreted the term *shuhada'*, cited in the verse, as meaning death in the name of Allah. Al-Baydawi identified the term with those who adhere to Allah's commands and serve as witnesses of Allah and His true revelation. Al-Baydawi, *Tafsir al-Baydawi*, pp. 213–215. Modern radical Islam, however, including in Palestine, highlighted the battlefield interpretation.

[53] See, e.g., *al-Risala*, June 21, 2001, and August 16, 2001.

Moreover, martyrdom for God and for the faith, according to the manifesto, constitutes not only a personal guarantee of rewards in paradise but also collective insurance for the emancipation of the entire community. As such, the religious conception was intertwined with national considerations, with the martyr becoming a cultural agent symbolizing revolution and liberation. In this context the text posits a cost-benefit doctrine (*maslaha*), which holds that the welfare of the public justifies an altruistic personal sacrifice. Ironically, whereas Muslim reformists enlist the doctrine of *maslaha* to diffuse sectarian and cultural tensions in response to the challenges of modernity, radical Islamists such as the Palestinian Islamic Jihad used this doctrine to reinforce the divisions between Islam and a more diverse cultural environment and to promote revolutionary activism.[54]

Linking individual salvation to collective emancipation paved the way for the Islamic Jihad to highlight the second element in justifying self-sacrifice, namely the existential nature of the struggle in Palestine in light of an infidel, suppressive occupier. Depicting the campaign in Palestine as defensive jihad created a sense of urgency. As such, the struggle was less subject to the traditional preconditions of the existence of a caliph, the normative rules of battlefield behavior outlined in Islamic judicial literature, and the imperative of tactical withdrawal in the event of inferior military resources vis-à-vis the enemy. Defensive jihad imposes the duty of personal enlistment on every believer who is sound in mind and body (*fard 'ayn*),[55] a duty defined by Ibn Taymiyya as second in importance only to the duty of belief in God (*shahada*) and taking precedence over prayer and other rites such as fasting or pilgrimage.[56] This interpretation reflected Islamic Jihad's aim to widen the battlefront against Israel.

To reinforce the notion of jihad in Palestine as a personal duty for every believer, the movement quoted extensively from the writings and fatwas of 'ulama' throughout the period of the Arab-Israeli conflict. As a movement

---

[54] On the concept of *maslaha* and its modern uses, see M. H. Kerr, *Islamic Reform* (Berkeley: University of California Press, 1966), pp. 103 ff; M. Khadduri, "Maslaha," *Encyclopaedia of Islam* 6 (1991), pp. 738–740; also Deina Abdelkader, "Modernity, the Principles of Public Welfare (maslaha) and the End Goals of Shari'a (maqasid) in Muslim Legal Thought," *Islam and Christian-Muslim Relations* 14 (2003), pp. 163–172.

[55] Also see the published work of Palestinian Shaykh 'Abdallah 'Azzam, who exerted a strong ideological influence on the emergence of Islamic radicalism in Palestine, although his first priority was Afghanistan. 'Azzam, *al-Difa' 'an aradi al-Muslimin* (al-Zarqa': Maktabat al-Manar, 1987); idem, *Fi'l-Jihad fiqh wa-ijtihad* (Pashawar: Maktab Khidmat al-Mujahidin, n.d.), pp. 6–12, 53–54.

[56] *Qira'a*, pp. 5–6, 13–14; also Chapter 2, note 8 in this book.

forged during the crucible of the late-twentieth-century Sunni revolution in
the Middle East, Islamic Jihad essentially viewed the 'ulama' as submissive
servants of infidel regimes and as distorters of Islam. However, the need to
generate broad support for the Palestinian cause and an awareness of the
sustained influence of the 'ulama' in the Arab public sphere prompted
Islamic Jihad to display a selectively restrained attitude toward them.[57]

Significantly, the manifesto under discussion goes beyond legitimizing
acts of self-sacrifice in Palestine on the grounds of defensive jihad whose
aim is regaining occupied Muslim territory. It elevates the status of
Palestinian territory as the focal point of the confrontation between
Muslims and their eternal enemies – that is, the Jews and the Christians.
It is a religio-historical confrontation over control of the sacred places,
especially Jerusalem and the al-Aqsa mosque, and is even more cataclysmic
than the Crusader occupation of the twelfth century. The existence of a
Jewish entity in Palestine under the protection of the West constitutes
nothing less than the axis of an imperialistic scheme to maintain a state
of divisiveness among Muslims. The outcome of the struggle in Palestine,
therefore, will determine the fate of the entire mission to revive and unify
the Muslim nation.[58]

By elevating the status of Palestine, Islamic Jihad sought first to broaden
the Arab-Islamic consensus regarding martyrdom as well as to create a
strategic depth of human and material resources to back the Islamic
agenda in Palestine – a stance adopted by Hamas (the Islamic Resistance
Movement) as well. The Islamization of Palestine did not mean rejecting
the geographic boundaries of this polity for the sake of a universal, pan-
Islamic vision but rather injecting metaphysical values into it. As such,
Palestinian Islam adhered to a broad thrust in Islamist thought incorporat-
ing national identity into the religious discourse.[59] Moreover, the need in
the Islamic Jihad narrative not only for heroes but also for villains is
reflected in the demonization of the Zionist presence in Palestine and its
global conspiratorial nature. The Zionist enemy, in "Readings in the Laws
of Martyrdom," is portrayed as the embodiment of evil on earth, standing
for "heresy, tyranny and hatred of both Islam and the Muslims. The

---

[57] *Qira'a*, p. 5. On the perception of the 'ulama' in Islamist radical discourse, see Sivan,
Radical Islam, pp. 50–56; also Chapter 7 in this book.
[58] *Qira'a*, pp. 4–5.
[59] Hatina, *Islam and Salvation*, pp. 48–53, 130–131, 165–167; Meir Litvak, "The
Islamization of the Palestinian-Israeli Conflict: The Case of Hamas," *Middle Eastern
Studies* 34 (1998), pp. 148–163.

Zionist presence in Palestine is tantamount to a cancerous tumor corrupting the entire body of the nation."[60]

The demonization of the Zionist enemy is accompanied by a delegitimation of those Arab and Muslim elements that neglect the duty of jihad or cast doubts about its validity in the modern era, especially in Palestine. These elements are silent Satans and even worse. Their avoidance of the struggle against Israel and their harassment or blocking of jihad fighters outside Palestine not only constitute a blatant violation of God's commands but also reflect the state of defeatism among Muslims in modern times. Such avoidance in itself is tantamount to self-immolation.[61]

The vociferous attack in the essay against contemporary Arab regimes, inspired by Sayyid Qutb's revolutionary approach, left Islamic Jihad without substantial support in the Arab political arena. Moreover, Shi'i Iran's bear hug did not improve the image of the movement among fellow Sunni in the region. If the Islamic Jihad defined itself as a bridge between Sunna and Shi'i, the movement's critics in the Sunni world perceived it as having become a front for Khomeini's Iran.[62]

The manifesto moves from disappointment with the Arab political elites to a new hope for the Muslim masses, who must be awakened and enlisted in the campaign to liberate Palestine, thereby enhancing their own fragile status in their countries. It plays on the sensitivities of Muslim believers everywhere, emphasizing that no one who prays facing the tomb of the Prophet and the sacred places in Mecca and Medina can possibly tolerate what is happening in Palestine. Historical examples of revolt and heroism against Western imperialism are cited, such as that of 'Abd al-Qadir al-Jaza'iri in Algeria, the Mahdi in Sudan, 'Umar Mukhtar in Libya, 'Abd al-Karim al-Khattabi in Morocco, and 'Izz al-Din al-Qassam in Palestine. Notably, the fleeting reference to al-Qassam (d. 1935) referred to the local Palestinian hero who wrought havoc in the British Mandate army and was mythologized in the 1980s as a role model in the hagiographic literature following the rise of the Islamic alternative and its ethos of self-sacrifice. His legacy was further legitimized with the

---

[60] Qira'a, pp. 4–5. A similar narrative was adopted by Shaykh As'ad Bayyud al-Tamimi (d. 1989), the leader of the Islamic Jihad Bayt al-Maqdis, in his book, Zawal Isra'il hatmiyya Qur'aniyya (Cairo: al-Mukhtar al-Islami, 1980).

[61] Qira'a, pp. 4–5, 11; also al-Jihad fi Filastin, pp. 84–89.

[62] Meir Hatina, "Iran and the Palestinian Islamic Movement," Orient 38 (March 1997), pp. 107–113.

formation of the 'Izz al-Din al-Qassam Brigades – the military arm of the Islamic Resistance Movement (Hamas).[63] The involvement of the Muslim Brethren under Hasan al-Banna in the 1948 War is also mentioned in the manifesto as an antithesis to the current impotence of his reformist followers in the Arab world.

If the manifesto encourages religious fervor, it emphasizes realpolitik no less. Inasmuch as a general enlistment of the Muslim world to join the struggle in Palestine is acknowledged as impractical, the main burden, at least in the initial phase, must fall on the Muslims of Palestine, the manifesto points out.[64] They are required "to display as much [fighting spirit] as they can, standing fast and defending the sacred places and the Islamic identity." They must adopt varied methods of resistance, both armed and unarmed. Some Palestinians will gather in the streets, raising the banner "There is no God except God." Others – the children, girls, and women – will throw stones. The armed men will conduct the military struggle. All this must be carried out with deep faith and conviction in the readiness for self-sacrifice. "Those who fight for God," the manifesto exhorts, "are buying the hereafter in exchange for the worldly life," and quoting the Qur'an: "Let those of you who are willing to trade the life of this world for the life to come, fight in God's way. To anyone who fights in God's way, whether killed or victorious, We shall give a great reward" (Sura 4: 74).[65] Thus, popular uprisings were defined as a type of jihad and the fallen as martyrs regardless of the circumstances of their death – whether in armed battle or following the bombardment and collapse of a building. By broadening the definition of the term *shahid* another incentive was added to enlist Palestinians in the struggle against Israel and to entrench its Islamic character.

Besides laying down the moral justification for sanctifying acts of self-sacrifice in Palestine, the manifesto defines operative guidelines. Although not disqualifying armed attack against the enemy by gunfire or hand grenades, it argues that because the enemy can seal off areas, thereby preventing the return of fighters to a safe place, they must continue fighting until death. Clearly, the essay gives primacy to "suicide" attacks. The

---

[63] See, e.g., 'Abd al-Satar Qasim, *al-Shaykh al-Mujahid 'Izz al-Din al-Qassam* (2nd ed., Nablus: Maktabat al-Risala, 1992); also S. Abdullah Schleifer, "Izz al-Din al-Qassam: Preacher and Mujahid," in Burke and Yaghoubian (eds.), *Struggle and Survival in the Modern Middle East*, pp. 164–178.

[64] *Qira'a*, pp. 4–6, 12.

[65] Ibid., pp. 5–6.

implication in practice is that these acts constitute a vital frontal encounter with the enemy, combining the element of surprise with determination.

Such acts can be accomplished by driving a booby-trapped car, penetrating a public building while carrying arms, or strapping explosives onto one's body (a "human bomb"). This type of combat is necessary, and, more importantly, effective. It causes multiple casualties and creates public demoralization in the enemy ranks, an optimal combination in any strategy for violence. By contrast, using roadside bombs and preparing escape routes exposes an operation to failure, given the high state of alert of the enemy forces. Even if the enemy might not manage to neutralize a planted bomb, it can evacuate people in time. Moreover, the success of the roadside bomb operation does not guarantee maximal damage to the enemy forces. This analysis implies a criticism of the armed struggle conducted by the PLO against Israel, which the Islamic Jihad viewed as a conventional struggle that lacked creative thinking or daring. It was dependent on a continuous supply of weapons and combat materials and enabled the enemy, with its superior operational capabilities, to neutralize such efforts to a considerable degree. The Palestinian struggle, the manifesto states, requires rejuvenation, which only the weapon of jihad and self-sacrifice has the power to provide.[66] Positioning the "human bomb" as an alternative to the "conventional bomb" implied the positioning of Palestinian Islam as an ideological and political alternative to the PLO.

In depicting the importance of the "human bomb" as a product of special circumstances and as compensation for the inferior military capability of the Palestinians, the Islamic Jihad, along with Hamas, sanctified "suicide" attacks as a means toward an end. Neither movement perceived it as a norm but rather as a circumscribed tactic that could be delayed or postponed in favor of other means of combat when necessary. This operative flexibility was aptly expressed in an internal Hamas document in response to the hard line adopted by the PA against the movement following a deadly wave of "suicide" attacks in Israeli cities in February–March 1996. The document stated explicitly:

Should we be required to halt the "suicide" attacks based on the argument that they harm the Palestinian cause, we will be forced to intensify our communal activity, penetrate all strata of society and take a firm hold of them. ... We will have to heighten our preaching against the Jews and their nature and enhance the praises of death in the service of God.[67]

---

[66] *Qira'a*, pp. 13–15; *Ma'rakat al-mujahid fi aqbiyat al-tahqiq* (n.p., n.d.), pp. 6–7.
[67] *Ma'ariv* (Tel Aviv), March 1, 1996.

This and other sources illuminated the calculated use of the "suicide" weapon depending on circumstances,[68] a feature that led one scholar to label its dispatchers "rational fanatics."[69]

The fact that the perpetrator's fate a priori is death, with no possibility of withdrawal or survival, so as to ensure the success of the operation impelled the Islamic Jihad movement to vigorously rebut possible criticism over the suicidal nature of such a measure. The manifesto argues, first, that because there is no escape from death, as stated in the Qur'an, "The death you run away from will come to meet you" (Sura 62: 8), there can be nothing more joyous and fulfilling than to meet death on the battlefield fighting the enemies of God.[70] Second, and more importantly, the very preaching of jihad entails advocating self-sacrifice. A study of the jihad march of the Prophet and of believers throughout Islamic history reveals a distinction between three levels of self-sacrifice when confronting the enemy. The first level is when the chances of dying or of surviving are equal, and "the combatant earns either martyrdom, or honor as a hero returning from war." The second level is when the probability of dying is greater than of surviving because of the material and military advantages of the enemy, which requires fiercer and more unconventional fighting. The highest level is when death is certain and the combatant approaches it imbued with the conviction that he will enter heaven. This last level is the most favorable, in the view of Islamic Jihad, and the one promoted by the movement within the Palestinian community. It involves an operation in which the combatant or combatants carry out an assault that destabilizes the enemy and engenders hope in the hearts of Muslims. Moreover, the loss of life in the Muslim camp is much less than in the enemy camp.

In this context, the manifesto cites two heroic historic accounts of self-sacrifice. The first concerns Abu 'Ubyad ibn Mas'ud (d. 635), who threw himself under the feet of the elephants of the Sasanian army to cut their bellies, inspiring other Muslims to follow suit. The second relates to al-Bara' ibn Malik (d. 641), who broke into the gate of a garden where a group of infidels had taken shelter, thereby enabling his fellow Muslims to enter the place and wipe them out. Ibn Mas'ud, ibn Malik, and other such martyrs restored the self-confidence of Muslims in times of crisis during the early history of Islam. Their role, the manifesto argues, is the same as

---

[68] *Qira'a*, p. 12.

[69] Ehud Sprinzak, "Rational Fanatics," *Foreign Policy*, no. 120 (September–October 2000), pp. 66–73.

[70] *Qira'a*, pp. 7–9; also *al-Jihad fi Filastin*, p. 93.

the role of those at present who wear explosive belts and blow themselves up. Both provide the human bridge on which Muslims march to victory.[71] Their real weapon is faith, thereby symbolizing what Mark Juergensmeyer has termed "divine power."[72]

Notably, the manifesto, which relies on early Muslim chronicles, documents both preceding acts of bravery only partially. In the case of ibn Mas'ud, his act indeed fortified the Muslims' fighting spirit, but when he fell, many of them fled the battlefield, with the Sasanians in hot pursuit. Moreover, there is no mention of a statement by 'Umar ibn al-Khattab, one of the Prophet's close associates and later the second caliph, who questioned the very engagement in battle with the Sasanians, as their military superiority in the field was clear. When news reached him of the searing defeat and the death of ibn Mas'ud, 'Umar declared that if ibn Mas'ud had retreated and not challenged death, "we would have been among his supporters now." In the case of ibn Malik, the manifesto does not mention that he was only wounded. Some Muslim commentators argued that he was denied the privilege of dying a martyr's death because he sought to glorify his name, thereby ruining his chances of dying a pure death for God. Moreover, ibn Malik's ongoing quest for a heroic death in the many battles he fought prompted 'Umar ibn al-Khattab to warn the commanders of the Muslim army not to use his services because of his "suicide tendency."[73]

The omission of these details by the Islamic Jihad points to a creative interpretation and a selective reading of classical Sunni traditions and chronicles to reinforce the ethos of self-sacrifice and create a heroic past, thereby counteracting the grim contemporary present. Hamas adopted similar practices, and it too made selective use of the ibn Malik story to foster martyrdom by individuals against enemy forces and thereby become role models for others.[74]

The glory of self-sacrifice in early Islam was highlighted and molded into a contemporary political ethos aimed at stimulating loyalty to Islamic Jihad and its platform. A large body of hagiographical literature was produced that embedded martyrs in the public memory, depicting them

---

[71] *Qira'a*, pp. 7–9.
[72] Mark Juergensmeyer, "The World-wide Rise of Religious Nationalism," *Journal of International Affairs* 50 (Summer 1996), pp. 15–16.
[73] Full accounts of ibn Mas'ud and ibn Malik appear in al-Tabari, *Ta'rikh al-rusul wa'l-muluk*, Vol. 3, pp. 454–455; Abu al-Hasan ibn al-Athir, *al-Kamil fi'l-ta'rikh* (Beirut: Dar Sadir, 1965–1966), Vol. 2, pp. 360–366, 438–440.
[74] *Filastin al-Muslima*, November 1995, p. 51.

as vital to the nation's past and future while paving the way for the
martyrs' movement to gain communal prestige.[75]

Although eschewing any claim that martyrdom has the power to drive
the enemy out of Palestine, "Readings in the Laws of Martyrdom"
perceives it as offering the Palestinians compensation for their inferior
tangible capacities and revealing their moral assets. Citing historical
proof of the power of determination and devotion, the manifesto refers
to the successful struggle of the Muslims against the Crusader invaders
in the twelfth century despite the imbalance of power and weaponry
between the two sides. The modern era, according to the manifesto,
has ushered in even greater difficulties for Muslim fighters, not only
because of the strength and cruelty of the enemy (Israel) and its patrons
(the West) but also because of the disunity and rifts among the Muslims.
Nevertheless, in keeping with the deterministic outlook of Islamic
Jihad, victory is assured even if it takes a long time to come, for it is
predestined, as written in the Qur'an. The struggle is essentially a
Manichean one between truth and falsehood, with the former destined
to gain the upper hand. Until this aspired turning point is reached, the
individual must focus on improving collective morality and heightening
ongoing sacrifice.[76]

A final point regarding the manifesto relates to the issue of attacking
civilians, which became the focus of the Palestinian "suicide" attacks, and
of the public discourse about them, from the mid-1990s onward. The text
itself, which was disseminated in the early stages of the first intifada, deals
with "suicide" attacks against Israeli security forces and settlers only.
Civilians – women and children – are not mentioned. In one place, the
manifesto emphasizes the difference between planting a roadside bomb,
which might miss the military target or hurt women and children, and a
"human bomb," which never misses its target.[77]

Nevertheless, a theological foundation for the possibility of attacking
Israel's civilian sector does exist in the manifesto: first, in citing the Qur'an

---

[75] See, e.g., *Shuhada' ma'a sabq al-israr* (n.p., 1993). The martyr's capacity to serve as a
moral compass and a source of inspiration for fellow Muslims was defined by radical
writers as one of the meanings of the term "living *shahid*," as in the verse, "And say not of
those slain in God's way, 'They are dead; rather they are living'" (Sura 2: 154). Qutb, *Fi
zilal al-Qur'an*, Vol. 1, pp. 143–144; also Laleh Khalili, *Heroes and Martyrs of Palestine:
The Politics of National Commemoration* (Cambridge, UK: Cambridge University Press,
2007).
[76] The movement's essay, *al-Mujahid amam al-tahqiq wa'l-ta'dhib*, which appears as a
supplement in *al-Islam wa-Filastin*, September 1, 1988, p. 16.
[77] *Qira'a*, p. 14.

regarding one of the goals of war, which is to cause demoralization in the enemy population, defined as a vital condition for victory; and second, more importantly, in projecting defensive jihad and death for the sake of God as a norm that applies in any time or place. How jihad is implemented in battles against infidels falls into the category of *al-siyasa al-shar'iyya* – that is, subject to political considerations. The original meaning of *al-siyasa al-shar'iyya* refers to the prerogative of the Muslim ruler to run the affairs of state, including in times of war. The Palestinian Islamic Jihad, however, shifted this prerogative to the Muslim public at large and to its vanguard, the Islamic movement, in light of the presence of an infidel occupier in the land. They are "required to defend their land with all the means and the power at their disposal."[78] The imperative of defensive jihad, and the absence of concrete guidelines as to how to conduct it, enabled an expansion of the scope of warfare to include non-combatants in the concept of enemy forces.[79]

This implicit theological basis for attacking civilians allowed for its implementation whenever circumstances were deemed to require it. In the Palestinian context, such circumstances were created when the momentum of the peace process reached a peak with the Oslo Accords and the establishment of the PA in 1993–1994. Harming civilians was justified by the argument that Israeli society was militaristic in essence. Women, the aged, workers, farmers, and others take part in Israeli war efforts by incitement or by providing material and moral support. Moreover, they inhabit stolen Muslim land and are prepared to defend it. Babies and small children are exempt, but the harm that befalls them is part of a necessary calculated risk. Their fate is similar to that of Muslims who serve the enemy as human shields against Muslim attack. If the possibility of harming a Muslim is permissible, then it is all the more permissible in the case of infidel children.[80]

Even without explicitly touching on the question of attacking civilians, the manifesto transforms self-sacrifice into a moral code that legitimizes "suicide" attacks and depicts their perpetrators as martyrs to be imitated. A succinct summary of the rationale for such acts is to be found toward the end of the manifesto:

---

[78] Ibid., pp. 4–5.
[79] Ibid.
[80] Nawaf Hayil Takruri (ed.), *al-'Amaliyyat al-istishhadiyya fi'l-mizan al-fiqhi* (2nd ed., Damascus: Dar al-Fikr, 1997), pp. 145–179.

["Suicide" attacks] restore the awe of Muslims after a long period of weakness and slackness and stimulate a growing number of new warriors to seek jihad for God. This is a blessed grace that empowers one or two fighters to actualize all this in one stroke, thereby reviving the nation's spirit of self-sacrifice and bringing the day of victory closer. . . . These acts revive the spirit of Muslims and imbue them with pride in the power of Islam to position God's words as supreme. He who charges forward does so not to escape life in desperation in the face of difficulties, or to kill himself. On the contrary, he is a devoted warrior . . . who sells his soul to God and earns martyrdom for the victory of Islam and the defeat of its enemies on earth. His aspired goal is to enter heaven and be close to the prophets and the righteous.[81]

This revolutionary message was enhanced by other materials published by the Islamic Jihad movement, especially its official organs, *al-Islam wa-Filastin* (Nicosia) and *al-Mujahid* (Beirut). These publications revealed that the martyrology concept had widened to extend beyond the battlefield and into the interrogation rooms of the enemy. In two essays, one published in September 1988 and the other in early 1990, the movement preached sustained endurance to captured Muslim fighters in the face of torture, mental abuse, and threat to life, on the basis of the religious concept of patience and fortitude (*sabr*).[82] In the words of the Qur'an, "[B]e mindful of God, and know that He is with those who are mindful of Him" (Sura 2: 194).

Captivity, the movement explained, is merely an entry into a new and critical stage in the confrontation with the vicious enemy. Even though the captive does not carry a weapon and is unable to fight physically, he still possesses firm faith and spiritual strength. Spiritual stamina or "a revolutionary will" (*al-irada al-thawriyya*) holds the key to victory over the enemy, who, by means of intensive interrogations, hopes to extract intelligence about the operational secrets of the movement.[83] Whereas the Israeli interrogator is perceived as merely doing his job, the captive *mujahid* is

---

[81] *Qira'a*, p. 14.

[82] The concept of *sabr* served as a key component in Islamist discourse, namely as a moral and psychological impetus for taking a firm stand in the struggle over the image of society in light of the political suppression and evils of Westernization. See, e.g., Qutb, *Fi zilal al-Qur'an*, Vol. 2, pp. 141–143; Yusuf al-Qaradawi, *al-Sabr fi'l-Qur'an* (Cairo: Maktabat Wahaba, 1970).

[83] *Ma'rakat al-mujahid*, pp. 3–18; *al-Mujahid amam al-tahqiq*. These two essays constitute a severe indictment of the record of the Palestinian struggle during 1967–1987, which failed to instill in its fighters the basic attributes of secrecy, discipline, commitment to the cause, and above all endurance during interrogations by the Israeli security services. The Westernized elements in Arab society were also criticized for disconnecting society from its Islamic cultural roots. The result was the quick breakdown and confession of fighters, stemming from fear and ignorance of the investigative methods of the Zionist interrogators, the essays pointed out. Notably, the two essays provide only one, rather general comment regarding death in captivity. Such a death can result from torture but can also

portrayed as bearing a historic mission inspired by a long tradition of self-sacrifice. This tradition began with Jesus, who was tortured by the Jews and the Romans, yet his message reached the people, while his torturers were doomed to hell. It continued with the early Muslims who were tortured by "the makers of the pit" (*ashab al-ukhdud*) but did not abandon their faith. It ended with 'Umar al-Mukhtar in Italian-controlled Libya and Sayyid Qutb in Nasserist Egypt, whose executions served as a model for those who followed them. "All these martyrs could have saved themselves, avoided torture, and chosen an easy life," the movements pointed out, "yet if they had done so their lives would have been miserable and forever devoid of peace of mind. They would have lost both this world and the one to come. Moreover, their nation would have lost the powerful educational lesson and the achievements of their sacrifice which underlay the victories."[84] The captive must never surrender or break down. The hereafter is more important to him than the mundane world, and his sole aspiration is to be a martyr. For the captive *mujahid*, God, the Prophet, and jihad are more beloved than his children, women, or the pleasures of life. Therefore, he must never reveal military information.[85]

Hamas' Perception of Martyrdom

Although by the late 1980s the Islamic Jihad had crossed a theological and moral threshold by internalizing martyrdom as a social norm,[86] Hamas remained a step behind, although it had no problem with the use of violence against Israel as part of its struggle against an infidel occupier. However, Hamas did not initially adopt the ethos of death developed by the Islamic Jihad.

---

result from the initiative of the captive himself (an act sanctioned by the shari'a as well), provided that the information he possesses is critical to Muslim interests.

[84] *Ma'rakat al-mujahid*, pp. 105–106.

[85] Ibid., pp. 33, 48, 105–106; *al-Mujahid amam al-tahqiq*, pp. 8–10. The accounts about Muslims who sacrificed their life for their faith during torture are discussed extensively in *al-Jihad fi Filastin*, pp. 111–126. See also the stance of prominent 'ulama', Mahmud Shaltut, *al-Fatawa*, pp. 419–421; Hasan Ayyub, *al-Shahid fi'l-Islam* (Beirut: Dar al-'Ilm li'l-Malayin, 1985), p. 55; idem, *al-Jihad wa'l-fida'iyya fi'l-Islam*, pp. 165–167.

[86] Apparently, there was also an attempt to imbue the Palestinian Jihad's perception of martyrdom with more impressive content when one of its woman activists, 'Atif 'Alyan, planned an unprecedented act "which will reinforce armed activity and bring it to a new stage" by driving a car bomb into the Israel government building in the Sheikh Jarrah neighborhood of Jerusalem and exploding it. However, she was arrested before performing the act and sentenced to fourteen years' imprisonment. She was released in 1997. *Filastin* (Gaza), no. 2 (March 1997), pp. 14–15.

The Hamas movement, which sprang from the Muslim Brethren in
the West Bank and the Gaza Strip in 1987, had a strongly communal
orientation (*da'wa*). Its covenant, published in August 1988 – that is, two
months after the appearance of the Islamic Jihad's "Readings in the Laws
of Martyrdom" – confined itself to a general statement about the duty of
jihad to liberate Palestine and redeem the exalted martyrs for God
combined with other means of struggle, predominantly preaching and
education.[87] Moreover, the Hamas covenant showed no evidence
of the impact of the Islamic Revolution in Iran, a vital source of
inspiration for the Islamic Jihad, especially regarding the issue of
martyrdom. Apparently, the historic animosity between the Sunna and
Shi'a, exacerbated by Khomeini's deviation from his ecumenical and
pan-Islamic attitude in the early 1980s, kept Hamas out of the
Iranian fold.[88]

Hamas did, however, make use of mythical martyrdom symbols from the
Muslim Arab past in its written works and wall posters. One example
was the story of the heroic death of Ja'far ibn Abi Talib, the Prophet's cousin
and close companion, who, in the battle against the Byzantines in 629,
continued carrying the Islamic flag proudly even after his hands were severed
one by one and died while draping the flag round his breast.[89] More recent
accounts of self-sacrifice in the struggles of the Muslim Brethren during the
1940s and 1950s were also used by Hamas.[90] However, Hamas made use of
these materials as symbols to stimulate enthusiasm and recruitment and not
as role models for acts of self-sacrifice.

[87] *The Hamas Covenant* (n.p., August 1988), Clauses 7, 8, 15, 19. For selected literature on
the emergence of Hamas and its formative history, see Ziad Abu 'Amr, *Islamic
Fundamentalism in the West Bank and the Gaza Strip* (Bloomington: Indiana University
Press, 1994); Shaul Mishal and Avraham Sela, *The Palestinian Hamas: Vision, Violence
and Coexistence* (2nd ed., New York: Columbia University Press, 2006), pp. 13–82;
Beverley Milton-Edwards and Stephen Farrell, *Hamas: The Islamic Resistance
Movement* (Cambridge: Polity, 2010), mainly pp. 52–84.
[88] The momentum of the peace process in the early 1990s engendered a rapprochement
between Hamas and Iran. Hamas sought to expand strategic support for the armed
struggle in Palestine, whereas Iran wanted to acquire a foothold in the Sunni world.
Nevertheless, the political partnership was limited, mainly because of reservations on the
part of Hamas – the product of its Sunni roots and close affinity with the Muslim Brethren
in the Arab world and the financial support it received from the wealthy Gulf states, rivals
of Iran. Hatina, "Iran and the Palestinian Islamic Movement," pp. 113–119.
[89] Quoted in Nachmani, "The Palestinian Intifada," pp. 90–91.
[90] A widely used book that was written by Kamil al-Sharif and Mustafa al-Siba'i, *al-Ikhwan
al-Muslimun fi harb Filastin* (3rd ed., Cairo: Maktabat Wahaba, n.d.).

Initially, Hamas' political rhetoric highlighted the "revolution of the stones" – that is, using stones, knives, and guns mainly to target soldiers and settlers. "Suicide" attacks were introduced into the movement only in 1993, prompted by a new political context: the Oslo Accords. At the same time, Israel's expulsion of 400 Hamas activists to Marj al-Zuhur in southern Lebanon brought them closer to Hizballah and the Iranian Revolutionary Guards.[91] The massacre of twenty-nine Arabs in Hebron perpetrated in April 1994 by a settler, Baruch Goldstein, reinforced religious approval for the phenomenon of "suicide" attacks and removed the remaining barrier to attacking Israel's civilian population, on the basis of the Qur'anic reciprocal principle of an eye for an eye (Sura 2: 194).[92]

Ultimately, Hamas took the lead in "suicide" attacks by virtue of its organizational ability and its claim to Palestinian leadership, while the Islamic Jihad, a small, quasi-underground organization with no communal infrastructure, lagged behind the larger movement. Its meager public support was a drawback but also an advantage in that the organization was less constrained by cost-benefit considerations and ideological questioning of the use of "suicide" attacks. In Hamas, as in Hizballah in the early 1980s, the growing use of the "suicide" weapon did not signify an alternative method replacing *da'wa*, or some other guerilla method, but rather the incorporation of all these means. "Suicide" attacks enhanced Hamas' public prestige, but the movement's primary raison d'être remained widespread community welfare activity, a base that allowed Hamas to carry out the attacks, as well as the capacity to survive countermeasures by Israel and to a lesser extent by the PA.[93]

By the time the al-Aqsa Intifada erupted in September 2000, self-sacrifice had become canonized and was a prominent feature of the intifada, adopted as well by nationalist factions identified with the PA. These factions, which consisted mainly of young activists from the poorest sectors, perceived the "suicide" weapon as a way of reinvigorating the national cause and as a political lever vis-à-vis the Islamists in the struggle over Palestinian public opinion.[94]

As time went by in the protracted conflict with Israel, the prized category of martyr was expanded to include those who were not killed in the context of "suicide" missions but rather died in direct military clashes with

---

[91] Hammad Hasanat, *Dhikrayat Marj al-Zuhur* (n.p., n.d.).

[92] *Filastin al-Muslima* (London), November 1994.

[93] This argument contrasts with that of Alshech, "Egoistic Martyrdom," pp. 42–47.

[94] Nasser Abufarha, *The Making of a Human Bomb: The Ethnography of Palestinian Resistance* (Durham: Duke University Press, 2009), pp. 194–221.

the Israeli army or as an indirect result of Israeli acts, such as blockades enforced by Israel that endangered the lives of the population by limiting their access to hospitals. Widening the term martyr to include a maximal number of fatalities was aimed at molding a powerful Palestinian ethos of human sacrifices as stepping stones to longed for national independence, conjuring up a procession of martyrs bearing the banner of struggle against the occupation.

"Suicide" perpetrators, however, remained at the apex of prestige and esteem as figures for whom jihad and self-sacrifice constituted the essence of their lives.[95] "Suicide" attacks became a cultural ethos.[96] They were depicted by Palestinians as the community's "daily bread," and their perpetrators were glorified as writing a new chapter in the history of their nation and restoring its lost dignity with their blood and their souls.[97] This indoctrination included the pedagogic sphere as well. Elementary schools taught a popular, "Song of the *Shahid*," whose lyrics were "Better my death than my stolen right and homeland; the sound of the explosion is pleasant to me and the flow of blood cheers me."[98] Public opinion polls showed a support rate of 65–75 percent for "suicide acts."[99] As the phenomenon expanded, the pool of perpetrators widened to include

[95] Orayb A. Najjar, "The Editorial Family of al-Kateb Bows in Respect: The Construction of Martyrdom Text Genre in One Palestinian Literary Magazine," *Discourse and Society* 7/4 (1996), pp. 499–530; Ahmad Bahar in *al-Risala*, April 3, 2003, and June 26, 2003.

[96] H. Sande, "Palestinian Martyr Widowhood: Emotional Needs in Conflict with the Role Expectations," *Social Science and Medicine* 34 (1992), pp. 710–716; Nasra Hassan, "An Arsenal of Believers: Talking to Human Bombs," *New Yorker*, November 2001, pp. 36–41; also *al-Islam wa-Filastin* 89 (June 2001).

[97] See, e.g., 'Abd al-Rahman 'Abbad, the official speaker of "The 'Ulama' Association in Palestine," a forum affiliated with Hamas, available at http://www.lailatalqadr.com/stories/p4220701.shtml (accessed September 7, 2011)

[98] *Ha'aretz*, January 28, 2002. Notably, in September 2002 Hamas launched a journal for children in hard copy and on the Internet, *al-Fatih*, dedicated inter alia to exalting martyrdom. See http://www.al-fateh.net (accessed September 12, 2011); Daphna Burdman, "Education, Indoctrination, and Incitement: Palestinian Children on Their Way to Martyrdom," *Terrorism and Political Violence* 15 (2003), pp. 96–123; Shafiq Masalha, "Children and Violent Conflict: A Look at the Inner World of Palestinian Children via Their Dreams," *Palestinian-Israeli Journal* 10 (2003), p. 66.

[99] See, e.g., several polls conducted by the Jerusalem Media and Communication Center (JMCC), in *Palestinian Opinion Pulse* 3/7 (January 2002), no. 8 (April 2002), no. 9 (June 2002); also Iyad al-Sarraj, director of the Gaza Community Mental Health Program (GCMHP), in *Journal of Palestine Studies* 31/4 (Summer 2002), pp. 72–74; Hafez, *Manufacturing Human Bombs*, pp. 8–10.

not only young unmarried males[100] but also older men, heads of families, and women.[101]

However, in contrast to support by nationalist and feminist groups in the Palestinian and Arab world for women perpetrators, women carrying out "suicide acts" remained taboo in Islamic circles, especially in Hamas. Hamas' spiritual leader, Shaykh Ahmad Yasin, argued that such a development was unnecessary: the number of men willing to sacrifice themselves was satisfactory, but more importantly, the martyrdom of women was dangerous because it would put the survival of the Palestinian people at risk. Combat was the province of men, Yasin implied, whereas the duty of women was essentially demographic – namely, producing children and increasing the power of the Muslim nation. Yasin's stance underscored Hamas' conservative communal vision, which, although assigning a key role to women in the resistance to the occupation, defined it as more a familial and communal than a military or leadership role.[102]

Other indications of Hamas' cautious use of the "suicide" weapon included the avoidance of forming permanent suicide units, for example, the Liberation Tigers of Tamil Eelam in Sri Lanka, whose candidates were recruited and trained on an ad hoc basis only and the prohibition of

---

[100] On the age factor, see Juergensmeyer, *Terror in the Mind of God*, p. 191.

[101] *Ha'aretz*, April 1, 2002; *al-Risala*, November 27, 2006. Based on interviews with survivors of failed "suicide" operations, their relatives, friends, and leaders, Barbara Victor argued that these women were almost all in desperate situations and were convinced that the only way they could redeem themselves and their family's honor was to become a national heroine through martyrdom. Victor, *Army of Roses: Inside the World of Palestinian Women Suicide Bombers* (Emmaus, PA: Rodale, 2003); also Nadia Taysir Dabbagh, *Suicide in Palestine: Narratives of Despair* (London: Hurst, 2005), pp. 135–177. Other scholars provided a more nuanced picture regarding the motivations of Palestinian female "suicide" bombers in which various motives – nationalist, religious, revenge, and defiance of the traditional gender hierarchy – were also at work: Yoram Schwitzer, "Palestinian Female Suicide Bombers: Virtuous Heroines or Damaged Goods?" in Cindy D. Ness (ed.), *Female Terrorism and Militancy: Agency, Utility, and Organization* (New York: Routledge, 2008), pp. 131–145; Anat Berko and Edna Erez, "Martyrs or Murderers? Victims or Victimizers? The Voices of Would-be Palestinian Female Suicide Bombers," in ibid., pp. 150–161; Aant Berko, *The Smarter Bomb: Women and Children as Suicide Bombers* (New York: Rowman and Littlefield Publishers, 2012); Caron E. Gentry, "Twisted Maternalism: From Peace to Violence," *International Feminist Journal of Politics* 11/2 (June 2009), pp. 235–252.

[102] *New York Times*, January 31, 2002, and February 4, 2002; *Ha'aretz*, February 10, 2002, March 3, 2002, and April 1, 2002. On the role of women in Hamas' ideology, see *Hamas Covenant*, Clauses 17–18. Hamas' stance did not differ essentially from the traditional content of Muslim commentaries. See, e.g., 'Abd al-Halim Mahmud, *Fatawa*, Vol. 2, pp. 110–111. A more favorable stance was displayed by the Islamic Jihad in Palestine, e.g., http://www.saraya.ps/index/php?act=Show&id=394 (accessed September 7, 2011).

recruiting children into this type of activity, following public criticism and even revulsion over the involvement of young teenage perpetrators. According to Isma'il Abu Shanab, a Hamas leader in the Gaza Strip, the "suicide" attacks were to be mounted by means of a well-thought-out plan under organizational leadership and with a defined target, usually in retaliation for an Israeli attack. They were not to be carried out by young children, and they were to be planned so that there was a realistic chance of inflicting damage on Israel. "These operations," Abu Shanab stated, "are not part of the regular resistance. They are carried out when the Israelis exceed the limits."[103] In a similar vein, Shaykh Ahmad Yasin depicted them as an extraordinary response to an exceptional emergency situation.[104]

Hamas thus aimed to avoid being labeled as a merely militaristic movement, in contrast to the Islamic Jihad. It wanted to show that although military jihad was central to its platform, it did not overshadow communal jihad, which was the focal point of its mother movement, the Muslim Brethren, during the two decades preceding the outbreak of the first intifada. Although Hamas' publicly stated opposition to using women or children for "suicide missions" did not resolve this issue completely, the small numbers of such perpetrators marginalized the phenomenon in the collective Palestinian and Arab perception.

MARTYRDOM IN THE MUSLIM PERIPHERY: THE CHECHEN CASE

Thus far, the discussion of the phenomenon of "suicide" attacks has centered on its historic, social, and political aspects in the Middle East, the core arena of the Islamic world and the central venue in which political Islam was shaped in modern times. The "suicide" attack phenomenon, however, also spilled over into peripheral regions of the Islamic world, such as in Central and South Asia, where they acquired additional emphases reflecting local circumstances. This was best exemplified in the Chechen case.

Since the early nineteenth century, Chechnya, located in northern Caucasia, has been in frequent revolt against the Russian presence, with Islam constituting an integral element of its ethnic national identity and a

---

[103] *Ha'aretz*, April 26, 2002; *Washington Post*, May 10, 2002.
[104] Yasin quoted in Anat Berko, *The Path to Paradise: The Inner World of Suicide Bombers and Their Dispatchers* (Westport, CT: Praeger Security International, 2007), p. 57.

key factor in its resentment of Russian rule. For Muslim Chechen believers, who constitute the vast majority of the Chechen population, any infringement of that faith was viewed as a national disaster, whereas protecting the faith signified their continued existence as a nation. The guardians of Chechen Islam were mainly the leaders of the local Sufi Naqshbandiyya and Qadiriyya orders, whose organizational capabilities and public influence enabled them to prevent the penetration of Communism. Large numbers of Chechens joined these orders, and pilgrimages to the graves of saints – some of whose biographies were closely intertwined with the anti-Russian and anti-Soviet struggle – became a fixture of the Chechen ethos.[105] Chechen Muslims were renowned for their tolerance of other religions, but the waves of religious resurgence in the Arab-Islamic milieu during the 1970s permeated the Caucasian region, giving rise to radical Islamist groups.

The Chechen struggle for national independence reached a climax in the late 1980s with the collapse of the Soviet Union and the bankruptcy of Communism. This breakdown intensified Islamic sentiment, leading to a surge in the construction of mosques and religious colleges and pilgrimages to Mecca, revealing Saudi Arabia as an important patron of Caucasian Islam by supplying preachers, teachers, and religious literature through the World Islamic League's global *da'wa* network. The political window of opportunity that was created was utilized by the Chechen leadership to declare their country a free and independent republic and, in so doing, challenged the coherence of the Russian Federation and the flow of oil and gas from the Caspian Sea that passes through Chechen territory.

The Russian response was severe. The Chechen aspiration for independence elicited a Russian military invasion in December 1994 lasting two years and spreading destruction and ruin in Chechnya. Nevertheless, stubborn guerilla warfare by Chechen rebels persisted following the penetration of radical Islam into northern Caucasia in the 1990s. As a result, Islamic culture in Chechnya became more diverse and was no longer led by Sufi orders.[106]

The radical message bearers were militant Islamists, mainly from Arab countries, who had fought Russia on several other fronts, including Afghanistan and Tajikistan. Prominent among them was Amir al-Khattab

---

[105] Alexandre Bennigsen and S. Enders Wimbush, *Muslims of the Soviet Empire: A Guide* (London: C. Hurst, 1985), pp. 21–23, 157–160.
[106] Robert Seely, *Russo-Chechen Conflict 1800–2000: A Deadly Embrace* (Portland, OR: Frank Cass, 2001), pp. 304–311.

(d. 2002), a member of a wealthy family from the Persian Gulf who headed the Arab *mujahidun* in Chechnya. In interviews, Khattab explained that he was inspired to come to Caucasia after viewing images of Chechen fighters wearing green headbands decorated with Islamic slogans. The influence of the foreign militants increased in parts of Chechnya. They provided financial aid to the needy and ideological indoctrination to the local fighters. Their activities met with increasing hostility from Sufi and 'ulama' circles, who perceived a threat to their status and traditional rituals posed by the fundamentalist version of Islam imported from abroad.[107]

However, despite contention with the traditional religious elite, radical Islam sank roots in the Chechen landscape, introducing Islamic conceptions into politics, mainly through demands for the establishment of an Islamic state as a remedy for society's infirmities.[108] This was particularly appealing to educated young people from poor families whose defiant political awareness was etched during the First Chechen War of 1994–1996. They were joined by armed militia units under the command of resistance leaders Shamil Basayev and Amir Khattab, who provided them with a sense of security and entitlement. Ongoing violence was aimed not only at the Russian army but also at Chechens who supported a political compromise with Moscow.

"Suicide" attacks were introduced into the national struggle in 2000. They were backed by ideological acceptance and religious approval from Muslim radicals in the Middle East who sought to broaden the "suicide" attack phenomenon and further implant it in the Islamic discourse, thereby neutralizing criticism of it by ideological rivals who opposed its use. Prominent in this effort was Yusuf al-'Uyayri, leader of al-Qa'ida in Saudi Arabia (killed in 2005), who glorified the Chechen struggle against Russia and defended their use of the "suicide" weapon as morally justified and militarily useful.[109] In al-'Uyayri's view:

[107] Sebastian Smith, *Allah's Mountains: The Battle for Chechnya* (revised ed., London: Tauris Parke Paperbacks, 2006), pp. 74–78, 153–154; Moshe Gammer, "Between Mecca and Moscow: Islam, Politics and Political Islam in Chechnya and Daghestan," *Middle Eastern Studies* 41 (November 2005), pp. 833–848.

[108] Gammer, "Between Mecca and Moscow," pp. 837–838.

[109] Yusuf al-'Uyayri, *Hal intaharat Hawwa' am istushhidat?* available at http://Wa.alsunnah.info/r?i=hqkfgsb2 (accessed February 6, 2013); for a short English translation, see *The Islamic Ruling of the Permissibility of Martyrdom Operations: Did Hawa Barayev Commit Suicide or Achieve Martyrdom?* available at http://www.religioscope.com/pdf/martyrdom.pdf (accessed February 6, 2013).

God showed us kindness in the land of Chechnya by preparing us to fight the infidel religions represented by the Russian army. We therefore ask God to strengthen us and help us, for every goodness is to be found in what He has ordained for us. Thus we praise Him for putting the heads of our enemies in our hands, [heads] which we severed systematically. As a result, some of us have died and some are waiting for death. God kept his promise to us and strengthened us by jihad after the humiliation meted out to us. Our brothers, the martyrs wrote history with their blood, for which we are proud and glorify them before the nations of the world. Their blood was spilled for the declaration of faith "There is no God except Allah.".... They saturated our lands and satisfied the wish of our Lord. For the sake of God people were torn to shreds and their heads were severed from their bodies, but this in no way deterred us from continuing in our path; rather, it only heightened our daring and our desire to become martyrs. Soon we will meet our loved ones, Muhammad and his companions, and how great will be the joy of he who meets God when He [God] is pleased by him, for he will rise up to life again with the prophets, the truthful, the *shahid*s, and the righteous.[110]

Ultimately, however, the "suicide" perpetrators were motivated more by revenge, despair, and an aspiration for an independent state than by religious zeal. In the first two years, during 2000–2001, the attacks were aimed at army bases in Chechnya only. The favored tactic was to drive Russian army trucks filled with explosives into chosen targets. The Russian army, reacting harshly, succeeded in reducing the attacks against its installations, pushing the Chechen resistance into a situation of distress. From 2002 onward, many of the Chechen attacks shifted to the Russian heartland, mainly to Moscow, with a rise in the number of civilian targets. During 2000–2006, 50 percent of the "suicide" attacks took place in Chechnya, 29 percent in Moscow, and 21 percent in southern Russia.[111] The most shocking attack took place in a theater in Moscow in October 2002, when more than 100 people were killed, causing severe reverberations. Some fifty perpetrators took part in the incident; eighteen of them were women wearing explosive belts. Their determination to blow themselves up was never in doubt, and all were killed in confrontations with the Russian security forces.[112]

During this period, 47 percent of the attacks were aimed at official or military targets located in civilian areas, 39 percent at Russian army bases, and 14 percent at governmental targets. In almost all these cases the perpetrators neither conveyed their intentions beforehand nor declared

---

[110] Al-ʿUyayri, *Hal intaharat Hawa umustushihdat?* p.1.
[111] Robert W. Kurz and Charles K. Bartles, "Chechen Suicide Bombers," *Journal of Slavic Military Studies* 20 (2007), pp. 532, 543–547.
[112] Fred Weir, "Chechen Rebels Go Kamikaze," *Christian Science Monitor*, June 7, 2000.

self-sacrifice for God. No posters with their pictures appeared in the streets. During 2003–2004 the scope of the attacks increased against a background of intensified Russian military action in Chechnya: 63 percent of all Chechen attacks took place then.[113]

Research has shown that most of the perpetrators were young and were victims of the war, having experienced trauma or loss following the killing, torturing, or wounding of a loved one or a family friend, leading them to a strong sense of commitment to a radical organization devoted to carrying out "suicide" attacks. Other factors, such as social estrangement, unemployment, and hopelessness, played a secondary role. Perpetrators underwent religious indoctrination aimed at overcoming the barrier of fear of death. Despite this religious orientation, however, political motives and the goal of revenge remained the first priority for the Chechen perpetrators. Radical Islam merely offered a convenient method to ease the perpetrator's mental and spiritual state in carrying out the act.[114]

Whereas other Islamist movements that accommodated "suicide" attacks, such as Hizballah and Hamas, discussed earlier, also offered a wide range of social support for this practice, this was not the case in Chechnya. Most of the Chechen population did not believe that carrying out "suicide" attacks would benefit the community. Ultimately, they favored compromise with the Russian authorities rather than ongoing violence to attain a degree of national independence.[115] Significantly, videos of "suicide" perpetrators in Chechnya were not distributed to the local population, in contrast to Palestine, Iraq,[116] and elsewhere where the perpetrators circulated videos to their supporters. Videos of Chechen perpetrators were, however, prepared primarily for external audiences in Islamic circles for fund-raising purposes to support what was promoted as a just struggle by freedom fighters against oppression, meriting financial, moral, and other support. Another difference in the Chechen context was that in addition to young unmarried perpetrators, older people who left children behind were also recruited.[117]

---

[113] For data on Chechen "suicide" attacks, see Anne Speckhard and Khapta Ahkmedova, "Black Widows and Beyond: Understanding the Motivations and Life Trajectories of Chechen Female Terrorists," in Ness (ed.), *Female Terrorism and Militancy*, pp. 100–104.

[114] Kurz and Bartles, "Chechen Suicide Bombers," pp. 529–534.

[115] Ibid., p. 535.

[116] For the Iraqi case, see Chapter 5 in this book.

[117] Kurz and Bartles, "Chechen Suicide Bombers," pp. 535–536; also Anne Nivat, "The Black Widows: Chechen Women Join the Fight for Independence – and Allah," in Ness (ed.), *Female Terrorism and Militancy*, pp. 122–130.

Important cultural differences also underlay the use of female perpetrators in Chechnya, in contrast to other zones of ethno-national conflict.[118] Radical Islamic movements generally involved women in violent acts only as a last resort and when operationally warranted, such as in passing through checkpoints unobtrusively. In the Palestinian case, this type of mission was perceived as a means for women to break away from their traditional roles and gain equality with men for a moment in history. In some cases, for women who had lost their honor (because of rape, infertility, or suspicion of an extramarital relationship), "suicide" attacks offered a prestigious alternative. This was not the case in Chechnya. Most of the female perpetrators there did not fit this profile. Anne Speckhard's research of families of Chechen female perpetrators found that those perpetrators were motivated by the same combination of circumstances as their male colleagues (trauma, harsh repression by the enemy, revenge, and a strong ideological commitment to the resistance cause), pointing to a more open social milieu. Although the Chechen family structure was traditional, the attainment of higher education by women was accepted, as was full-time employment outside the home. Notably, the first attack there, in 2000, was carried out by two women. From then on, statistical findings show that women were involved in 70 percent of the attacks and that 50 percent of the attacks were carried out entirely by women.[119]

Chechen women "suicide" attackers were labeled "black widows" by the Russian press when it became clear that many of them sought revenge for the death of husbands, brothers, or sons in the Chechen wars against Russia. The profile of female "suicide" attackers indicates a range of married and unmarried women ages fifteen to thirty-eight, and some of them having acquired higher education. Aside from revenge, psychological trauma also constituted a strong motive. Many of these women, as male perpetrators, lost family members in battle or in aerial bombings by the Russian army. Many others witnessed death, beatings, or abuse of family members by Russian soldiers. A psychological breakdown involving anger, depression, and self-blame at being unable to save family members paved the way to adopting violence and a jihad ideology.

Thus, for example, Tamara, a friend and neighbor of one of the perpetrators of the attack in the Moscow theater in 2002, addresses her brother who was killed in the war against the Russians: "In such a disgusting

---

[118] See notes 101–102.
[119] Anne Speckhard and Khapta Ahkmedova, "The Making of a Martyr: Chechen Suicide Terrorism," *Studies in Conflict and Terrorism* 29/5 (2006), pp. 1–65.

world, so unjust. ... O you my brother, who had always learned how to give me hope, now that you are not here anymore, I want to join you, I want to see you, I want to go to paradise too. I do not want to live in this world."[120]

Clearly, the trauma of loss of loved ones, and the widespread destruction, provided fertile ground for various sectors of the community to turn to radical Islam. Similarly, the incentives and the sense of tranquility offered by the notion of the next world in dying for God helped ease the trauma. Jihad was perceived as an act of retribution to an invading unbeliever and as reforming the universe. This new perception also involved a changed lifestyle – namely, a great deal more praying, greater devotion to good deeds, and wearing a veil. Statistics regarding sixty-four perpetrators revealed that forty-fie came from a secular background and only nineteen from a traditional background.[121]

These personal and social incentives prompted the perpetrators to seek refuge in a group environment, in contrast to Mark Sedgeman's analysis that the group network itself is the main incentive for carrying out attacks. In the Chechen case, personal trauma seems to be the motivating factor, alongside a strong preparedness to die as a martyr for the country, for social justice, or as revenge. The Chechen recruitment process took place through connections with family and friends. The recruits did not undergo prolonged or wide-ranging training. Once the radical ideology was adopted by the recruit, only a short time passed until the attack was carried out.

Chechen martyrdom was closely linked to a political agenda. A number of separatist Chechen groups assimilated the Islamist goal of establishing a sharia-based state into the national agenda of an independent state. This thrust was promoted vigorously by Amir Khattab who, together with Osama bin Laden, nurtured a version of Wahhabism that sought to create a single Islamic nation in the Caucasus. Khattab succeeded in forming a Caucasian front based in a broad network that encompassed all the Caucasian nations fighting against Russia. Reportedly, Chechens were trained in Afghanistan and were indoctrinated in Wahhabism in various study centers in Chechnya.[122]

Nevertheless, Chechen nationalist groups continued to declare that their primary goal was an independent state and were inclined toward dialogue

---

[120] Quoted in Nivat, "The Black Widows," p. 127.
[121] Speckhard and Ahkmedova, "The Making of a Martyr"; also idem, "Black Widows and Beyond," pp. 107–117.
[122] Gammer, "Between Mecca and Moscow," mainly pp. 836–839.

with Moscow. Reports pointed to a decline in "suicide" attacks in the latter part of the first decade of the twenty-first century, apparently because of an absence of wide communal support in Chechnya. Furthermore, there was a widespread sense among Chechens that resistance against Russia was hopeless. This was enhanced by the murders of key resistance leaders, including Shamil Baseyev in 2006. However, the "suicide" attack phenomenon did not disappear.[123]

NON-ISLAMIC PERSPECTIVES

Resistance groups in other, non-Muslim conflict zones during the 1990s, such as the Kurdish Worker's Party (PKK) in Turkey and the Liberation Tigers of Tamil Eelam (LTTE), also embraced this new guerilla warfare format. The main motive for using the weapon of self-sacrifice was stated clearly by an LTTE official: "Of course we use suicide bombers, because as a revolutionary organization we have limited resources."[124]

Initially, the military nature of the PKK resistance movement in southeast Turkey was conventional,[125] as can be learned from its guerilla handbook compiled in 1989 by the organization's leader, Abdullah Ocalan. Mainly, it laid down organizational rules and methods of recruiting the population to advance its goals, explicitly stating that attacks are to be aimed at regime personnel, the security forces, and collaborators within the Kurdish population. In instances when citizens were harmed, the organization explained that they were relatives of police agents or traitors or that the act was perpetrated without its knowledge by renegade Kurdish circles.[126]

The mid-1990s, which were influenced by Lebanese martyrology, gave rise to self-sacrificial forms of violence as part of an escalated propaganda campaign aimed at attracting public attention to the region. By the end of 2008, twenty-one out of thirty "suicide" attacks in southeast Turkey

---

[123] Kurz and Bartles, "Chechen Suicide Bombers," pp. 536–537.

[124] Quoted in the *New Yorker*, August 1, 2005, p. 56.

[125] On the PKK. see İsmet G. İmset, *The PKK: A Report on Separatist Violence in Turkey, 1973–1992* (Ankara: Turkish Daily News, 1992).

[126] Excerpts from the text appears in İmset, *The PKK*, pp. 149–154; also ibid., pp. 49–55, 98–104, 308–320; İmset, "The PKK: Terrorists or Freedom Fighters?" *International Journal of Kurdish Studies* 10/1–2 (1996), pp. 45–100; Gülistan Gürbey, "The Development of the Kurdish Nationalism Movement in Turkey since the 1980s," in R. Olson (ed.), *The Kurdish Nationalist Movement in the 1990s* (Lexington: University Press of Kentucky, 1996), pp. 9–37.

had been carried out by the PKK, aimed mainly at military and police targets. They were justified as part of the nationalist struggle against Turkish colonialism. They also included a sizeable number of female perpetrators who viewed martyrdom as a route to women's emancipation and the improvement of their status in the relatively conservative Kurdish society.[127]

Nevertheless, the use of the "suicide" weapon was not widespread in the Kurdish case and was never formalized or systematized. Moreover, its main focus remained mainly military and police targets. It waned in the wake of the success of the Turkish regime to suppress Kurdish violence in the late 1990s, including "suicide" attacks, by means of a focused campaign to isolate the organization, the capture of Abdullah Ocalan (in 1999), and the introduction of a dialogue regarding Kurdish aspirations in the region.[128]

In Sri Lanka the Tamil struggle for self-determination in the north and east of the country, led by the LTTE, incorporated national, linguistic, and religious aspects. It targeted the local regime, which was dominated by the Buddhist Sinhalese majority. The Tamils, who are Hindi – as are the vast majority of the population in neighboring India – constitute a minority in Sri Lanka. During 1983–2000 the LTTE, which acquired the image of a professional and ruthlessly dedicated fighting force, carried out 171 "suicide" attacks (killing some 1,500 persons), compared to the PKK's 21 attacks in Turkey and, in fact, more such attacks than any other movement at the time, including Hizballah and the Palestinian Islamic movements.

However, the Tamils' "suicide" attacks were directed primarily against political figures and government officials, including two prime ministers: Rajiv Ghandi of India and Ranasinghe Primadasa of Sri Lanka.[129] Moreover, their military goals were conventional: to capture territory, strategic assets, and weapons, to destroy enemy army resources, and to

---

[127] Hamit Bozarslan, *Violence in the Middle East: From Political Struggle to Self-sacrifice* (Princeton: Markus Wiener Publishers, 2004), pp. 21–38; Shaul Shay, *The Shahids: Islam and Suicide Attacks* (New Brunswick: Interdisciplinary Center, 2004), pp. 102–108.

[128] Ali Kemal Özcan, *Turkey's Kurds: A Theoretical Analysis of the PKK and Abdullah Öcalan* (London: Routledge, 2006); also Merari, *Driven to Death*, pp. 70–71. Notably, in March 2013, PKK leader Abdullah Ocalan announced a historic cease-fire with Turkey following three decades of conflict between them, calling on the Kurdish rebels to relinquish their arms and pass from armed struggle to democratic struggle.

[129] Stephen Hopgood, "Tamil Tigers 1987–2002," in Gambetta, *Making Sense of Suicide Missions*, pp. 43–76; Adam Dolnik, "Die and Let Die: Exploring Links between Suicide Terrorism and Terrorist Use of Chemical, Biological, Radiological, and Nuclear Weapons," *Studies in Conflict and Terrorism* 26/1 (2003), pp. 24–25.

cause maximal losses in enemy ranks. These were perceived as tactical moves in the context of a broad military strategy of insurgency against a stronger enemy force, as well as a means of distinguishing the LTTE from other, better established Tamil separatist groups. Harm to civilians was viewed as collateral damage inasmuch as political assassinations were generally carried out in public spaces where civilians congregated. The fighters showed a consistent readiness for death, explainable by the young age of the volunteers who were unencumbered by family or work commitments.[130]

The perpetrator did not always die in the act. When the goal was attained, escape was a possibility – that is, the missions were not purely suicidal. However, in most cases death was a certainty if the goal was to be achieved, and the fighters were trained in this spirit. Mental preparation, self-discipline, asceticism, and a cultlike loyalty to the leader were vital components of the preparatory process.[131]

The notion of suicide was rooted in the Tamil culture as a legitimate response to suffering. Sri Lanka has a high rate of suicide, although this does not mean that the Tamil fighters committed suicide out of desperation. Rather, their suicide was accepted with understanding. Additionally, the presence of a national struggle for independence and the suppressive Sinhala government contributed to recruitment. Notably, a high proportion of the recruits were women.

Until the 1960s, Tamil women were absent from the political and national arena. They became politically conscious during the 1960s with the growing separatist thrust of the Tamil minority in Sri Lanka. By the 1990s, women constituted between one-third and one-half of the elite unit of the LTTE, known as the Black Tigers. Another wing of the organization, in charge of attacks against the Sri Lankan navy, also had a sizable percentage of female perpetrators. As in the Kurdish case, the participation of women was pronounced (approximately 40 percent), as women could conceal explosives more easily and could more easily reach the target. These statistics showed that women played an important role, from the organization's viewpoint, and underwent rigorous training. They were also active in the political decision-making aspect, in addition to their combat tasks. The LTTE also had a women's branch. Women

---

[130] Hopgood, "Tamil Tigers 1987–2002," pp. 43–60; also Bruce Hoffman and Gordon H. McCormick, "Terrorism, Signaling, and Suicide Attack," *Studies in Conflict and Terrorism* 27 (2004), pp. 256–262.

[131] Hopgood, "Tamil Tigers 1987–2002," pp. 60–73.

took an active part in plans by this organization to assassinate more than twelve public figures.

The prominent presence of women was all the more significant in light of the conservative nature of Tamil society, replete with many social constraints for women that forced them into a traditionally subservient role. Tamil women challenged this role and joined underground movements that promised a radical change in their social status.[132]

Both the PKK and the LTTE demonstrated that a secular cause, too, could serve as a motivation for death. The fallen were also called martyrs. The weapon of "suicide" attacks constituted an additional method of widening the struggle for independence. In this respect there was little difference between them and the Sunni movements, which also defined themselves as being in a state of conquest.[133]

CONCLUDING NOTES

"Suicide" attacks introduced a daring and challenging dimension into Islamist discourse in the late twentieth century. The attacks began as a Shi'i phenomenon, with Iran as one of its first ideological formulators, and were first made operative by Hizballah in Lebanon. From there they permeated the Sunni realm, where they were incorporated into the Sunni tradition. The new discourse of self-sacrifice was presented as a foundation on which the survival of the political community was based. Nevertheless, whereas Iranian martyrdom was officially sanctioned and government sponsored, martyrdom in other regions was fostered by politically dissident and oppositionist groups that were fighting for power against internal and external rivals.

Martyrdom in Lebanon, Palestine, and Chechnya revealed a broad common denominator, namely sponsorship by religio-nationalist movements whose activities were focused within the geographic borders of their countries, thereby reasserting the territorial nature of the Islamist

[132] Debra D. Zedalis, *Female Suicide Bombers* (Honolulu, HI: University Press of the Pacific, 2004); Margaret Gonzalez-Perez, "From Freedom Birds to Water Buffaloes: Women Terrorists in Asia," in Ness (ed.), *Female Terrorism and Militancy*, pp. 185–188.

[133] Eventually, in the Tamili case, in 2006 the Sri Lankan army launched a major offensive against the Tigers, bringing the entire country under their control and defeating the LTTE military.

phenomenon. One result was that the boundaries between religion and nationalism became blurred.[134]

The leaders of these movements sought to represent the nation, with their primary concern liberation and state formation. The main asset available to them was the struggle against foreign occupation. For the Lebanese, Palestinians, and Chechens, religion served as an ethical marker in fortifying an indigenous identity against an infidel foreign threat, which was both cultural and military. Islam was fused with a culture of liberation, sanctifying a polarized concept of struggle between truth and falsehood, and believers and unbelievers. In this struggle the ultimate victory would be given to the righteous, even if the obstacles seemed insurmountable or the time prolonged. Sacrifice became a central ethos, presented as a defense of both faith and homeland and a victory of theology over technology.

A supportive sociological element for the notion of offensive martyrdom in the image of "suicide" attacks was, paradoxically, the built-in recoil to self-inflicted death, as reflected in the low suicide rate in the Arab Muslim population, sustained by religio-ethical prohibitions against such a death, and reinforced by traditional patterns of familial solidarity and mutual responsibility.[135] As far back as 1897, the French sociologist Émile Durkheim cited the affinity between suicide and social solidarity, pointing out that suicide is less common when the individual is part of a close-knit social environment with strong religious faith.[136]

Other supportive elements are cultural codes of revenge and honor;[137] masculinity (*rujula*), which is acquired in a brave and fearlessness deed;[138] and psychosocial patterns of beliefs about the justice of the cause, victimization, delegitimation of the rival or the enemy, and justification of hostile acts against them. Dehumanization aimed at precluding any possible

---

[134] Juergensmeyer, "The Worldwide Rise of Religious Nationalism," pp. 1–20. In the Palestinian case, see Loren D. Lybarger, *Identity and Religion in Palestine: The Struggle between Islamism and Secularism in the Occupied Territories* (Princeton, NJ: Princeton University Press, 2007), mainly chapters 1 and 4, and the epilogue.

[135] *Al-Ayyam*, June 2, 1997; *Ha'aretz*, May 31, 2002. Also As'ad Yusuf Abu Ghalyun in *Hadyu'l-Islam*, no. 158 (January–February 2003), pp. 91–97.

[136] Durkheim, *On Suicide*, pp. 152–276; Colin Pritchard, *The Ultimate Rejection? A Psycho-Social Study* (Buckingham: Open University Press, 1995), mainly the introduction.

[137] See, e.g., the Palestinian, Chechen, and Iraqi cases, Berko, *The Path to Paradise*, pp. 48–49; Kurz and Bartles, "Chechen Suicide Bombers," pp. 533–534; Hafez, *Suicide Bombers in Iraq*, pp. 144–145.

[138] See, e.g., Julie Peteet, "Male Gender and Rituals of Resistance in Palestinian Intifada: A Cultural Politics of Violence," in Samir Khalaf and Roseanne Saad Khalaf (eds.), *Arab Youth: Social Mobilization in Times of Risk* (London: Dar al-Saqi, 2011), pp. 201–203.

empathy for the rival. It ascribes negative attributes such as treachery, malice, aggression and wickedness to the other side. These characteristics help cast responsibility on the enemy for the outbreak of the dispute and its accompanying violence. Simultaneously, it enables the victim to justify his own behavior in a moral light, to reinforce his resilience, and to build up a consciousness of possible victory.[139]

Thus, the ethos of dispute is linked both to monistic politics directed inwardly to coalesce a community and to dualistic politics directed outwardly to create a total contradiction between two forces or ideas.[140] To use Frantz Fanon's anti-colonialist conceptualization, Islamist martyrdom constituted a new path, a new axis to destroy the power relationships between conqueror and conquered and between settler and inhabitant.[141] This observation is also valid regarding resistance groups in other, non-Muslim conflict zones, such as the PKK in Turkey and the LTTE in Sri Lanka, which also embraced this new format of guerilla warfare.

In all four Islamic cases discussed here, martyrdom was directed against a foreign occupier, but it also had a domestic agenda that was vital in upgrading the public status of the resistance movements involved. These movements were backed by charismatic leaders who led puritanical lifestyles, had expertise in mass communications, and offered a seemingly attractive bargain to those who joined their ranks. In return for loyalty, obedience, and self-sacrifice, they offered moral, psychological, and material rewards.

Viewed retrospectively, the use of self-sacrifice was not unrestrained but rather carefully thought out in response to specific needs – a reflection of the political realism of the Islamist movements that were anxious to avoid a military image. Significantly, controversy that was stirred in Arab-Muslim streets over the use of boys or women for this purpose had the effect of limiting the phenomenon of self-sacrifice and applying organizational and public control over it. Typically, the leader of the Palestinian Islamic Jihad, Shaykh 'Abdallah al-Shami, argued: "We do not take depressed people ... in order to be a martyr bomber, you have to want to live."[142] In the same

---

[139] Arendt, "On Violence," pp. 158–159; Daniel Bar-Tal, *Shared Beliefs in a Society: Social Psychological Analysis* (Thousand Oaks, CA: Sage Publications, 2000).

[140] T. Flanagan, "The Politics of Millennium," *Terrorism and Political Violence* 7/3 (Autumn 1995), pp. 164–172.

[141] Frantz Fanon, *The Wretched on the Earth* (New York: Grove Weidenfeld, 1991), mainly pp. 29–74.

[142] Shami, quoted in the *New Yorker*, July 9, 2001; also Shaykh Hasan Yusuf in *Middle East Affairs Journal* 7/3–4 (Summer/Fall 2001), pp. 249–251.

vein, Hamas spokesmen emphasized that those who explode themselves in the enemy's centers are "people of the mosques, aware of the prohibition against suicide and its fate in the next world."[143] Indisputably, however, this weapon metamorphosed into a cultural ethos of revolt and resistance, thus becoming an integral part of the symbolic repertory of the conquered society.

[143] *Filastin al-Muslima*, May 2001.

5

Al-Qa'ida: Transnational Martyrdom

Islamist movements that carried out "suicide" missions in Lebanon, Palestine, Chechnya, and elsewhere were careful to emphasize that this "suicide" weapon does not constitute a systematic or mass modus operandi but is implemented in emergency situations only and within defined Islamic parameters. Defending the faith and the homeland from the yoke of foreigners was a central theme, with its operative parameters conforming to the geographical borders of the specific entity in conflict. The geographic parameter also signified the distinctive difference between these religio-national movements and the transnational al-Qa'ida, which emerged in the early 1990s. Both networks nurtured martyrdom but in different contexts and with differing emphases. The core difference, aptly observed by Farhad Khosrokhavar, was that whereas religio-national movements sought to define their nation's place in a world of nations, al-Qa'ida's aim was to create a new world order.[1]

The emergence of al-Qa'ida introduced a new dimension in reviving the notion of global jihad that had been central in the early period of Islam, transcending geographic and ethnic boundaries, with no distinction between the West and its allies in the Middle East, Asia, and Africa. Thus, the boundary between "the realm of Islam" (in which the law of Islam prevailed) and "the realm of war" (the territories inhabited by infidels) that had developed over time in the Islamic tradition lost its validity.[2]

---

[1] Khosrokhavar, *Suicide Bombers*, pp. 225–226.
[2] For a selection of literature on al-Qa'ida, see, e.g., Gilles Kepel, *Jihad: The Trail of Political Islam* (Cambridge, MA: Belknap Press of Harvard University Press, 2002), pp. 299–322; Rohan Gunaratna, *Inside al-Qaeda: Global Network of Terror* (New York: Berkley Books, 2003); Peter Bergen, *Holy War, Inc.: Inside the Secret World of Osama bin Laden* (New

Jihad encased the globe, entwining the struggle against the West with a struggle as well against "apostate" regimes at home. The globalization of jihad also stimulated the creation of new symbols and a new collective identity, a redefinition of moral standards, the establishment of a rigid system of codes for normative behavior, and a legitimation of radical violence and the readiness to pay the ultimate price in the form of self-sacrifice.

An important foundation in the evolution of al-Qaʿida and its concept of martyrdom was provided by the struggle against the Soviet conquest of Afghanistan in which Arabs from the Middle East countries (the Arab Afghans) also participated. A key figure in this context was the Palestinian Shaykh ʿAbdallah ʿAzzam.

ʿABDALLAH ʿAZZAM'S MARTYRDOM LEGACY

Palestinian-born Shaykh ʿAbdallah ʿAzzam (d. 1989), a graduate of al-Azhar, was a member of the Jordanian Muslim Brethren for a period. After his dismissal from a university position in Jordan for political reasons, he moved to Saudi Arabia in 1981 where he lectured at King Abdulaziz University in Jedda. Shortly thereafter, he joined the struggle against the Soviets in Afghanistan, an experience that he described as a "rebirth."[3] For ʿAzzam, the Afghan model was a modern version of the Arabian Peninsula environment during the formative period of Islam, which served as the cradle of Islamic civilization. The Afghan environment – devoid of corrupting foreign influences – could foster the attainment of unity of body and spirit so necessary for bold and effective action on the enemy front. In fact, he wrote, it constitutes "the start of the historical turning of the whole world toward Islam."[4]

Although not stated explicitly, Afghanistan was perceived by ʿAzzam as suited to serve as an ideal geographic expanse for unifying and strengthening the community of believers, far from any corrupted environment, as

York: Simon and Schuster, 2002); Karen J. Greenberg, *al-Qaeda Now: Understanding Today's Terrorists* (New York: Cambridge University Press, 2005); Gerges, *The Far Enemy*; idem, *Journey of the Jihadist* (New York: Harcourt, 2007); idem, *The Rise and Fall of al-Qaeda* (Oxford: Oxford University Press, 2011); Raymond Ibrahim, *The al-Qaeda Reader* (New York: Broadway Books, 2007); Abdel Bari Atwan, *The Secret History of al-Qaeda* (Berkeley: University of California Press, 2008).

[3] On ʿAzzam's biography, see Husni Adham Jarrar, *al-Shahid ʿAbdallah ʿAzzam: rajul daʿwa wa-madrasat jihad* (Amman: Dar al-Diya', 1990); Hazim al-Amin, *al-Salafi al-yatim: al-wajh al-Filastini li'l-jihad al-ʿalami wa'l-Qaʿida* (Beirut: Dar al-Saqi, 2011), chapter 2.

[4] ʿAzzam, *Fi'l-Jihad*, pp. 5–6, 36–37, 156–157; Jarrar, *al-Shahid ʿAbdallah ʿAzzam*, pp. 170–171, 182.

exemplified by the Prophet's *hijra* from Mecca to Medina. There, in 'Azzam's words, the "solid basis" (*al-qa'ida al-sulba*) will be laid for the reestablishment of Muslim society of the future by force of raids (*ghazwa*) – another term linked to the Prophet's wars at the beginning of Islam. Whereas Muslim radicals who adopted the jihad weapon handed down by Sayyid Qutb and 'Abd al-Salam Faraj embarked on a spiritual *hijra* and focused on struggles against local regimes, 'Azzam and the Arab Afghans embarked additionally on a physical *hijra*, thereby paving the way for the internationalization of the Islamist struggle.

The role of the Arab Afghans in the struggle against the Soviet conquest was highlighted in 'Azzam's narrative in terms of both their leadership and their fighting ability, as befitting those who arrived from the heart of Islam.[5] Notably, on the practical level, and despite the common ground of jihad against the Soviets, the Arab volunteers tended to preserve their distinctive identity and did not mingle with the Afghan fighters (*mujahidun*).[6] Differences in language and culture were certainly factors.

Still, the role of the local Afghans was not neglected. The Afghan people, 'Azzam declared, were among the most ardent believers in the faith, possessing the attributes of a high moral level, discipline, and unity. Their bold struggle against the conquest reinforced the pride of Muslims throughout the world. Their endurance was mythical, 'Azzam wrote: "Where is Russia now? What is it [Russia] worth? ... All this [the conquest] has ended. The Russians are degraded and ridiculed." Still, 'Azzam pointed out with regret, in regions outside Afghanistan the injunction of jihad is neglected and forgotten, whether because of ignorance or in self-defense against Western detractors of Islam as a religion of the sword. This neglect of jihad, he observed, has revealed the deep crisis of the Muslim community and the absence of a talented, responsible leadership cadre.[7]

'Azzam's position on jihad in Afghanistan, as pointed out as well by Thomas Hegghammer, contrasted with the prevailing stance of the Islamic discourse at the time. Whereas 'Azzam insisted that jihad in Afghanistan

---

[5] 'Azzam, *Jihad sha'b Muslim* (n.p., n.d.), pp. 63–65.
[6] Mansfield, *His Own Words*, p. 40; Gerges, *The Far Enemy*, pp. 83–84.
[7] 'Azzam thereby attacked the low religious image attributed to the Afghan people by the molders of the Islamic discourse – namely as being religiously and morally weak, having no expertise in understanding the Qur'an, and being permissive of forbidden things such as drugs, which led to the absence of broad Islamic support for the Afghans' struggle against the Soviets. On the half-hearted Islamic discourse of jihad regarding Afghanistan, see, e.g., Thomas Hegghammer, *Jihad in Saudi Arabia* (Cambridge: Cambridge University Press, 2010), pp. 24–30, 40–42.

was an individual duty for all Muslims regardless of their nationality, religious scholars and Islamists argued that it was incumbent only on the Afghans. ʿAzzam thus set the stage for the globalization of the jihad cause, although focusing largely on occupied Muslim territories such as Afghanistan, Palestine, Eritrea, the Philippines, and Kosovo.[8]

Moreover, eschewing the somewhat apologetic tone adopted by Hasan al-Banna, Abu al-Aʿla Mawdudi, and Sayyid Qutb and demonstrating a radical new stance, ʿAzzam emphasized that Islam arose by the sword, as shown by the large number of passages in the Qurʾan (more than 100) relating to the term jihad. Anyone who proposes a contradictory interpretation of their straightforward meaning distorts the significance of going out to war, derides Islam, and should be shunned, he argued. He quoted primarily two verses that refer to the "sword": "Do not wrong your souls in these [four sacred] months – though you may fight the idolaters at any time, if they first fight you – remember that God is with those who are mindful of Him" (Sura 9: 36), and "When the [four] forbidden months are over, wherever you encounter the idolaters, kill them, seize them, besiege them, wait for them at every lookout post" (Sura 9: 5). Citing the authority of traditional commentators, ʿAzzam highlighted the second verse as constituting an order that overrides any other verse that might imply moderation toward non-Muslims, thereby seeking to fortify the duty of war and jihad.[9]

Furthermore, ʿAzzam held, jihad is a higher duty than frequent visits to, and praying in, the holy mosque of Mecca or renovating the mosque, and it is the only means to repel external aggression and establish the Islamic state. Thereby, the "human gods" will also be brought down from their lofty position to slavery, and absolute loyalty to God will be assured. This is the literal and practical meaning of the term jihad, he wrote, namely, "slaughter" (*dhabh*) of enemies.[10] Whoever shuns this duty "will be judged as someone who intentionally eats during the Ramadan fast and as someone who intentionally neglects prayer."[11] With this statement about jihad as war and the slaughter of enemies, ʿAzzam ratified ʿAbd al-Salam Faraj's stance in his book "The Absent Imperative"[12] written in

---

[8] Ibid., pp. 41–42.
[9] ʿAzzam's will, published in *al-Mujtamaʿ* (Kuwait), no. 944 (July 16, 1989), pp. 16–19, reprinted in Jarrar, *al-Shahid ʿAbdallah ʿAzzam*, pp. 137–144.
[10] ʿAzzam, *Fiʾl-Jihad*, pp. أ-ب, 4–6, 133–134; also Jarrar, *al-Shahid ʿAbdallah ʿAzzam*, pp. 136–144.
[11] ʿAzzam, *Fiʾl-Jihad*, p. 134.
[12] ʿImara (ed.), *al-Farida al-ghaʾiba*.

the late 1970s. Faraj too used the term slaughter. However, whereas Faraj aimed this message at local deviated regimes,[13] 'Azzam aimed it at non-Muslim invaders.

Just as prayer never ceases until a person's death, 'Azzam stated, the nature of jihad, which is systematically warlike and personal, is directed at present at repelling non-Muslim conquerors from the lands of Islam (*jihad al-daf*). It does not end until the fighter meets God. Even if the power of the Muslim side is inferior, there is no retreat from the duty of jihad.[14] Moreover, jihad and the defense of the lands of Islam from aggressive infidels constitute the preferred way of worship. "One hour spent fighting in the path of God is worth more than seventy years spent in praying at home."[15] Thus, martyrdom should be viewed as the jewel in the crown of Islam and the essence of Muslim life. In 'Azzam's view:

Nations are only brought to life by their beliefs and their convictions and they die only because of their desires and their lusts. The extent to which righteous convictions and correct beliefs spread within a nation, is the extent to which it plants its roots in the depths of the earth. . . . As for the Muslim Umma, it continues to exist throughout the course of history of humankind only by a divine ideology and the blood which flows as a result of spreading this divine ideology and implanting it in the real world. . . . History does not write its lines except with blood. Glory does not build its lofty edifice except with skulls. Honour and respect cannot be established except on a foundation of cripples and corpses.[16]

---

[13] In this context, Faraj quoted the hadith in which the Prophet said to the people of Quraysh: "I have come to slaughter you (*dhabh*)." 'Imara (ed.), *al-Farida al-gha'iba*, p. 82. The hadith is quoted in ibn Hanbal, *Musnad Ahmad*, Vol. 11, p. 610. Notably, in the context of refuting Faraj's militant approach in a fatwa published in 1983, Shaykh al-Azhar Jadd al-Haqq 'Ali Jadd al-Haqq held that the cited hadith did not deal with the original significance of the word *dhabh* – namely cutting the neck of an animal. This is because the Qur'an says that the Prophet is only the messenger of God, whose role is to pass on His message and not to slaughter people. Thus, the original significance of the word contradicts what is written in the Qur'an and contradicts the morality and the mercy that the Prophet displayed. Thus, the Prophet used the term *dhabh* in regard to the sons of Quraysh only metaphorically, and its meaning can be one of two possibilities: threatening to end their lives by the Prophet praying to God to act against them or purifying them from their pagan faith by adopting the right religion. In al-Haqq's view, the second option dovetailed with other hadiths in which the Prophet wished that the members of his tribe would take the right path and convert to Islam. Jadd al-Haqq 'Ali Jadd al-Haqq (with 'Atiyya Saqr), "Naqd al-farida al-gha'iba fatwa wa-munaqasha," *Majallat al-Azhar* (June–July 1993), pp. 21–24.

[14] 'Azzam, *Fi'l-Jihad*, pp. 4–5, 53–54, 86–87, 162–163.

[15] Ibid., pp. 2–4, 51–54.

[16] Extracts from two lectures delivered by 'Abdallah 'Azzam, which appear in http://www.almeshkat.net/vb/archive/index.php/t-16962.html (accessed May 24, 2010) and http://

'Azzam depicts those who build, mold, and write the glorious history of their nation as a small group numerically, but qualitative in values, especially the younger generation. Here, too, they are categorized in an internal hierarchy in ascending order: those who are devoted in faith and aspirations; those who detach themselves from their earthly life to spread and promote these aspirations; and, lastly, those who sacrifice their souls and their lives to bring about the victory of their values. The last are the "cherries in the cream" – role models whose path to paradise is more assured than others'. In shedding their blood they embed the religious truths of Islam more effectively than others. They transform the divine ideology from a metaphysical system to an empirical reality, infusing profane life with sacred values.

'Azzam's glorification of martyrdom also allowed him to defy rivals. One such group consisted of the establishment 'ulama', whom he derided as "scholars and jurists who are frozen to their chairs." The antithesis, which he sought to glorify, was provided by scholars whose hand that wielded the pen was the same hand that shed their own blood in the battlefield, thereby rejuvenating the nation. In his view, the religious leadership has a duty to take part in the Muslim march toward salvation, which entails agony, sweat, and blood. Clearly, 'Azzam also had his own image in mind, and his view suggests defiance of the well-known hadith: "The ink of scholars will outweigh the blood of martyrs on Judgment Day."[17] Another, more challenging set of rivals for 'Azzam were the communal-oriented movements, especially the Muslim Brethren, who, in his view, believed that states and societies could be altered without bloodshed and self-sacrifice and who thereby distort the essence of Islam and stray from the Prophet's path.[18]

Intent on intensifying the recruitment of Muslims for a jihad campaign, primarily in the Afghan arena, 'Azzam developed two additional themes. The first, a mystical or esoteric attribution of *karamat* from his personal testimony, associated with a group of Afghan fighters who, despite their numerical inferiority, were said to have defeated the Soviet planes and tanks and routed the Soviet forces, "who fled like mice chased by cats." In

www.yzeeed.com/vb/showthread.php?t=1827 (accessed May 24, 2010). For the English version titled, "Martyrs: The Building Blocks of Nations," see http://www.religioscope.com/info/doc/jihad/azzam_martyrs.htm (accessed May 24, 2010); also 'Azzam's article, "al-Tasmim 'ala al-mawt," *al-Jihad* 34 (September 1987), p. 3.

[17] Ahmad ibn 'Ali ibn Hajar al-'Asqalani, *Lisn al-mizan* (3rd ed., Beirut: Mu'asssat al-A'lami li'l-Matbu'at, 1986), Vol. 5, p. 225. According to al-'Asqalani, the cited hadith was a forgery.

[18] 'Azzam, *Fi'l-Jihad*, pp. 63–65; idem, "Martyrs."

another version, the clothing of Afghan fighters was seen to burn, yet their bodies were unscathed. These attributes were viewed as proof of God's support for the jihad path.[19] 'Azzam's second theme dealt with widening the definition of the *shahid*'s acts to include other types of death for God, such as training accidents, death by friendly fire, or falling from a high place. In such cases the fallen fighter is treated as a *shahid* – that is, his body is not washed, he is not wrapped in a shroud, prayers are not said for him, and his reward is assured in paradise.[20]

Although 'Azzam held that jihad is universal and should be carried out against non-Muslim occupiers wherever needed, he also cautioned that such jihad would be effective only if it had a strong geographical and political base as a point of departure for the promotion of the struggle in other arenas.[21] His priority was to create a strong base for Islam, rather than a sweeping global jihad.

'Azzam's first preference was Afghanistan, and only thereafter Palestine and elsewhere. His reasoning was practical rather than theological. In his view, although "Palestine is the highest issue in Islam, the heart of the Islamic world, and the blessed land," jihad must begin in Afghanistan for several reasons. First, the campaign against the Soviet army was still being carried on in full force there, including battles "such as Islamic history has not witnessed in many hundreds of years." Second, the flag raised in Afghanistan, in contrast to Palestine, was an explicitly Islamic flag, namely, there is no God except Allah, and the goal was clear: "So that God's message will be supreme." Third, the campaign in Afghanistan was led by members of the Islamic movement, whereas in Palestine many factions were involved – not only faithful Muslims but also Communists and Pan-Arabists who championed a secular state. Lastly, Afghanistan's borders were open to the *mujahidun*, whereas in Palestine the nature of the resistance was softer as a result of political maneuvers and divergent considerations.[22] 'Azzam's focus on Afghanistan was given practical content with the formation in 1984 of the Afghan Service Bureau (*Maktab Khidmat al-Mujahidun*), which handled preaching, fund-raising, importing Arab fighters, and training local fighters.

---

[19] 'Azzam, *Fi'l-Jihad*, pp. 30–31; also, his book, *'Ayat al-Rahman fi jihad al-Afghan* (Lahur: Ittihad al-Talaba al-Muslimin, 1983).

[20] 'Azzam, *Fi'l-Jihad*, pp. 42–43.

[21] Ibid., pp. 5, 116–117, 138.

[22] 'Azzam, *al-Difa' 'an aradi al-Muslimin*, pp. 36–37; idem, *Jihad sha'b Muslim*, pp. 82–83; also idem, *Dhikrayat Filastin* (Pashawar: Markaz al-Shahid 'Azzam, n.d.), also appearing in http://www.angelfire.com/id/azzam/images/41.zip (accessed June 3, 2010).

ʿAzzam's shelving of the Palestinian issue in practice, however, did not detract from his esteem for the Hamas movement and its leader, Shaykh Ahmad Yasin, for positioning themselves in the eye of the Muslim confrontation against the Jews in Palestine. He maintained contact with the movement consistently and also raised money for it.[23] Hamas, for its part, gave ʿAzzam a place of honor and recognition in its discourse as one of the central figures in Palestinian jihad, displaying a photograph of him next to Shaykh Yasin and Hasan al-Banna in the movement's publications. Part of this recognition stemmed from ʿAzzam's Palestinian origin, but it also filled a need in Hamas to display a religious scholarly genealogy of its own, which was lacking, while enhancing the status of jihad and martyrdom, including the image of "suicide" bombers – concepts that were reinforced by ʿAzzam.[24]

ʿAzzam's priorities and his sustained focus on the Afghan jihad created disputes and factionalization among the Arab Afghans. This resentment was exacerbated by the ambitions of ʿAzzam's protégé and partner, Osama bin Laden,[25] of Saudi origin, and his supporter, Ayman al-Zawahiri, the leader of the Egyptian Islamic Jihad movement,[26] both of whom sought to globalize the cause on the basis of the experience amassed in Afghanistan, targeting non-Muslim and Muslim regimes alike.[27] Nevertheless, the assertive legacy of jihad and martyrdom that ʿAzzam left behind became a cornerstone of al-Qaʿida, which crystallized in February 1998 with the formal establishment of the International Islamic Front for Jihad against the Jews and the Crusaders.

AL-QAʿIDA'S ETHOS OF DEATH

Al-Qaʿida's global character allowed it broader maneuverability than that of the territorial Islamist movements. Those movements created varied

---

[23] ʿAzzam, *Hamas: al-judhur al-taʾrikhiyya waʾl-mithaq* (Amman: n.p., 1990).

[24] Andrew McGregor, "'Jihad and the Rifle Alone': ʿAbdullah ʿAzzam and the Islamist Revolution," *Journal of Conflict Studies* 33/2 (Fall 2003), pp. 100–101.

[25] For an updated biography of bin Laden, see Michael Scheuer, *Osama bin Laden* (Oxford: Oxford University Press, 2011).

[26] For al-Zawahiri's biography, see Muntasir al-Zayyat, *The Road to al-Qaeda: The Story of Bin Laden's Right Hand* (London: Pluto Press, 2004).

[27] Apparently, ʿAzzam feared that the new organization would undermine his leadership and damage the service bureau infrastructure he had established, which was devoted to the Afghan struggle against the Soviets. He was assassinated in Peshawar, Pakistan, in 1989. Gunaratna, *Inside Al Qaeda*, pp. 23, 24, 62; al-Amin, *al-Salafi al-yatim*, p. 54.

levels of relationships with their central governments, ranging from cooperation to competition, disagreement, tension, and confrontation. By contrast, al-Qaʿida was freed from this modus vivendi in that it functioned as a supranational player that challenged existing power relationships.[28]

The concept of global jihad was waged by a charismatic leadership propelled by the success in driving out the Soviet army from Afghanistan in 1989 and facilitated by both material and human assets. The material asset was reflected in the phenomenon of globalization, which, although viewed as a "malignant evil" by Islamists who perceived it as a tool used by the West to enslave oppressed nations and obliterate their native cultures, nevertheless offered a window of opportunity for the relatively easy flow of people, funds, technical knowledge, and communications – the "flattening of the universe" in Thomas Friedman's phraseology.[29] In particular, the new communication technologies became widespread during the 1990s, around the same time as the appearance of al-Qaʿida. The organization quickly perceived the latent possibilities of cyberspace and exploited them to create two discourse audiences: one narrow and operative, linking the organization's activists through the transfer of messages and the planning of attacks; and the other broad and ideological, connecting Muslims throughout the world to the organization's concept of global jihad.[30] The

---

[28] For a structural profile of al-Qaʿida, see Kepel, *Jihad*, pp. 313–322; Denis MacAuley, "Ideology of Osama Bin Laden: Nation, Tribe and World Economy," *Journal of Political Ideologies* 10/3 (october 2005), pp. 269–287; Jack Kalpakian, "Building the Human Bomb: The Case of the 16 May 2003 Attacks in Casablanca," *Studies in Conflict and Terrorism* 28 (2005), pp. 113–127; *International Herald Tribune*, July 9–10, 2005; Shaul Mishal, "Al-Qaeda as a Dune Organization: Toward a Typology of Islamic Terrorist Organizations," *Studies in Conflict and Terrorism* 28/4 (2005), pp. 275–294; also Sageman, *Leaderless Jihad*, pp. 125–146; Assaf Moghadam, *The Globalization of Martyrdom: Al-Qaeda, Salafi Jihad and the Diffusion of Suicide Attacks* (Baltimore: Johns Hopkins University Press, 2008).

[29] Thomas Friedman, *The World is Flat: A Brief History of the Twenty-First Century* (New York: Farrar, Straus and Giroux, 2007).

[30] On the new media and its role in al-Qaʿida's activities, see Dale Eickelman and Jon W. Anderson (eds.), *New Media in the Muslim World: The Emerging Public Sphere* (Bloomington: Indiana University Press, 1999); Gary Bunt, *Islam in the Digital Age: E-Jihad, Online Fatwas and Cyber Islamic Environment* (London: Pluto Press, 2003); Gabriel Weimann, *Terror on the Internet* (Washington, DC: U.S. Institute of Peace Press, 2006); Bruce Hoffman, *Inside Terrorism* (New York: Columbia University Press, 2006), 131–155; Marc Sageman, *Leaderless Jihad: Terror Networks in the Twenty-First Century* (Philadelphia: University of Pennsylvania Press, 2004), pp. 109–124; Henry Schuster, "al-Qaeda's Media Strategy," in Karen J. Greenberg (ed.), *al-Qaeda Now: Understanding Today's Terrorists* (New York: Cambridge University Press, 2005), pp. 112–134.

use of multimedia, and especially the Internet, traversed the boundaries of the pan-Islamic Muslim community that al-Qaʿida sought to mold.[31]

The second – human – asset was located by al-Qaʿida in the countries of origin of its activists in the Arab-Muslim arena and in the Muslim dispersion in Western Europe. Empirical research by Marc Sageman examining the geographic origin of 172 members of global jihad shows that the first circle – essentially, the leadership layer – consisted mainly of Egyptians, who were the first to join in the formation of al-Qaʿida in the late 1980s and who already had an Islamist background, including periods in prison for political agitation. The remaining three circles consisted of activists from states in the Arab world (Saudi Arabia, Yemen, Kuwait, and others), from North Africa, and from Southeast Asia (primarily Indonesia and Malaysia).[32]

A few of the activists were young men who were second- or third-generation descendants of Muslim immigrants in Western Europe. They were mostly educated and middle class and had technological expertise – an important asset for al-Qaʿida's operational strategy. They felt disengaged and alien in their cultural and social environment, which they criticized as doing too little to integrate minorities in such areas as housing, education, and employment. Some found themselves at the bottom of the social and employment ladder. Others, particularly in France, had been in jail. This sense of alienation propelled such young people into the arms of al-Qaʿida, where they acquired a sense of belonging and a new mode of self-expression.[33]

More broadly, a middle-class status typified the social profile of al-Qaʿida recruits generally, with only marginal lower- and upper-class representation among the recruits. Most of the activists in Sageman's research were married, had higher, nonreligious education, and displayed

---

[31] A prominent al-Qaʿida Web site is *Minbar al-Tawhid waʾl-Jihad*, available at http://www.tawhed.ws. (accessed June 3, 2010). It first appeared in the early 2000s.

[32] Sageman, *Understanding Terror Networks*, pp. 70–73.

[33] On Muslims in Europe, see, e.g., Khosrokhavar, *Suicide Bombers*, pp. 184–200; Richard Barltrop (ed.), *Muslims in Europe, Post 9/11* (Oxford: St. Antony's College, 2003); Robert J. Pauly, *Islam in Europe: Integration or Marginalization?* (Aldershot: Ashgate, 2004); Jocelyne Cesari, *When Islam and Democracy Meet: Muslims in Europe and the United States* (New York: Palgrave, 2004), pp. 9–42; Joel S. Fetzer and J. Christopher Soper, *Muslims and the State in Britain, France and Germany* (New York: Cambridge University Press, 2005); Ruud Koopmans et al., *Contested Citizenship: Immigration and Cultural Diversity in Europe* (Minneapolis: University of Minnesota Press, 2005), mainly pp. 146–179; Alison Pargeter, *The New Frontiers of Jihad: Radical Islam in Europe* (London: I.B. Tauris, 2008); Kai Hafez, *Radicalism and Political Reform in the Islamic and Western Worlds* (Cambridge: Cambridge University Press, 2010).

a certain spiritual emptiness.[34] With the exception of marital status, the al-Qaʿida membership did not differ significantly from other Sunni Islamist movements, which points to the continued importance of the modern, educated middle class – the *effendiyya* – as an important resource pool for Sunni groups dating back to the 1920s.[35]

Unlike the Muslim Brethren, who functioned as a communal movement engaged in preaching, education, social welfare, and integration in official politics, al-Qaʿida focused on violence, carrying out large-scale attacks that were particularly lethal, and attracting media attention. Despite its global nature, al-Qaʿida, too, had begun as a territorial phenomenon focused on the Arab countries. Its founder, Osama bin Laden (d. 2011), initially devoted his efforts to Saudi Arabia, whereas his deputy, Ayman al-Zawahiri, focused on Egypt. Another leader, Abu Musʿab al-Suri (b. 1958), was involved in the local jihad in Syria before joining the global Islamic resistance. As discussed by Gabriel Almond, Scott Appleby, and Emanuel Sivan, fundamentalism is a phenomenon that generally develops in a particular location and ultimately carries on a struggle for cultural and political influence over the local "tribe."[36]

To what extent al-Qaʿida or its subgroups detached themselves from territorial Islam requires more detailed study. Clearly, however, at a certain point the organization widened its frontiers beyond the Middle East, a reflection of the lack of progress by the Sunni movements in the region in entrenching the Islamist agenda by the familiar means of political violence or communal activity.[37] Additionally, the enforced exile of key al-Qaʿida leaders

---

[34] Sageman, *Understanding Terror Networks*, pp. 73–80, 94.

[35] On the *effendiyya*, see Michael Eppel, "Note about the Term Effendiyya in the History of the Middle East," *International Journal of Middle East Studies* 41 (2009), pp. 535–539. For a sociopolitical and structural profile of al-Qaʿida, see Kepel, *Jihad*, pp. 313–322; Denis MacAuley, "Ideology of Osama Bin Laden: Nation, Tribe and World Economy," *Journal of Political Ideologies* 10/3 (october 2005), pp. 269–287; Kalpakian, "Building the Human Bomb"; also Moghadam, *The Globalization of Martyrdom*.

[36] Almond, Appleby and Sivan, *Strong Religion*, p. 242.

[37] For al-Qaʿida's critique of the thinking and strategies of Sunni movements, see, e.g., Meir Hatina, "Redeeming Sunni Islam: al-Qaʿida's Polemic against the Muslim Brethren," *British Journal of Middle Eastern Studies* 39/1 (April 2012), pp. 101–113; Holtman, *Abu Musʿab al-Suri's Jihad Concept*, pp. 91–111. In Zawahiri's thinking, the movement's global thrust did not mean neglect of the Arab arena. On the contrary, the struggle against the West was aimed as well at weakening their Arab allies. Moreover, creating an Islamic base in the heart of the Arab Middle East, al-Zawahiri argued, constitutes a precondition to Muslim victory over the "Western-Zionist alliance." *Al-Sharq al-Awsat*, December 12, 2001.

from their home countries, including bin Laden and al-Zawahiri, engendered a sense of borderlessness that may have also contributed to al-Qaʿida's global thrust.[38] Moreover, the fact that Sunni Islamists managed to take power in one state only – Sudan, which also proved to be a short-lived episode (1989–2000)[39] – was perceived by al-Qaʿida as proof of the poor Islamist record in the Middle East heartland.[40]

Al-Qaʿida's operations on a global scale from 1998 onward conveyed a powerful message that modern Islam was capable of doing more. What better means to do this than by focusing on the "Great Satan" – the United States and the West, symbols of hedonism – especially after the precedent of the collapse of the Soviet superpower, not least as a result of its humiliating defeat in Afghanistan by the *mujahidun*.[41] The organization's growing political appetite, along with the challenging presence of the American army in the Arabian Peninsula in the wake of the first Gulf War, prompted it to channel its violent energy toward the United States. According to bin Laden, the myth of American power had already been shattered by its shameful flight from Vietnam in 1969 and from Lebanon in 1983 as a result of guerilla warfare against it. Al-Qaʿida's role was to strike at America's vulnerable points and exhaust the Americans further.[42] This was reflected in violent attacks against American embassies in Kenya and Tanzania (August 1998), an attack against an American destroyer off the coast of Yemen (October 2000), and the dramatic climax – the series

---

[38] On the politics of exile, see, e.g., Gabriel Sheffer, *Diaspora Politics: At Home Abroad* (New York: Cambridge University Press, 2003), mainly pp. 1–31; idem, "Diasporas, Terrorism, and WMD," *International Studies Review* 7/1 (March 2005), pp. 160–162; Mario Sznaider and Luis Roniger, *The Politics of Exile in Latin America* (New York: Cambridge University Press, 2009), mainly pp. 1–139.

[39] In 2000 ʿUmar al-Bashir's military junta turned against the Muslim Brethren and subjected it to political repression. Khalid al-Mubarak, *Turabi's Islamist Venture and Implications* (Cairo: El Dar El Thaqafia, 2001); J. Millard and Robert Collins, *Revolutionary Sudan: Hasan al-Turabi and the Islamist State 1989–2000* (Leiden: Brill, 2003).

[40] Al-Zawahiri and Abu Musʿab al-Suri viewed the Muslim Brethren in Egypt, the largest of the Sunni movements, as primarily responsible for this failure. In his perception, their conciliatory stance toward the regime and their acceptance of the democratic political process served to heighten the crises of Islam in modern times. Al-Zawahiri, *al-Hisad al-murr* (Amman: Dar al-Bayariq, 1999); al-Suri, *Daʿwat al-muqawama al-Islamiyya al-ʿalamiyya*, available at http://www.4shared.com/office/bTr6J5ly/___.htm, pp. 1036–1051 (accessed July 3, 2012).

[41] On the Soviet campaign in Afghanistan, see Mark Galeotti, *Afghanistan: The Soviet Union's Last War* (London: Frank Cass, 1995). On al-Qaʿida's narrative, see Mansfield, *His Own Words*, pp. 37, 42.

[42] Bin Laden quoted in Bernard Lewis, "The Revolt of Islam," *New Yorker*, November 19, 2001, p. 63; *al-Majalla*, October 27, 2002; *Ruz al-Yusuf*, June 17, 1996.

of attacks within the United States (September 11, 2001), causing the death of more than 3,000 people.

The selection of the Twin Towers in New York as a target for mass attack was not accidental. It was aimed at striking at the integrity of the Western value system. According to bin Laden, "[W]hat were destroyed were not just the towers, but more importantly the moral towers in that country."[43] Certain researchers, including Stephen Holmes, argued that the choice of a symbolic site such as the Twin Towers was prompted essentially by political rather than religious motives. For bin Laden and for the mastermind of the attacks, Khalid Shaykh Muhammad, the Twin Towers symbolized the arrogant power of the United States, which, in their view, spoke pretentiously in the name of freedom and human rights and at the same time supported undemocratic regimes throughout the world that repress Muslims and others. Their intention in declaring a global war against America was to punish it for the injustice it embodied and to cause it to withdraw its forces from the Persian Gulf and end its support for the regimes in Saudi Arabia, Egypt, and Israel. Retaliation, punishment, and the destruction of local regimes, Holmes points out, reveals a secular rationale combined with historic circumstances, not a religious doctrine.[44]

Holmes' analysis is challenging, but it does not provide sufficient background to understand the al-Qa'ida phenomenon generally and its component of martyrdom in particular. Holmes discredits a one-sided religious motivation as an explanation for al-Qa'ida's declaration of war against the United States but posits another one-sided explanation in its place – a secular one, pointing to expedient political motives, which is no less problematic. His approach accords with that of another researcher, Diego Gambetta, who is similarly dissatisfied with ideological interpretations and sides with empirical evidence.[45] Both Holmes and, indirectly, Gambetta ignore the basic point of departure in the symbiotic relationship between religion and politics in Islam, which was prominent in the discourse of Islamist movements, including al-Qa'ida, thereby blurring the distinctions between "sacred" and "profane" violence. Furthermore, combating injustice and tyranny, or instilling fear in the enemy, is fundamental both to the jihad doctrine and to the Islamic doctrine of "forbidding wrong" and are intertwined. Notably, a secular national rationale does not necessarily conflict

---

with religious persuasion, especially if it is presented to the public in religious terms. In short, the struggle over the right of public representation, and the way the message is projected and received, is no less important than the analysis of the underlying motivations themselves.

Al-Qaʿida's brand of violence and fury was indeed projected as sacred, operating in the name of divine authority. However, it was also calculated. Targeting the Great Satan and exposing its fallibility by means of "suicide" missions gave al-Qaʿida maximal exposure to two publics: the West, where the point was to demonstrate the tangible presence of Islam in global affairs, and the Arab Muslim world, where the message was to reaffirm the vitality of Islam as a mobilizing, unifying, and revolutionary force. The organization's theological corpus revolved around several basic elements – namely, total loyalty to God, the defilement of modern society as neo-pagan, and the right to rise against deviant rulers.[46]

Al-Qaʿida, as a movement that sanctified a future golden age, was linked to utopianism and millennialism. It was based on the dualism of the battle of light against darkness, radiating certainty and perfection, and its struggle projecting an aura of cosmic drama in the expectation of imminent redemption. Its use of large numbers of recruits for "suicide" acts – some of these acts carried out simultaneously – was aimed at heightening this sense of drama. However, the importance of the al-Qaʿida phenomenon was more moralistic, psychological, and political than operative. Al-Qaʿida had internalized the basic assumption that asymmetrical warfare and cosmic jihad were not destined a priori to alter conventional power relations between Islam and the West or to defeat the United States. Rather, the essence of its strategic vision, as expounded by Abu ʿUbayd al-Qurashi, Abu Bakr Naji, and Abu Musʿab al-Suri, was to reinforce guerilla warfare over time and continue locating and taking control of convenient territory so as to exhaust the enemy and undermine its legitimacy. Thereby, they aroused the disadvantaged side of the equation – the Muslims – from their somnolence and imbued them with a spirit of resistance, dissidence, and protest against their extant sociopolitical situation. The targets of attacks could be military as well as economic, such as foreign banks or oil installations.[47]

---

[46] See, e.g., Hegghammer, *Jihad in Saudi Arabia*, pp. 4, 70–72, 83–98; Mamoun Fandy, *Saudi Arabia and the Politics of Dissent* (New York: Palgrave Macmillan, 2001).

[47] On the strategic vision of al-Qaʿida, see Devin R. Springer, James L. Regens, and David N. Edger, *Islamic Radicalism and Global Jihad* (Washington, DC: Georgetown University Press, 2009), pp. 89–95; Brynjar Lia, *Architect of Global Jihad: The Life of al-Qaida Strategist Abu Musʿab al-Suri* (New York: Columbia University Press, 2008); al-Suri, *Daʿwat al-muqawama*, pp. 903, 928–929, 1080–1086, 1091–1092, 1115–1118, 1370–1374.

Indeed, frontal confrontation (*muqawama sidamiyya*) served al-Qaʿida as its source of legitimation and the basis of modern Islamic activity. In al-Suri's perception:

Resistance is an act of collision and an agenda of violence. A most important fact should be stated clearly, namely that without the presence of strong armed violence and without total resistance – not simply a collection of acts of insurrection (*aʿmal al-intifadat*) – there is no value in any political and communicated theory of resistance. Resistance draws its sole existence and vitality from its armed strength in the battlefield, and its political and propaganda agendas draw their value from the bullets of the *mujahidun* and the thunder of the explosions of their attacks.[48]

Al-Suri and other al-Qaʿida spokesmen designated a key role in this concept of sweeping armed resistance to the "ideological fighter," posited as the antithesis of the ordinary fighter. In al-Suri's view:

Whoever does not fight for an ideology and a idea is incapable of showing resistance to defeat and prolonged suffering, and might soon reach a state of submission of honor and conscience to the enemy, and possibly even crossing over to the enemy if his material desires are satisfied or are fulfilled more than others have provided: possessions, women, high status, recognition, primacy, etc. He thus becomes an enemy and a traitor, or at least submits and retreats into his private life in order to be calm and safe, to make due with what he has attained or to be happy to be alive. By contrast, the ideological fighter stands firm, does not betray ... does not collaborate with his enemy and does not submit unless forced to do so if surrounded [by enemies]. ... He shows resistance and assumes that his suffering will earn him retribution in the next world. His peace of mind and his thoughts of his end constitute an incentive for him to show resistance and stand firm. His soul yearns for jihad and his conscience impels and stimulates him to carry out jihad for the sake of his lofty idealism. There is a huge difference between an ordinary fighter and an ideological fighter.[49]

The emphasis on religious identity and ideological conviction was a key component of al-Qaʿida's strategy, reflected in its strict interpretation of the doctrine of loyalty and enmity (*al-walaʾ waʾl-baraʾ*) and its dichotomous division of the world between the forces of tyranny vis-à-vis the Muslim nation and its spearhead, the *mujahidun*. Hatred of, or at least distancing from, the other and the non-Muslim guaranteed a perpetual state of dissonance and ultimately confrontation, which was one of al-Qaʿida's stated goals.[50]

---

[48] Al-Suri, *Daʿwat al-muqawama*, p. 1114.

[49] Ibid., p. 887.

[50] Ibrahim, *The al-Qaeda Reader*, pp. 66–115. Notably, al-Qaʿida's puritan perception of *al-walaʾ waʾl-baraʾ* was only one dimension of the more comprehensive nature of this concept. See, e.g., Wagemakers, *A Quietist Jihadi*, chapters 6 and 7.

The al-Qaʿida phenomenon reflected a combination of geographical and ideological extremism aimed at illuminating the defects of modern Islam and positing an alternative model that involved purity, daring, and total readiness for sacrifice for God. In an essay titled "Jihad, Martyrdom, and the Killing of Innocents," attributed to al-Zawahiri and written apparently before the September 11, 2001, attacks,[51] he defines the difference between suicide and self-sacrifice as based on intent: if the act was carried out as a result of despair, it is defined as suicide and is forbidden; if it is performed to serve Islam, it is self-sacrifice, and the perpetrator is "the best of all people." Thus, the test of intent is what matters and not whether the person was killed by his own act or by others.

In this context al-Zawahiri cited the hadith, "The King and the Lad," also known as "People of the Ditch" (*ashab al-ukhdud*), which recounts a legend about a despotic ruler who failed twice to execute a Muslim boy who refused to convert from Islam and remained steadfast in his faith in God. Seeing the king's despair, the boy showed him how to carry out the execution by crucifying him on a tree and shooting an arrow into his body while announcing to the crowd, "In the name of the lad's God." Hearing these words, all those present immediately declared their faith in the boy's God – Allah.[52]

This hadith allowed al-Zawahiri to argue that "suicide" attacks empower and magnify the faith. They reflect "firmness in the truth, and boldness with the truth in the face of kings, tyrants and oppressors – even if this leads to death."[53]

The fact that al-Zawahiri elaborated on this hadith was not coincidental. The use of the weapon of self-sacrifice, which conveys the ultimate ability to give, was limited by al-Zawahiri and al-Qaʿida mainly to boys and young men ages fifteen to twenty-five, on the basis of the following logic: A person cannot take care of himself, or is not aware of the significance of major events, until age fifteen, whereas after age twenty-five a person takes on family responsibilities, finishes college, and

---

[51] The translated essay appears in Ibrahim, *The al-Qaeda Reader*, pp. 141–171.

[52] Ibid., pp. 146–150. The hadith was also cited by another al-Qaʿida leader, Yusuf al-ʿUyayri, in his *Hal intaharat Hawwaʾ am istushhidat?* pp. 7–8. "People of the Ditch" were the despotic king's men, who were instructed to throw Muslim believers into a pit and burn them to death. The incident is hinted at in the Qurʾan (Sura 85: 4–11). For the hadith, see Muslim, *Sahih Muslim*, Vol. 4, pp. 2299–2300. This hadith also reinforced Ibn Taymiyya in ruling that a Muslim may attack unbelievers if he is certain they will kill him, so long as this benefits Muslims. *Majmuʿat al-fatawa*, Vol. 28, pp. 501–502, 540.

[53] Ibrahim, *The al-Qaeda Reader*, pp. 149–150.

is committed to work to support his wife and children. The more the mind grows in maturity, the weaker the person's ability to give. Who will take care of the children? Who will support them? Thus, only young people have the strength to devote themselves to jihad and self-sacrifice.[54]

The readiness of young people to give for the benefit of the collective leads al-Zawahiri to sanctify the lofty nature of "suicide" attacks, which is the case even when the perpetrator operates alone against the enemy, embedded in the legal concept of *inghimas* (plunging into the enemy). There is no impediment in this situation, al-Zawahiri ruled, so long as the perpetrator believes that he can spread death in the enemy's ranks, thereby gaining an advantage for Muslims in the battlefield.[55] This examination of intent (*niyya*) also led al-Zawahiri to sanctify other circumstances in which self-death is permitted, such as not allowing oneself to be taken captive by infidels, not giving away secrets, or not abandoning one's faith under torture.[56]

Al-Zawahiri's colleague, Yusuf al-ʿUyayri, a high-ranking leader of al-Qaʿida in Saudi Arabia (killed in 2005), further upgraded the importance of intention in the training of "suicide" attackers. In his view, if the attacker's intention is true and pure to spread destruction in the ranks of the enemy and elevate the message of God, this suffices to legitimize the deed, even if the rest of the conditions are absent or exist only partially, for example, the perpetrator's understanding that there are no other means at hand that can guarantee his safety or his certainty that the enemy will suffer physical damage and damage to morale. In al-ʿUyayri's view, "If the first condition [intention] is absent, the deed is worthless, but if it is satisfied, while some others are lacking, then it is not the best thing, but this does not necessarily mean that the *mujahid* is not a *shahid*."[57]

Support for al-Zawahiri's and al-ʿUyayri's stance was provided by Abu Musʿab al-Suri, who stated that if the *mujahid* is aware that he will not be able to cause losses but that his act will spread fear in the enemy ranks or will instill courage among the Muslims to follow his example so that they will be killed but also will cause heavy losses to the enemy, then his act is in no way disqualified. This is also true, al-Suri added, regarding a *mujahid* who only hopes that other Muslims will follow him and complete the work

---

[54] Ibid., pp. 267–270; also ʿAzzam, "Martyrs."
[55] Ibrahim, *The al-Qaeda Reader*, pp. 146–157. On the concept of *inghimas*, see Chapter 2 in this book, notes 34–36.
[56] Ibrahim, *The al-Qaeda Reader*, pp. 157–161.
[57] Al-ʿUyayri, *Hal intaharat Hawwaʾ am istushhidat?* pp. 46–47.

he started. "Conceivably he might even receive retribution for this in the next world."[58]

The al-Qaʿida leaders' determined stance regarding the legitimacy of the "suicide" weapon did not deter them from addressing the issue of harming civilians during attacks against unbelievers – namely, women, children, *dhimmi*s, and Muslims – an issue that was and remained controversial in the Arab Muslim discourse despite al-Qaʿida's efforts to reinterpret it. Al-Zawahiri was diligent in citing traditional legal opinions on the issue, namely the sweeping prohibition of it by the Maliki and the Awzaʿi schools of thought and, by contrast, the pronounced permission for it by the Hanafi school, some Hanbalis, and later Malikis, which permitted bombing unbelievers where women, children, *dhimmi*s, and Muslims were present. A third opinion, that of the Shafiʿis and Hanbalis, permitted bombing unbelievers even if Muslims or others who were protected by Islam were present, so long as there was a need or a duty for Muslims to do so or if not doing so would cause a delay in carrying out jihad. Al-Zawahiri declared that his organization supported the third opinion. The act of jihad, he explained, obliges the use of all types of effective weapons, including explosives and rockets, because reaching the prime targets is made difficult by strict security measures. The use of firepower is therefore permitted.

Citing the majority legal opinion, al-Zawahiri also discredited the minority Maliki and Awzaʿi opinion by arguing that their view relates to offensive jihad. When the issue is defensive jihad, however – that is, when Muslims struggle against an enemy who tries to take control of their lands – there can be no dilemma regarding killing those who ought not be killed except circumstantially and without intent. In such instances, danger threatens every Muslim if the struggle is abandoned.[59] Another al-Qaʿida leader, Abu Musʿab al-Suri, justified "suicide" attacks and the killing of civilians on both legal and military grounds – namely these attacks follow the Qurʾanic injunction that aggression against Muslims requires retaliation in kind (Sura 2: 194), while they also serve as a strategy of deterrence.[60]

Some of the religious justifications for "suicide" attacks were identical with those of Palestinian Hamas and Islamic Jihad. Conceivably, in adopting this weapon, al-Qaʿida recognized its effectiveness in the arena of the

---

[58] Al-Suri, *Daʿwat al-muqawama*, p. 1146.
[59] Ibrahim, *The al-Qaeda Reader*, pp. 161–171.
[60] Holtmann, *Abu Musʿab al-Suri's Jihad Concept*, pp. 119–121, 138–147.

conflict with Israel as well. Notable in this context is the appearance in al-Qaʿida's official Web sites of the book, "Martyrdom Acts on the Ideological Balance-sheet" (*al-ʿAmaliyyat al-istishhadiyya fiʾl-mizan al-fiqhi*, 1996) by Nawaf Hayil Takruri,[61] a Hamas activist in Damascus dedicated to the religious endorsement of "suicide" attacks. In contrast to Hamas, however, al-Qaʿida widened the religious legitimation of the attacks as applying to the entire world. The enemy is to be found in Europe and the United States, as well as everywhere else, including the Middle East, Asia, and Africa. This theme is well articulated in a widely influential manifesto, "Manual for a Raid"[62] that was used as a preparatory guide in the planning of the September 11 attack.

"MANUAL FOR A RAID"

The manifesto, which was translated into English along with commentaries by Kanan Makiya and Hassan Mneimneh,[63] is basically an operative document but is imbued with ideological themes. It was attributed to Muhammad ʿAta, an Egyptian who commanded the al-Qaʿida hijackers in the September 11, 2001, attacks in the United States. The essay offers valuable insights into the mindset of the al-Qaʿida perpetrators before they embarked on their mission.[64] It draws extensively on the Qurʾan as well as on moralistic themes derived from Sufism, apparently related to ʿAta's own biography and the influence of Sufism during his childhood. These themes emphasize that purity of soul and firmness of intention are necessary preconditions for embarking on the "greater jihad" directed against one's own evil nature, which precedes embarking on the "little jihad" of fighting infidels.[65] Such a two-step process is supported by the

---

[61] Takruri (ed.), *al-ʿAmaliyyat al-istishhadiyya.*

[62] For the Arabic text, tilted *innaha ghazwa fi sabil allah*, see *al-Sharq al-Awsat*, September 20, 2011. An English translation is provided by Kanan Makiya and Hassan Mneimneh, "Manual for a Raid," in R. B. Silvers (ed.), *Striking Terror: America's New War* (New York: Publishers Group West, 2002), pp. 319–327. All references, unless otherwise stated, are from this version.

[63] Makiya and Mneimneh, "Manual for a Raid."

[64] For the profiles of the perpetrators of the September 11 attacks, see Terry MacDermott, *Perfect Soldiers: The Hijackers – Who They Were, Why They did it* (New York: HarperCollins, 2005); also Davis, *Martyrs*, pp. 85–89.

[65] Makiya and Mneimneh, "Manual for a Raid," pp. 306–307, 319–320; also Cook, "Suicide Attacks or 'Martyrdom Operations,'" p. 24.

Qurʾanic verse, "Strive hard for God as is His due" (Sura 22: 78), which is interpreted as jihad against both the believer's lusts and the infidels. The importance of this inner journey is also referred to in the manifesto by citing the mystic, Abu al-Qasim al-Junayd (d. 910): "Man cannot fight his visible enemy without first fighting his internal enemies."[66] This approach was shared as well by several critics of Sufism, such as the medieval jurist Ibn Qayyim al-Jawziyya, who posited the struggle both against the soul and against the infidels as conditional on fulfilling a third jihad – that aimed at Satan, which restrains man's base instincts and demonstrates the need to give up the pleasures of life and accept the burden of fighting against the enemies of Islam.[67]

Clearly, Sufi culture provided a spiritual stimulus for Islamist activism despite the Islamists' widespread opposition to it. The Sufi influence on Hasan al-Banna, founder of the Muslim Brethren in Egypt, was evident and even more pronounced in the case of al-Banna's follower, Saʿid Hawwa (d. 1989), the prominent ideologist of the Brethren in Syria.[68] The forerunner of Sunni radicalism, Sayyid Qutb, although rejecting the Sufi notion of an endless quest for spiritual perfection by the believer, was in accord with the Sufi principle of the "greater jihad" against one's temptations as mental preparation for the military "little jihad" aimed at the removal of tyrants who expropriated God's sovereignty.[69] A similar view was expounded by the Shiʿi cleric Muhammad Husayn Fadallah in Lebanon.[70]

"Manual for a Raid" is conceived as an authoritative religious guide as well as an operational handbook. It projects composure, focus, and devotion to the mission. It includes two sets of instructions: mental preparation,

---

[66] Ibn Kathir, *Tafsir ibn Kathir*, Vol. 3, p. 288; Ibn Qayyim al-Jawziyya, *Zad al-maʿad*, Vol. 2, pp. 39–42; idem, *al-Fawaʾid* (2nd ed., Beirut: Dar al-Kutub al-ʿIlmiyya, 1973), p. 59; also *Mahmud, Fatawa*, Vol. 1, pp. 320–321.

[67] Ibn Qayyim al-Jawziyya, *Zad al-maʿad*, Vol. 2, pp. 43–44.

[68] Jumʿa Amin ʿAbd al-ʿAziz, *Fahm al-Islam* (Alexandria: Dar al-Daʿwa, 1990), pp. 56–63; Hawwa, *al-Madkhal ila daʿwat al-Ihwan al-Muslimin* (Amman: Dar al-Arqam, n.d.), pp. 49–173.

[69] Qutb, "al-Jihad fi sabil Allah," pp. 141–142; idem, *Maʿalim fiʾl-tariq*, pp. 75–76. However, Qutb's follower, Muhammad ʿAbd al-Salam Faraj, showed less patience for spiritual jihad. The same is true for ʿAbadallah ʿAzzam, although (as cited in note 15) he made use of the theme of *karamat* to reinforce the attractiveness of jihad. ʿImara (ed.), *al-Farida al-ghaʾiba*, pp. 24–25; ʿAzzam, *Fiʾl-Jihad*, pp. 162–164; also idem, *Jihad shaʿb Muslim*, pp. 36–37.

[70] Richard Bonney, *Jihad: From the Quran to Bin Laden* (New York: Palgrave, 2004), pp. 297–298.

including intensive prayer, the recitation of Qur'anic verses, and the avoidance of disagreement to entrench discipline and sustain determination; and operational preparation, such as memorizing orders, maintaining strict secrecy, and meticulously handling relevant documents and equipment. This dual set of instructions was aimed at the coalescence of a unified group imbued with a sense of elite status, moral truth, high motivation, and determined commitment to the goal and the operation. Every movement by the perpetrator was calculated to ensure the success of the mission by confronting the devil's camp with inner calm and a practiced mode of behavior in which the ultimate result was the aspired encounter with God and the enjoyment of the pleasures of heaven.[71]

An important element in the mental and operational preparation of the perpetrator was his connection with his mission group, which provided mutual support and solidarity and reaffirmed the significance of death and what lies beyond. The group dynamic was reflected, for example, in a section in the manual instructing the perpetrators, before leaving for their mission, to remind each other about the supplications and their meanings, to perform the morning prayers in a group, and to hold onto each other's shoulder on the way out of the apartment, in the airport, when entering the plane, and in the cabin, to remind each other that this act is for the sake of God.[72] The manual, similar to the wills of the perpetrators in Hizballah in Lebanon, and Hamas and Islamic Jihad in Palestine, also referred to the incentive of marriage to black-eyed beauties on entering paradise, for example:

Be happy and cheerful, be relaxed and feel secure because you are engaged in an action that God loves and is satisfied by it. You will be soon, with God's permission, with your heavenly brides in Heaven. ... Know that the Heavens have raised their most beautiful decoration for you, and that your heavenly brides are calling you, "Come O follower of God," while wearing their most beautiful jewelry.[73]

Essentially, the focus of the manual is on the perpetrator and his spiritual and physical purification in the context of the mythical environment of the Prophet. The essay emphasizes that the Prophet established the Islamic order in the seventh century based on a series of military expeditions (*ghazwa*) aimed not for booty or territorial assets but entirely to please

---

[71] Makiya and Mneimneh, "Manual for a Raid," pp. 319–327; also Holmes, "al-Qaeda, September 11, 2001," pp. 151–152; Yuval Neria et al., "The al-Qaeda 9/11 Instructions: A Study in the Construction of Religious Martyrdom," *Religion* 35 (2005), pp. 1–11.

[72] Makiya and Mneimneh, "Manual for a Raid," pp. 321, 326.

[73] Ibid., pp. 323, 325.

God, as an offering or sacrifice.[74] The theme of an offering to God is also mentioned in an early will prepared by Muhammad ʿAta in 1996 when he lived in Hamburg in which he referred to the narrative of the sacrifice of Isaac and Abraham's preparedness to sacrifice his only son by divine command without objection or second thoughts.[75] The "Manual for a Raid," in relating to self-sacrifice as a ritual act, seeks to imbue it with a lofty spiritual aura and to promote an awareness that faith is not only a declarative act but also a purposeful one.

The link between the theological and the political dimensions of jihad missions is nearly unmentioned in the essay, except for a general observation about the struggle against the infidel enemy and the enemy's technological superiority and about Muslims who are addicted to the corrupt Western culture, depicted as "followers of Satan." There is no hint of ideological or judicial reservations about such a mission either in terms of its benefits to the Muslim community, on the one hand, or the killing of civilians, on the other. The focus is entirely on the perpetrator and his spiritual and physical perfection. This is reflected as well in Muhammad ʿAta's will, cited earlier, which devotes a significant portion to the type of care of the perpetrator's body, his burial, and the disbursement of his possessions and books, which must be carried out according to Islamic rules.[76]

THE ISSUE OF KILLING CIVILIANS

Notably, bin Laden stated in a fatwa in 1998 that there is no such thing as innocent civilians; they are all soldiers of "the realm of war" (*dar al-harb*).[77] His close associate, al-Zawahiri, reinforced this ruling in 2002 by adding a prohibition against showing compassion or affection for unbelievers or their families as an integral part of demonstrating complete faith in God, thereby seeking to guarantee the perpetrator's composure and preventing feelings of remorse during attacks in civilian milieus.[78] Moreover, according to bin Laden, taking prisoners of war was

---

[74] Ibid., pp. 323–324.

[75] ʿAta's will in http://www.islamonline.net/Arabic/news/2001-10/07/article22.shtml (accessed October 12, 2011); also Davis, *Martyrs*, p. 88.

[76] ʿAta's will in http://www.islamonline.net/Arabic/news/2001-10/07/article22.shtml (accessed October 12, 2011).

[77] *Al-Quds al-ʿArabi* (London), February 23, 1998.

[78] Al-Zawahiri quoted in Ibrahim, *The al-Qaeda Reader*, pp. 75–79.

also forbidden, in contrast to the traditional Islamic view that the purpose of war is to defeat the enemy, not to slaughter captives and certainly not to harm innocent civilians. In this, bin Laden also deviated from the basic approach of such founders of Sunni activism in the twentieth century as Rashid Rida, Hasan al-Banna, Taqi al-Din al-Nabhani, Abu al-A'la Mawdudi, and Sayyid Qutb.

Those thinkers explicitly emphasized humane rules of warfare and the duty of the Muslim to serve as a symbol and example of mercy and compassion by eschewing the abuse of slain bodies or of prisoners, the killing of children, women, and the aged, and the mistreatment of monks.[79] Qutb traced the essence of refraining from harming noncombatants to the verse, "Fight in God's cause against those who fight you, but do not overstep the limits: God does not love those who overstep the limits" (2: 190). He defined the first part of the verse as the objective of jihad, namely to make God's word supreme in the world and to protect the believers from repression, and he defined the second part as the ethical limits of war, namely to avoid attacking civilians who pose no threat to Muslims or to their community. Qutb quoted two hadiths in this context: "Believers avoid killing immorally more than all others," and "Attack in the name of God and for the sake of God, kill anyone who disbelieves in God. Attack, but do not commit any treacherous act, and do not abuse slain bodies and do not kill babies."[80] Preserving the rules of war fixed by Islam, Qutb noted, was a legacy from the first believers even in the face of enemies who attempted to convert them from the faith by means of harsh torture. In Qutb's view, such scrupulousness is integral in the faith; it shows obedience to God, and it is this that promises victory in war.

Bin Laden, by contrast, deviated from his ideological mentor, 'Abdallah 'Azzam, who justified attacking civilians only if they provided moral or material assistance to the enemy. 'Azzam devoted a lengthy discussion to refraining from harming children in view of their young age, which prevents them from acting like adult infidels, and women, because to

---

[79] Rida, *Tafsir al-Qur'an al-hakim*, Vol. 2, pp. 208–209; al-Banna, "Risalat al-jihad," pp. 262–263; idem, *al-Salam fi'l-Islam*, pp. 59–65; Nabahani, *al-Shakhsiyya al-Islamiyya*, pp. 186–191; Mawdudi, "al-Jihad fi sabil Allah," pp. 55–60; idem, *Shari'at al-Islam fi'l-jihad wa'l-'alaqat al-duwaliyya* (Cairo: Dar al-Sahwa, 1985). See also al-Qasimi, *al-Jihad wa'l-huquq al-duwaliyya*, pp. 314–338, 522–529.

[80] Qutb, *Fi zilal al-Qur'an*, Vol. 1, pp. 177–191. For the two hadiths, see Abu Dawud Sulayman ibn al-Ash'ath al-Sijistani al-Azdi, *Sunan Abi Dawud* (Beirut: Dar al-Fikr, n.d.), Vol. 3, p. 37; ibid., p. 53.

their weakness. The prohibition against killing children and women also extended to taking them captive: they could be enslaved but not killed. Other civilian categories similarly exempted included elders, the ill, farmers, tradesmen, and cloistered monks.[81]

ʿAzzam's arguments are both moralistic and expedient. In his view, an intentional, demonstrative attack on progeny and the helpless creates hatred that lasts for generations and, moreover, does not serve the goal of Islam, which seeks to bring people close to God and His Prophet through love and persuasion.

The only instance of killing civilians that ʿAzzam allowed was when Muslim fighters cannot attack infidels/unbelievers without harming women and children who are nearby, for example, during nighttime attacks on infidel cities or gathering places or when helpless civilians are used by infidels as a human shield. In this respect, thereby, ʿAzzam sided with the Hanafi school of thought and expressed surprise at the stance taken by Abu ʿAmr al-Awzaʿi (d. 774), founder of the Awzaʿi school of law, and Imam Malik ibn Anas (d. 795), founder of the Maliki school of law, who forbade killing women and children absolutely, even when the enemy uses them as human shields in its bases on land or in its boats at sea. ʿAzzam defined their position as "exaggerated," especially when there is a legal consensus (*ijmaʿ*) permitting the killing of Muslims when unbelievers use them as shields. "Is the sanctity of the blood of the wives and children of unbelievers holier than the blood of Muslims?" he asks.[82]

Aside from the issue of harming civilians, ʿAzzam also held a divergent position from bin Laden's on the subject of prisoners of war in ratifying the existence of the status of prisoners of war in the Islamic tradition and defining the range of possibilities faced by the ruler – namely execution, slavery, or freedom – and forbidding abuse. By contrast, bin Laden denied the very existence of this status, thereby redesigning the rules of war in Islam by rejecting the extensive body of legal literature on the subject as part of his broader goal of reorganizing the Islamist discourse. This was reflected as well in al-Qaʿida's perception of martyrdom, as manifested in the "Manual for a Raid":[83] a perception was put into practice optimally in

---

[81] Nevertheless, ʿAzzam sweepingly permitted killing women who were Communists, because of their atheistic beliefs, even if they played no role in fighting or in supporting the fighting some other way. ʿAzzam, *Iʿlan al-jihad* (Pashawar: Maktab Khidmat al-Mujahidin, 1990), pp. 36–37, 110–120; also idem, *Fiʾl-Jihad, ʾadab wa-ahkam*, pp. 5–16, 24, 41.

[82] ʿAzzam, *Iʿlan al-jihad*, pp. 120–127. Also *Fiʾl-Jihad, ʾadab wa-ahkam*, pp. 9–16; Peters, *Jihad in Classical and Modern Islam*, pp. 19–23.

[83] ʿAzzam, *Fiʾl-Jihad, ʾadab wa-ahkam*, pp. 41–53.

Iraq in the wake of the American incursion in 2003 in which some 514 "suicide" attacks were recorded by 2006, turning it into the arena that induced the largest scale of this type of martyrdom ever.[84]

Al-Qaʿida viewed Iraq, the cradle of Muslim civilization, as an alternate, and more qualitative, arena of activity than Afghanistan, where its grip had been weakened as a result of the overturn of Taliban rule by the American incursion in 2001. Pakistan, too, had distanced itself from al-Qaʿida when it joined the United States in the struggle against global terrorism.[85] Al-Qaʿida also hoped to revive from a sense of Sunni degradation and a growing dissonance with the Shiʿa, who, with the assistance of the Americans, became the masters of Iraq. Not surprisingly, Iraq, with the support of al-Qaʿida, became a magnet for Sunni radicals of various nationalities, along with a new generation of Arab Afghans trained in camps in Afghanistan and Pakistan during the 1990s. Their arrival to fight and die in Iraq was made possible by recruiting networks in neighboring countries and in Europe as a means of developing and reinforcing an identity devoted to a common cause. "Suicide" ammunition arrived together with the volunteer jihadists[86] for use against the coalition forces, Shiʿa Muslims, and their allies within the Sunni community, justified by the so-called Crusader-Shiʿa plot against Islam and an emphasis on the necessity to expunge Sunni degradation in the wake of the conquest.

As in other arenas, self-sacrifice in Iraq was nurtured not only on the battlefield but also in the ideological realm through martyrdom literature consisting of recorded video wills, biographical dictionaries, and online magazines. These commemorative materials were aimed both at the small circle of fighters to reinforce their commitment and determination regarding self-sacrifice and at the broad Iraqi and Muslim public to gain its support, utilizing cultural code words that resonated in Iraqi society such as *sharaf* (nobility), *ʿird* (honor), and *muruʾah* (chivalry).[87]

---

[84] For extensive data, see Hafez, *Suicide Bombers in Iraq*, pp. 93–109.

[85] Shai, *The Shahids*, pp. 101–102; also, Muhammad Tahir ul-Qadri, *Fatwa on Terrorism and Suicide Bombings* (London: Minhaj ul-Qurʾan International, 2001).

[86] Hafez, *Suicide Bombers in Iraq*, chapters 6 and 7; also Nick Ayers, "Ghost Martyrs in Iraq: An Assessment of the Applicability of Rationalist Models to Explain Suicide Attacks in Iraq," *Studies in Conflict and Terrorism* 31/9 (September 2008), pp. 856–882.

[87] Hafez, *Suicide Bombers in Iraq*, chapters 4 and 5; Meir Litvak, "'More Harmful than the Jews': Anti-Shiʿi Polemics in Modern Radical Sunni Discourse," in Mohammad Ali Amir-Moezzi, Meir M. Bar-Asher, and Simon Hopkins (eds.), *Le shiʿisme imamite quarante ans après* (Turnhout: Brepols, 2009), pp. 309–311.

Ultimately, al-Qaʿida projected a cult of death, described by Makiya and Mneimneh as a form of nihilism or self-destruction, and by other commentators as a "passion for the real" – that is, making use of violent and spectacular means to regain self-identity. Still others viewed al-Qaʿida's violence as stemming from the paranoia of threatened individuals and groups who perceive their culture to be under siege and in a struggle for survival.[88]

---

[88] Makiya and Mneimneh, "Manual for a Raid," pp. 317–318; also Salvoj Žižek, *Welcome to the Desert of the Real* (New York: Verso, 2002), pp. 9–15, 51–52; Benjamin Barber, *Jihad vs. MacWorld* (new ed., London: Corgi Books, 2003), pp. xii–xiv; J. Harold Ellens, "Jihad in the Qur'an, Then and Now," in idem (ed.), *The Destructive Power of Religion* (London: Praeger, 2004), Vol. 3, pp. 42–43, 48–49.

6

Martyrs as Preachers

The phenomenon of martyrdom has had three main functions for the Islamist movements that embraced it, centering on the affinity between theology and power and between ethos and politics. These functions may be categorized as effectiveness and efficiency, the humiliation of the enemy, and the symbolic empowerment of the weak.

Indisputably, "human bombs," despite constituting a negligible percentage of all violent Islamist activity globally (3.3 percent according to an American estimate in 2007),[1] have proven to be an effective and efficient means of warfare, blending the elements of surprise, accuracy, and shock. They have produced high losses, destruction, and demoralization in the enemy ranks – an optimal combination in any strategy of violence. The strategy also involves relatively low expenditure, eliminates the need to plan an escape route, bypasses the danger of capture and subsequent interrogation, and gains wide media exposure, which brings the movement's grievances and demands to the fore. It serves as a powerful means of arousing popular Muslim support and reinforcing the political alternative put forward by the movement. These advantages were recognized increasingly as the phenomenon intensified.[2]

---

[1] This rate appears in Merari, *Driven to Death*, p. 4.

[2] On the effectiveness of this means of warfare, see Crenshaw, "The Logic of Terrorism," in Reich (ed.), Origins of Terrorism, pp. 18–19; Weimann, *Terror on the Internet*. The American political scientist Robert Pape calculated that "suicide" attacks accounted for 48% of those killed in violent attacks throughout the world between 1980 and 2003. Robert A. Pape, *Dying to Win: The Strategic Logic of Suicide Terrorism* (New York: Random House, 2005), p. 28; also *al-Sabil*, July 3–9, 2001, p. 19; http://www.palestine-info.info/arabic/fatawa/alfatawa/alfatawa/htm (accessed August 4, 2010); al-'Uyayri, *Hal intaharat Hawwa' am istushhidat?* enumerating the advantages of "suicide" operations, mainly pp. 4–6.

A pronounced example of such effectiveness was demonstrated in the Lebanese arena when "suicide" attacks by Hizballah during 1983–1985 served to hasten the departure of American and French soldiers stationed in Beirut and later the withdrawal of Israeli army forces from a narrow strip in Lebanon north of the Lebanese-Israeli border. Another example was the Palestinian arena in the late 1990s and early 2000s when "suicide" attacks became the showcase of the Palestinian struggle and constituted the bulk of casualties on the Israeli side.[3] The fact that national secular movements such as the PLO in Palestine, the PKK in Turkey, and the Tamils in Sri Lanka adopted this tactic as well pointed to its effectiveness.[4] Additionally, another example is attacks by al-Qaʿida and its offshoots in the United States and Europe, which have forced Western governments to heighten security, sometimes even at the expense of civil rights.

The element of surprising the enemy, leaving him helpless if possible, and causing demoralization in his ranks also involves humiliation. This is the second function of martyrdom. Humiliation, one of the declared goals of jihad, instills fear of Islam in its enemies while restoring the dignity of the believers, as explained explicitly by the Shiʿi ideologist ʿAli Shariʿati as far as back as the early 1970s:

> By shedding his own blood, the shahid is not in a position to cause the fall of the enemy [for he cannot do so]. He wants to humiliate the enemy, and he does so. . . . By his death, he condemns the oppressor and provides commitment for the oppressed. He exposes aggression and revives what has hitherto been negated. He reminds the people of what has already been forgotten. In the icy hearts of a people he bestows the blood of life, resurrection and movement. For those who have become accustomed to captivity and thus think of captivity as a permanent state, the blood of a shahid is a rescue vessel.[5]

Shariʿati's Sunni colleague in Palestine, Hamas leader ʿAbd al-ʿAziz al-Rantisi (d. 2001), supported this rationale, asserting that the "suicide" attacks had brought the Israelis to such a condition of exhaustion, fear, and concern, that they visit mental health clinics. As a result,

their lives have become an unbearable hell. This is in addition to their loss of self-confidence, which has convinced them that they have no future in Palestine. The

---

[3] Based on data provided by Assaf Moghadam. Between 1993 and 2002 more than 135 "suicide" bombers exploded themselves in the proximity of Israeli civilians or soldiers. During the Second Intifada (September 2000–August 2002) nearly 44% of all Israeli casualties resulted from "suicide" attacks. Moghadam, "Palestinian Suicide Terrorism," p. 65.

[4] Ibid., pp. 82–83; also Chapter 4 of this book.

[5] Shariʿati, "A Discussion of Shahid," pp. 240–241.

psychological defeat is a prelude to defeat in the battlefield, and causes it, as the hadith says: "God made me victorious by awe frightening my enemies, even if they are at a distance of a month's journey."[6]

In the wake of September 11, Western intellectuals, too, dealt extensively with the issue of damage to the morale and the perceived power of the United States. The French philosopher Jean Baudrillard, in his book, *The Spirit of Terrorism and Requiem for the Twin Towers* (2002),[7] noted that from the point of view of the world's greatest power – the United States – the worst of all is not being attacked or destroyed, but being humiliated. The destruction of the Twin Towers on September 11, he observed, was not aimed at defeating the world system, whether politically or economically. "Something else is at issue here: the stunning impact of the attack, the insolence of its success and, as a result, the loss of credibility, the collapse of image."[8]

The reverse side of the bankruptcy of the power image is the glorification of the weak side of the equation: the Muslims. This is the third function of martyrdom – "symbolic empowerment," namely, providing a sense of power to the powerless, whether vis-à-vis Israel in the case of Hamas in Palestine, Russia in the case of the Chechen jihad, or the West and its allies in the case of al-Qaʿida. Martyrdom signaled possession of spiritual power, which is regarded by its protagonists as even more important than material power, as it provides the endurance to carry on with a confrontation that is difficult to win, given the asymmetry between the forces.

In mastering their fate by taking their own lives when and where they chose, and in rendering their victims helpless, the martyred perpetrators claimed power for those who were powerless in the name of a superior metaphysical authority. They were "dead men walking,"[9] who, in their death, symbolized the victory of theology over the mundane world. Their act was presented as the single advantage held by Muslims in their struggle against their modern enemies, as noted by Hasan Nasrallah, leader of Hizballah, and his deputy, Naʿim Qasim. In Nasrallah's words, "Having martyrs means that we are capable of striking at the heart of the enemy anywhere, no matter how advanced his technologies and how modest

[6] Al-Rantisi quoted in *al-Sabil*, July 3–9, 2001, p. 19. On the cited hadith, see al-Bukhari, *Sahih al-Bukhari*, Vol. 1, p. 128; also ibn Hanbal, *Musnad Ahmad*, Vol. 35, p. 343, Vol. 36, p. 452.
[7] Jean Baudrillard, *The Spirit of Terrorism and Requiem for the Twin Towers*, trans. by Chris Turner (London: Verso, 2002).
[8] Baudrillard, *The Spirit of Terrorism*, mainly chapter 4; the quote is on p. 82.
[9] Emmanuel Sivan, *Ha'aretz*, April 21, 2002.

ours."[10] In a similar vein, an al-Qaʿida leader in Saudi Arabia, Yusuf al-ʿUyayri, stated that "there is no other technique which strikes as much terror in the enemy hearts and which shatters their spirit as much."[11]

In a broader cultural sense, the "suicide" perpetrators, in Thomas Friedman's view, embodied the resilience of the olive tree vis-à-vis the Lexus – that is, an authentic, rooted identity vis-à-vis Western progress that strives for global cultural homogeneity.[12] The transfer of a sense of empowerment preserves the believers' capacity for resistance, humiliates the enemy, and leaves an indelible impression of Islam etched in the consciousness of the enemy.[13] This emotional, psychological, and cultural function is well reflected in the image of the perpetrator or martyr and his role in the drama, as viewed in the written and video-recorded will or testament (*wasiyya*) he has prepared before embarking on the mission from which there is no return.

The wills left behind by the Muslim martyrs may be classified as ethical wills, constituting a sub-genre of morality literature such as is found both in Jewish literature, especially of the seventeenth and eighteenth centuries, and in Christianity, primarily in its formative period. Such wills provide an important source of knowledge about attitudes toward death, values, and changes in moral norms. They are short and generalized, with whatever personal information offered by the martyr about himself and his life framed in a collective, societal context,[14] reflecting the essentially didactic aim of these wills. This holds true for the wills in the present discussion, which constituted an important pedagogic medium for transmitting the martyrdom ethos, bringing the ideological platform of the martyrs' movements onto the street and into the homes of the public. The content of the wills projected a message of power, determination, and commitment to Islamic and national causes, highlighting the altruistic rather than personal motives of the perpetrators.

---

[10] Nasrallah quoted in *al-ʿAhd*, April 5, 1996; Qasim, *Hizbullah*, p. 50; also *al-Sunna*, April 2002.

[11] Al-ʿUyayri, *Hal intaharat Hawwaʾ am istushhidat?* p. 4.

[12] Thomas Friedman, *The Lexus and the Olive Tree* (New York: Farrar, 1999), pp. 7–13, 25–37.

[13] See, e.g., Hamas leader ʿAbd al-ʿAziz al-Rantisi (d. 2004) in *al-Sabil*, July 3–9, 2001.

[14] Avriel Bar-Levav, "When I was Alive: Jewish Ethical Wills as Egodocuments," in Rudolf Dekker (ed.), *Egodocuments and History: Autobiographical Writing in Its Historical Context since the Middle Ages* (Rotterdam: Erasmus University Rotterdam, 2002), pp. 47–59. The main format of the wills in the Islamic tradition was that of inheritance. R. Peters, "Wasiyya," *Encyclopaedia of Islam* 1 (1960), pp. 171–172.

Although the fate of the perpetrator is known from the start, the narrative in the wills carefully details the method of the act of self-sacrifice, endowing it with a heroic status. In this, the function of the Islamist wills is not very different from letters smuggled out of prisons by martyrs during the early Christian period or by prisoners of the revolutionary movement Narodnaya Vola ("For the People") in Russia in the mid-nineteenth century, exhorting their relatives and friends to show devotion to their credo, prepare themselves for self-sacrifice, and stand up for their views. However, the advantage of the written, and especially the recorded, Islamist wills was their visual exposure electronically, which imbued them with greater dramatic influence. Publicizing these wills was widespread in Hizballah, Hamas, and al-Qaʿida, although much less so in the Chechen Jihad, where the tactic of "suicide" attacks was not as prevalent or as widely endorsed by the local community. Nevertheless, Chechen attackers did leave personal letters for their families, which was important pedagogically and in raising morale not only within the family but also in a wider circle of people who were exposed through the letters to the personal motivations and lofty goals of the act of self-sacrifice.[15] Ultimately, these letters and other personal materials served as valuable content in martyrdom literature.

Foreign observers and researchers tend to minimize the importance of the use of the wills postmortem and question their authenticity, as they do regarding letters left by martyrs. Critics viewed these materials as part of a body of martyrological literature that was largely fabricated. In their perception, the wills were displayed as a written text read aloud by the future martyr in a routinely staged video format, thereby reducing the martyr to a statistic or a cog in the system. Some scholars held that the aim of the will was to seal the fate of the perpetrator and prevent him from changing his mind at the last minute, lest he be perceived as a traitor and shamed.[16] These critics, however, overlook the ideological and cultural functions of the projected will. In analyzing the wills, it is clear that the martyr is presented not merely as an operative player executing a violent act but rather as a pedagogic agent, a preacher, and role model setting a sacred example for the living and, thereby, invested with moral authority to guide the reader or viewer. The wills can thus be classified as ethical wills, aimed at providing spiritual and practical guidance for both the individual and the collective.

---

[15] Nivat, "The Black Widows," pp. 126–127.
[16] Bakken, "The Anatomy of Suicide Terrorism," p. 6; Merari, *Driven to Death*, pp. 266–267; also Hoffman and McCormick, "Terrorism, Signaling, and Suicide Attack," pp. 252–256.

Notably, a striking resemblance may be found between the perception of death of the contemporary Muslim martyr and the perception of the revolutionary Russian martyr of the mid-nineteenth century in the Narodnaya movement. Despite disparate ideological viewpoints (religious vs. socialist) and a different format of the act of self-sacrifice (pre-planned vs. execution by the state), similarities are also apparent – namely a protest against exploitation and humiliation and the determination to put an end to these evils by self-sacrifice. Many of the members of Narodnaya were executed by hanging after they planned or carried out acts of sabotage. Their primary aim was to arouse the public regarding the evils of the Czarist system and to destroy the system's legitimacy by means of a victory of conscience over force. Some members left farewell letters resembling wills, emphasizing their ideology, which were used intensively by the movement for recruitment and increased anti-Czarist activity. S. Ya. Vittenberg, executed in 1879, left the following message:

Naturally I do not want to die. To say that I'm dying willingly would be a lie. But this fact must not cast a shadow on my faith and on the certainty of my convictions. Remember that the highest example of honour and sacrificial spirit was without doubt shown by the Saviour. Yet even he prayed 'take this cup away from me.' And so how can I not pray also? And yet I too, like Him, tell myself, If no other way is possible, if it is necessary that my blood should be shed for the triumph of Socialism, if the move from the present to a better organization can only be made by trampling over our bodies, then let our blood be shed and flow to redeem humanity; let it serve as manure for the soil in which the seeds of Socialism will sprout. Let Socialism triumph and triumph soon. That is my faith.[17]

In the Islamic context, the art of preaching fills two main functions: conveying basic religious knowledge and encouraging ethical behavior.[18] Indeed, this is how the function of the modern martyrs is perceived. Their image as preachers underscores the fragmentation of religious authority in modern times, with the martyrs now added to the growing list of lay *du'at*

---

[17] Venturi, *Roots of Revolution*, p. 635, also, pp. 635–638. There were also quite a few Narodniki women – most prominently Vera Zasulich – who devoted and sacrificed their lives for the cause. See Margaret Maxwell, *Narodniki Women: Russian Women Who Sacrificed Themselves for the Dream of Freedom* (New York: Pergamon Press, 1990).

[18] See, e.g., Jonathan P. Berkey, *Popular Preaching and Religious Authority in the Medieval Islamic Near East* (Seattle: University of Washington Press, 2001); also Boaz Shoshan, *Popular Culture in Medieval Cairo* (Cambridge: Cambridge University Press, 1993), mainly pp. 9–22, 67–78.

(preachers), in this case conveying their convictions through written, electronic, and digital media platforms.[19]

The martyrs bring the political ideology of their movement to the public in the most direct way possible. Moreover, the time elapsed between their act and the publication of their will is brief, especially in the case of audiovisual wills, thereby guaranteeing the continuity of the drama. Essentially, written and video wills aim to create a covenant sealed in blood between the movement and the audience, with the martyrs functioning as the connecting link. The martyrs declare their total devotion to their group while at the same time serving as a recruitment tool for future candidates.

THE WILLS: FORM AND CONTENT

In the written wills the text is central, with the decorative aspect limited to a photograph of the martyrs and, usually, a few printed details about their identity, the act they performed, and its motives. Using these elements, the movement to which the martyrs belonged sets the tone for the commemoration of their exalted deed for the purpose of recruitment and indoctrination.

In audiovisual wills, the visual backdrop is more elaborate, imbuing the will with greater vitality and drama. Here the martyrs are shown in full figure and in an impressive stance. They appear confident and determined, generally wearing a flak jacket equipped with explosives and holding a Qur'an, with flags and religious slogans displayed in the background. The opening and closing segments are accompanied by rousing instrumental music and singing. The video is largely documentary and projects authenticity, viewed on TV or computer screens by an audience that experiences the drama as if in real time. It is a visual presentation that radiates moral fortitude, courage, and commitment. Thus, for example, a recorded will prepared by al-Qaʿida as part of its operations against the American forces in Iraq, dated February 2007, shows a young perpetrator, Abu Anas al-Najdi, calmly and with impressive self-confidence addressing a group gathered around him in a circle, suggesting a lesson or sermon delivered by a shaykh to his pupils. The fact that he holds a pistol in his hand is meant to

[19] Eickelman and Anderson, "Redefining Muslim Publics," pp. 1–18; Gudrun Krämer and Sabine Schmidtke, "Introduction: Religious Authority and Religious Authorities in Muslim Societies: A Critical Overview," in Gudrun Krämer and Sabine Schmidtke (eds.), *Speaking for Islam: Religious Authorities in Muslim Societies* (Leiden: Brill, 2006), pp. 12–13.

highlight the knot between preaching and jihad and defiance toward those who do not accept this view.

Al-Najdi explains that the duty of the believer – from child to elder – to repel the non-Muslim aggressor who enters the land of the Muslims is second only to the belief in God. Whoever does not join the *mujahidun*, he warns, is a sinner. In the final segment of the video, the martyr bids farewell to his friends, who respond with smiles and strong embraces, while a song in the background promises that they will soon be reunited in paradise.[20]

The content of the wills functions as a mobilizing narrative preaching martyrdom in the name of a metaphysical authority. The reliance on a sublime authority aims to remove doubts and defuse the tragedy, the recoil from the act, and the extremism of it, especially if it is aimed at civilians. This piety bears a resemblance to the Christian notion of "holy cruelty" (*sancta crudelitas*).[21]

The wills present a Manichean picture of a fateful struggle between righteousness and heresy, and heroes and villains, supported by an array of quoted Qur'anic verses, hadiths, and judicial imperatives. They project a message of piety, morality, and power, highlighting the perpetrators' altruistic rather than personal motives. Muhammad Sa'd, one of Hizballah's first martyrs in the early 1980s, declared in his will that a person who is motivated to fight by a sense of ethnic or tribal fanaticism, or to garner praise for his courage, has no place in the next world. His acts must stem from complete loyalty to God and not from an ambition to achieve a material interest.[22] Sa'd's Palestinian colleague, Jamal 'Abd al-Ghani al-Nasir, a young Hamas activist from Nablus, broadened this list of motives in his will, dated April 2001:

> By God, what prompted me to this path was nothing but: first, my love of God and martyrdom; second, my love of al-Aqsa and Palestine and the defense of them; and third, the desire to avenge the blood of martyrs at a time when the leaders of the Arabs and the Muslims forsook the defense of Palestine and sufficed with certain types of aid. I tell you: We do not want your money, your flour and your medications, but we want your armies so that they will conquer Palestine. My brothers ... by God, a single act of sacrifice performed by a Muslim young man shakes the Zionist entity and causes it losses greater than those caused by all the Arab armies together in their wars against the Zionists.[23]

---

[20] http://irak-info.blogspot.com/2009/01/cosecha-comprendida-para-diciembre-del.html (accessed February 2, 2011).

[21] Kedar, *Crusade and Mission*, pp. 17–18.

[22] *Al-'Ahd*, May 24, 1985.

[23] For the published will, see *al-Sabil*, July 3–9, 2001, p. 5.

The issue of revenge is a central motif in the wills, reflecting the principle of an eye for an eye as reprisal and, in the view of the sponsoring movement, constituting a balance of deterrence vis-à-vis the enemy. Jamal ʿAbd al-Ghani al-Nasir articulated this motif thus:

Who among us is not angry and does not feel a desire for revenge when he walks in the funeral processions of the *shahid*s, especially the mass processions in Nablus? Who among us is not angry and doesn't want revenge when seeing the mothers, wives and children of the shahids on television? Who among us does not identify with the owners of the homes that were destroyed in Khan Yunis and the shops in Hebron? Who among us is not angry when children are murdered, trees cut down and cities bombed? ... By the life of God, the Jews tore the land and destroyed it greatly! ... I truly wanted to take revenge, but I didn't know how. I wanted to take revenge upon them, to kill as many among them as possible and cause them as many losses as possible. Of course, the road to my goal is resistance, the road of Yahya ʿAyyash, Sharif, ʿAwad, Hamran and ʿAbayat. I chose one of the methods of resistance, namely acts of self-sacrifice.[24]

Citing the names of previous martyrs was intended to identify the perpetrator as a link in the distinguished and growing genealogy (*silsila*) of jihad fighters and martyrs, thereby heightening the legitimacy and sanctity of his act. This rationale also guided the Jordanian Muslim Brethren newspaper, *al-Sabil*, which listed all the wills of the Palestinian martyrs of the 2001 al-Aqsa Intifada in numerical order, specifically, *Shahid* No. 1, *Shahid* No. 2, and so forth. Moreover, in an effort to project an egalitarian image of shared fate and solidarity, most of the wills do not refer to the martyrs' social standing.[25] The theme of solidarity appears as well in wills from the Lebanese arena, describing the martyrs there as belonging to the entire Lebanese nation. This included Shiʿi martyrs, too, reflecting the growing thrust by Hizballah in the 1990s to participate in parliamentary politics and in the government and to project itself as an all-Lebanese movement with a national rather than ethnic agenda.[26]

Unity was presented even more systematically in the wills of the Salafi jihadists in Iraq, who, in contrast to their Jordanian, Palestinian, and Lebanese counterparts, came from various areas in the Middle East, Asia, and Europe. However, geographic and national identities were blurred and a shared fate was emphasized, with the destruction and

---

[24] Ibid.
[25] Ibid. For a similar observance in Israel's commemoration of fallen soldiers, see Azaryahu, *State Cults*, p. 126.
[26] See, e.g., Eli Hurvitz, *The Military Wing of Hizballah: A Social Profile* (Tel Aviv: The Moshe Dayan Center, December 1999), pp. 27–29, 64–72 (in Hebrew).

humiliation in Iraq projected as reflecting a broader reality of total war against Islam and its believers by arrogant invaders and their local allies.[27]

In essence, the wills provide an alternative reading of reality and the encounter with its challenges. Martyrdom is self-sacrifice impelled not by despair but rather by hope and the anticipation of the approaching redemption. Whoever strives for this and actualizes it belongs to the elite, for "the privilege of martyrdom is not granted to all men on earth, but is the privilege of he whom God values." Moreover, he alone is a true believer.[28] In a recorded will dated May 2001, Mahmud Muhammad Marmash, a Hamas activist, pointed out that the option of resistance is the only option, for the pioneers who give up their lives weaken the self-confidence of the Zionist entity. He dedicates his act to every loyal Muslim who willingly accepts God as God, Islam as religion and Muhammad as messenger, and to every Muslim who loves martyrdom and strives to achieve it.[29] In a slightly different version in his written will, Marmash assumes the role of preacher of the correct path:

> As for my brothers and sisters, I call upon them to cling to this religion, which is the correct path to this life, and be vigilant regarding prayers and the commandments which God, may his name be praised and exalted, has imposed. I remind you about the precious deposit which is your responsibility, namely my mother, who has suffered in this world for your comfort. And there is another deposit, namely your little children. God, may He be praised and exalted, imposed this responsibility upon you so that you raise them in the path of Islam, for you will be questioned about this on the day of resurrection.[30]

Muhammad 'Ata, one of the leaders of the September 11 "suicide" bombers, also requested in the will he prepared in 1996 that his family and all others read his will mandating awe of God, following the Sunni creed, and refraining from the temptations of life, thereby proving themselves to be true believers.[31]

Preaching for the right path is often highlighted in the wills in cases in which the martyrs' image had previously been tarnished socially or morally for reasons such as drug use, infidelity, or collaboration with the

---

[27] Hafez, *Suicide Bombers in Iraq*, pp. 142–147.
[28] The will of Hanadi Jaradat, member of the Palestinian Islamic Jihad, who carried out a "suicide" attack in Haifa in October 2003, available at http://www.saraya/ps/index/php?act=Show&id=2382 (accessed September 7, 2011).
[29] http://al-fateh.net/hide/arch/fa-29/wasiya29.htm (accessed September 7, 2011).
[30] *Al-Sabil*, July 3–9, 2001, p. 6.
[31] 'Ata's will quoted in http://www.islamonline.net/Arabic/news/2001–10/07/article22.shtml (accessed October 12, 2011); also Davis, *Martyrs*, pp. 88–89.

enemy. Through martyrdom, such persons seek repentance for their deeds and purification of their souls as a proper preparation for entering paradise and removing the mark of shame from themselves and their family. This pattern has been described by some scholars as "instrumental martyrdom" – that is, the use of wills as a platform not only for the purification of the soul but also for the social rehabilitation of the martyrs and their relatives. Instrumental martyrdom was also attributed to Palestinian women as an honorable way out of social ostracism stemming from divorce, infertility, and the like.[32] The sponsoring movements themselves encouraged repentance, termed "returning to oneself," and emphasized that the gates of repentance are open to every living soul.[33] Still, ideological motives and the desire for political activism should not be ignored, for example, regarding Palestinian women martyrs, as discussed by Caron E. Gentry. The analysis of the motivations of female Palestinian *shahid*s during the al-Aqsa Intifada, Gentry argues, suggested a maternalistic prism of shattered dreams regarding marriage and children – a view that reflects a perception of women's primary role as mother and wife.[34]

The wills contain a series of fixed tenets that repeat themselves in a standard format aimed at entrenching the ethos of martyrdom in the public consciousness so that it becomes canonical. The wills begin by presenting the personal identity of the martyrs, followed by an explanation of the motives for the deed, and instructions to the family regarding how to accept the sought for death, including refraining from crying, distributing candies, and following the path of jihad and faith. The martyrs' departure from their mother is given a special status, meant to impart a compassionate aura to them in emphasizing her critical role in producing a jihad fighter.

According to Muslim tradition, a mythological figure, the poetess Tumadir bint 'Umar (d. 664), nicknamed al-Khansa', is considered the "mother of the *shahid*s," having lost her four sons in the Battle of al-Qadisiyya (637) where the Muslims defeated the Persians, thereby paving the way for the spread of Islam. As far as is known, she did not compose any lament for her sons, but rather ordered them to fight in the jihad war, and when notified of their death, said, "Praise be God who honored me by their death." Al-Khansa' was adopted by Hamas as the symbol of

---

[32] Victor, *Army of Roses*; also Mira Tzoref, "The Palestinian Shahida," in Yoram Schweitzer (ed.), *Female Suicide Bombers: Dying for Equality* (Tel Aviv: Jaffe Center for Strategic Studies, 2006), pp. 13–22.

[33] See, e.g., Yasin quoted in Berko, *The Path to Paradise*, pp. 60–61.

[34] Gentry, "Twisted Maternalism: From Peace to Violence," pp. 235–252.

Palestinian motherhood. A thick volume published by Hamas, titled *Khansa' fi Filastin* (2008),[35] accorded the mothers of martyrs a place of honor, quoting their thoughts at length, highlighting their role in encouraging their sons' act of self-sacrifice, and describing their joy on the fulfillment of their wish. This, the book declared, made the mothers full partners in the struggle for the liberation of Palestine.[36] In a similar vein, al-Qa'ida published a periodical for women, titled *al-Khansa'*, urging them to take part in jihad.[37]

If al-Khansa' symbolized the woman's jihad role in the Sunni world, the image of Fatima (d. 633), the Prophet's daughter and wife of 'Ali, founder of the Shi'a, represented the ideal in the Shi'a community. Fatima was associated with sacrificing her sons, Hasan and Husayn, on the alter of faith and justice. In the awakening Shi'a, she became a symbol in opposing oppression and of the ideal pious mother, who is ready to send her sons to fight and die in defense of Islam without showing sorrow or shedding a tear.[38]

Other forums dedicated to women and to Islamic family life were conducted in Islamic Web sites, which encouraged women to support jihad with donations and through the education of their children and to play an active role in this effort. One of them stated:

The woman is one of the primary influential facilitators of the victory of Islam. Moreover, if she had not fulfilled her role with maximal courage and self-sacrifice ... Islam would not have achieved victory during its periods of success over the unbeliever states which had such advantages of quantity, equipment and

---

[35] Ghassan Da'war, *Khansa' fi Filastin* (Giza: Markaz al-I'lam al-'Arabi, 2008).

[36] Ibid. See also Iris Jean-Klein, "Palestinian Martyrdom Revisited: Critical Reflections on Topical Cultures of Explanation," *Pragmatism, Law and Governmentality* Paper 5 (2000), mainly pp. 11–22: http://scholarship.law.cornell.edu/ealccs_plg/5 (accessed April 7, 2013). The most prominent Hamas "Khansa'" was Miriam Farahat, or "Um Nidal," who also served as a Hamas member of Parliament. Her name became widespread during the al-Aqsa Intifada when three of her children and one of her grandsons were killed during armed clashes with Israeli forces. These sacrifices did not deter her from continuing to call for jihad and self-sacrifice against Israel. Her death from illness in 2013 was marked by Hamas in Gaza with an official funeral and memorial ceremonies. http://www.almasryalyoum.com/node/1572566 (accessed April 7, 2013).

[37] Al-'Uyayri, *Hal intaharat Hawa umustushihdat?* pp. 1–2.

[38] Al-Sadr, *Fadak fi'l-ta'rikh*; Shari'ati, "Fatima is Fatima." See also Aghaie, *The Martyrs of Karbala*, pp. 123–125; Faegheh Shirazi, *The Veil Unveiled: The Hijab in Modern Culture* (Gainesville: University Press of Florida, 2001), pp. 92–103; idem, "The Islamic Republic of Iran and Women's Images: Masters of Exploitation," in idem (ed.), *Muslim Women in War and Crisis: Representation and Reality* (Austin: University of Texas Press, 2010), pp. 109–138.

money. . . . It is she who educates her children for jihad, and she who guards the honor and possessions of the man who sets out for jihad. It is she who steadfastly faces the difficulties and encourages her children and those under her responsibility to stand fast and continue in this path. Indeed, behind every great jihad fighter stands a woman.[39]

The sanctified trio of mother-*shahid*-redeemer of the nation is interwoven in the wills, intended first and foremost to codify the normative nature of the act of self-sacrifice, which receives its ultimate approval from the mother, thereby neutralizing the prospect that was indeed displayed by some mothers, such as in the Palestinian milieu, of opposing the sacrifice of their children on the alter of faith and homeland.

The wills provide the means by which the martyrs convey moral significance to their community, illuminate their flaws, and pave the way to their ultimate redemption. In the vocabulary of Shiʿi martyrdom, the martyrs' fate may be compared to a candle which, in burning itself, lights the path of society that is overshadowed by the darkness of repression.

In as much as the martyrs write the heroic history of their nation with their own blood, and in light of their altruistic sacrifice, they are worthy of claiming authority and obedience both on their own behalf and that of their political movement. Notably, until the act itself, and the exposure of their identity, the martyrs are anonymous figures. They burst into public awareness by virtue of their act, not beforehand. They project their personal and moral qualities only retrospectively. Their charisma and status stem from the act and its success. Their origin is unknown. In Max Weber's sociological terminology, the martyrs lack the charisma of "office" by virtue of a high post, while also lacking the charisma of "kinship" by virtue of high genealogical status, or what historian Yaʿakov Raz terms "the genetic of greatness."[40] They are unknown soldiers, generally from a low social background, acquiring glory only after death.

In this sense, the martyrs ostensibly fit the criteria of "authority claimed" rather than "authority recognized"; however, this is not necessarily so, as the martyrs belong to a political movement that has already established its authority, which is extended to them. Moreover, the

---

[39] Yusuf al-ʿUyayri, *Dawr al-nisaʾ fi jihad al-aʿdaʾ*, available at http://www.tawhed.ws/r1?i=3509&x=8fsj2em2 (accessed May 5, 2013).

[40] S. N. Eisenstadt (ed.), *Max Weber on Charisma and Institution Building* (Chicago: University of Chicago Press, 1968), pp. xxi–xxii, 18–27; Yaʾakov Raz's preface to Raʿnan Rein's book, *Populism and Charisma: Peronist Argentina 1943–1955* (Tel Aviv: Modan, 1998), p. 8 (in Hebrew).

martyrs speak in the name of a higher, divine authority. Conceivably, therefore, their authority is both claimed and recognized.

The character of the Muslim martyrs embodies their sponsoring movement, just as the early Christians embodied the church. The movement, which not only challenges the enemy but also demands recognition within its community as a moral avant-garde that leads, thereby merits authority and loyalty.[41] Altruistic martyrdom, therefore, is not a one-sided gift but rather entails obligations and reciprocity.[42] Like charity, it is an effective way of signaling and demanding status, allegiance, prestige, and superiority within a group or a nation.[43]

Ultimately, the individual character of the act of self-sacrifice, as noted by Hannah Arendt, does not blur the fact that "power is never the property of an individual; it belongs to a group and remains in existence only so long as the group keeps together. When we say of somebody that he is in 'power' we actually refer to his being empowered by a certain number of people to act in their name."[44] In the same vein, anthropologist Karin Andriolo pointed out that when suicide is linked to a group and is motivated, planned, and executed within the organizational framework of the group, "the highly private, individual, and volatile progression toward ending one's life marches to the beat of an ideological movement seeking violent recognition."[45]

COMMEMORATING THE MARTYRS

The involvement of the Islamist movement with which the martyrs are affiliated does not end with the political capital it gains from the exposure of the printed or video will or with the organized mass funeral of the

---

[41] *Filastin al-Muslima*, October 1995, pp. 51–52; Hasan Fadlallah, *Harb al-iradat: sira' al-muqawama wa'l-ihtilal al-Isra'ili fi Lubnan* (Beirut: Dar al-Muhajir, 1998).

[42] Self-sacrifice evokes an analogy with a gift, perceived by sociologists as a form of exchange and a form of contractual morality. See, e.g., Marcel Mauss, *The Gift: The Form and Reason for Exchange in Archaic Societies* (London: Routledge, 1990). For a more reserved approach, see Ilana F. Silber, "Echoes of Sacrifice? Repertoires of Giving in the Great Religions," in Albert I. Baumgarten (ed.), *Sacrifice in Religious Experience* (Leiden: Brill, 2002), pp. 291–312.

[43] On charity as a utility investment, see Amy Singer, *Charity in Muslim Societies* (Cambridge: Cambridge University Press, 2008), pp. 9–10. Singer borrows from the world of biology in citing altruistic behavior in animals, as examined by Amotz and Avishag Zahavi in *The Handicap Principle: A Missing Piece of Darwin's Puzzle* (New York: Oxford University Press, 1997), pp. xv–xvi.

[44] Arendt, "On Violence," p. 143.

[45] Andriolo, "Murder by Suicide," p. 736.

martyrs. The movement, sometimes in cooperation with the community, also translates its symbolic gratitude for the act of self-sacrifice by the martyrs into a series of financial and ethical obligations to their family. These consist of pilgrimages to the family home, a monthly grant to the family, study scholarships for the children or relatives of the *shahid*, sermons in their honor in the mosque, and invitations to the family to take part in commemorative and festive assemblies. Such recognition also heightens the social prestige of the family, which is especially significant in the case of families with a low socioeconomic background, from rural areas, or living in refugee camps.[46] Others who benefit are the dispatchers of the martyrs, especially if they are arrested and imprisoned, as in the Palestinian case. There they are respected by their comrades, who regard them as normatively moral.[47]

The movement also makes intensive efforts to perpetuate the martyrs' image through commemorative enterprises. Commemoration, as various scholars have shown, is in effect a social ritual involving both official and vernacular agents that compete for public representation and the molding of the collective memory. Rituals, as defined by Julie Peteet, can be read as texts of empowerment, which in a political context represent the social order of hierarchies and relations of domination or, alternatively, a reversal and a vindication of them.[48] Commemoration grants internal cohesion and historical significance, provides a psychological conduit of endurance, formulates a vision, and defines the distinctiveness of a specific group or community in comparison with others. Commemoration is thus an ongoing activity devoted to preservation and perpetuation,[49]

---

[46] Moghadam, "Palestinian Suicide Terrorism," p. 72; *al-Mujahid*, December 15, 1993; also al-Sarraj's interview in *Journal of Palestine Studies*, pp. 74–75.

[47] Berko, *The Path to Paradise*, pp. 36–43.

[48] Peteet, "Male Gender and Rituals of Resistance in the Palestinian Intifada," pp. 198–199; also Pitcher, "The Divine Impatience," p. 28.

[49] For literature on memorial activity and its link to politics, see Barry Schwartz, "The Social Context of Commemoration: A Study in Collective Memory," *Social Forces* 61 (December 1982), pp. 374–376; Paul Connerton, *How Societies Remember* (Cambridge: Cambridge University Press, 1989), pp. 1–5, 44–53; George L. Mosse, *Fallen Soldiers: Reshaping the Memory of the World Wars* (New York: Oxford University Press, 1990), mainly chapters 3 and 5; Maurice Halbwachs, *On Collective Memory* (Chicago: University of Chicago Press, 1992), pp. 25–26, 84–104, 116–118; John Gillis (ed.), *Commemorations: The Politics of National Identity* (Princeton, NJ: Princeton University Press, 1994); Jay Winter and Emmanuel Sivan, "Setting the Framework," in J. Winter and E. Sivan (eds.), *War and Remembrance in the Twentieth Century* (Cambridge: Cambridge University Press, 1999), pp. 6–37.

because "memory survives only in repetitions."[50] It creates "commemorative density," in Yael Zrubavel's terminology, to transmit the legacy more effectively.[51]

In the Islamic context, modern conflicts in Lebanon, Palestine, Afghanistan, Chechnya, and Iraq have produced a large corps of martyrs and a vast body of popular literature to celebrate their deeds in well-organized commemorative and hagiographic campaigns. An important element in this process is the presentation of the biographies of the martyrs, which are usually brief and telegraphic. They include personal details about the martyrs, a photograph of them, a description of the act itself, the number of fatalities and wounded caused by the act, and the martyrs' will. This material is widely circulated in newspapers, anthologies, and special martyr venues in TV programs and on the Internet.[52] A survey of lists of martyrs among the Afghan *mujahidun* and in Hamas in Palestine shows that not all were "suicide" perpetrators: some were killed in military clashes with the enemy or as a result of targeted attacks against them. Their inclusion in the martyrs' lists was aimed at reinforcing the ethos of self-sacrifice and projecting an image of an egalitarian movement endowed with true social solidarity.[53]

The martyrs' biographies, written in a style similar to biographical lexicons of 'ulama' and Sufis in Muslim history, aimed to present a religious and ethical model to be imitated while also placing the specific figure in the wider context, thereby reinforcing his/her influence.[54] Thus, the biographical image underwent a process of reconstruction to conform to the desired ideal to be imitated and to display loyalty to the sponsoring movement's political paradigm. This unified and standardized image created by the biographies ensured the projection of a coherent message.

---

[50] Quoted in Varzi, *Warring Souls*, p. 103.

[51] Yael Zerubavel, *Recovered Roots: Collective Memory and the Making of Israeli National Tradition* (Chicago: Chicago University Press, 1995), p. 8; also idem, *The Nation and Death: History, Memory and Politics* (Tel Aviv: Dvir, 2002), pp. 13–15 (in Hebrew).

[52] See, e.g., Hizballah Web site at http://www.moqawama.org (accessed March 2, 2012); Hamas Web sites at http://www.palestine-info.info/arabic/hamas/shuhda/2003/alla/syrah.htm (accessed March 2, 2012), http://al-fateh.net/hide/arch/fa-29/wasiya29.htm (accessed March 2, 2012), and http://www.alqassam.ps/arabic/sohdaa.php (accessed March 2, 2012); Islamic Jihad in Palestine at http://www.saraya.ps/index.php?act (accessed March 2, 2012).

[53] See, e.g., *Filastin al-Muslima*, November 1994, p. 14; 'Azzam, *'Ayat al-rahman fi jihad al-Afghan*.

[54] Daphna Ephrat, *Spiritual Wayfarers, Leaders in Piety: Sufis and the Dissemination of Islam in Medieval Palestine* (Cambridge, MA: Harvard Center for Middle Eastern Studies, 2008), pp. 139–152.

FIGURE 6.1 The image of Ahmad Qasir is shown above the ruins of an Israeli military installation in Tyre.
Source: *Al-ʿAhd*, May 24, 1985.

A survey of the biographies of the martyrs reveals an image of chosen individuals endowed with knowledge, piety, and high moral qualities – a narrative reinforced by comments from family members (mainly parents) for greater emphasis and authenticity. Thus, for example, Hizballah in Lebanon describes Ahmad Qasir, who carried out a "suicide" attack on the Israeli army command headquarters in Tyre in 1982, as "religiously pious, often spent time in the mosque and in reading the Qurʾan, and became close to ʿulamaʾ." Qasir holds an important pioneering place in Hizballah's martyrdom genealogy as a "hero of the Khaybar operation" and as someone "whose drops of blood created the dawn of acts of self-sacrifice."[55]

Another martyr, Bilal Fahs, who drove a "suicide" car bomb into an Israeli army convoy in Southern Lebanon in 1984, was honored with the appellation "Laureate of Southern Lebanon" (*ʿaris al-janub*) and was compared to Bilal the Abyssinian, the Prophet's trusted friend and the

[55] *Al-ʿAhd*, May 24, 1985, and November 14, 1986.

first muezzin in Islam (d. ca. 640). The first Bilal announced, "I testify that there is no God except Allah," while the contemporary Bilal translated this pronouncement into a deed through an act of self-sacrifice, announcing that tyrants merit death, and subordination and bowing are reserved for God only. Both Bilals, Hizballah asserted, "represent a single message . . . the message of initiative, endeavor and sacrifice."[56]

Islamic Jihad in Palestine depicted the piety of Hanadi Jaradat, a lawyer from Jenin who carried out a "suicide" act in the Maxim Restaurant in Haifa in 2003, in similar terms, thus:

Hanadi was an ideal model for faithful Palestinian women. Her behavior belied her youth, and her biography differed from young women her age. She prayed at the appointed times, awaking at night to be close to God by every means. She fasted and studied the Qur'an, completing it entirely seven times. Her last two months before sacrificing herself were spent in fasting. She was a devoted believer with great forbearance and when she sacrificed herself she was still fasting.[57]

Some of the accounts in the biographical anthologies describe the martyrs as having relinquished comfort, money, and possessions and as leaving behind families and children as an act of purification of body and soul for the sake of sacrifice on the alter of faith and community. Many of these martyrs were described as having been involved in the past in resistance activity and confrontations with the enemy. The imprisonment of several of them was portrayed as a hothouse environment that fortified their spirit and reinforced their religious and patriotic awareness. The prison experience was presented in the martyrological literature as an additional, "softer" arena for expressing dissidence and as a living testimony to the ability to endure and to the sense of mission by the believers, as God and justice stand by their side against a cruel and demonic rival, while the final victory is in their hands.

Some martyrs were depicted as being put to a test to evaluate their determination, namely by people sent to them to try to weaken their resolve. However, they remained steadfast.[58] The details of their religious preparation, including their visit to the mosque on the day of the assignment, were also described in a detailed, almost epic style. All these steps

[56] *Al-'Ahd*, June 29, 1984; *al-Safir*, June 17, 1984; also Jaber, *Hizballah*, 89–90.
[57] http://www.saraya/ps/index/php?act=Show&id=2382 (accessed September 7, 2011).
[58] Hafez, *Suicide Bombers in Iraq*, pp. 148–149. See also the account of Ahmad Qasir who carried out the attack on the Israel Defence Forces soldiers in Tyre, November 1982, cited in Fadlallah, *Harb al-Iradat*, pp. 129–133; also 'Abd al-Hamid al-Shuaybani, *Siyar al-shuhada': durus wa-'ibar* (Riyadh: Dar al-Watan, 1999), pp. 5–9.

were aimed to purify the act spiritually, distance it from any personal, mundane, or political consideration, and elevate it to an eschatological level, thereby also lessening the fear of death in the public consciousness.[59] The very fact of projecting the act in the public discourse in two contexts – the religious, as martyrdom, and the communal, as a collective act necessary to continued survival and resistance to oppression – was aimed at turning killing into a positive act.

A study of the biographies also reveals the representation of the martyrs as the movement's ideal, embodying – in their image and in their death – the lofty values of the community and the reason for its continued existence. Depicting their act not only as one of bravery but also as one of absolute self-sacrifice on the alter of faith or homeland aims at evoking deep emotion, especially in the case of young people whose life and future are still before them, yet they choose to relinquish them for an exalted goal. This is the same message as that projected in the narrative of the family, and especially by the martyrs' mother, as shown in some of the biographies.

Depicting the martyrs in a universal terminology – for example, using the familiar saying, "In their death they commanded us to live" – conveyed the message that these acts were not impelled by a death wish. On the contrary, the movements' spokesmen pointed out, the sanctification of life is an exalted commandment, yet the readiness for self-sacrifice and bravery for the lofty goal of preserving the independent existence of the people is a legitimate demand.[60] Although the longing by some individuals for the privilege of eternal life in paradise evoked a great deal of attention, as did the wills of Hamas activists during the Second Intifada (2000–2005), the description of these phenomena as acts of "egoistic martyrdom" bordering on eschatological extremism, as argued, for example, by Eli Alshech,[61] is questionable. Personal redemption was closely entwined with collective redemption in the here and now. The fact that an organized martyrological thrust functioned under the aegis of a mother movement that competed for political primacy in its community and stood for resistance against conquest essentially reinforced the individual/collective dualism and restrained the egoistic element of the act.

[59] See, e.g., Hassan, "An Arsenal of Believers"; idem, "Are You Ready? Tomorrow You Will Be in Paradise," *Times*, July 14, 2005, available at http://www.timesonline.co.uk/tol/life_ and _style/article543551.ece (accessed July 11, 2011).

[60] See, e.g., the *shahid* sections in *al-Risala* and *al-Istiqlal* in Gaza. For the Shiʿi Iranian case, see Liora-Baavor Hendelman, *The Middle East Research Institute*, no. 25 (February 24, 2000).

[61] Alshech, "Egoistic Martyrdom," pp. 32–37.

Moreover, a substantial portion of the justifications of the act of self-sacrifice as stated in the wills, especially in light of increasing attacks against civilians, were distinctly communal in nature (for example, defense of the homeland, humiliation, revenge, and the superior morality of Muslims) and were supported in Islamic tradition. Thus, the phenomenon of self-sacrifice was projected as closely linked to the idea of resistance to the conquest – a link that endowed the act – in the movements' discourse and in their approach to the public, with an altruistic rather than egoistic character.

A similar process of commemorating the martyrs is evident as well in non-Muslim secular movements that fostered martyrdom, as exemplified by the Tamil Tigers in Sri Lanka. Reportedly, every "suicide" fighter there was granted a last meal and a photograph with the leader. This served to project symbolic power, a personal model of self-sacrifice for the Tamil cause, and the personal closeness between leader and fighter as part of political recruitment. As in the Islamic case, the motif of sacrifice was supported by embedded cultural norms that were highlighted because of new circumstances, such as the concept of *arppanippu* (dedication, in this case of man to God) and *balidan* (sacrifice as a gift of life).[62]

All Tamil fighters celebrated Heroes Day. In addition, the elite suicide units – the Black Tigers – had their own day of commemoration marking the first attack against the Sri Lankan army in May 1987. This special day was covered intensively in the media both in northern and southern Sri Lanka. Certain regions conducted memorial events for the "suicide" fighters who came from their area. Their photographs were widely disseminated so that the public would pay them due respect. Their burial stones were differentiated from others by the words "Black Tiger." Their death dates were listed in the Tamil independence calendar, and their names were closely bound up with the redemption of the nation in speeches and broadcasting stations such as the Voice of Tigers. The founder and leader of the organization, Velupiiai Prabhakaran, speaking in one such broadcast, said:

The death of a liberation hero is not a normal event of death. This is an event of history, a lofty ideal, a miraculous event which bestows life. The truth is that a liberation fighter does not die. . . . Indeed, what is called "flame of his aim," which has shone for his life, will not be extinguished. This aim is like a fire, like a force in history, and it takes hold of others. The national soul of the people has been touched and awakened.[63]

---

[62] Hopgood, "Tamil Tigers," p. 63.
[63] Prabhakaran quoted in Hopgood, "Tamil Tigers." The quote appeared originally in Peter Schalk, "Resistance and Martyrdom in the Process of State Formation in Tamililam," in

The goal was to demonstrate determination and strengthen morale. This also explains the meticulous training for the act, for if such fighters served as a source of honor, they must be soldiers of merit.

The heroic account of the martyrs, whether in the Muslim or the non-Muslim context, served as a morality story that filled both a pedagogic role and a recruitment role. The martyrs became the symbol of the revolution, embodying the struggle for independence as an issue of retrieving by force what had been taken by force. Their image became objectified and the memory of them was effectively channeled into the collective memory, thereby fulfilling the aim of the commemorative rituals that surrounded their death.

The realms of martyrdom memory, in Pierre Nora's depiction,[64] were reflected in varied memorial sites: print and memoir texts, funeral and burial ceremonies, parades, speeches, songs, graphics, audiovisual tapes, and Web sites. Public spaces were also utilized for commemoration, including streets and schools named for martyrs, as well as mosques, walls, traffic round-abouts, town centers, social clubs, and restaurants decorated with martyrs' photographs. Handbooks were also distributed, which, in addition to the commemoration of fallen martyrs, functioned as a guide to fixed religious behavior based on daily and weekly rituals such as purification, prayer, the study of Qur'an verses before bedtime, a weekly fast, and going to the mosque on Friday.[65] One handbook explained that "strengthening one's spirit is the only way to overcome our inner lusts and our enemies that surround us on all sides."[66]

School textbooks were of special importance. They created a display of objective knowledge which in reality consisted of the desirable knowledge that the specific movement wished to convey in the schools, inter alia reflecting power struggles with rival groups.[67] Emphasis was placed on a legacy of heroic martyrdom, instilling a sense of shared fate and communal

Joyce Pettigrew (ed.), *Martyrdom and Political Resistance: Essays from Asia and Europe* (Amsterdam: VU University Press, 1997), p. 79.

[64] Pierre Nora, *Realms of Memory: Rethinking the French Past*, trans. by Arthur Goldhammer (New York: Columbia University Press, 1996–1998).

[65] See, e.g., in the Lebanese case, *Nur al-'ashiqin* (Beirut: Mu'assasat Bint al-Hady, n.d.); *al-'Ishq al-Karbala'i* (Beirut: n.p., n.d.).

[66] *Nur al-'ashiqin*, pp. 7–6.

[67] See, e.g., Michael W. Apple, *Official Knowledge: Democratic Education in a Conservative Age* (2nd ed., New York: Routledge, 2000); Allan Luke, *Literacy, Textbooks and Ideology* (London: Falmer Press, 1998); Elie Podeh, *The Arab-Israel Conflict in Israeli History Textbooks 1948–2000* (Westport, CT: Bergin and Garvey, 2002), pp. 1–7.

solidarity by means of a dramatic narrative with heroes and villains.[68] For example, in the Palestinian context, an online magazine aimed at the twelve- to eighteen-year age group, *al-Fath*, conveys the ethos of martyr-dom through stories, poems, and riddles. Two regular columns, titled "The Story of a Martyr" and "The Legacy of a Martyr," describe heroic epics of the Islamic past and present, such as the struggle against the Crusaders in the twelfth century and the resistance movement led by Shaykh 'Izz al-Din al-Qassam in Palestine during the 1930s.[69]

Calendars were also used for commemorative purposes. They delineated sacred times as separate from mundane and routine time, during which believers identified with the martyrs and their lofty sacrifice and, thereby, were exposed to the movement's revolutionary message and political agenda. The plethora of memorial days, side by side with Islamic holy days – first and foremost the month of Ramadan, as well as mythological commemorations of the past such as the Battles of Badr (624) and Uhud (625) in the Sunna tradition and the battle of Karbala (680) in the Shi'a tradition – created a historical continuity of sacrifice and an aura of holiness.

The visible public commemoration of the martyrs, especially in the urban environment, guaranteed the martyrs' symbolic eternal life, thereby becoming a cultural norm, accessible to all. Inevitably, this accessibility was part of a process by which, as pointed out by George Mosse, the ritual of the fallen becomes public property through material means.[70]

The commemoration of Muslim martyrdom was primarily textual, visual, and virtual and less physical and ichnographic, as in monuments and statues in the public space. Burial places, too, were more modest than usual and did not serve as sites for periodic ceremonies or pilgrimages, as

[68] Anne Marie Oliver and Paul F. Steinberg, *The Road to Martyrs' Square: A Journey into the World of the Suicide Bomber* (New York: Oxford University Press, 2005).
[69] Chernitzki, *Constructing Collective Palestinian Identity*, pp. 7–8, 33–38. In an interview, Dr. Iyad Sarajj, a Palestinian psychiatrist in Gaza, pointed out that the martyr has become a role model for young people. "Once, the Israeli soldier was a symbol of power, and when we would ask children to play a game in which they imagined themselves as Arabs or Jews, all of them wanted to be a Jewish soldier. Today he is replaced by the martyr. This is the image that fills them with pride, self-respect, and a sense of empowerment." The martyr is also viewed by the child as high in status in his community. To be a martyr is to be socially accepted. Sarajj, quoted in *Ha'aretz*, April 1, 2002.
[70] Mosse, *Fallen Soldiers*, chapter 7. See also Anthony D. Smith, *National Identity* (London: Reno: University of Nevada Press, 1991), p. 77; Allen, "Getting by the Occupation," pp. 453–487.

do national military cemeteries in modern times[71] or as sites for mystical visits to the graves of holy figures in both the premodern and modern eras.[72] Apparently, this minimization stemmed from the desire of the sponsoring political movements to contain the phenomenon and prevent endangering the transcendental status of God. In this, they were following the legal tradition that prohibits erecting a structure or a mosque over a grave or decorating it with flags and written messages praising the deceased – and all the more so in the case of martyrs – lest this harm the reward that they merit in the next world and constitute a deviation from Sunni rules.[73]

Nevertheless, it was difficult to discourage the spread of stories about miracles and folk beliefs such as perfumed aromas (musk) that rise from the graves of *shahids*[74] or the supernatural powers attributed to them[75] – beliefs held as well by early Christian martyrs. The attribution of divine blessings to the martyrs is not surprising, as the martyrs are depicted as ever present and remembered, their spirit embodied in each member of their community, while they themselves are to be found in the ambiance of the prophets, righteous figures, and fellow martyrs. They therefore had the power to serve as a conduit or mediator (*wisata*) for requests for healing, fertility, livelihood, and so forth.

---

[71] Mosse, *Fallen Soldiers*, mainly chapters 3 and 5; Sivan, *The 1948 Generation*. An exception is the case of Iran, as discussed by Joyce Davis, where special cemeteries were built for martyrs whose graves were decorated with photos of smiling young faces. Davis, *Martyrs*, pp. 46–47.

[72] Peter Brown, *The Cult of Saints: Its Rise and Function in Latin Christianity* (Chicago: University of Chicago Press, 1981), mainly pp. 1–22; Christoph S. Taylor, *In the Vicinity of the Righteous: Ziyara and the Veneration of Muslim Saints in Late Medieval Egypt* (Boston: Brill, 1999).

[73] See, e.g., Abu 'Abdallah Muhammad al-Shaybani, *al-Mabsut li'l-Shaybani* (Karatchi: Idarat al-Qur'an wa'l-'Ulum al-Islamiyya, n.d.), Vol. 1, p. 422; al-Sarakhsi, *al-Mabsut*, Vol. 2, p. 62; Muslim, *Sahih Muslim*, Vol. 2, p. 667; also 'Azzam, *Fi'l-Jihad, 'adab wa-ahkam*, pp. 93–95; al-Suri, *Da'wat al-muqawama*, p. 1604; Ayoub, "Martyrdom in Christianity and Islam," p. 70; Khalid, *al-Shahid fi'l-Islam*, p. 75.

[74] The belief in musk is based on the Prophet's ruling after the Battle of Uhud (625): "Do not wash the shahids, for on the day of judgment their wound will exude the scent of musk." Another hadith quotes the Prophet as saying, "Whoever is wounded for the sake of God – and God knows who was wounded for him – on the day of judgment his color will be the color of blood and his scent the scent of musk." Al-Bukhari, *Sahih al-Bukhari*, Vol. 3, p. 1032; also Ayoub, "Martyrdom in Christianity and Islam," p. 70.

[75] Alshech, "Egoistic Martyrdom," pp. 36 (n. 40), 40–41; idem, "The Emergence of the Infallible Jihad Fighter – The Salafi Jihadists' Quest for Religious Legitimacy," *Middle East Media Research Institute: Inquiry and Analysis* 30 (June 2008), pp. 1–11.

These and other virtues attributed to the martyrs, including dream visions, appeared in the brief biographies issued by the *mujahidun* in Afghanistan, Hamas in Palestine, and al-Qaʿida in Iraq.[76] They contributed to the reinforcement of the charismatic image of the martyrs as bearing a metaphysical message and as chosen by God, who speaks to them directly, putting them beyond criticism or doubt regarding the purity of their motives – criticism that intensified with the spread of the phenomenon (see Chapter 7). The martyrs were depicted as counted among the friends of God (*awliya'*), with their blessing derived from their adherence to the Prophet's commandments and prohibitions. God has infused His spirit and light in them and bestowed virtues and miracles on them (*karamat*).

The use of such terms as *awliya'* and *karamat* (taken primarily from the Sufi repertoire) in the creation of hagiographic martyrdom literature points to the complex attitude toward Sufism in the Islamist discourse. This attitude was expressed not only in ritual and glorification but also in the adoption and appreciation of various Sufi values and practices, molding them to accord with an activist vision. This embodies the essence of the transvalue strategy – the representation or evaluation of something according to a new principle. Thus, Sufi themes of self-purification, total loyalty to a spiritual teacher (*suhba*), and social altruism (*ihsan*) became, under Islamist mentors, an important tool in molding a pure, disciplined, and obedient believer inspired by the mission to alter a historic reality. In the context of Islamic martyrdom, the concepts of holiness and the attributes of miracle making also underwent a renewed and refined interpretation regarding martyrs, stressing their devotion to the sharʿia but eliminating the custom of prostration or constructing mosques on their graves, so that their religious credentials are entirely a function of their act of jihad in the battlefield.[77]

The primary originator of Sunni hagiography of martyrs and its blend with Sufi inspiration was Shaykh ʿAbdallah ʿAzzam, whereas the immediate context was provided by the Afghan fighters in their struggle against the Soviet army and its local allies in Afghanistan. The biographies of the fallen among these fighters, descriptions of how they died, their wills and farewell letters to their families, and their virtues were documented by

[76] Hafez, *Suicide Bombers in Iraq*, pp. 157–158.
[77] Hatina, "Restoring a Lost Identity," p. 308; Itzchak Weismann, "Modernity from Within: Islamic Fundamentalism and Sufism," *Der Islam* 86 (2011), pp. 142–170; H. Lauzière, "Post-Islamism and the Religious Discourse of ʿAbd al-Salam Yasin," *International Journal of Middle East Studies* 37 (2005), pp. 241–261.

'Azzam in two books written in the early 1980s: *'Ushshaq al-hur* ("Lovers of the Fair Black-Eyed Women"), and especially *'Ayat al-Rahman fi jihad al-Afghan* ("Verses from the Qur'an about the Jihad of the Afghans").[78] 'Azzam praised their religious sincerity, modesty, communal altruism, avoidance of internal disputes, and the honor and obedience they showed to the authority figures among them. He refers to them as masters, commanders, and kings for they are "the guardians of the tree of knowledge that did not dry up or wither, in as much as this tree is irrigated with blood," and, in sacrificing their souls, they are the drafters of the glorious history of their nations. In the matter of *karamat* of the martyrs, 'Azzam mainly addresses the preservation of their bodies over time and the perfumed scents that emanate from them over long distances.[79] Although both books relate primarily to jihad fighters who died in battle, and not to "suicide" bombers (who were introduced in the Afghanistan arena at a later stage, mainly from 2001, upon the American conquest of the country), this distinction is blurred in later editions.

Visual hagiography played an important role alongside the textual hagiography. Maximal use was made of outdoor signage, mass assemblies, plays, documentary and fictional films, and video clips as part of a culture of resistance aimed at reconstructing the martyrs' act of self-sacrifice while introducing them to the community, thereby creating a persona that is incorporated in the public consciousness.

The veneration of the martyrs' heroic deed by various means of transmission shifts their identity from the private and familial realm to the public domain so that they become an icon of the collective. This shift from anonymity to public recognition as cultural heroes – in this case symbols of revolution and liberation – make the martyrs worthy of emulation.

---

[78] 'Azzam, *'Ushshaq al-hur*, available at http://www.4shared.com/dir/dEglkHus/_online. html (accessed May 5, 2011); idem, *'Ayat al-rahman fi jihad al-Afghan.*
[79] 'Azzam, *'Ushshaq al-hur*, pp. 7–9.

7

Debating "Suicide" Attacks

"Suicide" attacks in ethnic, national, and global conflicts between Muslims and non-Muslims ignited disputes and polemics in Islamic circles over religious legitimacy regarding both the self-inflicted death of the perpetrator and the killing of civilians. Various elements in the Islamic spectrum took part in this debate, ranging from lay reformists and radicals to establishment 'ulama', attesting to the fragmentation of religious authority and the contest over the soul of the believers.

Whereas advocates held that such acts were an ultimate realization of God's will and would be rewarded by the pleasures of paradise, critics argued that these were pure acts of violence and suicide, punishable by torment in hell. Both sides drew on the same religio-legal sources but came to different conclusions on the basis of creative commentary or by making use of vague Qur'anic passages or disputes between Muslim jurists. Of the two narratives, the advocates had the upper hand.

A vocal voice in debating "suicide" attacks was provided by the religious scholarship community, graduates of *madrasa*s and religious colleges – the 'ulama' – particularly in the Sunni Arab world. Their proficiency in the traditional rulings, in contrast to the majority of Islamists whose background was autodidactic, contributed an extensive religious discourse about the new phenomenon that came their way and required their immediate consideration in terms of what was permitted or prohibited. Notably, the challenge in the religio-legal context was important but not exclusive: the intense involvement of 'ulama' with the issue also reflected their desire to regain religious authority in the areas of guidance and judicial rulings that they had lost to lay Islamists or to charismatic Salafi 'ulama' in modern times. As aptly observed by a Muslim imam in

California, Shaykh Hamza Yusuf, "Fatwas were once issued primarily by recognized religious authorities of a country or Islamic university, but now every Tom, Dick and Abdullah gives a fatwa (legal opinion)."[1]

The proliferation of new actors in the Islamic spectrum, with the martyrs constituting the latest link in the chain, attested to a crisis of legal authority in Islam. Although the crisis was evident from the late nineteenth century onward, with the spread of literacy, mass education, and mass communications,[2] it became more acute with the introduction of the electronic media, especially the Internet. The new communication technologies led to the emergence of a network society that connected distant Muslim communities throughout the world, including Muslim immigrant communities, while also illuminating the diffusion of Islam and the competition over the authority to represent it. This engendered a critical dialogue, disputation, and various alternatives. Some of the 'ulama' lacked communication skills or charisma and had difficulty expanding their influence beyond the traditional Friday sermons, lectures in *madrasas*, and written fatwas. Others, however, were endowed with these attributes and quickly established a virtual presence. Global scholarly networks such as the International Islamic University of Malaysia, the European Council for Fatwa and Research (ECFT), and the International Union of Muslim Scholars (IUMS) also made extensive use of the new media.[3]

Both lower-level and senior 'ulama' throughout the Arab Muslim world debated the "suicide" phenomenon in statements, interviews, and fatwas. The wide exposure of the fatwas – the traditional venue for religious and moral guidance[4] – in mosques and in print and especially the electronic

---

[1] Hamza, quoted in the *New York Times*, September 20, 2001; also Emily Wax, "The Mufti in the Chat Room," *Washington Post*, July 31, 1999; Miriam Netzer, "One Voice? The Crisis of Legal Authority in Islam," *al-Nakhla* (Spring 2004), pp. 1–5.

[2] Ami Ayalon, *The Press in the Arab Middle East: A History* (Oxford: Oxford University Press, 1995).

[3] See Eickelman and Anderson, "Redefining Muslim Publics," pp. 5–7; Peter G. Mandaville, "Reimagining the Umma?" in Ali Mohammadi (ed.), *Islam Encountering Globalization* (London: Routledge, 2002), pp. 61–90; idem, *Global Political Islam* (London: Routledge, 2007), pp. 312–331; Bryan S. Terner, "Religious Authority and the New Media," *Theory, Culture and Society* 24/2 (2007), pp. 117–134.

[4] On the institution of fatwas and its development in modern times, see M. K. Masud, B. Messick, and D. S. Powers, "Muftis, Fatwas and Islamic Legal Interpretation," in M. K. Masud, B. Messick, and D. S. Powers (eds.), *Islamic Legal Interpretation: Muftis and Their Fatwas* (Cambridge, MA: Harvard University Press, 1996), pp. 3–26; Jakob Skovgaard-Petersen, "Fatwas in Print," *Culture and History* 16 (1997), pp. 73–88; idem, "In Defence of Muhammad: 'Ulama', Da'iya and the New Islamic Internationalism," in Meir Hatina (ed.), *Guardians of Faith in Modern Times: 'Ulama' in the Middle East* (Leiden: Brill, 2008), pp. 291–309.

media made fatwas an effective means of projecting the 'ulama' authoritative stance on "suicide" attacks. Nevertheless, the position among Sunni
jurists was split: a situation stemming partly from the absence of a hierarchical and central religious authority, in contrast, for example, to the
much greater coherence of the Shi'i establishment, especially in Iran.
Another factor was the influence of environmental parameters on the
Sunni 'ulama' stance and their need to heed them – namely their governments' political agenda as well as public opinion in their countries.

The extensive body of religio-legal literature provides an opportunity to
trace the internal Islamic debate over the phenomenon of "suicide" attacks
and its affinity with power struggles for authority and state-related politics.
The scholarly debate centered on the religious legitimacy both of the self-
inflicted death of the perpetrator and the killing of civilians.

SACRED VIOLENCE

Advocates of "suicide" attacks perceived no dilemma in the use of such
violence, in as much as the struggle was against unbelievers, not Muslims.
Regarding the fear that such acts would be interpreted as suicide, they held
that the situation at hand was one of defensive jihad, which creates a sense
of urgency and necessity. In such a situation, all means are valid, including
"suicide" attacks. Such operations fulfill the two main requirements for
martyrdom, as stipulated in the legal literature: the test of intention,
namely to become a martyr in the service of the faith; and the test of the
result, namely causing damage to enemy forces. Moreover, as argued by
supportive 'ulama', such determinations are not the province of the perpetrator but rather of experienced persons with military and political knowledge in the perpetrator's sponsoring movement.[5]

The reality of living under infidels rule also minimized dilemmas regarding harming civilians, such as women, workers, farmers, and others, who
were depicted as contributing to the enemy's war effort by providing moral
or material support, especially because they were living on conquered
Muslim land. Children and infants, by comparison, were depicted as
exempt, and any harm to them was considered to be unintentional, akin
to collateral damage.

'Ulama' in high official positions played a key role on three main levels:
the canonization of "suicide" attacks in the Arab Muslim discourse as the
fulfillment of the ideal of jihad – that is, "walking in the path of God in

---

[5] See, e.g., the fatwa by the Saudi Shaykh Salman al-'Awda in *al-Sabil*, July 3–9, 2001, p. 18.

promoting good, justice and truth";[6] the enhancement of the religious dimension of ethno-national conflicts; and, thereby, the entrenchment of the 'ulama' status as exponents of Islam.

Seeking to reestablish their authority in regions such as Palestine, Chechnya, and Kashmir, 'ulama' in the Muslim world took advantage of the Islamist movements' need for religious sanction of the "suicide"-attack type of combat strategy to win over local public opinion. These movements demarcated Islam as the legitimate standard bearer of the struggle against infidel occupiers but failed to produce prestigious 'ulama' of their own, as had emerged in Cairo, Riyadh, Damascus, and Amman. Furthermore, their spokesmen were concerned that "suicide" attacks would be interpreted as an act of despair over the ongoing occupation and, as such, damage the attraction of Islam as a theology of liberation and as the only path to bring about the final victory. Outside religious sanction was therefore sought to legitimize the "suicide" phenomenon, a need that enhanced the prestige of the 'ulama'.

Fatwas that they issued provided the theological depth needed to legitimize "suicide" acts and sharpened the distinction between martyrdom in the battlefield – representing the epitome of faith in God – and forbidden suicide, meriting eternal damnation and torture in hell. According to Shaykh Ibrahim al-'Ali of Jordan, self-immolation reflects discontent with God's will, whereas martyrdom reflects an elevated transaction in which God buys the soul and the property of the believer, who thereby earns a place in paradise. The fact that, in the Palestinian case, the target was Israel provided diverse religious justifications for such attacks, on the basis of the depiction of Israel in modern Islamic historiography as an aggressive infidel entity threatening the sanctity of Islam and the Palestinian people. The struggle against Israel was presented as a defensive jihad that obligates the recruitment of every sound and healthy believer to join the campaign.[7]

---

[6] See an earlier stance by Shaykh al-Azhar 'Abd al-Halim Mahmud, *Fatawa*, Vol. 2, pp. 111–113.

[7] See, e.g., *Filastin al-Muslima*, October 1995, May 1996, September 1996; *al-Sabil*, March 18, 1996; *al-Ra'y al-'Amm* (Kuwait), July 31, 1997; *Fatawa 'ulama' al-Islam fi masa'il jihadiyya wa-hukm al-'amaliyyat al-istishhadiyya* (Beirut: Dar al-Wahda al-Islamiyya, 2002), pp. 25–41. Another eminent, albeit unaffiliated scholar, the exiled Egyptian Shaykh Yusuf al-Qaradawi in Qatar, referring specifically to the struggles in Palestine, Chechnya, and Kashmir, ruled that "a man's defense of his homeland, honor, people and religion is the highest level of jihad." In his view, Muslims living in *ribat* (border) regions function as guards of Islam who defend its frontiers against the attacks of unbelievers. The

In depicting the campaign in these contentious regions as a defensive jihad – in contrast to an offensive jihad that aims at expanding Islamic rule over territories inhabited by infidels – the 'ulama' underscored the issue of protecting Muslim territory and people or regaining occupied Muslim territory. The notion of a defensive jihad created a sense of existential urgency and, as such, was less subject to the normative rules of battlefield behavior outlined extensively in Islamic judicial literature (for example, rules regarding an armistice, the treatment of noncombatants, or the avoidance of an indiscriminate use of arms).

Relating "suicide" acts to the concept of jihad – which was identified primarily with the duty to reaffirm the superior morality of Islam – also facilitated a reliance on ancient legalist traditions that explicitly prioritized martyrdom over the sanctity of life. These traditions held that a fighter is permitted to attack enemy troops if his intent is to become a true martyr and if there is a chance that he will strike one of them. Otherwise, such an act is a forbidden suicide. Obviously, a fighter equipped with explosives would likely cause serious damage to the enemy, and consequently the suicide perpetrators easily fulfilled the requirements for martyrdom and entry into paradise. In this sense, no difference existed between someone who carried a rifle and someone who exploded himself.[8]

Advocates of "suicide" attacks thus posited two conditions that must be met by the perpetrators – the sincerity of the candidate's intention and the resulting damage caused to the enemy forces. Notably, the eminent Shaykh Yusuf al-Qaradawi, an unaffiliated scholar often depicted as the global mufti, was satisfied with the fulfillment of the first condition only, thereby reducing the requirement for the legitimacy of the act. In his view, even if the fighter does not expect to cause losses but seeks only to spread fear within the enemy ranks, his attack is not disqualified, as he benefits Muslims.[9]

more dangerous the frontier region, the more essential the presence there, which is preferable to rituals, including pilgrimages to Mecca and Medina, and deserves a higher reward in the next world. In this context, al-Qaradawi cited a hadith about Abu Hurayra (d. 676), one of the Prophet's friends, who, for the sake of God, preferred being in *ribat* than to be near the Ka'ba in Mecca on the night of al-Qadar, quoted in *Palestinian Time*, April 1996, p. 11. For al-Qaradawi's earlier stance, see *al-Liwa' al-Islami*, May 1977. See also Jalal al-Din al-Mahalli and Jalal al-Din al-Suyuti, *al-Qur'an al-karim* (Beirut: Dar al-Ma'rifa, 1983), p. 96.

[8] Kohlberg, "Martyrdom and Self-sacrifice in Classical Islam," p. 22; al-Ghazali, *Ihya' 'ulum al-din*, Vol. 2, p. 408; *Filastin al-Muslima*, October 1995.

[9] Al-Qaradawi, quoted in *Filastin al-Muslima*, September 1996. Al-Qaradawi relied on al-Qurtubi (d. 1272) and al-Shawkani (d. 1839). Muhammad ibn Ahmad al-Qurtubi, *al-Jami' li-ahkam al-Qur'an* (2nd ed., Cairo: Dar al-Sha'b, 1952–1953), Vol. 2, p. 363;

The large body of fatwas issued by 'ulama' in support of "suicide" attacks related essentially to the absence of any theological barrier to martyrdom in the cause of fighting the infidel. This was in stark contrast to the prohibition against internal Muslim strife (*fitna*), which had left a traumatic mark on early Islamic history. The 'ulama' took care, therefore, to position jihad and self-sacrifice in a proper historical and geographical context, namely as a struggle solely against an occupier, defined a priori as infidel, and not against Muslims or their rulers.

A detailed discussion of this issue was provided by Shaykh Salman al-'Awda of Saudi Arabia, who pointed out that one of the conditions for sanctioning the type of attacks under consideration is that they be aimed only against infidel countries that declared war against the Muslims or took over Muslim land, as in Palestine or Chechnya.[10] Pakistani 'ulama' also held this view, expressed in a fatwa published in 2005 denouncing the "suicide" attack phenomenon perpetrated against Muslims, and on Pakistani soil, rather than in Muslim regions under foreign occupation, such as Kashmir, Iraq, and Palestine.[11]

In contrast to the relatively restrained position of their Sunni colleagues, Shi'i 'ulama' in Tehran and Beirut displayed a more assertive stance, utilizing the "suicide" attacks to strike at the Arab regimes by projecting the attacks as demonstrating the fortitude of revolutionary Islam, which alone has the strength to put an end to regional disputes and perverse domestic politics.[12] The supportive approach toward "suicide" attacks in the Islamic religious discourse also undermined ecumenical efforts by senior Christian clerics in the Western world to form a unified religious front against "killing in the name of God," relegating these efforts to an intellectual exercise.[13]

In the Palestinian case, high-ranking 'ulama' also played a key role in the obstruction of normalization (*tatbi'*) with Israel in the wake of the Egyptian-Israeli peace accord in 1979, and even more so regarding the Palestinian-Israeli Oslo Accords in 1993. Some 'ulama' ruled that Muslims

---

Muhammad ibn 'Ali al-Shawkani, *Fath al-qadir: al-jami' bayna fannay al-riwaya wa'l-diraya min 'ilm al-tafsir* (Beirut: Dar al-Fikr, n.d.), Vol. 1, p. 193. A similar approach was adopted by 'Umar al-Ashkar, head of Shari'a Studies in the University of Jordan in Amman, in *al-Sabil*, July 3–9, 2001, p. 16.

[10] The fatwa is quoted in *al-Sabils* July 3–9, 2001. For the hadith, see al-Bukhari, *Sahih al-Bukhari*, Vol. 3, p. 1155.

[11] *The Hindu International* (online version), May 19, 2005.

[12] *Kiyan* (Tehran), March 11, 1996; *al-'Ahd* (Beirut), April 5, 1996; *Jomhuri-ye Islami* (Tehran), April 20, 1996; *Der Spiegel* (Hamburg), October 14, 1996.

[13] *Ha'aretz*, February 22, 2002.

who visited Israel or cooperated with it in the economic sphere risked exposure to hardship, disease, and even punishment on basis of the Islamic imperative to forbid wrongdoing. The fate of such a Muslim in the next world was portrayed as dire, as he would be subject to punishment for hypocrisy (*nifaq*), having betrayed Islam and violated the contract of solidarity with the nation of believers.[14] The enlistment of other opinion molders – both from the religious and the secular intelligentsia – in the anti-normalization campaign rendered the Israeli desire for not only political but also cultural inclusion in the region alien to the Arab collective consciousness.

The resolute stance of 'ulama' officials regarding the Arab-Israeli conflict, as well as their position regarding the broader issue of Islam in the public sphere, calls into question the scholarly narrative regarding the eroded status of the Sunni 'ulama' in modern times. These 'ulama' often found themselves between a rock and a hard place, forced to comply with the reformist policies of their regimes and, at the same time, reaffirming their loyalty to Islam under threat of degradation by the Islamist opposition. Still, they displayed considerable assertiveness on issues they perceived as vital in such areas as ensuring the superior position of the shari'a in matters of personal status, the maintaining of a visible Islamic presence in the public domain, and the reinforcement of local Arab opposition to integrating Israel into the regional milieu. In this sense, observations by Western commentators regarding the relegation of Sunni 'ulama' to the status of mere state preachers, or their diminished relevance to Islamic politics, are inaccurate and bear reexamination.[15]

PURE VIOLENCE

Other opinions in the scholarly religious community were critical of the perpetrators of "suicide" acts, denouncing them as bereft of faith in God and unfit for reward in paradise. These dissident voices, however, were drowned out by the outpouring of supportive declarations and fatwas and did not attain significant airing in public or in the scholarly discourse. Studying these critical views reveals a considerable degree of religious conviction and judicial restraint, as well as creative interpretation inspired by political considerations.

[14] See, e.g., *al-Sabil*, August 23, 1994; *Filastin al-Muslima*, October 1995.
[15] See, e.g., Meir Hatina, "Introduction," in idem (ed.), *Guardians of Faith in Modern Times*, pp. 1–21.

The counterarguments were diverse, ranging from emphasizing the moral and pacifistic nature of Islam, which prohibits the premeditated killing of any person, to the institutional nature of the jihad imperative, which requires the a priori presence of a caliph or military commander familiar with the rules of war and how to conduct it. Shaykh 'Abdallah Nimr Darwish, founder of the Islamic movement in Israel and its spiritual leader for many years, emphasized that in contrast to the militaristic image attributed to the Prophet Muhammad by 'ulama' who supported the jihad against Israel, the Prophet had engaged as much in political and social activity as in military campaigns. His goal was the establishment of a stable and harmonious society. In Darwish's view, the 'ulama', in expressing support of, or alternatively, remaining silent over, the "suicide" phenomenon, projected a message of death, distorting the image of Muslims and shaming them in the eyes of the world. These 'ulama', he said, must assemble immediately and adopt a political solution as the only option for settling the Arab-Israeli conflict. Other Arab 'ulama' in Israel backed Drawish's appeal, expressing concern over the increasingly fragile coexistence between Arabs and Jews in Israel.[16]

Denunciation was also voiced by Iranian 'ulama' exiled in Paris, such as Mahdi Ruhani, who was considered one of the leaders of the Shi'i population in Europe, and by Turkish 'ulama' under the leadership of the mufti of Istanbul, Salah al-Din al-Qiyya. Qiyya's rejection of Palestinian "suicide" acts carried out in early 1996 also reflected its domestic agenda in containing militant leftist groups and the Kurdish labor movement (the PKK), which also used the "suicide" weapon.[17]

Some 'ulama' did not share the vision of coexistence with Israel, yet opposed the current "suicide" trend. They glorified self-sacrifice for Islam as the pinnacle of jihad, exemplified by the individual who attacks the enemy and causes casualties and demoralization in its ranks, knowing that he will not be saved – as by sinking a ship or taking over a factory or a military camp. However, these 'ulama' rejected the specific type of warfare in which the perpetrator wears a belt of explosives and blows himself up, an act they defined as self-immolation and strictly forbidden in Islam.

An earlier voice in this respect was Shaykh Hasan Ayyub, a Lebanese jurist who served as mufti of Lebanon in the early 1970s. In the second

[16] Voice of Palestine (official radio station of the PA, broadcast from Jericho), March 4 and 6, 1996; *al-Mithaq* (Acre), November 21, 1997.
[17] *Ha'aretz*, March 6, 1996. However, the northern branch of the Arab Muslim Brethren in Israel, headed by Shaykh Ra'id Salah, displayed a more ambivalent stance. *Ha'aretz*, September 11, 2001, October 26, 2001.

edition of his well-known book, "Jihad and Sacrifice in Islam" (1983), Ayyub, apparently in response to "suicide" acts against Western and Israeli forces by Hizballah, ruled definitively that a person may expose himself to a situation in which he might be killed, but he may not kill himself on purpose.

Ayyub's point of departure was that the aim of war against enemies is to cause them damage until they surrender and accept Islam and Muslim rule. Every act by Muslims that leads to this goal is permissible and is even a Muslim duty. Acts of self-sacrifice, which by nature are extremely danger-ous, also fall into this category. The rule concerning the perpetrator is that he cannot expect to live but must carry out the act first and foremost with the intent to kill. This pertains as well to a lone perpetrator who faces a large enemy, which presents two possible situations: If the perpetrator knows that he will kill the person he attacks and he himself will be saved, the act is for the good. If he knows or assumes with high probability that he will be killed but will wreak damage or will otherwise bring about an advantage for Muslims, this act, too, is permitted. Ayyub cites as examples the sinking of a boat with enemies aboard, with the perpetrator among them; the take-over of a hotel with the aim of killing the fighters in it, knowing that he will be killed with them; and the of planting explosives in an army camp or army headquarters to wipe out whoever is there, with the knowledge that he will not survive.[18]

The *mujahid* in all these instances meets his death after causing serious losses to the enemy, killing, and destroying. This constitutes the height of sacrifice, for a man redeems his creed and his brothers with his soul. However, Ayyub points out, he is not permitted to wear an explosive belt to blow himself up together with those nearby. The difference is that in the first instance he kills his enemy and is killed in its wake. By contrast, in the second instance he kills himself first to kill his enemy. Conceivably, he might also fail to kill anyone else except himself. Ayyub's concern, therefore, is the fact not only that the death is pre-planned, but also that it embodies the possibility of the failure of the act, so that the perpetrator dies without causing damage to the enemy.[19]

Ayyub, who was known as a committed supporter of martyrdom, wrote a book about the subject in the early 1970s. In it he claimed that the nation's martyrs are viewed as the base of a building: the structure of the nation rests on their bodies, rising up until it proudly reaches the clouds. The martyrs are likened to souls who, when abandoned, render the body

[18] Ayyub, *al-Jihad wa'l-fida'iyya fi'l-Islam*, pp. 160–163.
[19] Ibid., pp. 163–164.

useless, yet their "pure red blood" is required all the more at present in light of the struggles of the Arab and Muslim world against imperialism and Zionism.[20] Ayyub devoted these words of praise to the fighters who were killed in circumstantial deaths as a result of jihad acts, but not to those who died in a premeditated death, such as in "suicide" attacks, in which case he considered them to be self-immolated in every respect.[21]

A similar line of thinking was later adopted in the 1990s by the Saudi-born Shaykh Muhammad ibn Salih ibn 'Uthaymin and the Albanian-born Muhammad Nasir al-Din al-Albani. Ibn 'Uthaymin quoted the hadith: "Whoever kills himself with an iron weapon will retain this weapon in his hand, thrusting it in his stomach in the fires of hell forever and ever."[22] Ibn 'Uthaymin and al-Albani did not rule out the possibility that a suicide might gain God's mercy if he had acted out of ignorance and had assumed that he was fulfilling the will of God. However, they pointed out that the prohibition of self-immolation is well known, and the ignorant can easily seek the council of knowledgeable persons, namely the 'ulama', to avoid committing a grave sin. He who avoids doing so seeks only blind revenge by any means, permissible or forbidden.

Not only did the two shaykhs forbid "suicide" acts, but also they prohibited all jihad acts against enemies if these were not preceded by an order from an emir, caliph, or military commander. "Is there an Islamic army fighting for God today?" al-Albani asked, and answered in the negative. In his view, a jihad based on shari'a orders with a commander who organizes the campaign and permits a certain individual to commit suicide to kill several unbelievers is permitted. This situation does not exist at present. Therefore, the gate must be closed until a climate is created that has a caliph, a commander who will carry out the orders of the caliph, and soldiers who will obey him.

For his part, Ibn 'Uthaymin pointed to the broad significance of the jihad perception, which also includes struggling with inner lusts, preaching for God, instructing the believer in the right path, and prohibiting indecency in the public sphere. Moreover, in a challenge to the lay radicals, he declared that implementing jihad without the individual, his mentors, or commanders acquiring proficiency in the Islamic injunctions is forbidden

---

[20] Ayyub, *al-Shahid fi'l-Islam*, pp. 137–141.

[21] Ayyub, *al-Jihad wa'l-fida'iyya fi'l-Islam*, pp. 163–164.

[22] This hadith is quoted in al-Bukhari, *al-Jami' al-Sahih*, Vol. 5, p. 72. See also al-Qurtubi, *al-Mufhim* (Cairo: Dar al-Kitab al-Misri, 1992), Vol. 1, pp. 291–311.

and thus will be of no use to them in the next world.[23] Such a person does not benefit Muslims either, for the killing of tens or hundreds of infidels will not bring their community to embrace Islam. On the contrary, they will become more embittered and determined to take revenge against the Muslims. Suffice to cite the brutal retaliation by the Jews in Palestine against the Palestinians for every suicide attack on their citizens. Ibn 'Uthaymin thus sanctified the welfare of the public (*maslaha*) on the basis of the judicial principle that preventing damage or harm is preferable to bringing about benefits.[24]

Criticism of "suicide" acts also emanated from religious circles close to the PA. This censure was colored by political antipathy for Hamas and the Islamic Jihad, which adopted an oppositionist stance to the PA's peace policy following the Oslo Accords. In 1996, Shaykh Majdi Hasan Badah of the Palestinian Ministry of Religious Endowments declared that war and martyrdom are not the essence of the life of the believer unless they are forced on him. Even then, before he can earn the title of *shahid*, his conduct must fulfill several conditions such as showing total loyalty to God and acting to benefit his community. Otherwise his act is self-immolation for the sake of succor from the hardships of life. Such conditions, Badah claimed, are not fulfilled in the current reality. On the contrary, he argued, the impulse for "suicide" acts is for the most part material and sectarian, aimed at gaining political advantage or covering up the organizational impotence of the Islamic movements. Moreover, the damage from such acts exceeds the benefit and detracts from the constructive work of the newly independent Palestinian entity.[25]

This critical attitude, however, was not shared by most Palestinian 'ulama', who ruled out conciliation with Israel despite the declared PA

---

[23] Takruri (ed.), *al-'Amaliyyat al-istishhadiyya*, pp. 85–86; *al-Sharq al-Awsat*, May 8, 2001; Muhammad ibn Salih ibn 'Uthaymin, *Sharh riyad al-salihin min kalam sayyid al-mursalin* (Riyadh: Madar al-Watan li'l-Nashr, 2005), Vol. 1, pp. 165–166; Vol. 3, pp. 344–359, 368, 376; also al-Albani's fatwas from the early 1990s in 'Ukasha 'Abd al-Mannan al-Tibi (ed.), *Fatawa al-Shaykh al-Albani* (Cairo: Maktabat al-Turath al-Islami, 1994), pp. 294–310.

[24] Ibn 'Uthaymin, *Sharh riyad al-salihin*, Vol. 1, pp. 165–166; also *al-Liwa' al-Islami*, September 30, 2010. On the doctrine of *maslaha* and the principle of harm versus benefits, see, e.g., Mustafa Zayd, *al-Maslaha fi'l-tashri' al-Islami* (2nd ed., Cairo: Dar al-Fikr al-Islami, 1964), pp. 17–61; Majid Khadduri, "Maslaha," *EI* VI (1991), pp. 738–740.

[25] Majdi Hasan Badah in *al-Bayan* (Gaza), April 1996, pp. 32–33, May 1996, pp. 32–34; Ahmad Yusuf in ibid., January 1996, pp. 9–11. Reservations were also voiced by the secretary-general of the Palestinian Islamic Front, Shaykh Salah 'Abd al-'Al, and several Hamas figures, including Shaykh Jamil Hamami of the West Bank, who stated that he does not have "anything good to say about the February-March suicide attacks." Voice of Palestine, March 3, 1996; *al-Bayan*, May 1996, pp. 50–51.

policy. Their stance revealed that their co-option into the bureaucratic structure of the PA was weak and only partial. Typically, the mufti of Jerusalem, 'Ikrima Sabri, praised the virtue of martyrdom, pointing to it as the key distinction between the Palestinian and the Israeli value systems. Israeli society, he observed, is "a selfish society that loves life. These are not people who are eager to die for their country and their God. The Jew will leave this land rather than die for it, but the Muslim is happy to die [for it]."[26] Sabri's colleague, 'Abd al-Salam Abu Shukhaydim, the mufti of the Palestinian security forces, described the seven rewards for such a Muslim, beginning with the purging of all his sins so that he suffers no torment in his grave, through the marriage to seventy dark-eyed virgins, and, finally, the guarantee of a place in heaven for seventy of his relatives.[27]

The religious polemic against "suicide" acts by a dissident minority of 'ulama' during the 1990s prompted a "war" of fatwas but did not gain momentum. Most of its spokesmen lacked the religious and moral prestige of their adversaries in the scholarly community and, as such, had little impact on the judicial discourse on the issue. This judicial inferiority was exacerbated in the Palestinian case by the eruption of the Second Intifada in September 2000. The intifada, with its emphasis on the sanctity of the al-Aqsa mosque, reinforced the historical narrative promoted by Hamas and the Islamic Jihad with regard to the nature of the struggle in Palestine as being religious and cultural rather than territorial. The violent events also forged areas of coalescence between the Islamist narrative and the national narrative of the PA on such loaded issues as Jerusalem, the refugee problem, and the settlements. Despite the pronounced asymmetry in power vis-à-vis Israel, the Palestinians succeeded in creating a certain deterrent balance during the intifada. Their main weapon for this was "suicide" attacks.

If the First Intifada (1987–1992) witnessed the canonization of civic resistance, the Second Intifada (2000–2004) witnessed the sanctification of "suicide" acts. The sharp increase in these attacks as part of the violent confrontation with Israel also resulted in an increase in the scale of Israeli fatalities and casualties, mainly of civilians.[28] This development

---

[26] Sabri's statement, dating back to 1988, quoted in the *New Yorker*, July 9, 2001, p. 36.

[27] Abu Shukhaydim, quoted in *al-Hayat al-Jadida* (Gaza), September 17, 1999; also Muhammad al-Asi, "The Struggle in the Holy Land," *Middle East Affairs Journal* 8/1–2 (2002), pp. 13–15.

[28] For statistics on the "suicide" phenomenon, see Joe Stork, *Erased in a Moment: Suicide Bombing Attacks against Israeli Civilians* (New York: Human Rights Watch, October 2002), pp. 150–152; Pape, *Dying to Win*, Appendix 1; *Ha'aretz*, September 29, 2002.

revealed the effectiveness of the "suicide" weapon, which, in the Palestinians' perception, placed their side on a more equal footing vis-à-vis Israel's conventional and sophisticated armaments, exposing Israel's Achilles' heel. Accordingly, Hamas leader 'Abd al-'Aziz al-Rantisi argued that this development signaled a "true revolution" in Palestinian history, positioning Hamas as "the ultimate defender of the homeland."[29] The Palestinian mythologization was aptly summarized by the British Palestinian academic and political activist 'Azzam Tamimi, who was also known as a Hamas sympathizer:

Do not call them suicide bombers; call them *shuhada'*, as they have not escaped the miseries of life. Life is sacred, but some things, like truth and justice, are more sacred than life. The *shuhada'* are not desperate, they are hopeful. . . . The al-Aqsa Intifada is horrendous, and there have been many casualties, but the Palestinians are not complaining. They are the victims, and they have the right to fight. The Israelis have guns, we have the human bomb. We love death, they love life. . . . Our history is made by blood and sweat.[30]

Although the primary factor responsible for turning "suicide" attacks into the ultimate Palestinian weapon was the Islamist movements, they were eventually joined by nationalist groups that were identified with the PA during the course of the al-Aqsa Intifada. The enlistment of these groups initiated a process of mass indoctrination that helped entrench the concept of martyrdom in the Palestinian collective memory as a symbol of strength.

The canonization of "suicide" attacks in the al-Aqsa Intifada, followed by Israeli military retaliations, captured the Arab imagination and evoked widespread praise for the Palestinian cult of death. The London-based *al-Quds al-'Arabi* wrote that "the culture of martyrdom has become acceptable and a model for imitation, just as the [throwing of] stones symbolized the previous Intifada."[31] Arab political elements, too, justified the Palestinian "suicide" acts, whether explicitly or implicitly, as a litmus test for support of the Palestinian cause. As a consequence, the Islamic judicial discourse on the issue constricted, with fewer critical voices fueling it.

---

[29] Al-Rantisi quoted in http://www.amin.org/views/abdulaziz_rantisi/2002/jun17.html (accessed September 7, 2011).

[30] For 'Azzam's full text, see http://www.aqsa.org.uk/activities/africa.html (accessed August 21, 2011); also quoted in *al-Quds al-'Arabi*, September 2, 2004; idem, *Hamas: A History from Within* (Northampton, MA: Olive Branch Press, 2007), pp. 171–186.

[31] *Al-Quds al-'Arabi*, April 1, 2002; also a manifesto by Sudanese 'ulama' in *al-Sunna* (Birmingham), May 2002.

A prominent exception was a statement by the mufti of Saudi Arabia, 'Abd al-'Aziz ibn 'Abdallah 'Al al-Shaykh, who in April 2001 ruled that although war against the enemy is obligatory and whoever shirks it should be put to death, it must be conducted only in ways determined by religious law. These do not include "suicide" acts, which constitute self-immolation per se or the hijacking of ships and airplanes whose passengers might be Muslims, protected subjects (*dhimmi*s), or protected foreign citizens (*musta'minin*). The mufti also denounced the practice of accusations of heresy against Muslim individuals and rulers ostensibly in the name of the Qur'anic imperative to "forbid wrongdoing." Whoever carries out such a mission must possess religious knowledge, the mufti argued. Some forbidden things can be removed by force, which is the province of political authorities, whereas others can be resolved by preaching, which offers a wide range of possibilities.

This analysis led him to the conclusion that both issues – military jihad and denouncing Muslims as apostates – are too sensitive to be left in the hands of laymen. In this, he defied the militant Islamists, whom he described as devoid of religious or moral authority and as motivated solely by alien considerations that lead to social anarchy.[32]

In renouncing the radicals, 'Al al-Shaykh was following a conservative tradition by such Saudi muftis as 'Abd al-'Aziz ibn Baz (d. 1999), who warned against distorting God's words, discrediting the authority of the 'ulama' as the "heirs of the Prophets," or revolting against legitimate rulers. In their view, the elimination of immoral phenomena in society must be accomplished only by spiritual and communal jihad through dialogue and reproof. Where enforcement was required, the only authorized bodies to do so were the government and the judiciary.[33]

Conceivably, the timing of this critical pronouncement (2001) by the Saudi mufti regarding "suicide" acts was not coincidental and was directed more at domestic Saudi affairs than at the Palestinian arena. The statement

---

[32] 'Al al-Shaykh's interview in *al-Sahrq al-Awsat*, April 21, 2001; also *al-Dustur*, April 22, 2001. For other statements by Saudi 'ulama', including the imam of the Grand Mosque of Mecca Muhammad al-Sabil, see *al-Sahrq al-Awsat*, May 5, 2001; *al-Hayat*, January 13, 2001; *al-Ahram Weekly*, December 13–19, 2001. On the Islamic stance toward musta'-minin, see Ibn Qayyim al-Jawziyya, *Kitab ahkam ahl al-dhimma* (Damascus: Matba'at Jami'at Dimashq, 1961), Vol. 1, p. 372.

[33] See, e.g., Muhammad bin 'Abd al-'Aziz al-Musnad (ed.), *Fatawa Islamiyya* (Riyadh: Dar al-Watan, 1994), Vol. 4, pp. 257–296; 'Ali ibn Husayn Abu Lawz (ed.), *Fitnat al-takfir* (Riyadh: Dar Ibn Khuzayma, 1997). See also ibn 'Uthaymin, *Sharh riyad al-salihin*, Vol. 2, p. 109.

was issued some time after the "suicide" attack against an American ship in the port of Aden in October 2000 and the hijacking of a Saudi plane flying from Jidda to London that same month. These and other acts were attributed to the al-Qaʿida network, whose opposition to the West and to the Saudi royal family had become increasingly violent.[34] Notably, in his statement, the Saudi mufti did sanction military jihad against an enemy who conquers Muslim territory and declared that a person who dies in defense of his property, his life, or his people is a martyr, blurring the significance of his pronouncement about "suicide" attacks against Israel to some extent. His statement in its entirety, nevertheless, gained wide coverage in the Arab and Western media and evoked angry responses within the ʿulamaʾ ranks. Most of them dismissed his ruling as religiously baseless, certainly with regard to the Palestinian case in which all means of fighting the Jews were viewed as legitimate.[35] Instead of exalting jihad, they charged, ʿulamaʾ in high offices busy themselves with matters they consider to be more important.[36] Others dismissed the status of the critical ʿulamaʾ as marginal and lacking public recognition in the Arab and Palestinian streets.[37]

Still other ʿulamaʾ, such as Yusuf al-Qaradawi, went further and questioned the integrity of the mufti's motivation for issuing such a controversial fatwa, in as much as he owed his eminent position to the Saudi royal family. According to al-Qaradawi, any jurist who rules against "suicide" attacks belongs to "those who are ignorant of religion and its laws."[38] A more prestigious counter-ruling was sought to refute that of the mufti in Mecca, one of the centers of religious scholarship in the Muslim world.

---

[34] Reuven Paz, "The Saudi Fatwah against Suicide Terrorism," *PeaceWatch*, no. 323, May 2, 2001, in: http://www.ict.org.il/Articles/tabid/66/Articlsid/63/currentpage/34/Default.aspx (accessed August 13, 2010); J. Teitelbaum, *Holier than Thou: Saudi Arabia's Islamic Opposition* (Washington: Washington Institute for Near East Policy, 2000), pp. 73–82; Kepel, *Jihad*, pp. 299–322.

[35] *Al-Quds al-ʿArabi*, April 24, 2001; *al-Hayat*, April 25, 2001; *al-Hayat al-Jadida*, April 27, 2001; *al-Sharq al-Awsat*, May 8, 2001; Voice of Palestine, May 25, 2001. For a more balanced attitude toward ʾAl al-Shaykh's statement, see *al-Sharq al-Awsat*, May 8, 2001. For the reaction by Hamas and Islamic Jihad, see *al-Hayat*, April 25, 2001; *Filastin al-Muslima*, May 2001; *New Yorker*, July 9, 2001, pp. 35–36.

[36] *Al-Quds al-ʿArabi*, April 24, 2001.

[37] *Al-Sabil*, July 3–9, 2001, p. 19.

[38] *Al-Sharq al-Awsat*, May 8, 2001; *al-Ahram Weekly*, December 13–19, 2001; *al-Quds al-ʿArabi*, April 24, 2001. On Qaradawi's stance toward Palestinian "suicide" acts, see *Filastin al-Muslima*, September 1996, pp. 50–51; *al-Istiqlal* (Gaza), August 20, 1999; *al-Ahram al-ʿArabi* (Cairo), February 3, 2001; *al-Raʾy* (Amman), April 25, 2001; *al Ahram Weekly*, December 13–19, 2001.

Such a counterweight was soon provided by the religious authorities in Cairo, a center of Islam whose status was no less distinguished.

The grand mufti of Egypt Nasir Farid al-Wasil declared in May 2001 that Palestinian "suicide" attacks constitute legitimate jihad aimed at putting an end to injustice, protecting the places sacred to Islam, and providing a suitable response to Israeli aggression. He called on all Arabs to assist the Palestinians with funding and weapons, and boycotting Israeli products, which he perceived as a jihadi act and a weapon of a just war. Should political and economic jihad fail, Wasil ruled, the solution is military jihad.[39] In the same vein, a group of 'ulama' from al-Azhar University, the bastion of orthodoxy in Egypt, stated in a signed manifesto that the jihad in Palestine is a personal obligation that encompasses children as well, even without their parents' permission.[40]

A more nuanced position was taken by the rector of al-Azhar, Muhammad Sayyid Tantawi (d. 2010), reflecting the dilemma of a religious scholar who had to maneuver between three elements: jurisprudence, public opinion, and the interests of his political patrons. Tantawi had a record of relative openness on such current public issues as improving the social status of women, allowing bank interest, and permitting organ transplants. He was also known for his ecumenical approach in promoting interfaith dialogue between Muslims, Christians, and Jews. From this perspective, he was more attuned to the government's national agenda than his predecessor, Jadd al-Haqq 'Ali Jadd al-Haqq.[41] His relative openness, however, angered many of his colleagues in al-Azhar and obliged him to walk a narrow intellectual line with regard to the issue of "suicide" attacks against Israel.

In various statements that gained the status of fatwas, Tantawi argued that the Palestinians' "suicide" attacks constitute self-defense against an enemy who kills their people and defiles their homeland and that the perpetrators of such acts are martyrs. This applies, however, so long as

---

[39] *Al-Shuruq* (Sharja), February 28, 2000; *Ha'aretz*, May 11, 2001. Wasil's successor as mufti of Egypt Ahmad al-Tayyib, was more restrained in his public statements, but he, too, supported Palestinian "suicide" acts. *Al-Liwa' al-Islami*, November 7, 2002; On boycott as a jihadi act, see Leor Halevi, "The Consumer Jihad: Boycott Fatwas and Nonviolent Resistance on the World Wide Web," *International Journal of Middle East Studies* 44 (2012), pp. 45–70.

[40] *Al-Hayat al-Jadida*, April 27, 2001.

[41] On Tantawi and his rulings, see Salim 'Abd al-Jalil, *al-Imam al-Akbar Muhammad Sayyid Tantawi: min Bani Salim ila al-Madina al-Munawara* (Cairo: Lajnat al-Buhuth, 2010); J. Skovgaard-Petersen, *Defining Islam for the Egyptian State* (Leiden: Brill, 1997), pp. 251–290.

the aim is to kill enemy fighters but not the weak among the enemy – women, children, and the aged – because such an act violates the commandments of Islam and of humanity at large.[42]

Tantawi's statements were perceived as reinforcing the ruling of the Saudi mufti and elicited bitter criticism by his rivals in Egypt and the Arab world. In turn, the religious debate that raged through fatwas and counter-fatwas prompted various commentators to try to neutralize the controversy by creative interpretation that would present a unified stance in support of "suicide" attacks in Palestine. One such figure was the Egyptian jurist Tawfiq al-Shawi, who argued that the negative position of the Saudi mufti referred to times of peace, which indeed prevailed in the Muslim countries far from Palestine. However, the mufti's adversaries referred to times of war, as in Palestine, where sacrifice for the homeland is a religious duty.[43]

The moral dilemma addressed by the Saudi mufti and the rector of al-Azhar involved not only the self-inflicted death of the perpetrator but also the death of innocent civilians as well. The mufti's and rector's stance was reinforced by several Arab intellectuals and public figures who called for a halt to attacks on civilians, which distort and debase the image of the struggle against the occupation.[44] A joint opinion published by some fifty-five Palestinian writers and public figures in June 2002 demanded an end to "suicide" attacks, as they could endanger the existence of the PA and its diplomatic achievements.[45] The well-known cultural critic and advocate for Palestinian rights Edward Said went a step further toward a more moralistic position, pointing out that "suicide" attacks dehumanize the Palestinian liberation cause. "All liberation movements in history have affirmed that their struggle is about life, not about death. Why should ours be an exception?" Said argued.[46]

---

[42] *Al-Hayat*, April 27, 2001; *Ruz al-Yusuf* (Cairo), May 18, 2001; *al-Liwa' al-Islami*, June 14, 2001; Tantawi's articles in *al-Ahram*, January 10 and 17, 2002, November 15, 2002. Apparently, severe criticism by his adversaries impelled Tantawi to adjust his attitude. In a later fatwa he retracted the immunity from attacking women and children in Israeli settlements, pointing to the difficulty in distinguishing between them and male fighters. *Ha'aretz*, March 22, 2002.

[43] Al-Shawi quoted in *al-Hayat*, April 27, 2001.

[44] *Al-Quds* (Jerusalem), June 20, 2002; *al-Watani* (Cairo), July 7, 2002.

[45] *Ha'aretz*, May 27, 2002, June 24, 2002; *al-Hayat al-Jadida*, April 23, 2001; Abu Amr quoted in the *New Yorker*, July 9, 2001, p. 36; *al-Ayyam* (Ramallah), October 1, 2004.

[46] Said quoted in *al-Ahram Weekly*, May 16–22, 2002; also al-Sarraj's interview in *Journal of Palestine Studies*, p. 74.

"Suicide" attacks also prompted liberal circles in the Arab world to widen their attack against their Islamic rivals and to promote a more general revision in the perception of Islam, presenting it as a cultural and ethical code rather than a judicial codex and a political theology. Liberals argued that the right to armed resistance is subject to limitations, and "suicide" attacks in Palestine, Chechnya, Kashmir, or Iraq, which were portrayed as jihad for God, simply represent an act of degeneracy. The "ritual of death" involves a distortion of the perception of the struggle and a cheapening of the sanctity of life. The liberals pointed an accusing finger primarily at religious officials who flood the public discourse with fatwas praising and defending the phenomenon or, alternatively, adopting an ambiguous position toward it.[47] In the opinion of one writer: "We are entitled to guidance from eminent 'ulama' in the darkness of this ordeal. The 'ulama' must not leave the long-suffering Muslims in confusion and perplexity."[48] More acutely, Shakir al-Nabulsi, a Jordanian liberal, demanded that the UN establish a court for acts of terror, where anyone who publishes quotations from the religious legal literature encouraging terror would be put on trial.[49]

Ultimately, the sensitive issue of civilians was placed on the Islamic public agenda and advocates of "suicide" acts were compelled to provide persuasive judicial support for their stance, as the notion of attacking civilians went to the heart of the message of Islam and became a primary issue of debate. On the doctrinal level, those 'ulama' who justified attacking civilians ruled that Islam prohibits killing civilians such as women, small children, the aged, the blind, farmers, and workers attending to their jobs. There are, however, two exceptional situations: when these civilians take part in war or assist it by incitement and the provision of material or moral assistance and when harming them is unavoidable because of the difficulty of distinguishing them from soldiers or when they serve as human shields against a Muslim attack.

On the practical level, the 'ulama' who supported the "suicide" phenomenon narrowed the category of immune civilians to babies, children, and the mentally unfit. Women, they pointed out, are capable of carrying arms and can be drafted in wartime. Furthermore, they corrupt the

---

[47] *Jedda Arab News*, November 5, 2001; *al-Watani*, July 7, 2002; *al-Sharq al-Awsat*, September 3, 2004; *al-Ra'i al-'Amm*, September 5, 2004; *al-Ayyam* (Bahrain), September 7, 2004; *al-Hayat*, February 1, 2007.

[48] *Al-Sharq al-Awsat*, October 4, 2001.

[49] Al-Elaph, September 3, 2004.

morality of young Muslims and estrange them from religion. The other groups, such as elders, farmers, and workers, inhabit land expropriated from Muslims and are prepared to defend it at all times.[50] Another judicial theme cited to justify harming civilians was the principle of reciprocity (*al-muʿamala biʾl-mithl*) dealt with in the Qurʾan (Sura 2: 194), which allows deviation from the rules of war when the aggressor deviates from them first. In this respect, for example, the Jews' crimes against the Palestinian people are brutal and well known to all, the ʿulamaʾ argued.[51] Some ʿulamaʾ used their adversaries' point of departure – the rejection of killing civilians – to justify such an act. Even if "suicide" attacks are evil, these ʿulamaʾ reasoned, they constitute a legitimate deviation from the shariʿa on the basis of the doctrine of necessity (*al-darura*) and all the more so in the case of a far worse evil as represented by infidel conquests of Muslim land. In assessing the two evils – "suicide" attacks and occupation – they found the first to be the lesser evil.[52]

AN ANTI-QAʿIDA CONSENSUS

"Suicide" operations in ethno-national conflicts were perceived by the broad center of the Islamic spectrum as outside the realm of internal Muslim strife (*fitna*) and, moreover, as targeting entities that throughout twentieth-century Islamic historiography were defined as inhabited by infidels and oppressors.[53] The loosening of religious restraints regarding the means of warfare in ethno-national conflicts contrasted with the overall condemnation of al-Qaʿida, which was depicted as a modern version of the Kharijites of early Islam and, thus, outside the consensus.[54]

The revelation of the involvement of Arabs – Saudis, Egyptians, Yemenis, and others – in planning and carrying out the September 11

---

[50] Takruri (ed.), *al-ʿAmaliyyat al-istishhadiyya*, pp. 16–17, 147–171; Qaradawi in *al-Raʾy*, April 25, 2001.

[51] *Al-Hayat*, April 25 and 27, 2001.

[52] *Al-Hayat*, April 27, 2001; Takruri, (ed.), *al-ʿAmaliyyat al-istishhadiyya*, pp. 127–128.

[53] *Majallat al-Azhar*, May–June 2002; *al-Hayat*, April 4, 2002.

[54] On the term Kharijites and its modern significance, see Wilfred Madelung, *Religious Trends in Early Islamic Iran* (Albany, NY: Bibliotheca Persica, 1988), pp. 54–76; Jeffery T. Kenney, *Muslim Rebels: Kharijites and the Politics of Extremism in Egypt* (Oxford: Oxford University Press, 2006), chapter 1; Hussam S. Timni, *Modern Intellectual Readings of the Kharijites* (New York: Peter Lang, 2008); Joas Wagemakers, "'Seceders' and 'Postponers'? An Analysis of the 'Khawarij' and 'Murjiʾa' Labels in Polemical Debates between Quietist and Jihadi-Salafis," in Jeevan Deol and Zaheer Kazmi (eds.), *Contextualising Jihadi Thought* (New York: Columbia University Press, 2011), pp. 145–164.

attacks prompted the 'ulama' to firmly denounce bin Laden's acts as criminal (*'amaliyyat ijramiyya*), violating Islamic morality and conducted against noncombatants. Two main foci of denunciation were Cairo and Riyadh, venues that also contended with militant attacks on their soil. Both al-Azhar and the Saudi *madrasa*s, which had been religious rivals over time, especially during the Nasserist era, found themselves on the same front vis-à-vis al-Qaʿida, which, inter alia, posed a challenge to the widespread *daʿwa* (communal) networks operating throughout the Muslim and the Western worlds.

The religious establishment feared the tarnishing of Islam by extremism and violence. It also felt impelled to show conformity with the condemnation of the attacks by the Arab regimes, given the deteriorating image of the Arab countries in Western public opinion.[55] Thus, Shaykh al-Azhar Tantawi and the Saudi Mufti Al al-Shaykh depicted the al-Qaʿida perpetrators as despised terrorists, although they urged Washington not to accuse any party without evidence.[56] Their spokesmen pointed to the fact that the attacks were carried out in non-Muslim territory, which belied bin Laden's claim that they were part of defensive jihad. Moreover, they emphasized, permission to take the life of an individual or a group can be granted only by religious leaders and authorized officials.[57]

Other 'ulama', including in Europe and the United States, took on the responsibility of clarifying the distinction between self-sacrifice and suicide to the younger generation – al-Qaʿida's favored target audience – leaving no doubt that the latter category must be applied to al-Qaʿida followers, who traded their religious faith for political and national interests or to gain mass media exposure.[58] The true meaning of jihad, these 'ulama' explained, is to spread the values of tolerance and stability, which expose bin Laden and al-Qaʿida as nothing more than "a web of fanatics" who will be subject to the gravest likelihood of eternal punishment after death. In their view, al-Qaʿida's atrocities violated the ethics of battle spelled out

---

[55] The Saudi clerics were prominent in such condemnation, in view of Saudi citizenship held by 15 of the 19 perpetrators of the September 11 attacks. *Paris Le Monde*, October 5, 2001; *al-Hayat*, September 15, 16, 18, and 20, 2001; *al-Musawwar* (Cairo), September 21, 2001; *al-Sharq al-Awsat*, October 19, 2001; *New York Times*, September 30, 2001.

[56] *Al-Hayat*, September 15, 16, and 18, 2001; *al-Quds al-ʿArabi*, October 19, 2001; Mena (Egyptian News Agency), September 25, 2001.

[57] *Al-Hayat*, January 13, 2002; also Muhammad al-Atawneh, "Shahada versus Terror in Contemporary Islamic Legal Thought: The Problem of Suicide Bombers," *Journal of Islamic Law and Culture* 10/1 (April 2008), pp. 26–27.

[58] *Al-Sharq al-Awsat*, May 8, 2001, June 29, 2006.

by the Prophet Muhammad, which renounces any deliberate violence outside the context of organized warfare based on self-defense.[59] Some even urged the Islamic government in Kabul to extradite bin Laden to the United States so as to prevent a graver evil – namely a destructive war against the Afghan people.[60]

Al-Qaʻida elicited sharp criticism from the Muslim Brethren as well, particularly in Egypt, where the Brethren rejected al-Qaʻida's ideology out of hand as contentious, distorted, and fomenting factionalism among the believers. By contrast, the Brethren underscored the virtues of *daʻwa* – preaching, education, and persuasion – which alone, in their view, could widen the influence of Islam, especially through the Muslim communities in the West. The Brethren depicted *daʻwa* as the key to their resilience and prolonged survival, thereby providing an indicator of the marginality of their rivals.[61]

A significant reinforcement of the viability of the Brethren's evolutionary strategy and their ability to make inroads in civil society was demonstrated during the Arab Spring of 2011 when they promoted a demand for political and democratic freedom, while proving their status as the best organized of the oppositionist movements. An indisputable indication of this was provided by the electoral parliamentary victories of the Egyptian Brethren in 2011–2012 and of the Nahda (Revival) movement in Tunisia in October 2011. In demonstrating the existence of a strong civil presence, the Brethren, along with other communal movements, sought to expose al-Qaʻida as a purely military organization without popular support, which nevertheless insisted on projecting itself as speaking for all Muslims.

Shiʻi clerics also denounced al-Qaʻida's martyrdom. Significantly, the spiritual mentor of Hizballah in Lebanon, Muhammad Husayn Fadlallah,

---

[59] *Al-Hayat*, September 17 and 18, 2001; *New York Times*, September 30, 2001; Jedda Arab News, October 29, 2001; ul-Qadri, *Fatwa on Terrorism and Suicide Bombings*. See also Brigitte Maréchal, *The Muslim Brothers in Europe: Roots and Discourse* (Leiden: Brill, 2008), pp. 220–221.

[60] In this the ʻulamaʼ were reacting to a fatwa issued by the Afghan ʻulamaʼ council that prohibited the forced extradition of bin Laden, urging him to leave only "at the time he chooses." This fatwa was depicted as issued by "students who did not complete their studies in jurisprudence." *Al-Hayat*, September 21, 2001; *al-Sharq al-Awsat*, October 9, 2001.

[61] See, e.g., *al-Mukhtar al-Islami* (October 24, 2006); Jean-Piere Filiu, "The Brotherhood vs. Al-Qadeda: A Moment of Truth?" *Current Trends in Islamist Ideology* 9 (November 12, 2009). http://www.currenttrends.org/research/detail/the-brotherhood-vs-al-qaeda-a-moment-of-truth (accessed January 10, 2011).

rejected the religious legitimation of the September 11 attacks, noting that even if the perpetrators had good intentions, the method was mistaken and contradicted Islamic doctrine. It cannot be considered as jihad and self-sacrifice, he explained, for two reasons: a moral one, relating to the killing of civilians who had no link to the American government or its foreign policy and, more importantly, damaging Muslim interests throughout the world. The September 11 attacks provided the United States with an opportunity, in the name of a war against terrorism, to destroy every movement that opposes American policy in the region. The world was thereby wide open to America, which seeks to subvert the world to its rule, Fadlallah declared.[62]

Although some who denounced al-Qaʻida found themselves in a dilemma in light of the American occupation of Afghanistan and Iraq, and censured Western aggression, this did not blur their negative stance against al-Qaʻida.[63] Only a small number of ʻulamaʼ justified the organization's violent acts.[64] Prominent among them were Saudi clerics, led by Hammud ibn ʻUqala al-Shuʻaybi, who defended the September 11 attacks and labeled the United States an infidel state that threatens Islam. They pressed the Muslim public not to assist in turning in al-Qaʻida activists, and to help their brothers in the Taliban movement in Afghanistan.[65] Several ʻulamaʼ, led by Salman al-ʻAwda, were arrested by the Saudi authorities and, in the wake of al-Qaʻida attacks in Riyadh in May and November 2003, disassociated themselves publicly from their support of the organization. Their main argument was that these were attacks against Muslims and members of other religions in Muslim-ruled countries – attacks that border on anarchy, which is forbidden by Islam.[66]

Anarchy and loss of control were also the themes dealt with by the Jordanian Abu Muhammad al-Maqdisi, considered the ideological mentor of Abu Musʻab al-Zarqawi, leader of al-Qaʻida in Iraq.[67] Al-Maqdisi, however, disassociated himself from the organization's indiscriminate

---

[62] Fadlallah's interview in *Journal of Palestinian Studies*, 31/2 (Winter 2002), pp. 78–84.

[63] *Islamabad News*, November 5, 2001.

[64] See, e.g., *al-Hayat*, September 20, 2001

[65] *Al-Quds al-ʻArabi*, October 18, 2001.

[66] On these ʻulamaʼ, who belonged to the *sahwa* (awakening) movement in Saudi Arabia, and their revised stance toward al-Qaʻida, see Hegghammer, *Jihad in Saudi Arabia*, pp. 147–155; Madawi al-Rasheed, *Contesting the Saudi State* (New York: Cambridge University Press, 2007), pp. 59–101; Stephane Lacroix, *Awakening Islam: The Politics of Religious Dissent in Contemporary Saudi Arabia* (Cambridge, MA: Harvard University Press, 2011), Chapters 2 and 3.

[67] Wagemakers, *A Quietist Jihadi*.

attacks against civilians and against Shi'is in Iraq, defining these acts as contrary to the Shari'a and as transforming their perpetrators into neo-*Kharijites*. In an essay he published in 2004, republished in an expanded version in 2007, titled *Waqafat ma'a thamarat al-jihad* ("Positions on the Fruits of Jihad"), al-Maqdisi sought to curb the "suicide" attack phenomenon, along with the religious pretentiousness of its lay dispatchers in ruling on jihad matters. In his view, the "suicide" weapon may be used only when there is an acutely clear and necessary interest and when an unbeliever or a group of unbelievers cannot be killed with a pistol or rifle.[68]

Al-Maqdisi was concerned not with the question of whether the act was suicide or self-sacrifice, or whether killing enemy civilians was or was not justified – although he commented elsewhere that attacking people praying in church, elderly tourists, or representatives of international aid organizations does not serve the interests of Islam.[69] More important to him, as to the Saudi Salafi scholars, was the issue of attacking innocent Muslims who were present in the area of the attack – in the street, the marketplace, the plaza, or the vicinity of a foreign embassy where an explosive car could be positioned. Enemy targets were no longer pinpointed and the attacks had shifted to the Muslim public space, he charged, sometimes missing the enemy entirely.

The blood of Muslims is holy in Islam, al-Maqdisi pointed out – even that of wayward Muslims – and eschewing the killing of a thousand unbelievers is preferable to spilling the blood of one believer. Moreover, such bloodletting only detracts from public support for the *mujahidun* and eases the non-Muslim aggressors' efforts to take control, as proven by the Iraqi case. Al-Maqdisi ascribed the anarchy in the use of "suicide" attacks to social and intellectual emptiness and the unrestrained fervor of youngsters who have not bothered to deepen their religious knowledge regarding jihad under the tutelage of accredited 'ulama' and have not considered the results of their acts in terms of the welfare of Muslims. Positing an antithesis for these young people, al-Maqdisi analyzed the perpetrators of the September 11 attacks as characterized not by courage or self-sacrifice but by self-restraint, group work, and careful preparation during the attacks. In this he sought to illuminate the lesser intellectual as well as military

---

[68] Abu Muhammad al-Maqdisi, *Waqafat ma'a thamarat al-jihad: bayna al-jahl fi'l-shar' wa'l-jahl bi'l-waqi'* (http://www.tawhed.ws or http://www.almaqdese.net; 2004, expanded edition, 2007), pp. 2–9 (accessed June 10, 2010).

[69] Ibid., pp. 7–8.

quality of the contemporary al-Qaʿida activists and to rechannel their fervor along more constructive lines.[70]

Another ideologue, Sayyid Imam al-Sharif (also known as ʿAbd al-Qadir ibn ʿAbd al-ʿAziz or Dr. Fadl), a former leader of the Egyptian Jihad who was extradited from Yemen to Egypt in 2005 and imprisoned there, went a step further. Whereas his published work from the 1980s and early 1990s served as a source of inspiration for radical Islam, including al-Qaʿida, reflecting his view that jihad is a constant state and self-sacrifice is the ultimate religious act, his written work from the late 1990s shows a complete disassociation from acts of violence, including "suicide" attacks. In his later view, an important condition before attempting jihad is the ability to carry it out and to attain a victory for religion. In as much as the current state of the Islamic faithful is poor, he wrote, ranging from paralysis (ʿajz) to weakness and suppression (istidhʿaf), the option of jihad and victory is nil. Moreover, the Qurʾan provides a variety of possibilities for action aside from jihad, depending on the variable abilities of the believer: concealing faith, withdrawing and emigrating, or censuring verbally and by acts.

Al-Sharif thus finds proof that God and his Prophet praise prudent warfare rather than blind confrontation, which can cause more harm than benefit to the believers. In vetoing jihad in the present circumstances, al-Sharif also vetoes self-sacrifice, which in his view has become inflated to unprecedented proportions as a result of al-Qaʿida's strategy and sows the killing of innocents. Entering non-Muslim countries legally, he points out,

---

[70] Ibid., pp. 19–20, 30, 49, 106. Notably, Nelly Lahoud argues that al-Maqdisi's criticism of al-Qaʿida's modes of warfare was not the result of moderation or inner conviction but of his desire to get a more lenient prison sentence from the Jordanian authorities. Moreover, other writings of al-Maqdisi, which did not gain much media exposure, reveal his ongoing rigid and extreme views. Joas Wagemakers also raises doubts about al-Maqdisi's revisionist stance regarding violent jihad activity, arguing that his critique aimed at gaining greater scholarly control of a trend that in his view had become the prerogative of warriors rather than scholars. Lahoud, "In Search of Philosopher-Jihadis: Abu Muhammad al-Maqdisi's Jihadi Philosophy," *Totalitarian Movements and Political Religions* 10/2 (June 2009), pp. 205–220; Wagemakers, "Reclaiming Scholarly Authority: Abu Muhammad al-Maqdisi's Critique of Jihadi Practices," *Studies in Conflict and Terrorism* 34/7 (2011), pp. 523–539. Whatever al-Maqdisi's motives were, no less important was the fact that his critical stance was made public and gained wide attention, thereby reinforcing internal tension in the Salafi Jihad camp regarding the best strategy to adopt while providing a convenient tool for rival high-ranking ʿulamaʾ as well as the Muslim Brethren, who opposed global jihad.

is perceived by Islam as a contractual connection that forbids harming the subjects of those countries, whether military personnel or civilians, as is the case in airplanes, hotels, and so forth.[71]

Such internal cracks in al-Qaʿida's ranks during the 2000s embarrassed its leaders, prompting them, in contrast to the past, to defend the legitimacy of acts aimed at all venues with an American presence, especially an imposed presence as in Iraq, or by agreement as in Saudi Arabia, which, in al-Qaʿida's view, turned the rulers there into unbelievers. Al-Qaʿida's legal justifications for the attacks were accompanied by scorn for the religious credentials of the critical Salafi scholars, including al-Maqdisi, for contenting themselves with textual rhetoric and not taking action. Only those who participate physically on the battlefield can claim authority and even immunity regarding jihad, al-Qaʿida declared. In the same vein, the organization sought to revise the hadith, "The ink of scholars will outweigh the blood of martyrs on Judgment Day," by positioning the martyrs as preferred. In this, al-Qaʿida went beyond ʿAbdallah ʿAzzam, an *ʿalim* by training, who demanded that religious study be integrated with the jihad act, blending the ink of the pen with the blood of the martyrs.[72]

Increasingly, al-Qaʿida's dispute with its rivals turned the issue of religious authority into a lawless arena. Sunni criticism merged with a more general defiance of al-Qaʿida, a challenging rival in the Islamic arena. Reformists and radicals alike accused al-Qaʿida of tarnishing Islam in the eyes of outsiders, who branded it as a religion of extremism and indiscriminate killing, exposing Muslim communities in the West to hostile acts and restrictions and weakening the ability of the faithful to face the challenges of modernity.[73]

One writer depicted the dilemma faced by Muslim society concisely: "We have no other option: either we'll be modern, or we'll not be at

---

[71] Sayyid Imam al-Sharif, *Wathiqat tarshid al-ʿamal al-jihadi fi Misr waʾl-ʿalam*, available at http://www.e-prism.org/images/TARSHID_AL-JIHAD.pdf (accessed January 8, 2011); also Simon Wolfgang Fuchs, *Proper Signposts for the Camp* (Wurzburg: Ergon Verlag, 2011); Daniel Lav, "Jihadists and Jurisprudents: The 'Revisions' Literature of Sayyid Imam and Al-Gamaʾa Al-Islamiyya," in Joseph Morrison Skelly (ed.), *Political Islam from Muhammad to Ahmadinejad* (Santa Barbara, CA: Praeger Security International, 2010), pp. 105–146.

[72] See Chapter 5, note 15; Jarar, *al-Shahid ʿAbdallah ʿAzzam*, p. 141; also ʿAzzam, "What Jihad Taught Me," in Ibrahim Abu Rabiʿ (ed.), *The Contemporary Arab Reader on Political Islam* (London: Pluto Press, 2010), p. 45.

[73] *Jedda Arab News*, October 29, 2001; *Le Monde diplomatique* (Paris), November 2001.

all."[74] In the same vein, a Pakistani writer, in an open letter to bin Laden in November 2001, concluded: "The last thing Muslims need is the growing darkness in your caves. ... True jihad today is not in the hijacking of planes, but in the manufacturing of them."[75] Additional ammunition for such criticism was provided by a series of "suicide" incidents in Muslim countries such as Saudi Arabia (mid-2003) and primarily in Iraq in the wake of attacks against Shi'i Muslims there and the intensification of hostility between Sunnis and Shi'is.

Twenty-six Saudi religious leaders signed a manifesto addressed to the Iraqi people in August 2004, declaring that opposition to the American forces in Iraq is the personal responsibility of every Muslim, with the goal of liberating the land. However, at the same time, the manifesto laid down theological and legal parameters for the moral behavior of the Muslim fighters, forbidding the taking of prisoners or attacking non-fighters and persons who do not display animosity, for example, journalists or persons who perform humanitarian or any other type of tasks that are totally unrelated to the American war effort. To support this, the 'ulama' cited the Qur'anic verse, "Fight in God's cause against those who fight you, but do not overstep the limits: God does not love those who overstep the limits" (Sura 2: 190), and the hadith which states that the Prophet did not kill the hypocrites (*munafiqun*) so that "people will not say that Muhammad murders his friends." If the Prophet himself teaches to let alone someone who in principle deserves death, it is all the more incumbent on everyone to behave so.[76]

This military ethic was aimed primarily at al-Qa'ida, which was described as a fifth column in the service of imperialism and Zionism, attacking Islam and its believers by acts that appear as resistance but are actually a distortion of it. The organization, the manifesto declared, also threatens to tear apart the delicate social fabric in Iraq by encouraging religious animosity, when what is required is a united front to eject the occupation and build a unified state.[77] The attack against Muslim believers, several of the critical 'ulama' charged, is a grave crime and a declaration of war against God, for He viewed them as supreme in status,

---

[74] *Al-Hayat*, January 13, 2002; also *al-Ayyam* (Bahrain), August 17, 2004.

[75] Quoted in Thomas Friedman, *Longitudes and Attitudes: Exploring the World after September 2001* (New York: Farrar, 2002), p. 105.

[76] The manifesto was published August 11, 2004 and reprinted in *al-Wai'*, no. 215 (Beirut), pp. 6–9. For the cited hadith, see Muslim, *Sahih Muslim*, Vol. 4, p. 1998.

[77] Ibid.

as can be learned from the hadith: "God deems the perishing of the entire world as less severe than the killing of one Muslim."[78]

Reacting, al-Qaʿida highlighted American aggression in Iraq and the degradation of the local population, including the destruction of mosques, the masses of bodies lying in the streets, and the violent interrogations, as well as the corruption of the Iraqi government, which functions as a puppet of the infidel conquest. In al-Qaʿida's narrative, faith and self-sacrifice are the solution to this sick reality. The martyrs were projected as pure in their faith and their path, as redeemers of the state and the land and as avengers of the acts of the West.

Eventually, the dispute engendered fissures between the organization's leaders and their representatives in Iraq. In a letter from Ayman al-Zawahiri to Abu Musʿab al-Zarqawi in July 2005, al-Zawahiri thanks al-Zarqawi for bringing the campaign to the heart of the Muslim world and asserts that al-Qaʿida will never rest until an Islamic state is established in the heart of the Islamic world, especially in the Levant, Egypt, the Arabian Peninsula, and Iraq. The support for local struggles in Afghanistan, Bosnia, Chechnya, and Kashmir, he stated, constitute merely the establishment of a base for the forthcoming struggle for the heart of the Islamic world. In this context, Zawahiri emphasized that the jihad fighters in Iraq are more exalted than those in Egypt or Syria, as their primary mission is to establish an Islamic emirate in Iraq that will gradually spread out and lead to widening the jihad circle to include all of Iraq's neighbors. Meanwhile, al-Zarqawi's task was to establish an Islamic theocracy, protect it, and preserve it forever rather than to simply defeat the American forces. The strongest weapon that the *mujahidun* have is the popular support of the Muslim population in Iraq and its neighboring countries, al-Zawahari stressed.

Focusing on the issue of popular support, al-Zawahiri emphasized to al-Zarqawi that victory will not be achieved without such support, even if apostate rulers should suddenly be brought down, as this will not happen without public dissatisfaction. Popular support is the parameter that separates victory from defeat. Without popular support, the struggle between al-Qaʿida and the state authorities will be limited to prison cellars far from the public eye. This is exactly what the secular

---

[78] See, e.g., Shaykh al-Azhar ʿAli Gumʿa, quoted in *al-Liwaʾ al-Islami*, September 30, 2010. The hadith is quoted in Ahmad ibn Shuʿayb al-Nasaʾi, *al-Sunan al-kubraʾ* (Beirut: Muʾassasat al-Risala, 2001), Vol. 3, p. 417.

regimes wish for. They do not want to destroy al-Qaʿida but rather to distance it from the frightened, unguided masses. Thus, the organization cannot rest on power alone; it must act to recruit the general public in its struggle to embrace the fighters. The Muslim population will not rally around the jihad flag unless it is aimed at the foreign occupation, whether Jewish or American. In this al-Zawahiri voiced his opposition to the harsh policy adopted by al-Zarqawi in Iraq, including cruel public executions of prisoners, besmirching the reputations of influential senior Sunni ʿulamaʾ, and damaging Shiʿi ritual sites and holy places. These acts, al-Zawahiri asserted, detracted from Iraqi Sunni support for al-Qaʿida and from speeding up the withdrawal of American forces.[79]

The specific dilemma revealed by al-Zawahiri regarding the type of struggle waged by al-Qaʿida in Iraq became more acute in the wake of the Arab Spring of 2011. These events posed the option of nonviolent civil uprisings in the Middle East, bringing down authoritarian regimes in Tunisia, Egypt, and Libya and forcing the revolutionary style of al-Qaʿida's adherents into a state of distress. By contrast, the long-term evolutionary strategy of communal and legal effort from top down, led primarily by the Muslim Brethren, was the main beneficiary of the Arab revolutions.

The Brethren, as well as official ʿulamaʾ and other Islamic bodies, rejected al-Qaʿida's sweeping goal of global jihad against the United States and the West. Notably, their polemic revealed how anachronistic the ethos of universal jihad against the world of the infidels had become in modern Islamic thought. It had been replaced by an acceptance of the post–World War I political order and a shift of emphasis to the struggle over the moral image of the territorial polity. Al-Qaʿida itself experienced a decline in its organizational and public status, especially in light of its absence from the central arena of the Arab Spring and the killing of its revered leader, Osama bin Laden, in June 2011. Some researchers, such as Fawaz Gerges, went so far as to assert that al-Qaʿida had ended its historic role and had vanished.[80]

However, denouncing jihad against the great Satan – America – did not mean disengaging from jihad against the little Satans – Israel, in the

---

[79] These statements were taken from a letter sent by al-Zawahiri to al-Zarqawi in October 2005 and appear at https://www.fas.org/irp/news/2005/10/letter_in_arabic.pdf (accessed February 15, 2012). See also Mansfield, *His Own Words*, pp. 208–209.

[80] Fawaz A. Gerges, *The Rise and Fall of al-Qaeda* (Oxford: Oxford University Press, 2011), mainly pp. 3–28, 104–126, 192–214.

case of the Palestinians, and Russia, in the case of the Chechens. Those states and others, such as India, in the Kashmir arena,[81] continued to dominate the Islamic discourse, and the jihad against them was crowned in heroic terms as a struggle of the deprived against an oppressive enemy.[82]

[81] On the Kashmiri jihad, although not quite endorsing "suicide" attacks, see, e.g., Šumit Ganguly, *The Crisis in Kashmir* (Cambridge: Cambridge University Press, 1997), pp. xiii–xiv, 20–42; Michael T. Rinder, *The Evolution of Religion Nationalism in Pakistan: Islamic Identity, Ideology and State Power* (PhD dissertation; Cambridge, MA: Harvard University, 2007), mainly pp. 238–259; Stephen Tankel, *Storming the World Stage: The Story of Lashkar-e-Taiba* (London: C. Hurst, 2010).
[82] See also the resolutions adopted by the Organization of Islamic Conference (OIC), Kuala Lumpur, Malaysia, April 1–3, 2002, in *al-Hayat*, September 18, 2001, April 4, 2002; *New York Times*, September 30, 2001; al-Qaradawi quoted in *al-Aharm al-ʿArabi*, October 26, 2002.

8

Approaching "Suicide" Attacks

A COMPARATIVE HISTORICAL PERSPECTIVE

Self-destruction for ideological or political reasons is not a new phenomenon. It can be found in the ancient Japanese culture of warfare in which the samurai fighter who faced loss or defeat in war killed himself by disembowelment for the sake of an honorable death. In a modern version of the samurai legacy, kamikaze (literally: divine winds) Japanese fighter pilots – mostly students whose recruitment had been deferred and who were called up to defend their country – died by crashing their aircraft into American targets in the Pacific Ocean at the end of World War II.[1] The term "divine winds" was the name given to a typhoon that destroyed the Mongolian navy during an attempt to invade Japan in the thirteenth century.

Kamikaze epitomized the pinnacle of religious and nationalistic indoctrination stressing duty to nation and emperor and was introduced in the Japanese education system at the start of the twentieth century. Some 200 air sorties were carried out by kamikaze pilots during the war causing the destruction of approximately 35 American ships and the death of more than 4,900 sailors. The implementation of kamikaze created a new paradigm of behavior in modern warfare when facing the realization that the war is lost: organized offensive suicide. Those chosen to serve as human bombs were imbued with the sense that they were the last defense and the

---

[1] Dennis Warner, *The Sacred Warriors: Japan's Suicide Legions* (New York: Van Nostrand Reinhold Co., 1982).

last hope of saving the nation from a life of degradation, suffering, and perpetual danger that could barely be called living.

Idealism, patriotism, and a sense of responsibility for the fate of the Japanese homeland and society stemmed in part from the overall ethos nurtured in high schools and universities – the source from which most of the pilots were drafted. They were convinced that they were the shields of their nation and the bearers of the historic legacy of the ancient warriors. Still others were impelled by group pressure – unable to remain aloof when their friends and comrades stepped forward and offered their lives.[2] Part of the kamikaze indoctrination included rewards. One of the Japanese military commanders was quoted as declaring, "Having stepped up to the task, you have all become young gods with no earthly desires." A successful mission in which no member returned invoked honor, whereas a failed mission in the form of fliers who returned to the home base was branded with shame.[3]

Viewed comparatively, several similarities between the Japanese kamikaze and the Muslim "suicide" bombers seem evident, including the reliance on traditional imperatives, a sense of conviction and idealism, and the human profile of the recruits: young students, mainly unmarried, with no children. Moreover, in both cases the "suicide" mission was held in esteem by the community and was commemorated in the public sphere.[4] Nevertheless, the kamikaze category differs from the category of "suicide" attackers in that the perpetrators were army soldiers who attacked military rather than civilian targets – a differentiation that was blurred in the research literature of the 1990s. For example, David Sears, a military scholar, referred to the kamikaze by the contemporary term "suicide bombers," making a connection between the al-Qaʻida attack against the American *Cole* flotilla off Yemen in 2000 and the kamikaze attacks on the seaplane base at *Kerama Retto* in 1944–1945. Raphael Israeli, a Middle East scholar, posited a close identification between the Japanese and the Islamic phenomena, coining the term "Islamikaza."[5]

---

[2] Emiko Ohnuki-Tierney, *Kamikaze, Cherry Blossoms and Nationalisms* (Chicago: University of Chicago Press, 2002), pp. 157–175; for the world view of some of the pilots, see ibid. Chapter 6; also Merari, *Driven to Death*, pp. 265–266.

[3] David Sears, *At War with the Wind: The Epic Struggle with Japan's World War II Suicide Bombers* (New York: Citadel, 2008), pp. 139, 145–146, 152.

[4] However, in both cases, voices of criticism and protest by family members, friends, and local observers have been documented. See Ohnuki-Tierney, *Kamikaze*, pp. 175–182; Chapter 4, notes 103, 115, and Chapter 7, of this book.

[5] Sears, *At War with the Wind*, pp. 1–10; Raphael Israeli, *Islamikaza: Manifestations of Islamic Martyrology* (London: Frank Cass, 2003).

Notably, Shi'a and Sunni observers also associated "suicide" attacks in modern Islam with the Japanese kamikaze actions in an effort to place them in a broader context of similar historical developments, thereby blunting the dispute over the phenomenon (see Chapter 7). In an essay in 1986, the Lebanese writer Sa'd Abu Diya praised the kamikaze phenomenon as a clear expression of the determination and daring of the people of the East. The Saudi Shaykh Salman al-'Awda, arguing that acts of self-sacrifice are part of guerilla warfare, also cited the example of the kamikaze phenomenon during the World War II.[6]

Other examples of self-destruction in various cultures include Buddhist monks who immolated themselves during the Vietnam War in protest against the American occupation and its local allies,[7] and imprisoned soldiers in the Irish Republican Army (IRA) who went on hunger strikes to the death during the 1970s. These acts reflected displays of commitment, military tactics, and protest, which are evident in Islamist-motivated "suicide" attacks as well.[8] However, the Islamist pattern introduced new dimensions involving the systematization of active self-sacrifice in which the perpetrator blows himself up together with a chosen target by means of a rigged car that he drives or an explosive belt on his body. His death is also a necessary precondition for the success of the act, thereby placing him on a level different from that of a conventional fighter for whom death is a reasonable possibility but not unavoidable.[9]

In Islamic perspective, self-destruction can be traced to early Muslim history, and especially to the Assassins, a radical offshoot of the Isma'ili Shi'i sect in northern Persia in the late eleventh century.[10] Similarities can be noted in that the fighters of the past, as their modern-day colleagues the "suicide" bombers were not mainly misfits. Those who chose to die did not do so as a result of emotional depression, mental disorder, or a desire not to live. Moreover, an important incentive for them

---

[6] Abu Diya, *Dirasa tahliliyya fi'l-'amaliyyat al-istishhadiyya*, p. 24; Salman al-'Awda quoted in *al-Sabil*, July 3–9, 2001, p. 18.

[7] Michael Biggs, "Dying without Killing: Self-Immolations 1963–2002," in Gambetta (ed.), *Making Sense of Suicide Missions*, pp. 178–180.

[8] Adam Dolnik, "Die and Let Die: Exploring Links between Suicide Terrorism and Terrorist Use of Chemical, Biological, Radiological, and Nuclear Weapons," *Studies in Conflict and Terrorism* 26/1 (2003), p. 20.

[9] Yoram Schweitzer, "Suicide Bombings: The Ultimate Weapon?" *International Policy* (Herzliya: Institute for Counter-Terrorism, August 7, 2001), available at http://www.ict.org.il/Articles/tabid/66/Articlsid/68/Default.aspx (accessed June 23, 2010).

[10] For a historic survey of the Assassins, see Bernard Lewis, *The Assassins: A Radical Sect in Islam* (New York: Basic Books, 1976).

was the reward of paradise. This promise required support elements to neutralize the expectation or fear of death, uncertainties about the passage from the present world into the next world, and entry into paradise – support that was provided by the leader and the group. Both in the Assassins' and the contemporary Muslim concepts of martyrdom, the time between death and the entry into paradise had to be reduced to nil. The speeding up of this process was reflected in the Shi'a image of a flying white horse that carries the martyr to paradise, while in the Sunna version green birds of paradise carry the souls of the martyrs to God.

Another similarity between the historical Assassins' and contemporary "suicide" perpetrators was their dual nature: they were a tool of the weak against a stronger force, and they signified the last resort of resistance, thus posing serious problems for the rulers of the time in both periods. Another similarity was the perceived loftiness of the moral mission of shattering a repressive ruler to achieve justice, which made a strong impression on young people and was incorporated in religious rituals thereafter.

Still, several elements differentiated the martyrdom of the Assassins from modern martyrdom. First, their victims in early Muslim history were invariably political, military or religious leaders. Second, the method was always targeted assassination and always by the same technique: stabbing by a dagger, which resulted in immediate death, while the perpe-trator did not expect to survive and was inevitably killed by his captors. Thus, the death of the perpetrator was not planned but was caused by the reaction of the enemy to the attack. Third, his death was not viewed as an essential condition for the success of the attacks, as in contemporary times when the perpetrator wears an explosive belt. Some of the early Assassins allowed the enemy to kill them, whereas others killed themselves. Neither of these options exist for the contemporary "suicide" attackers, who choose intentional death.[11]

Such assertive martyrdom inflamed the imagination of the Muslim masses, reinforced by the appearance of al-Qa'ida on the world scene, which intro-duced its globalization. Not only did the phenomenon became part of the Arab Muslim agenda, but also it became part of the Western agenda when jihad violence that reached its doorstep from the late 1990s onward turned the intellectual engagement with Islam into a civil security issue.[12]

---

[11] See also Gambetta, "Can We Make Sense of Suicide Missions?" pp. 279–283.

[12] See, e.g., a bibliography of "suicide" attacks listed in the Dudley Knox Library, Naval Postgraduate School, Marlatt, United States, available at http://www.nps.edu/Library (accessed June 23, 2010).

For some Western governments, such as Spain and England, which experienced "suicide" attacks at home in the early 2000s, this development also raised doubts regarding their adherence to a multiculturalism model that enabled immigrant communities to maintain a cultural identity separate from the national culture.[13] As a result, the dispute among Western observers regarding the link between Islam, violence, and tyranny intensified.

WESTERN DISCOURSE ON "SUICIDE" ATTACKS: A CRITICAL REVIEW

Some commentators argued that Islam in its very essence is characterized by a low threshold of tolerance for other cultures and by its opposition of enlightenment.[14] The French philosopher Gilbert Dulou held that the readiness of Muslims to die on the alter of Islam is prompted by a thirst for blood, stemming from a fantasy that their acts will bring them to paradise.[15] Others were guided by the frustration-aggression theory,[16] attributing Islamic violence to the corrupt political climate and the depressed socioeconomic reality in the Muslim world or to living under foreign military occupation.[17] According to the American scholar Roxanne L. Euben, jihad for those who endorse it constitutes a "political effort to bring into existence a public sphere in which true justice, equality and freedom are possible."[18] Another observer, the anthropologist Linda M. Pitcher, observed that the practice of martyrdom, as in the Palestinian case, underscores the dilemma of young people who live on the margins of

---

[13] Michael Barone, "Cultures Aren't Equal," *U.S. News and World Report*, August 15–22, 2005, available at http://www.usnews.com/usnews/opinion/articles/050815/15barone.htm. (accessed May 25, 2010).

[14] See, e.g., Barber, *Jihad vs. MacWorld*; Gilbert Dulou, *Le Problème Islamique* (Paris: n.p., 2002); Roland Jacquard, *Fatwa contre l'Occident* (Paris: A. Michel, 1998).

[15] Dulou, *Le Problème Islamique*, mainly chapter 5.

[16] John Dollard et al., *Frustration and Aggression* (New Haven: Yale University Press, 1939).

[17] Bozarslan, *Violence in the Middle East*; Amin Maalouf, *In the Name of Identity: Violence and the Need to Belong* (New York: Penguin Books, 2000); Roxanne L. Euben, "Killing (for) Politics: Jihad, Martyrdom and Political Action," *Political Theory* 30/1 (2001), pp. 4–35; Éric Rouleau, "Politics in the Name of the Prophet," *Le Monde Diplomatique*, English edition, November 2001, available at http://mondediplo.com/2001/11/09prophet (accessed May 25, 2010); Pape, *Dying to Win*, pp. 27–37, 45–60, 79–101; Adam L. Silverman, "Just War, Jihad and Terrorism, A Comparison of Western and Islamic Norms for the Use of Political Violence," *Journal of Church and State* 44/1 (Winter 2002), pp. 73–92; Christoph Reuter, *My Life Is a Weapon: A Modern History of Suicide Bombing* (Princeton, NJ: Princeton University Press, 2004), mainly pp. 1–18; Abufarha, *The Making of a Human Bomb*, pp. 1–22; also *al-Ahram Weekly*, July 4–10, 2002.

[18] Euben, "Killing (for) Politics," p. 385.

society. They speak through the ritual of *shahada*. "They enact a performance that enables a voice to escape the confines of [Israeli] military
occupation."[19]

However, the American writer Thomas Friedman, attributed the
essence of the problem to globalization, which flattens out the world and
allows for more direct contact between cultures. Some cultures were
prepared for this type of change, collaborated with it, and blossomed,
whereas others, such as Islam, felt threatened, frustrated, and even
degraded in the wake of this direct contact, which enabled them to see
where they stood in relation to others. In Friedman's view, "terrorism is
not spawned by the poverty of money. It is spawned by the poverty of
dignity" – a position adopted as well by the German writer and poet Hans
Magnus Enzensberger.[20]

Some scholars looked beyond the two conflicting narratives: religious
fanaticism vis-à-vis injustice and frustration, which are the province of the
weak and the powerless. Most prominently, the American anthropologist
Talal Asad argued that there is no justifiable terror, just as there is no just
war. He called for a critical examination of the topic of killing and death in
modern politics. The military death machine of nations, including Western
nations, Asad contended, seeks to ensure the defeat of the rival by means of
killing civilians, destroying their environment, and disrupting the ordinary
course of their lives more than any terrorist act. The humanitarian laws of
war do not provide clear rules for the conduct of moral wars. This logic of
violence holds true for terrorists and sovereign states alike. Moreover, the
readiness to die together with the enemy is not alien to Western thought,
and it ought to be considered simply as a tool of armed struggle, with the
use of religion allowing for a more effective condemnation and degradation of the other. Asad thereby seeks to erase the religious element in the
"suicide" attack phenomenon and place it in the general context of uni-

---

[19] Pitcher's thesis refers mainly to martyrdom that resulted from clashes with Israeli soldiers,
but its rationale also applies to "suicide" attacks. Linda M. Pitcher, "'The Divine
Impatience': Ritual, Narrative, and Symbolization in the Practice of Martyrdom," in
Medical Anthropology Quarterly 12/1 (1998), pp. 8–30; also Lori Allen, "Getting by
the Occupation: How Violence Became Normal during the Second Palestinian Intifada,"
Cultural Anthropology 23/3 (2008), pp. 453–487.

[20] Thomas L. Friedman, *The World Is Flat: A Brief History of the Globalized World in the
Twenty-first Century* (New York: Farrar, Straus and Giroux, 2005), pp. 391–406 (the
quote is on p. 400); Hans Magnus Enzensberger, "Globalization and the Radical Loser,"
New Perspectives Quarterly 23/3 (June 2006), pp. 34–36.

versal cruelty, in which the liberal and secular West has also played a significant role.[21]

These scholarly and moralistic debates, however, did not blur the reality that the notion of martyrdom embodied by "suicide" attacks preoccupied Western observers who had long since ceased to regard religion as a central priority. Some had even announced the "end of history," as evidenced by the final victory of the liberal-secular order over other competing ideologies.[22] Once Western man had ceased to regard religion as his primary consideration, he also ceased to believe that other people could behave differently and resort to "sanctified" violence, especially when carried out in a systematic, controlled, and conscious fashion. In an age of self-preoccupation, loosened communal ties, and cynicism, the willingness to die for a conviction or cause was viewed with incredulity and as the waste of a precious life. Some observers and commentators in the West perceived such violence as pure fanaticism, explicit evil, and a clear manifestation of a "culture of death"[23] or, alternatively, as an activist version of nihilism. Such nihilistic behavior, in this view, does not sanctify higher moral values but rather satisfies a self-destructive instinct, an urge to ruin for the sake of ruination, reflecting a pessimistic outlook which holds that everything in the modern world is worthless.[24] In a depiction of such nihilistic behavior, Nietzsche noted that "existence is regarded as a punishment and conceived as an error."[25]

Other observers embraced a psychosociological viewpoint. In psychologist Mordechai Rotenberg's view, the explanation for this mindset lies in an ongoing monitory, one-sided indoctrination of a single truth (including by means of prayer and meditation) that is indisputable and which nurtures behavior that is robotic and obedient and can lead to murderous suicide. Rotenberg also noted the use made by various religions of the denial of death by projecting images of eternal life replete with limitless sexuality. The emphasis on this motif, which appears not only in the Qur'an but also in the iconic legends of *One Thousand and One*

---

[21] Asad, *On Suicide Bombing*, mainly chapter 2; idem, quoted in *Arab Studies Journal* (Fall 2007/Spring 2008), pp. 123–130; also idem, *Formations of the Secular: Christianity, Islam and Modernity* (Stanford, CA: Stanford University Press, 2003), pp. 100–126.

[22] Francis Fukuyama, *The End of History and the Last Man* (New York: Free Press, 1992).

[23] Israel W. Cherny, *Fighting Suicide Bombing: A Worldwide Campaign for Life* (Westport, CT: Praeger Security International, 2007), mainly pp. 2–10, 79–99.

[24] See, e.g., Landkford, *The Myth of Martyrdom*.

[25] On Nietzsche's concept of nihilism, see his book, *The Will to Power* (New York: Russell & Russell, 1964), Vol. 1, pp. 8–31.

Nights,[26] illuminates the molding of the Muslim's behavior in internalizing these messages during childhood. Based on Ernst Becker's thesis of the denial of death, Rotenberg observed that the culture of Islam succeeded in imbuing its believers with a metaphysical resistance to the fear of death largely as a result of its detailed enumeration and reinforcement of future rewards. Muslims deny the fear of old age and death, transforming these fears into the anticipated eternal youth of the next world as embodied in the Qur'anic tradition.[27]

Another approach attributes the robotic behavior and the hedonistic sexual temptations awaiting the jihad recruit in the next world to a distorted and pathological love for a father figure – in this case God – who is perceived as authorizing killings and who provides an outlet for the frustrations and the conflicted souls of candidates for "suicide" missions in the form of acts of mass destruction and extermination. In psychologist Ruth Stein's view, based on an analysis of a letter by Muhammad 'Ata (discussed in Chapter 6), the basic submissiveness of the "suicide" perpetrator to "the father" reveals a developmental regression. Rather than fight against the repressive father, who demands sacrifice and death, the perpetrator prefers to submit to him entirely. The "suicide"-attacker son, who is about to kill and be killed, thereby demonstrates a deep sense of alienation from the outside world. With this, after satisfying the father's demand, the son will pass from a life of abasement and scorn to a significant and coveted life.[28]

The theme of a quest for significant and coveted life also constituted the essence of the analysis pointing to the sexual frustration of young people unable to socialize with the opposite sex because of restrictive moral and social codes characteristic of traditional societies. In this context, the sexual reward projected for perpetuators in the form of seventy dark-eyed virgins awaiting them in paradise was given special emphasis.[29]

[26] *Stories from the Thousand and One Nights*, trans. by Edward William Lane (New York: P.F. Collier, 1909).

[27] Mordechai Rotenberg, *From Mikdash to Midrash: Psychology of Fundamentalism and Judaism* (Tel Aviv: Schocken Publishing House, 2001), pp. 21–39 (in Hebrew); idem, *Heaven, Hell and Immortality: Christianity, Islam and Judaism* (Jerusalem: Rubin Mass Ltd. 2008; in Hebrew); Aziz al-Azmeh, "Rhetoric for the Senses: A Consideration of Muslim Paradise Narratives," *Journal of Arabic Literature* 26 (1995), pp. 215–231.

[28] Ruth Stein, "Vertical Mystical Homoeros," *Studies in Gender and Sexuality* 4/1 (Winter 2003), pp. 38–58.

[29] See Juergensmeyer, *Terror in the Mind of God*, pp. 197–198. On the relationship between sexual repression and political aggressiveness, see Wilhelm Reich, *The Mass Psychology of Fascism* (Harmondsworth: Penguin Books, 1970), pp. 59–67.

These psychological analyses, however, project more perplexity than empirical insight in the attempt to explain a willingness not only to kill but also to die. They reveal the limitations of Western rationalization, which tend to reject the existence of a world beyond logic and yet are unable to provide what religion does provide: a satisfying response to the penultimate vexing issue of the finality of life and the ruination of the body. This limitation is well reflected in a book by philosopher and publicist Sam Harris, *The End of Faith*, which makes the sobering point that "Without death, the influence of faith-based religion would be unthinkable. Clearly, the fact of death is intolerable to us, and faith is little more than a shadow cast by our hope for a better life beyond the grave."[30] Indeed, religious faith aspires to fill the gap in knowledge about the next world by emphasizing the existence of heaven and hell, while also emphasizing the worthlessness of life as compared to the greatness of the soul and an absolute devotion to God.

Even if a response of rage is posited as an explanation, rage is not necessarily an irrational reaction. It might also, and even primarily, stem from a sense on the part of the side that adopts violence that justice will be betrayed if one does not respond with rage and that violence is the only way to expose the ugly face of the enemy and express one's truth openly.[31]

Similarly, regarding the sexual impetus, which sparked the imagination in Western discourse, a careful examination of radical Islamist texts and the wills of perpetrators shows that this motif is actually downplayed and is consistently presented in the context of the jihad discourse as only one of many celestial rewards that await the *shahid* in paradise. This holds true for Hizballah, Hamas, and al-Qa'ida alike. Islamist writers, responding to criticism and ridicule regarding the issue of sexual rewards as an incentive for self-sacrifice, justified this aspect as part of God's plan for those who fight for his path. Nevertheless, these writers pointed to the importance of striving for a higher level of self-sacrifice not for reward but from a yearning for God and a longing to be close to him. They quoted Ibn al-Qayyim al-Jawziyya (d. 1350) in this context, who stated that the yearning for food, drink, and the sight of paradise is far less

[30] Sam Harris, *The End of Faith: Religion, Terror, and the Future of Reason* (New York: W.W. Norton, 2004), mainly chapter 1; also Mark Lilla, *The Stillborn God: Religion, Politics and the Modern West* (New York: Knopf, 2007); Geertz, *Interpretation of Cultures*, pp. 87–125.
[31] See Arendt's observation, "On Violence," pp. 160–161.

than the yearning of those who love God, and the two cannot even be compared.[32]

Moreover, if an assumption is made that "suicide" attackers nevertheless embody an act of self-immolation, despite the repression of this element in the Islamist narrative, they might be classified in the typology posited by Durkheim under the category of "altruistic suicide," which, in contrast to "egoistic suicide," is carried out in response to a higher command, whether religious or political. Such a command is expressed and nurtured by the group or organization with which the recruit is affiliated.[33] Another researcher, Jeffrey Riemer, following Durkheim's approach, coined the term "heroic suicide"[34] in that the impersonal nature of the act and the religious aura surrounding it entitle its perpetrator and his family to prestige rather than social condemnation.

Thus, side by side with the psychological interpretation of "suicide" attacks, a theological interpretation of the phenomenon is called for that will tie it to political, sociological, and pedagogic aspects as well. Rather than minimizing the importance of ideas as guides to historical events, their weight should be enhanced.[35] Instead of focusing on boring into the soul of the lone attacker, his pedagogical functioning and his political state of mind should be evaluated, and the modus operandi and agenda of the movement behind him should be analyzed. Lastly, rather than cataloging the "suicide" weapon as irrational and unrestrained, it should be examined as functional weaponry and as an expression of a political strategy. Its planners should be viewed as "rational fanatics" rather than pure fanatics, based on the historical perspective of thirty years since the first appearance

---

[32] See, e.g., ʿAzzam, *ʿUshshaq al-hur*, p. 2; Bakr ibn ʿAbd al-ʿAziz al-Athari, available at http://www.tawhed.ws/r?i=21110905&str=%D8%AD%D9%88%D8%B1 (accessed February 19, 2011); and ʿAbd al-Karim ʿAbd al-Hamid, available at http://www.tawhed.ws/dl?i=faaq4rsv (accessed May 5, 2011). For the reference to Ibn Qayyim al-Jawziyya, see his book, *Madarij al-salikin byna manazil iyyaka naʿbudu wa-iyyaka nastaʿin* (Beirut: Dar al-Kitab al-ʿArabi, 1996), Vol. 3, p. 58.

[33] Durkheim, *On Suicide*, pp. 217–240; also Bruce Hoffman and Gordon H. McCormick, "Terrorism, Signaling, and Suicide Attack," *Studies in Conflict and Terrorism* 27 (2004), pp. 243–281; Nicholas W. Bakken, "The Anatomy of Suicide Terrorism: A Durkheimian Analysis" (University of Delaware, 2007), pp. 3–5, 7–8, available at http://www.ifpo.org/wp-content/uploads/2013/08/Bakken_Suicide_Terrorism.pdf (accessed July 11, 2011).

[34] Jeffrey W. Riemer, "Durkheim's Heroic Suicide in Military Combat," *Armed Forces and Society* 25 (Fall 1998), pp. 103–120.

[35] See Weiner and Weiner, *The Martyr's Conviction*, pp. 1–2, 125–126, 131–138.

of this manifestation on the world stage in early 1980.[36] The "suicide" attack weapon also satisfied the impatience of the leaders of radical movements, their strong desire for action, and their competition with rival groups for local communal support. Moreover, as Martha Crenshaw points out, they perceived this weapon as a "catalyzer, not a substitute, for a mass revolt."[37] The role of "suicide" attacks, therefore, should not be exaggerated, nor should their popular support be viewed as a critical point in Islam, as discussed, for example, by David Cook.[38]

With the exception of al-Qaʿida, most, if not all, the movements surveyed here offered a broad array of social services that overshadowed their military activity, especially as several of these movements, such as Hizballah in Lebanon and Hamas in Palestine, became involved in state politics and their leaders even held governmental positions, thereby developing more complex political agendas. They were primarily communal movements, representing broad collective goals while developing mobilizing structures such as mosques, welfare and educational associations, medical services, and political institutions.[39] These bodies also served as agents of religious indoctrination and as points of interaction with the local population. Diligent investment in long-term communal needs accorded with the perception by these movements of *sabr*, or forbearance, in the gradual Islamization of the polity. Moreover, the context of a foreign conquest legitimized the "suicide" bomber phenomenon both religiously and politically, thereby positioning it as only one component, albeit an important one, in a general resistance strategy.

---

[36] See Sprinzak, "Rational Fanatics," pp. 66–73; Crenshaw, "The Logic of Terrorism," pp. 7–24; Pape, *Dying to Win*; idem, "The Strategic Logic of Suicide Terrorism," *American Political Science Review* 97 (August 2003), pp. 343–361. Pape's main argument is that "suicide" attacks are designed to achieve specific political purposes: to coerce a targeted government to change its policy or make significant political concessions.

[37] Crenshaw, "The Logic of Terrorism," p. 19; also Gambetta, "Can We Make Sense of Suicide Missions?" p. 260; See also Mia Bloom, "Dying to Kill: Motivations for Suicide Terrorism," in Ami Pedahzur (ed.), *Root Causes of Suicide Terrorism: The Globalization of Martyrdom* (London: Routledge, 2006), pp. 25–53.

[38] David Cook, "The Implications of 'Martyrdom Operations' for Contemporary Islam," *Journal of Religious Ethics* 32 (2004), pp. 130, 141.

[39] On social movement theory and its application to Middle Eastern studies, see Doug McAdam et al. (eds.), *Comparative Perspectives on Social Movements: Political Opportunities, Mobilizing Structures, and Cultural Framings* (Cambridge: Cambridge University Press, 1996); Charles Tilly, *Social Movements 1768–2004* (Boulder: Paradigm Publishers, 2004), mainly pp. 1–15; Quintan Wiktorowicz, "Introduction: Islamic Activism – A Social Movement Theory," in idem (ed.), *Islamic Activism: A Social Movement Theory Approach* (Bloomington: Indiana University Press, 2004), pp. 1–34; also Glenn E. Robinson, "Hamas as Social Movement," in ibid., pp. 112–139.

The multi-faceted background of "suicide" attacks is supported as well by quantitative empirical research. Studies conducted by Ariel Merari in 1990 and 2005 of "suicide" bombers from Hizballah and Amal in Lebanon, and Hamas and the Islamic Jihad in Palestine, suggest that there is no single psychological profile for a "suicide" perpetrator and that religious indoctrination and strong diverse motives such as group pressure, patriotism, hatred of the enemy, and a sense of victimization underlie the readiness to die.[40] Quantitative research by Pénélop Larzillièr and Lamis Andoni added another aspect to the study of Palestinian martyrdom in their findings that no specific social cause, such as economic distress, could be singled out.[41] Studies of Chechen martyrdom by Anne Speckhard and Khapta Akhmedova negated the aspect of personal dysfunction and pointed to emotional trauma and a desire for revenge as primary motives for "suicide" acts, with religion serving as a convenient conduit to ease the perpetrator's spiritual and mental state in preparation for carrying out the act.[42]

Mark Sageman's research, which examined more than 100 al-Qaʿida activists, also negated the claim of dysfunction as a motivation for such acts. Rather, his findings point to the importance of social networks (ties of friendship, blood ties, and close ties between mentor and recruit), which provided support and identity for the activists.[43] Similarly, the importance of social networks that were unofficial and nonpublic in the conventional sense was highlighted by Mohammed Hafez as an explanation for the supranational martyrdom phenomenon in post-Saddam Iraq.[44] These networks, described by Alberto Melucci as networks of shared

---

[40] Ariel Merari, "The Readiness to Kill and Die," pp. 192–207; idem, "Social, Organizational and Psychological Factors in Suicide Terrorism," in Tore Bjørgo (ed.), *Root Causes of Terrorism* (London: Routledge, 2005), pp. 70–86; idem, *Driven to Death*, mainly pp. 261–271.

[41] Pénélop Larzillièr, "Le 'martyre' des jeunes Palestiniens pendant l'intifada Al Aqsa: analyse et comparaison," *Politique étrangère* 4 (octobre–décembre 2001), pp. 937–951; Lamis Andoni, "Searching for Answers: Gaza's Suicide Bombers," *Journal of Palestine Studies* 24/4 (1997), pp. 33–45.

[42] Speckhard and Khapta, "Black Widows and Beyond," pp. 100–121.

[43] Sageman, *Understanding Terror Networks*, pp. 80–91, 114–118; also Khosrokhavar, *Suicide Bombers*, pp. 2–3.

[44] Hafez, *Suicide Bombers in Iraq*, pp. 16–18, 21–23, 165–212; also Diane Singerman, "The Networked World of Islamist Social Movements," in Wiktorowicz (ed.), *Islamic Activism*, pp. 149–158.

meaning, were typified by a strong connection between collective identity, mobilization, and activism.[45]

These and other studies reveal that there is no support for the notion that dysfunction or nihilism are motivators of "suicide" bombers. There is, however, evidence for personal motivations such as lack of education, unemployment, emotional trauma, a vendetta as a result of imprisonment or defamation of family members, or the anticipation of acquiring honor and admiration after death, which would radiate as well to the rest of the family. However, the importance of personal motives must not be exaggerated, nor can a single psychological or sociological profile be constructed. Notably, such motivations are more relevant to the Palestinian and Chechen arenas in which a number of empirical and quantitative studies have been carried out.[46] Other arenas, however, remain largely unexplored. Moreover, personal motivations must be examined as part of the larger martyrdom phenomenon in which religious and ideological justifications regarding paradise and hell and the struggle against an unbeliever enemy or conqueror play an important role.

Ultimately, as the study of social history shows, the perpetrator does not function in a vacuum but rather in a given social and cultural milieu in which he creates the content of his personal and social status. Moreover, he is empowered by a political movement that imbues his act with significance

---

[45] Alberto Melucci, "The Process of Collective Identity," in Hank Johnston and Bert Klandermans (eds.), *Social Movements and Culture* (Minneapolis: University of Minnesota Press, 1995), pp. 41–63; also idem, *Challenging Codes: Collective Action in the Information Age* (Cambridge: Cambridge University Press, 1996), mainly pp. 287–301, 344–347.

[46] See, e.g., Dolnik, "Die and Let Die," pp. 22–23; Assaf Moghadam, "Palestinian Suicide Terrorism in the Second Intifada: Motivations and Organizational Aspects," *Studies in Conflict and Terrorism* 26/2 (2003), pp. 69–76; Rona M. Fields, Salman Elbedour, and Fadel Abu Hein, "Palestinian Suicide Bombers," in Chris E. Stout (ed.), *Psychology of Terrorism: Clinical Aspects and Responses* (Westport, CT: Praeger Publishers, 2002), Vol. 2, pp. 193–223; Berko, *The Smarter Bomb*; Mohammed M. Hafez, "Dying to be Martyrs: The Symbolic Dimension of Suicide Terrorism," in Pedahzur (ed.), *Root Causes of Suicide Terrorism*, pp. 54–55; Speckhard and Akhmedova, "Black Widows"; idem, "Mechanisms of Generating Suicide Terrorism: Trauma and Bereavement as Psychological Vulnerabilities in Human Security – The Chechen Case," in Jill Donnelly et al (ed.), *Developing Strategies to Deal with Trauma in Children* (Amsterdam: IOS Press, 2005), pp. 54–69: available at http://ebooks.iospress.nl/volume/developing-strategies-to-deal-with-trauma-in-children (accessed July 6, 2010). Some empirical data on al-Qaʿida recruits, especially in North Africa and Europe, can also be found, but no single profile of global jihad has emerged. Edwin Bakker, "Jihadi Terrorists in Europe and Global Salafi Jihadis," in Rik Coolsaet (ed.), *Jihadi Terrorism and the Radicalisation Challenge in Europe* (Hampshire: Ashgate, 2008), pp. 69–84; Barltrop (ed.), *Muslims in Europe.*

and molds his postmortem image in the public at large through written and recorded wills and hagiographic literature (see Chapter 6). Essentially, as reflected in the record of the "suicide" bomber phenomenon, it is the movement that translates the willingness of the individual to die as a martyr into the act itself, supplying the means, knowledge, and required logistic planning.

Conclusion

The essence of religious faith lies in its provision of meaning to human existence. In its most radical dimension, as reflected in the three humanistic religions, it posits the sacrifice of life for God.

Ideologically, self-sacrifice was perceived as a religious act that ensures the survival and flourishing of faith and evokes intimacy with God. It was seen as the true embodiment of the "culture of devotion," to adopt Frank Graziano's notion in reference to popular saints of Latin America.[1] However, self-sacrifice is not devoid of social elements. In sociological terms, a martyr is an individual who lives and functions in a specific social and cultural setting. In a situation of confrontation with another, stronger group, martyrdom is an effective tool in fortifying group morale, thereby ensuring future volunteers. Put another way, martyrdom may be seen as a manifestation of power politics.

Viewed historically, Judaism and Christianity, which preceded Islam, influenced the perception of death in Islam in many ways (for example, as testimony to the power of belief and the pleasures of paradise) but differed from it in patterns of martyrdom. Whereas the ideal of sacrifice in the first two religions was put into practice defensively – in Christianity in its early history and in Judaism for long periods thereafter – at the hands of oppressors in interrogation rooms and public squares, the ideal of sacrifice in Islam was put into practice offensively against unbelievers on the battle-field. Martyrdom in Islam elicited laudatory literature as a branch of

---

[1] Frank Graziano, *Cultures of Devotion: Folk Saints of Spanish America* (Oxford: Oxford University Press, 2007).

military jihad aimed at elevating the word of God or, alternatively, repelling an external aggression against his believers.

Muslim history, which included periods of political and military quiescence, did not always adhere to the ideal of sacrifice. On the contrary, the ideal underwent erosion over time and lost its supremacy over other forms of death, such as death resulting from asceticism, illnesses, or natural disasters, although it remained a key ethos in Muslim tradition. It attracted renewed glorification in recent times by revivalist movements, both Sunna and Shi'a, which viewed it as a means of verifying the moral superiority of Islam over other cultures perceived as hedonistic and as a lever for group cohesion and a demonstration of endurance in the face of political repression.

With this, the motif of martyrdom evoked varied interpretations, an indication of the multifaceted nature of modern Islamist thought and changing historical circumstances. Indeed, a careful analysis of ideological writing, side by side with evaluating the historical and political realties in which they were molded, reveals a diverse religious discourse on martyrdom: trends toward restraint alongside those typified by extremism and the elevation of death in anticipation of Islamic salvation. The Muslim Brethren in the 1930s and 1940s adopted communal jihad and preached altruism for the benefit of the community, but radical organizations from the 1950s onward promoted jihad and revolution against secular nationalism as conceptualized by Nasser and the Ba'th Party. A revolutionary ideology was implemented as well by the awakening Shi'a against the Shah's regime in Iran.

In parallel, the radicals upgraded the status of the simple believer from a silent voice to a sounder of the alarm and the bearer of a mission who holds the keys to the establishment of the Kingdom of God. In their perception, the true believer is committed to fight to the death against a corrupted and unjust regime, although his primary mission is to attack and kill without exposing himself to deliberate death. Moreover, civilians are excluded from the range of harm. These two parameters of the *mujahid* – circumstantial death and nonviolence against civilians – reflected a moral restraint on the basis of the theological prohibition of suicide and the killing of civilians in societies that were Muslim. These parameters also constituted the dividing line between the early radicals of the 1970s and 1980s and the 1990s and thereafter, who adopted "suicide" attacks or missions inspired ideologically by revolutionary Iran.

Fueled by a sense of humiliation, and nurturing an eschatological expectation of salvation, the awakening Shi'a advocated initiated offensive martyrdom. The Iranian model was embraced and further developed by dissident Islamist movements mainly in ethnic-national conflicts, most prominently in Lebanon, Palestine, Chechnya, and Afghanistan. These movements waged a dual struggle: militarily against foreign occupation and politically over supremacy in their own communities. In these arenas "suicide" attacks were viewed as part of guerrilla warfare and as a weapon of the weak in their struggle against a foreign oppressor.

"Suicide" attacks in ethnic and national conflicts between Muslims and non-Muslims engendered a debate in Islamic circles during the 1990s over religious legitimacy regarding both the self-inflicted death of the perpetrator and the killing of civilians. Whereas critics renounced "suicide" acts as unfit for reward in paradise, others viewed these acts as the epitome of faith in God, highlighting the issue of protecting Muslim territory and people or of regaining occupied Muslim territory. They depicted the notion of defensive jihad as instilling a sense of urgency and, as such, outside the bounds of ethical rules of warfare outlined extensively in Islamic judicial literature (as, for example, the acceptability of armistice, the just treatment of noncombatants, or the avoidance of an indiscriminate use of arms). Typically, Shaykh Muhammad Husayn Fadlallah, the late spiritual leader of Hizballah in Lebanon, ruled: "There is no difference between dying with a gun in your hand or exploding yourself. In a situation of struggle or holy war, you have to find the best means to achieve your goals."[2]

Relating "suicide" acts to the concept of jihad – which was identified primarily with the duty to reaffirm the superior morality of Islam – also engendered a reliance on earlier legalist traditions that explicitly prioritized martyrdom over the sanctity of life. The context of infidel occupation also loosened restraints regarding harming civilians, women, farm workers, and others who were depicted as supporting the military effort of the enemy morally or materially and, moreover, inhabiting occupied Muslim land.

Islamist movements that carried out "suicide" attacks, and their supporters from the mainstream religious spectrum, were careful to emphasize that this weapon does not constitute a systematic or mass modus operandi but is implemented in emergency situations only and within specific Islamic parameters. Defending the faith and the homeland was a central theme, with its operative parameters conforming to the geographical borders of the specific entity in conflict. The geographic parameter, side by side with a calculated martyrdom, also signified the distinctive difference between

---

[2] Fadlallah quoted by Ranstorp, "Terrorism in the Name of Religion," p. 55.

these religio-national movements and the al-Qaʿida organization that emerged in the early 1990s.

Al-Qaʿida replaced territorial and calculated martyrdom with a transnational and sweeping martyrdom aimed at the entire West and its allies in the Arab Muslim world. This concept of global jihad, which fostered perpetual war between Islam and its enemies, was reinforced by the elements of a charismatic leadership, operational mobility, and a new human reservoir in the Western European Muslim diaspora and elsewhere.

Al-Qaʿida's strategy of global jihad against the "new Crusade" inflamed the imagination of the Muslim masses although it failed to gain a footing in Islamic discourse. A variety of Islamic sectors, communal and militant alike, perceived al-Qaʿida's universal vision as utopian and as eroding the meager resources of the Islamists in their struggle against the modern state. Nevertheless, the emergence of al-Qaʿida infused the phenomenon of martyrdom with new vitality, culminating in the September 11, 2001, attacks in the United States.

Besides constituting an effective tool of guerilla warfare, "suicide" attacks also functioned as a political statement in the name of divine authority, projecting the option of protest and resistance over that of compromise and rapprochement. Furthermore, "suicide" attacks constituted an important pedagogic medium by which the perpetrators brought the ideological platform of their movements into the street and into the homes of the public. Their dramatic death, followed by the exhibition of their written and recorded wills prepared prior to embarking on their mission, conveyed a message of piety, power, determination, and commitment. Commemorations of their exalted altruism took place in a variety of venues: printed memoir texts, funeral and burial ceremonies, songs, graphics, audiovisual tapes, and the Internet.

These means of instilling the ethos of self-sacrifice constituted an important aspect of popular culture, which, in situations of confrontation, can become a tool in political struggles, or "wars of position" in Antonio Gramsci's wording.[3] Methodologically, this type of culture may be termed a culture of resistance aimed at influencing the masses or at demonstrating broad oppositionist trends to the powers that be.[4] Popular culture can thus

---

[3] Quintin Hoare and Geoffrey Nowell-Smith (eds.), *Selections from the Prison Notebook of Antonio Gramsci* (New York: International Publishers, 1971), pp. 238–239.

[4] See, e.g., Rebecca L. Stein and Ted Swedenburg, "Popular Culture, Rational History and the Question of Power in Palestine and Israel," *Journal of Palestinian Studies* 33/4 (Summer 2004), pp. 6–9.

reflect political events and power struggles no less accurately than can the study of politics or diplomatic history.

Intensive commemorative campaigns constructed an ideal image of the martyrs as chosen by God, projecting charisma on the basis of moral and ascetic conduct, social altruism, courage, and dissidence, yet also based on the attributes of divine grace and spiritual powers. Islamic martyrologists, mainly Sunnis, who were charged with the production of popular martyrdom literature, were not satisfied with perpetuating an ethical type of martyr only but sought to project a martyr with such Sufi attributes as *karamat* as well, revealing an awareness that a heroic death in battle was insufficient to establish authority and secure the devotion of the Muslim activist who seeks religious arousal. Moreover, by positioning the martyrs as conduits of divine blessings and as mild ascetics, their affiliated movements aimed at elevating the purity of their motives beyond any doubt or criticism, thereby also enhancing their own public appeal. Eventually, the expropriation of sources of guidance and authority from other cultural agents, in this case Sufis, led to a more interactive relationship between radical Islam and mysticism, in modern times, than is assumed in the scholarly literature.

Retrospectively, modern Muslim radicals who cherished the ethos of battlefield martyrdom shared what Max Weber defined as the "ethics of ultimate ends," which tends to project a set of exalted ideas in the name of justice. In such a perception, religion represents the means of ultimate order, thereby enabling the proper handling of the disorder of modern times.[5] Moreover, in this view, according to anthropologist Clifford Geertz, religion not only encourages self-sacrifice but also demands it.[6]

Such a mindset also fostered a direct link between a return to the golden age of early Islam and the restoration of the pure and powerful community, which is characterized by devotion and a sense of superiority.[7] The rehabilitation of Islam as a system of governance, in this thinking, may take a

---

[5] Max Weber, "Politics as a Vocation," in H. H. Gerth and C. W. Mills (eds.), *From Max Weber: Essays in Sociology* (New York: Oxford University Press, 1946), pp. 120–123.

[6] Geertz, *The Interpretation of Cultures*, p. 126.

[7] Some Muslim radicals advocated the restoration of the "textual community," which evolved around the core scriptures – the Qur'an and the Sunna – depicted by these radical circles as the "hard religion," while making selective use of judicial literature produced thereafter. See, e.g., Muhammad Abu Halima, who was involved in the World Trade Center explosions in New York in 1993, cited in M. Juergensmeyer, "Terror in the Name of God," *Current History* 100 (November 2001), p. 359. The term "textual community" is taken from Brian Stock, *The Implications of Literacy: Written Language and Models of Interpretation in the Eleventh and Twelfth Centuries* (Princeton, NJ: Princeton University

long time, but it will occur in the end: every new difficulty is merely a passing episode in the victorious march of the truth.[8] Historical evidence supporting this outlook was cited by al-Qaʿida's al-Zawahiri in the form of the Crusader occupation of Syria and Palestine, the French occupation of Algeria, and the British occupation of Egypt, which lasted decades or more but were eventually terminated by the Muslims.[9]

Additionally, Muslim radicals upgraded the status of jihad and self-sacrifice in Islam, perceiving them as a vital condition for a correct and innate understanding of the religion and for the reestablishment of its supremacy. In this perception, relinquishing jihad meant self-destruction. However, it was here that the radicals differed in approach.

For early radicals, as in Egypt and Syria in the 1960s and 1970s, self-sacrifice revealed a measured jihad subject to moral restrictions because of the nature of the environment in which it was to be implemented – namely Muslim society. It was directed against local regimes only, and the death of the perpetrator was circumstantial, not deliberate. For later radicals in ethno-national conflicts, such as in Lebanon, Palestine, and Chechnya in the 1980s and 1990s, self-sacrifice demonstrated an assertive jihad against an infidel occupier through "suicide" operations that implicitly targeted civilians as well. However, their discourse also revealed an awareness of the dilemmas – and their attempts to resolve them – regarding the affinity between martyrdom and self-immolation and the issue of targeting civilians. Lastly, for al-Qaʿida and Salafi-jihadists, martyrdom meant a sweeping jihad against the Crusader West and its Arab-Muslim allies, including in Iraq and Saudi Arabia, without reservations or apologetics and without differentiation between enemy soldiers, prisoners of war, and civilians.

Of the three radical narratives, only the ethno-national one gained wide theological backing from the broad center of the Islamic spectrum: the Muslim Brethren and the religious establishment. Jihad and martyrdom in ethno-national conflicts, including "suicide" attacks, did not evoke internal Muslim strife (*fitna*). Moreover, they targeted defamed entities that were defined throughout twentieth-century Islamic historiography as infidel and repressive, with jihad against them viewed as equal to the jihad waged by the believers in early Islam.[10] The two other narrative poles were

---

Press, 1983), p. 90. See also M. Eliade, *Myth and Reality* (New York: Harper & Row, 1975), pp. 21–38; Qutb, *Maʿalim fiʾl-tariq*, pp. 11–19.

[8] See, e.g., al-Zawahiri quoted in *al-Sharq al-Awsat*, December 8, 2001.

[9] Ibid; Also al-Suri, *Daʿwat al-muqawama al-Islamiyya*, pp. 922–923.

[10] See, e.g., the rulings of Shaykh ʿAbd al-Halim Mahmud in his *Fatawa*, Vol. 2, pp. 111, 113.

excluded from the realm of sanctity in that they advocated mere violence. Domestic jihad, as espoused by the Egyptian Jihad and other radical movements, was dismissed as constituting a modern version of the Kharijites of early Islam – that is, outside the consensus – whereas the global jihad of al-Qa'ida was denounced as apostasy.[11]

The renunciation of domestic jihad against Arab regimes reflected the primacy of the legalist orientation, which advocated *da'wa*, or communal activity, whereas the renunciation of cosmic jihad against the Christian West reflected the primacy of territorial Islam, which focused on upgrading its status within a defined political community. According to the Muslim Brethren and similar groups, *da'wa* – namely preaching, education, and persuasion – alone has the ability to broaden the influence of Islam. It also explains the secret of the strength of these groups and their ability to survive over the years in comparison with the weakness and marginality of their adversaries.

In challenging the radical circles, Brethren spokesmen emphasized that the basis for bringing about change in society and in the state is the principle of gradualism rather than hastiness – a policy of patience rather than an impulsive reaction. Theological support for this stance was cited by the Brethren in the Prophet's activity in Mecca, which was typified by preaching, in light of the weakness of the community of believers. This is the reality in the modern era as well, and thus communal work is the right path.[12]

The extent to which the *da'wa* strategy embraced compromise in religious ideals is a topic for separate discussion.[13] However, clearly, it gained a superior place in Islamist discourse, heightening an awareness of the importance of diligent "field work" and the establishment of physical networks rooted in the community rather than in virtual spheres or politics as an agent of change. The reinforcement of the option of communal jihad

---

[11] *Jedda Arab News*, October 29, 2001; *Le Monde diplomatique* (Paris), November 2001.

[12] *Al-Mukhtar al-Islami*, October 14, 2006, p. 36; also Marc Lynch, "Islam Divided between Salafi-Jihadi and the Ikhwan," *Studies in Conflict and Terrorism* 33/6 (May 3, 2010), pp. 467–487.

[13] See, e.g., Mona El-Ghobashy, "The Metamorphosis of the Egyptian Brethren," *International Journal of Middle East Studies* 37 (2005), pp. 373–395; Jillian Schwedler, *Faith in Moderation: Islamist Parties in Jordan and Yemen* (Cambridge: Cambridge University Press, 2006); Asef Bayat, *Making Islam Democratic: Social Movements and the Post-Islamist Turn* (Stanford: Stanford University Press, 2007), mainly pp. 1–15, 194–197; Yoram Meital, "The Struggle over Political Order in Egypt: The 2005 Elections," *Middle East Journal* 60/2 (Spring 2006), pp. 257–279; Christoph Schumann, "Freiheit und Staat im islamistischen Diskurs," in *Islam und Moderner Nationalstaat* (Paderborn: Wilhelm Fink Verlag, forthcoming).

over revolutionary jihad led to an erosion in the status of militant martyrdom but did not abolish its importance as a component of guerrilla warfare
and a symbolic repertory of defiance and opposition. This was especially
true in ethno-national conflict arenas still struggling for political viability
and deeply involved in state building.

Bibliography

Newspapers and Periodicals

Al-'Ahd (Beirut)
Al-Ahram al-'Arabi (Cairo)
Al-Ahram Weekly (Cairo)
Al-'Alam (London)
Arab Studies Journal
Al-Ayyam (Bahrain)
Al-Ayyam (Ramallah)
Al-Bayan (Gaza)
Al-Da'wa (Cairo)
Al-Dustur (Amman)
Der Spiegel (Hamburg)
Elaph (London)
Filastin (Gaza)
Filastin al-Muslima (London)
Filastin al-Thawra (Beirut)
Foreign Report (London)
Ha'aretz (Tel Aviv)
Al-Hayat (London)
Al-Hayat al-Jadida (Gaza)
International Herald Tribune (London)
Al-'Irfan (Lebanon)
Al-Islam wa-Fialstin (Nicosia)
Al-Istiqlal (Gaza)
Jerusalem Report (Jerusalem)
Al-Jihad (Pashawar)
Jomhuri-ye Islami (Tehran)
Journal of Palestine Studies (Washington)
Kayhan International (Tehran)

Al-Khalij (Abu Dhabi)
Kiyan (Tehran)
Le Monde diplomatique (Paris)
Al-Liwaʾ al-Islami (Cairo)
Maʿariv (Tel Aviv)
Al-Majalla (London)
Majallat al-Azhar (Cairo)
Al-Manar (Lebanon)
Mena (Egyptian News Agency)
Middle East Insight (Washington)
Al-Mithaq (Acre)
Al-Mujahid (Beirut)
Al-Mujtamaʿ (Kuwait)
Al-Mukhtar al-Islami (Cairo)
Al-Musawwar (Cairo)
New York Times (New York)
New Yorker (New York)
News International (Islamabad)
Palestinian Times (London)
Al-Qabas (Kuwait)
Al-Quds (Jerusalem)
Al-Quds al-ʿArabi (London)
Al-Raʾy (Amman)
Al-Raʾy al-ʿAmm (Kuwait)
al-Risala (Gaza)
Ruz al-Yusuf (Cairo)
Al-Sabil (Oslo)
Al-Sharq al-Awsat (London)
Al-Shuruq (Sharja)
Al-Sunna (Birmingham)
Al-Taliʿa al-Islamiyya (London)
Washington Post (Washington)
Al-Watani (Cairo)

Books and Articles in Arabic

ʿAbd al-ʿAziz, Jumʿa Amin. *Fahm al-Islam*. Alexandria: Dar al-Daʿwa, 1993.

ʿAbd al-Jalil, Salim. *al-Imam al-Akbar Muhammad Sayyid Tantawi: min Bani Salim ila al-Madina al-Munawara*. Cairo: Lajnat al-Buhuth, 2010.

ʿAbd al-Rahim, Muhammad. *Arbaʿun hadithan fi fadl al-shahid waʾl-shahada*. Damascus: al-Hikma, 1995.

Abu Bashir, Salah Masʿud. *Jihad shaʿb Filastin khilala nisf qarn*. Beirut: Dar al-Fath, 1968.

Abu Diya, Saʿd. *Dirasa tahliliyya fiʾl-ʿamaliyyat al-istishhadiyya fi Janub Lubnan*. Amman: Jamʿiyyat ʿUmmal al-Matabiʿ al-Taʿawuniyya, 1986.

Abu Husayn. *Ya thar Allah: latamat Husayniyya*. Tehran: n.p., 1984.

Abu Lawz, ʿAli ibn Husayn (ed.). *Fitnat al-takfir*. Riyadh: Dar Ibn Khuzayma, 1997.

Ahmad, Jawad Muhammad (ed.). *Fatawa al-Azhar fi wujub al-jihad wa-tahrim al-taʿamul maʿ al-kiyan al-Sahyuni*. Cairo: Marakz Yafa, 1998.

Ahmad, Rifʿat Sayyid (ed.). *Rihlat al-dam al-ladhi hazama al-sayf*. 2 vols. Cairo: Markaz Yafa, 1997.

Al-Amin, Hazim. *al-Salafi al-yatim: al-wajh al-Filastini liʾl-jihad al-ʿalami waʾl-qaʿida*. Beirut: Dar al-Saqi, 2011.

Al-Isbahani, Ismaʿil ibn Muhammad. *al-Targhib waʾl-tarhib*. 3 vols. Cairo: Dar al-Hadith, 1993.

Al-ʿAsqalani, ibn Hajar. *Fath al-bari fi sharh sahih al-Bukhari*. 13 vols. Beirut: Dar al-maʿrifa, 1959
  Lisan al-mizan. 10 vols. 3rd ed. Beirut: Muʾasssat al-Iʿlami liʾl-Matbuʿat, 1986.

Ayyub, Hasan. *al-Jihad waʾl-fidaʾiyya fiʾl-Islam*. 2nd ed. Beirut: Dar al-Nadwa al-Jadida, 1983.
  Al-Shahid fiʾl-Islam. Beirut: Dar al-ʿIlm liʾl-Malayin, 1985.

Al-Azdi, Abu Dawud Sulayman ibn al-Ashʿath al-Sijistani. *Sunan Abi Dawud*. Beirut: Dar al-Fikr, n.d.

ʿAzzam, ʿAbdallah. *ʾAyat al-rahman fi jihad al-Afghan*. Lahur: Ittihad al-Talaba al-Muslimin, 1983.
  Al-Difaʿ ʿan aradi al-Muslimin. Al-Zarqaʾ: Maktabat al-Manar, 1987.
  Fiʾl-Jihad, ʾadab wa-ahkam. N.p.: Matbuʿat al-Jihad, 1987.
  "Al-Tasmim ʿala al-mawt," *al-Jihad* 34 (September 1987), p. 3.
  Iʿlan al-jihad. Pashawar: Maktab Khidmat al-Mujahidin, 1990.
  Hamas: al-judhur al-taʾrikhiyya waʾl-mithaq. Amman: n.p., 1990.
  Fiʾl-Jihad: fiqh wa-ijtihad. Pashawar: Maktab Khidmat al-Mujahidin, n.d.
  Jihad shaʿb Muslim. N.p., n.d.
  Dhikrayat Filastin. Pashawar: Markaz al-Shahid ʿAzzam, n.d. Also available at: http://www.angelfire.com/id/azzam/images/41.zip. (accessed June 3, 2010)
  ʿUshshaq al-hur. Available at: http://www.4shared.com/dir/dEglkHus/_online.html (accessed May 5, 2011).

Bahansi, Ahmad Fathi. *al-Siyasa al-jinaʾiyya fiʾl-shariʿa al-Islamiyya*. Cairo: Dar al-Shuruq, 1988.

Al-Balkhi, Muqatil ibn Sulayman ibn Bashir al-Azdi. *Tafsir Muqatil ibn Sulayman*. 5 vols. Beirut: Dar Ihyaʾ al-Turath, 2003.

Al-Banna, Hasan. "Sinaʿat al-mawt," *al-Nadhir*, no. 18 (September 26, 1938), pp. 3–5; reprinted in *al-Imam al-shahid yatahadadith ila shabab al-ʿalam al-Islami*. Beirut: Dar al-Qalam, 1974, pp. 129–132.
  Al-Salam fiʾl-Islam. 2nd ed. Cairo: Manshurat al-ʿAsr al-Hadith, 1971.
  "Al-Jihad fi sabil Allah wa-manzilatuhu min al-Islam," *al-Taliʿa al-Islamiyya* (London), January 1, 1981, pp. 16–21.
  Majmuʿat rasaʾil al-imam al-shahid. Beirut: al-Muʾassasa al-Islamiyya, n.d.
  "Risalat al-jihad," in idem, *Majmuʿat rasaʾil al-imam al-shahid*. Beirut: al-Muʾassasa al-Islamiyya, n.d., pp. 246–264.

Al-Baydawi, Nasir al-Din ʿAbdallah ibn ʿUmar. *Tafsir al-Baydawi*. 5 vols. Beirut: Dar al-Fikr, 1996.

Al-Bukhari, Abu ʿAbdallah Muhammad ibn Ismaʿil. *al-Jamiʿ al-sahih*. Beirut: Muʾassasat al-Halabi, 1960.
   Sahih al-Bukhari. 7 vols. 3rd ed. Beirut: Dar Ibn Kathir, 1987.
Al-Darimi, Abu Muhammad ʿAbd Allah ibn ʿAbd al-Rahman. *Sunan al-Darimi*. 2 vols. Beirut: Dar al-Kitab al-ʿArabi, 1987.
Della Vida, G. Levi. "Khāridjites," The Encyclopaedia of Islam 4 (1997), pp. 1074–1077.
Diwan al-qaʿid al-shahid Marwan Hadid. N.p., 1983. Available at: http://www.tawhed.ws/a?a=zodhchjh (accessed February 28, 2012).
Fadlallah, Hasan. *Harb al-iradat: siraʿ al-muqawama waʾl-ihtilal al-Israʾili fi Lubnan*. Beirut: Dar al-Muhajir, 1998.
Fadlallah, Muhammad Husayn. *ʿAla tariq Karbalaʾ*. Beirut: Dar al-Tayyar al-Jadid, 1984.
   Kitab al-jihad. Beirut: Dar al-Malak, 1996.
   Al-Islam wa-mantiq al-quwwa. 4th ed. Beirut: Dar al-Malak, 2003.
Faraj, Muhammad ʿAbd al-Salam. *al-Farida al-ghaʾiba*. N.p., n.d.
Fatawa ʿulamaʾ al-Islam fi masaʾil jihadiyya wa-hukm al-ʿamaliyyat al-istishhadiyya. Beirut: Dar al-Wahda al-Islamiyya, 2002.
Al-Ghazali, Abu Hamid, *Ihyaʾ ʿulum al-din*. 2 vols. Cairo: Muʾassasat al-Halabi, 1967.
Al-Ghazali, Muhammad. *Maʿa Allah: dirasat fiʾl-daʿwa waʾl-duʿat*. 3rd ed. Cairo: Dar al- Hadith, 1965.
Harun, ʿAbd al-Salam. *al-Alf al-mukhtara min Sahih al-Bukhari*. 4 vols. Cairo: Dar al-Maʿarif, 1960.
Hasanat, Hammad. *Dhikrayat Marj al-Zuhur*. N.p., n.d.
Hawwa, Saʿid. *Fi ʾAfaq al-taʿlim*. Cairo: Maktabat Wahaba, 1980.
   Jund Allah. 2nd ed. N.p., 1991.
   Al-Madkhal ila daʿwat al-Ihwan al-Muslimin. Amman: Dar al-Arqam, n.d.
Haykal, Muhammad Khayr. *al-Jihad waʾl qital fiʾl-siyasa al-shariʿiyya*. 3 vols. Beirut: Dar al-Bayariq, 1993.
Al-Haythami, ʿAli ibn Abi Bakr. *Majmuʿ al-zawaʾid*. 5 vols. Cairo: Dar al-Rayyan liʾl-Turath, 1987.
Ibn Abi al-Dunya, ʿAbdallah ibn Muhammad. *Kitab al-manamat*. Beirut: Muʾassasat al-Kutub al-Thaqafiyya, 1993.
Ibn Abi Shayba, Abu Bakr ʿAbdallah ibn Muhammad. *Musannaf ibn Abi Shayba*. 7 vols. Riyadh: Maktabat al-Rushd, 1989.
Ibn Anas, Malik. *Muwattaʾ al-Imam Malik*. 2 vols. Beirut: Muʾassasat al-Risala, 1992.
Ibn al-Athir, Abu al-Hasan. *al-Kamil fiʾl-taʾrikh*. 13 vols. Beirut: Dar Sadir, 1965–1966.
Ibn Hanbal, Abu ʿAbdallah Ahmad. *Musnad Ahmad*. 45 vols. Beirut: Muʾassasat al-Risala, 2001.
Ibn Kathir, Abu al-Fidaʾ Ismaʿil ibn ʿUmar. *Tafsir Ibn Kathir*. 4 vols. Beirut: Dar al-Fikr, 1980–1981.
Ibn Majah, Abu ʿAbdallah Muhammad ibn Yazid. *Sunan ibn Majah*. 2 vols. Cairo: Ihyaʾ al-Kutub al-ʿArabiya, n.d.
Ibn al-Mubarak, Abdallah. *Kitab al-jihad*. Beirut: Dar al-Nur, 1971.

Ibn Qayyim al-Jawziyya. *Zad al-maʿad fi hady khayr al-ʿibad.* 5 vols. Cairo: al-Matbaʿa al-Misriyya, 1959–1960.

    Kitab ahkam ahl al-dhimma. 2 vols. Damascus: Matbaʿat Jamiʿat Dimashq, 1961.

    al-Fawaʾid. 2nd ed. Beirut: Dar al-Kutub al-ʿIlmiyya, 1973.

    Madarij al-salikin byna manazil iyyaka naʿbudu wa-iyyaka nastaʿin. 3 vols. Beirut: Dar al-Kitab al-ʿArabi, 1996.

Ibn Taymiyya, Taqi al-Din. *al-Fatawa al-kubra.* 6 vols. Beirut: Dar al-Maʿrifa, n.d.

    Majmuʿat al-fatawa. 37 vols. Cairo: Maktabat Ibn Taymiyya, n.d.

    Qaʿida fiʾl-inghimas fiʾl-ʿaduww hal yubah? Riyad: Maktabat al-Salaf, 2002.

Ibn ʿUthaymin, Muhammad ibn Salih. *Sharh riyad al-salihin min kalam sayyid al-mursalin.* 6 vols. Riyadh: Madar al-Watan liʾl-Nashr, 2005.

Al-ʿImad, Salwa. *al-Imam al-shahid fiʾl-taʾrikh waʾl-idiolojiyya: shahid al-Shiʿa muqabil batal al-Sunna.* Beirut: al-Muʾassasa al-ʿArabiyya, 2000.

ʿImara, Muhammad (ed.). *al-Farida al-ghaʾiba: judhur wa-hiwarart, dirasat wa-nusus.* New ed. Cairo: Nahadat Misr, n.d.

Al-ʿIshq al-Karbalaʾi. Beirut: n.p., n.d.

Jabir, Husayn ibn ʿAli. *al-Tariq ila jamaʿat al-Muslimin.* Kuwait: Dar al-Daʿwa, 1969.

Jadd al-Haqq, Jadd al-Haqq ʿAli (with ʿAtiyya Saqr). "Naqd al-farida al-ghaʾiba fatwa wa-munaqasha," *Majallat al-Azhar* (June–July 1993), pp. 3–54.

Al-Jazari, ʿAbd al-Rahman. *Kitab al-fiqh ʿala al-madhahib al-arbaʿa.* Cairo: Dar al-Kutub, 1939.

Jarrar, Husni Adham. *al-Shahid ʿAbdallah ʿAzzam: rajul daʿwa wa-madrasat jihad.* Amman: Dar al-Diyaʾ, 1990.

Al-Jihad fi Filastin farida sharʿiyya wa-darura harakiyya. N.p, 1982.

Jubran, Ghassan Dawʿar. *Khansaʾ fi Filastin.* Giza: Markaz al-Iʿlam al-ʿArabi, 2008.

Khalid, Hasan. *al-Shahid fiʾl-Islam.* Beirut: Dar al-ʿIlm liʾl-Malayin, 1971.

Al-Mahalli, Jalal al-Din, and Jalal al-Din al-Suyuti. *al-Qurʾan al-karim.* Beirut: Dar al-Maʿrifa, 1983.

    Tafsir al-jalalayn. Cairo: Maktabat Misr, n.d.

Al-Mahdi, Muhammad Ahmad ibn ʿAbdallah. *Manshurat al-Imam al-Mahdi al-ahkam waʾl-ʾadab.* 4 vols. Khartum: Wizarat al-Dakhiliyya, 1964.

Mahmud, ʿAbd al-Halim. *Kitab al-jihad.* Cairo: Dar al-Maʿrif, 1983.

    Fatawa. 2 vols. 4th ed. Cairo: Dar al-Maʿarif, 1996.

Mahumd, ʿAli ʿAbd al-Halim. *Wasaʾil al-tarbiya ʿind al-Ikhwan al-Muslimin.* 4th ed. Mansura: Dar al-Wafaʾ, 1990.

Al-Maqdisi, Abu Muhammad. *Waqafat maʿa thamarat al-jihad: bayna al-jahl fiʾl-sharʿ waʾl-jahl biʾl-waqiʿ.* 2004. Expanded edition, 2007. Available at: http://www.tawhed.ws or http://www.almaqdese.net; (accessed June 10, 2010).

Maʿrakat al-mujahid fi aqbiyat al-tahqiq. N.p., n.d.

Mawdudi, Abu al-Aʿla. *Shariʿat al-Islam fiʾl-jihad waʾl-ʿalaqat al-duwaliyya.* Cairo: Dar al-Sahwa, 1985.

    "Al-Jihad fi sabil Allah," in *Thalath rasaʾil fiʾl-jihad.* Amman: Dar al-ʿUmr, 1992, pp. 5–65.

Muslim, ibn al-Hajjaj al-Qushayri. *Sahih Muslim*. 5 vols. Beirut: Dar Ihya' al-Turath al-ʿArabi, n.d.

Al-Musnad, Muhammad ibn ʿAbd al-ʿAziz (ed.). *Fatawa Islamiyya*. 8 vols. Riyadh: Dar al-Watan, 1994.

Al-Mujahid amam al-tahqiq wa'l-taʿdhib, an appendix in *al-Islam wa-Filastin*, September 1, 1988, pp. 3–16.

Al-Nabhani, Taqi al-Din. *Nizam al-hukm fi'l-Islam mafahim Hizb al-Tahrir*. 2nd ed. Jerusalem: Manshurat Hizb al-Tahrir, 1953.

al-Shakhsiyya al-Islamiyya. 3 vols. 5th ed. Beirut: Dar al-Umma, 2003–2005.

Nadwi, Abul Hasan ʿAli. *Idha habbat rih al-iman*. New ed. Beirut: Mu'assasat al-Risala, 1985.

Tarshid al-sahwa al-Islamiyya, lecture delivered in Abu Dabi in November 1988, quoted in http://www.wadelhilew.ahlamontada.com/t111-topic. (accessed January 4, 2012).

Tasa'ulat fi tahaddiyat ʿala tariq al-daʿwa. Cairo: Dar al-Kalima, 1998.

Izalat asbab al-khudhlan ahamm wa-aqdam min izalat ʿathar al-ʿudwan. India: Dar al-ʿArafat, n.d.

Al-Nasa'i, Ahmad ibn Shuʿayb. *al-Sunan al-kubra'*. 10 vols. Beirut: Mu'assasat al-Risala, 2001.

Nur al-ʿashiqin. Beirut: Mu'assasat Bint al-Hady, n.d.

Al-Naysaburi, Abu ʿAbdallah Muhammad. *al-Musdatrak ʿala al-sahihayn*. 4 vols. Beirut: Dar al-Kutub al-ʿIlmiyya, 1990.

Al-Qaradawi, Yusuf. *al-Sabr fi'l-Qur'an*. Cairo: Maktabat Wahaba, 1970.

Al-Tarbiya al-Islamiyya wa-madrasat Hasan al-Banna. Cairo: Maktabat Wahaba, 1979.

Qira'a fi fiqh al-shahada, appendix to *al-Islam wa-Filastin*, June 5, 1988, pp. 1–15.

Qasim, ʿAbd al-Sattar. *al-Shaykh al-Mujahid ʿIzz al-Din al-Qassam*. 2nd ed. Nablus: Maktabat al-Risala, 1992.

Al-Qasimi, Zafir. *al-Jihad wa'l-huquq al-duwaliyya al-ʿamma fi'l-Islam*. Beirut: Dar al-ʿIlm li'l-Malayin, 1982.

Al-Qurtubi, Muhammad ibn Ahmad. *al-Jamiʿ li-ahkam al-Qur'an*. 22 vols. 2nd ed. Cairo: Dar al-Sha'b, 1952–1953.

Al-Mufhim. 4 vols. Cairo: Dar al-Kitab al-Misri, 1992.

Qutb, Sayyid. *Fi Zilal al-Qur'an*. 6 vols. New ed. Beirut: Dar al-Shuruq, 1986.

"Al-Jihad fi sabil Allah," in *Thalath rasa'il fi'l-jihad*. Amman: Dar al-ʿUmr, 1992, pp. 107–148.

Al-Razi, Fakhr al-Din. *Mafatih al-ghayb: al-tafsir al-kabir*. 32 vols. 3rd ed. Beirut: Dar Ihya' al-Turath al-ʿArabi, 2000.

Rida, Muhammad Rashid. *Tafsir al-Qur'an al-hakim*. 12 vols. 2nd ed. Cairo: Matb'at al-Manar, 1931–1932.

Saʿada, Antun. *fi mughtarabihi al-qasri al-aʿmal al-kamila*. N.p., 1942.

Al-Muhadharat al-ʿashr. N.p., 1948.

al-Islam fi risaltihi al-Masihiyya wa'l-Muhamadiyya. 4th ed. Beirut: n.p., 1980.

Fi'l-Mas'ala al-Lubnaniyya. 2nd ed. Beirut: Dar al-Fikr, 1991.

Al-Sadr, Muhammad Baqir. *Fadak fi'l-ta'rikh*. Beirut: Dar al- Taʿaruf al-Islami, 1990.

Salah, Mahmud. *Hakadha qatalna al-Sadat: 'i'tirafat Khalid al-Islambuli wa-zumalaihi fi hadith al-minassa*. Cairo: Maktabat Madbuli al-Saghir, 1995.

Al-San'ani, Abu Bakr 'Abd al-Razzaq ibn Hammam. *al-Musannaf*. 12 vols. Beirut: al-Majlis al-'Ilmi, 1970.

Al-Sarakhsi, Abu Bakr Muhammad. *al-Mabsut li'l-Sarakhsi*. Beirut: Dar al-Ma'rifa, 1985/1986.

Shaltut, Mahmud. *al-Fatawa*. Cairo: Dar al-Qalam, n.d.

Shams al-Din, Muhammad Mahdi. *Fiqh al-'unf al-musallah fi'l-Islam*. Baghdad: Markaz Dirasat Falsafat al-Din, 2004.

Sha'rawi, Muhammad Mutawalli. *al-Hayat wa'l-mawt*. Cairo: Akhbar al-Yaum, 1991.

Al-Sharif, Kamil, and Mustafa al-Sibai'. *al-Ikhwan al-Muslimun fi harb Filastin*. 3rd ed. Cairo: Maktabat Wahaba, n.d.

Al-Sharif, Sayyid Imam. *Wathiqat tarshid al-'amal al-jihadi fi Misr wa'l-'alam*. Available at: http://www.e-prism.org/images/TARSHID_AL-JIHAD.pdf (accessed January 8, 2011).

Al-Shawkani, Muhammad ibn 'Ali. *Fath al-qadir: al-jami' bayna fannay al-riwaya wa'l-diraya min 'ilm al-tafsir*. 5 vols. Beirut: Dar al-Fikr, n.d.

Shawkat, Sami. *Hadhihi ahdafuna*. Baghdad: Matba'at al-Tafid al-Ahliyya, 1939.

Al-Shaybani, Abu 'Abdallah Muhammad. *al-Mabsut li'l-Shaybani*. 5 vols. Karachi: Idarat al-Qur'an wa'l-'Ulum al-Islamiyya, n.d.

Al-Shuaybani, 'Abd al-Hamid. *Siyar al-shuhada': durus wa-'ibar*. Riyadh: Dar al-Watan, 1999.

Shuhada' ma'a sabq al-israr. N.p., 1993.

Al-Suri, Abu Mus'ab. *Da'wat al-muqawama al-Islamiyya al-'alamiyya*. Available at: http://www.4shared.com/office/bTr6J5ly/___.htm) (accessed July 3, 2012).

Al-Suyuti, Jalal al-Din. *Abwab al-sa'ada fi asbab al-shahada*. Cairo: al-Maktaba al-Qayyima, 1987.

Al-Tabari, Abu Ja'far Muhammad ibn Jarir. *Ta'rikh al-rusul wa'l-muluk*. 11 vols. Cairo: Dar al-Ma'arif, 1968.

Takruri, Nawaf Hayil (ed.). *al-'Amaliyyat al-istishhadiyya fi'l-mizan al-fiqhi*. 2nd ed. Damascus: Dar al-Fikr, 1997.

Al-Tamimi, As'ad Bayyud. *Zawal Isra'il hatmiyya Qur'aniyya*. Cairo: al-Mukhtar al-Islami, 1980.

Al-Tibi, 'Ukasha 'Abd al-Mannan (ed.). *Shahada wa'l-istishhad fi zilal al-Qur'an li'l-Shaykh Sayyid Qutb*. New ed. Cairo: Maktabat al-Turath al-Islami, 1994.

(ed.) *Fatawa al-Shaykh al-Albani*. Cairo: Maktabat al-Turth al-Islami, 1994.

Al-Tirmidhi, Muhammad ibn 'Isa. *Sunan al-Tirmidhi*. 5 vols. Beirut: Dar Ihya' al-Turath al-'Arabi, 1991.

Al-Tustari, Abu Muhammad Sahl ibn 'Abdallah. *Tafsir al-Qur'an al-'Azim*. Cairo: Dar al-Kutub al-'Arabiyya al-Kubra, 1911.

Al-'Uyayri, Yusuf. *Hal intaharat Hawwa' am istushhidat?* Available at: http://www.Wa.alsunnah.info/r?i=hqkfgsb2 (accessed February 6, 2013).

Dawr al-nisa' fi jihad al-a'da'. Available at: http://www.tawhed.ws/rl?i=3509&x=8fsj2em2 (accessed May 5, 2013).

Yakan, Fathi. *Nahwa haraka Islamiyya 'alamiyya wahida*. 3rd ed. Beirut: Dar al-Imam, 1977.

Madha ya'ni intima'i li'l-Islam. Beirut: Mu'assasat al-Risala, 1977.

Abjadiyyat al-tasawwur al-haraki li'l-ʿamal al-Islami. Beirut: Muʾassasat al-Risala, 1981.

Abjadiyyat al-tasawwur al-haraki li'l-ʿamal al-Islami. Beirut: Muʾassasat al-Risala, 1987.

Mushkilat al-daʿwa wa'l-daʿiya. Beirut: Muʾassasat al-Risala, 1987.

Yasin, Muhammad Naʿim. *Athar al-Islam fi takwin al-shakhsiyya al-jihadiyya li'l-fard wa'l-jamaʿa.* Kuwait: Dar al-Arqam, 1984.

Al-Zawahiri, Ayman. *al-Hisad al-murr.* Amman: Dar al-Bayariq, 1999.

Zayd, Mustafa. *al-Maslaha fi'l-tashriʿ al-Islami.* 2nd ed. Cairo: Dar al-Fikr al-Islami, 1964.

Al-Zirkili, Khayr al-Din. *al-Aʿlam: qamus wa-tarajim.* 15th ed. Beirut: Dar al-ʿIlm li'l-Malayyin, 2002.

Books and Articles in Other Languages

Abd-Allah, Umar F. *The Islamic Struggle in Syria.* Berkeley: Mizan Press, 1983.

Abdel Haleem, M. A. S. *The Qurʾan: A New Translation.* Oxford: Oxford University Press, 2004.

Abdelkader, Deina. "Modernity, the Principles of Public Welfare (maslaha) and the End Goals of Shari'a (maqasid) in Muslim Legal Thought," *Islam and Christian-Muslim Relations* 14 (2003), pp. 163–172.

Abedi, M., and G. Legenhausen (eds.). *Jihad and Shahadat: Struggle and Martyrdom in Islam.* Houston: Institute for Research and Islamic Studies, 1986.

Abrahamian, Ervand. *The Iranian Mojahedin.* New Haven: Yale University Press, 1989.

Abu ʿAmr, Ziad. *Islamic Fundamentalism in the West Bank and the Gaza Strip.* Bloomington: Indiana University Press, 1994.

Abufarha, Nasser. *The Making of a Human Bomb: The Ethnography of Palestinian Resistance.* Durham: Duke University Press, 2009.

El-Affendi, Abdelwahab. *Turabi's Revolution: Islam and Power in Sudan.* London: Grey Seal, 1991.

Afsaruddin, Asma. "Competing Perspectives on Jihad and Martyrdom in Early Islamic Sources," in Brian Wicker (ed.), *Witnesses to Faith? Martyrdom in Christianity and Islam.* Aldershot, Hants: Ashgate, 2006, pp. 15–31.

Aghaie, Kamran. *The Martyrs of Karbala: Shii Symbols and Rituals in Modern Iran.* Washington, DC: University of Washington Press, 2004.

Ajami, Fouad. *The Vanished Imam: Musa al-Sadr and the Shia of Lebanon.* London: I.B. Tauris, 1986.

Algar, Hamid. *Islam and Revolution: Writings and Declarations of Imam Khomeini.* Berkeley: Mizan Press, 1981.

Society and Economics in Islam: Writings and Declarations of Ayatullah Sayyid Mahmud Taleghani. Berkeley, CA: Mizan Press, 1982.

Allen, Lori. "Getting by the Occupation: How Violence Became Normal during the Second Palestinian Intifada," *Cultural Anthropology* 23/3 (2008), pp. 453–487.

Almond, Gabriel A., R. Scott Appleby and Emmanuel Sivan. *Strong Religion: The Rise of Fundamentalisms around the World.* Chicago: Chicago University Press, 2003.

Alshech, Eli. "The Emergence of the Infallible Jihad Fighter – The Salafi Jihadists' Quest for Religious Legitimacy," *Middle East Media Research Institute; Inquiry and Analysis* 30 (June 2008), pp. 1–11.

"Egoistic Martyrdom and Hamas' Success in the 2005 Municipal Elections: A Study of Hamas Martyrs' Ethical Wills, Biographies and Eulogies," *Die Welt des Islams* 48 (2008), pp. 23–49.

Andoni, Lamis. "Searching for Answers: Gaza's Suicide Bombers," *Journal of Palestine Studies* 24/4 (1997), pp. 33–45.

Andriolo, Karin. "Murder by Suicide: Episodes from Muslim History," *American Anthropologist* 104/3 (September 2002), pp. 736–742.

Anyat, Hamid. *Modern Islamic Political Thought.* Austin: University of Texas Press, 1982.

Apple, Michael W. *Official Knowledge: Democratic Education in a Conservative Age.* 2nd ed. New York: Routledge, 2000.

Arendt, Hannah. "On Violence," in idem, *Crises of the Republic* (New York: Harcourt Brace, 1972), pp. 105–112, 134–146.

Asad, Muhammad. *The Message of the Qur'an.* Gibraltar: Dar al-Andalus, 1980.

Asad, Talal. *Formations of the Secular: Christianity, Islam and Modernity.* Stanford, CA: Stanford University Press, 2003.

On Suicide Bombing. New York: Cambridge University Press, 2007.

Al-Asi, Muhammad. "The Struggle in the Holy Land," *Middle East Affairs Journal* 8/1–2 (2002), pp. 13–15.

Al-Atawneh, Muhammad. "Shahada versus Terror in Contemporary Islamic Legal Thought: The Problem of Suicide Bombers," *Journal of Islamic Law and Culture* 10/1 (April 2008), pp. 18–28.

Atwan, Abdel Bari. *The Secret History of al-Qaeda.* Berkeley: University of California Press, 2008.

Ayalon, Ami. *The Press in the Arab Middle East: A History.* Oxford: Oxford University Press, 1995.

Ayers, Nick. "Ghost Martyrs in Iraq: An Assessment of the Applicability of Rationalist Models to Explain Suicide Attacks in Iraq," *Studies in Conflict and Terrorism* 31/9 (September 2008), pp. 856–882.

Ayoub, Mahmoud Mahmoud. "Martyrdom in Christianity and Islam," in R. T. Antoun and M. E. Hegland (eds.), *Religious Resurgence: Contemporary Cases in Islam, Christianity and Judaism.* New York: Syracuse University Press, 1987, pp. 67–77.

Azaryahu, Maoz. *State Cults: Celebrating Independence and Commemorating the Fallen in Israel 1948–1956.* Beer Sheva: The Ben-Gurion Research Center, 1995.

Aziz, T. M. "The Role of Muhammad Baqir al-Sadr in Shi'i Political Activism in Iraq from 1958 to 1980," *International Journal of Middle East Studies* 25/2 (1993), pp. 207–222.

Al-Azmeh, Aziz. "Rhetoric for the Senses: A Consideration of Muslim Paradise Narratives," *Journal of Arabic Literature* 26 (1995), pp. 215–231.

'Azzam, 'Abdallah. *Join the Caravan.* 2nd ed. London: Azzam Publications, 2001.

"What Jihad Taught Me," in Ibrahim Abu Rabi' (ed.), *The Contemporary Arab Reader on Political Islam.* London: Pluto Press, 2010, pp. 42–47

"Martyrs: the Building Blocks of Nations." Available at: http://www.reli gioscope.com/info/doc/jihad/azzam_martyrs.htm (accessed May 24, 2010).

Bagchi, David. "Luther and the Problem of Martyrdom," in Dian Wood (ed.), *Martyrs and Martyrologies*. Cambridge, MA: Blackwell Publishers, 1993, pp. 209–219.

Bakken, Nicholas W. "The Anatomy of Suicide Terrorism: A Durkheimian Analysis," University of Delaware, 2007, pp. 1–11. Available at: http:// www.ifpo.org/wp-content/uploads/2013/08/Bakken_Suicide_Terrorism.pdf (accessed July 11, 2011).

Bakker, Edwin. "Jihadi Terrorists in Europe and Global Salafi Jihadis," in Rik Coolsaet (ed.), *Jihadi Terrorism and the Radicalisation Challenge in Europe*. Hampshire: Ashgate, 2008, pp. 69–84.

Barber, Benjamin. *Jihad vs. MacWorld*. New ed. London: Corgi Books, 2003.

Bar-Levav, Avriel. "When I was Alive: Jewish Ethical Wills as Egodocuments," in Rudolf Dekker (ed.), *Egodocuments and History: Autobiographical Writing in its Historical Context since the Middle Ages*. Rotterdam: Erasmus University Rotterdam, 2002, pp. 47–59.

Barltrop, Richard (ed.). *Muslims in Europe, Post 9/11*. Oxford: St. Antony's College, 2003.

Barone, Michael. "Cultures Aren't Equal," *U.S. News and World Report*, August 15–22, 2005. Available at: http://www.usnews.com/usnews/opinion/articles/ 050815/15barone.htm (accessed May 25, 2010).

Bar-Tal, Daniel. *Shared Beliefs in a Society: Social Psychological Analysis*. Thousand Oaks, CA: Sage Publications, 2000.

Baudrillard, Jean. *The Spirit of Terrorism and Requiem for the Twin Towers*, trans. by Chris Turner. London: Verso, 2002.

Bayat, Asef. *Making Islam Democratic: Social Movements and the Post-Islamist Turn*. Stanford: Stanford University Press, 2007.

Beeman, William O. *Iranian Performance Traditions*. Los Angeles: Mazda Press, 2010.

Behbudi, M. B. *The Qur'an – A New Interpretation*. Richmond, UK: Curzon Press, 1997.

Ben-Amos, Avner. *Funerals, Politics and Memory in Modern France 1789–1996*. Oxford: Oxford University Press, 2000.

Ben-Amos, Avner, and Daniel Bar-Tal. "Patriotism as a Psychological-Sociological Phenomenon," in idem (eds.), *Patriotism: Homeland Love*. Tel Aviv: Hakibbutz Hameuchad, 2004, pp. 13–28 (in Hebrew).

Bennigsen, Alexandre, and S. Enders Wimbush. *Muslim of the Soviet Empire: A Guide*. London: C. Hurst, 1985.

Berenbaum, Michael, and Reuven Firestone. "The Theology of Martyrdom," in Rona M. Fields et al. (eds.), *Martyrdom: The Psychology, Theology and Politics of Self-sacrifice*. Westport, CT: Praeger Publishers, 2004, pp. 117–145.

Bergen, Peter. *Holy War, Inc.: Inside the Secret World of Osama bin Laden*. New York: Simon and Schuster, 2002.

Bergen, Peter, and Paul Cruickshank. "The Unraveling: The Jihadist Revolt Against bin Laden," *New Republic*, June 11, 2008. Available at: http://www.tnr.com/article/the-unraveling (accessed October 8, 2010).

Berkey, Jonathan P. *Popular Preaching and Religious Authority in the Medieval Islamic Near East*. Seattle: University of Washington Press, 2001.

Berko, Anat. *The Path to Paradise: The Inner World of Suicide Bombers and Their Dispatchers*. Westport, CT: Praeger Security International, 2007.

   The Smarter Bomb: Women and Children as Suicide Bombers. New York: Rowman and Littlefield Publishers, 2012.

Berko, Anat, and Edna Erez. "Martyrs or Murderers? Victims or Victimizers? The Voices of Would-be Palestinian Female Suicide Bombers," in Cindy D. Ness (ed.), *Female Terrorism and Militancy: Agency, Utility, and Organization*. New York: Routledge, 2008, pp. 146–166.

Biggs, Michael. "Dying without Killing: Self-Immolations 1963–2002," in Diego Gambetta (ed.), *Making Sense of Suicide Missions*. Oxford: Oxford University Press, 2005, pp. 173–208.

Blidstein, Gerald J. *Political Concepts in Maimonidean Halakha*. Ramat-Gan: Bar-Ilan University, 1983.

Bloom, Mia. *Dying to Kill*. New York: Columbia University Press, 2005.

   "Dying to Kill: Motivations for Suicide Terrorism," in Ami Pedahzur (ed.), *Root Causes of Suicide Terrorism: The Globalization of Martyrdom*. London: Routledge, 2006, pp. 25–53.

Bonner, Michael. *Jihad in Islamic History*. Princeton, NJ: Princeton University Press, 2006.

Bonney, Richard. *Jihad: From the Quran to Bin Laden*. New York: Palgrave, 2004.

Bowersock, Glen W. *Martyrdom and Rome*. Cambridge: Cambridge University Press, 1995.

Boyarin, Daniel. *Dying for God: Martyrdom and the Making of Christianity and Judaism*. Stanford, CA: Stanford University Press, 1999.

Bozarslan, Hamit. *Violence in the Middle East: From Political Struggle to Self-Sacrifice*. Princeton: Markus Wiener Publishers, 2004.

Browers, Michaelle. "The Secular Bias of Ideology Studies and the Problem of Islamism," *Journal of Political Ideologies* 10 (2005), pp. 75–93.

Brown, Peter. *The Cult of Saints: Its Rise and Function in Latin Christianity*. Chicago: University of Chicago Press, 1981.

Bunt, Gary. *Islam in the Digital Age: E-Jihad, Online Fatwas and Cyber Islamic Environment*. London: Pluto Press, 2003.

Burdman, Daphna. "Education, Indoctrination, and Incitement: Palestinian Children on Their Way to Martyrdom," *Terrorism and Political Violence* 15 (2003), pp. 96–123.

Burke, Edmund, and David N. Yaghoubian. "Middle Eastern Societies and Ordinary People's Lives," in idems, *Struggle and Survival in the Modern Middle East*. London: I.B. Tauris, 1993, pp. 1–32.

Castelli, Elizabeth A. *Martyrdom and Memory: Early Christian Culture Making*. New York: Columbia University Press, 2004.

Cesari, Jocelyne. *When Islam and Democracy Meet: Muslims in Europe and the United States*. New York: Palgrave, 2004.

Chabbi, J. "Ribat," *Encylopaedia of Islam* 8 (1995), pp. 493–506.

Chelkowski, Peter (ed.). *Ta'ziyeh: Ritual and Drama in Iran*. New York: University Press, 1979.

Cherny, Israel W. *Fighting Suicide Bombing: A Worldwide Campaign for Life*. Westport, CT: Praeger Security International, 2007.

Chubin, Shahram, and Charles Tripp. *Iran and Iraq at War*. Boulders: Westview Press, 1991.

Clancy-Smith, Julia. "Saints, Mahdis, and Arms: Religion and Resistance in Nineteenth-Century North Africa," in Ira M. Lapidus and Edmund Burke (eds.), *Islam, Politics and Social Movements*. Berkeley: University of California Press, 1988, pp. 60–80.

Cohen, Amnon. *Political Parties in the West Bank under the Jordanian Regime, 1949–1967*. Ithaca: Yale University Press, 1982.

Cohen, Jeremy. *Sanctifying the Name of God: Jewish Martyrs and Jewish Memories of the First Crusade*. Philadelphia: University of Pennsylvania Press, 2004.

Cohen, Uri S. *Survival: Senses of Death between the World Wars*. Tel Aviv: Resling Publishing, 2007 (in Hebrew).

Cole, Juan R. *Sacred Space and Holy War: The Politics, Culture and History of Shi'ite Islam*. London: I.B. Tauris, 2002.

Connerton, Paul. *How Societies Remember*. Cambridge: Cambridge University Press, 1989.

Cook, David. "Suicide Attacks or 'Martyrdom Operations' in Contemporary Jihad Literature," *Novo Religio* 6 (2002), pp. 20–24.

"The Implications of 'Martyrdom Operations' for Contemporary Islam," *Journal of Religious Ethics* 32 (2004), pp. 129–151.

Understanding Jihad. Berkeley: University of California Press, 2005.

Martyrdom in Islam. New York: Cambridge University Press, 2007.

Cook, David, and Olivia Allison. *Understanding and Addressing Suicide Attacks: The Faith and Politics of Martyrdom Operations*. Westport, CT: Praeger Security International, 2007.

Cook, Michael. *Commanding Right and Forbidding Wrong in Islamic Thought*. Cambridge: Cambridge University Press, 2000.

Cormack, Margaret (ed.). *Sacrificing the Self: Perspectives on Martyrdom and Religion*. Oxford: Oxford University Press, 2002.

Council for the Preservation of Monuments. *Scenes of Fighting and Martyrdom Guide: War Years in Poland 1939–45*. Warsaw: Sport Turystyka Publication, 1968.

Crenshaw, Martha. "The Logic of Terrorism," in Walter Reich (ed.), *Origins of Terrorism*. Cambridge: Cambridge University Press, 1990, pp. 7–24.

Cunningham, Lawrence S. "Cause Non Poena: On the Contemporary Martyrs," in Johan Leemans (ed.), *More than a Memory: The Discourse of Martyrdom and the Construction of Christian Identity in the History of Christianity*. Leuven: Peeters, 2005, pp. 451–464.

Dabashi, Hamid. *Theology of Discontent*. New York: New York University Press, 1993.

Shi'ism: A Religion of Protest. Cambridge, MA: The Belknap Press of Harvard University Press, 2011.

Dabbagh, Nadia Taysir. *Suicide in Palestine: Narratives of Despair*. London: Hurst, 2005.

Dakake, Maria Massi. *The Charismatic Community: Shi'ite Identity in Early Islam*. New York: State University of New York Press, 2007.

Dale, Stephen Frederic. "Religious Suicide in Islamic Asia," *Journal of Conflict Resolution* 32/1 (March 1988), pp. 37–59.

Davis, Joyce M. *Martyrs: Innocence, Vengeance and Despair in the Middle East*. New York: Palgrave Macmillan, 2003.

Delooz, Pierre. "Towards a Sociological Study of Canonized Sainthood in the Catholic Church," in Stephan Wilson (ed.), *Saints and Their Cults*. London: Cambridge University Press, 1985, pp. 189–216.

Dollard, John et al. *Frustration and Aggression*. New Haven: Yale University Press, 1939.

Dolnik, Adam. "Die and Let Die: Exploring Links between Suicide Terrorism and Terrorist Use of Chemical, Biological, Radiological, and Nuclear Weapons," *Studies in Conflict and Terrorism* 26/1 (2003), pp. 17–35.

Donner, Fred M. "The Sources of Islamic Conceptions," in John Kelsay and James T. Johnson (eds.), *Just War and Jihad*. New York: Greenwood Press, 1991, pp. 31–69.

Dulou, Gilbert. *Le Problème Islamique*. Paris: n.p., 2002.

Durkheim, Émile. *On Suicide: A Study in Sociology*, trans. by John A. Spaulding and George Simpson. New ed. New York: The Free Press, 1966.

Eickelman, Dale, and Jon W. Anderson (eds.). *New Media in the Muslim World: The Emerging Public Sphere*. Bloomington: Indiana University Press, 1999.

"Redefining Muslim Publics," in idem. *New Media in the Muslim World: The Emerging Public Sphere*. Bloomington: Indiana University Press, 1999, pp. 1–18.

Eisenstadt, S. N. (ed.). *Max Weber on Charisma and Institution Building*. Chicago: University of Chicago Press, 1968.

Eliade, M. *Myth and Reality*. New York: Harper & Row, 1975.

Ellens, J. Harold. "Jihad in the Qur'an, Then and Now," in idem (ed.), *The Destructive Power of Religion*. London: Praeger, 2004, vol. 3, pp. 39–52.

Enzensberger, Hans Magnus. "Globalization and the Radical Loser," *New Perspectives Quarterly* 23/3 (June 2006), pp. 41–62.

Ephrat, Daphna. *Spiritual Wayfarers, Leaders in Piety: Sufis and the Dissemination of Islam in Medieval Palestine*. Cambridge, MA: Harvard Center for Middle Eastern Studies, 2008.

Eppel, Michael. "Note about the Term Effendiyya in the History of the Middle East," *International Journal of Middle East Studies* 41 (2009), pp. 535–539.

Eraqi-Klorman, Bat-Zion. "Muslim Society as an Alternative: Jews Converting to Islam," *Jewish Social Studies* 14/1 (Fall 2007), pp. 89–118.

Euben, Roxanne L. "Killing (for) Politics: Jihad, Martyrdom and Political Action," *Political Theory* 30/1 (2001), pp. 4–35.

Ewing, J. Franklin. "Juramentado: Institutionalized Suicide among the Moros of the Philippines," *Anthropological Quarterly* 28/4 (October 1955), pp. 148–155.

Ezzati, Abu al-Fazl. *The Spread of Islam: The Contributing Factors*. 4th ed. London: Islamic College for Advanced Studies Press, 2002.

Fandy, Mamoun. *Saudi Arabia and the Politics of Dissent*. New York: Palgrave Macmillan, 2001.

Fanon, Frantz. *The Wretched on the Earth*. New York: Grove Press, 1966.

Farnell, Lewis R. *Greek Hero Cult and Ideas of Immortality*. Oxford: Clarendon Press, 1921.

Farzaneh, Mateo Mohammad. "Shi'i Ideology, Iranian Secular Nationalism and the Iran-Iraq War," *Studies in Ethnicity and Nationalism* 7/1 (2007), pp. 86–103.

Fetzer, Joel S., and J. Christopher Soper. *Muslims and the State in Britain, France and Germany*. New York: Cambridge University Press, 2005.

Fields, Rona M., Salman Elbedour and Fadel Abu Hein, "Palestinian Suicide Bombers," in Chris E. Stout (ed.), *Psychology of Terrorism: Clinical Aspects and Responses*. Westport, CT: Praeger Publishers, 2002, vol. 2, pp. 193–223.

Filiu, Jean-Pierre. "The Brotherhood vs. Al-Qaeda: A Moment of Truth?" *Current Trends in Islamist Ideology* 9 (November 12, 2009). Available at: http://www.currenttrends.org/research/detail/the-brotherhood-vs-al-qaeda-a-moment-of-truth (accessed January 10, 2011).

Fish, Stanley Eugene. *Is There a Text in This Class? The Authority of Interpretive Communities*. Cambridge, MA: Harvard University Press, 1980.

Flanagan, T. "The Politics of Millennium," *Terrorism and Political Violence* 7/3 (Autumn 1995), pp. 164–172.

Flusser, David. "Martyrdom during the Period of the Second Temple and Early Christianity," in *Holy War and Martyrdom*. Jerusalem: Israeli Historical Society, 1968, pp. 61–71 (in Hebrew).

Freamon, Bernard K. "Martyrdom, Suicide and the Islamic Law of War: A Short Legal History," *Fordham International Law Journal* 27 (2003), pp. 299–369.

Frellich, Morris. "In the Relevance of Culture," in idem (ed.), *Masked Suicide and Culture*. New York: Bergin and Garvey, 1993, pp. 165–186.

Friedman, Thomas. *The Lexus and the Olive Tree*. New York: Farrar, 1999.
  Longitudes and Attitudes: Exploring the World after September 2001. New York: Farrar, 2002.
  The World is Flat: A Brief History of the Globalized World in the Twenty-first Century. New York: Farrar, Straus and Giroux, 2005.

Fuchs, Simon Wolfgang. *Proper Signposts for the Camp*. Wurzburg: Ergon Verlag, 2011.

Fukuyama, Francis. *The End of History and the Last Man*. New York: Free Press, 1992.

Gage, Richard L. (ed.). *Choose Life: A Dialogue – Arnold Toynbee and Disaku Lkeda*. London: Oxford University Press, 1976.

Galeotti, Mark. *Afghanistan: The Soviet Union's Last War*. London: Frank Cass, 1995.

Gambetta, Diego. "Forward," in idem. *Making Sense of Suicide Missions*. Oxford: Oxford University Press, 2005, pp. 259–299.
  "Can We Make Sense of Suicide Missions?" in idem, *Making Sense of Suicide Missions*. Oxford: Oxford University Press, 2005, pp. 279–283.

Gammer, Moshe. "Between Mecca and Moscow: Islam, Politics and Political Islam in Chechnya and Daghestan," *Middle Eastern Studies* 41 (November 2005), pp. 833–848.

Ganor, Boaz. "Suicide's Terrorism: An Overview," *Countering Suicide Terrorism* (journal online), 2000. Available at: http://www.ict.org (accessed July 15, 2010).

Geertz, C. *The Interpretation of Cultures.* New York: Basic Books, 1973.

Gensen, J. J. G. *The Neglected Duty.* New York: Macmillan, 1986.

Gentry, Caron E. "Twisted Maternalism: From Peace to Violence," *International Feminist Journal of Politics* 11/2 (June 2009), pp. 235–252.

Gerges, Fawaz A. *The Far Enemy: Why Jihad Went Global.* New York: Cambridge University Press, 2005.

Journey of the Jihadist. New York: Harcourt, 2007.

The Rise and Fall of al-Qaeda. Oxford: Oxford University Press, 2011.

Gerth, H. H., and C. Wright Mills (eds.). *From Max Weber: Essays in Sociology.* London: Kegan Paul, 1947.

El-Ghobashy, Mona. "The Metamorphosis of the Egyptian Brethren," *International Journal of Middle East Studies* 37 (2005), pp. 373–395.

Gillis, John R. (ed.). *Commemorations: The Politics of National Identity.* Princeton, NJ: Princeton University Press, 1994.

Ginzburg, Carlo. "Microhistory: Two or Three Things That I know about It," *Critical Inquiry* 20/1 (1993), pp. 10–35.

Gonzalez-Perez, Margaret. "From Freedom Birds to Water Buffaloes: Women Terrorists in Asia," in Cindy D. Ness (ed.), *Female Terrorism and Militancy: Agency, Utility, and Organization.* New York: Routledge, 2008, pp. 183–200.

Goodich, Michael. "The Politics of Canonization in the Thirteenth Century: Lay and Mendicant Saints," in Stephan Wilson (ed.), *Saints and Their Cults.* London: Cambridge University Press, 1985, pp. 169–187.

Graziano, Frank. *Cultures of Devotion: Folk Saints of Spanish America.* Oxford: Oxford University Press, 2007.

Greenberg, Karen J. *al-Qaeda Now: Understanding Today's Terrorists.* New York: Cambridge University Press, 2005.

Gregory, Brad S. *Salvation at Stake: Christian Martyrdom in Early Modern Europe.* Cambridge, MA: Harvard University Press, 1999.

Grossman, Avraham. "Martyrdom in the Eleventh and Twelfth Centuries: Between Ashkenaz and the Muslim World," *Pe'amim* 75 (Spring 1998), pp. 27–46 (in Hebrew).

Gunaratna, Rohan. *Inside al-Qaeda: Global Network of Terror.* New York: Rohan Gunaratna, 2003.

Gürbey, Gülistan. "The Development of the Kurdish Nationalism Movement in Turkey since the 1980s," in R. Olson (ed.), *The Kurdish Nationalist Movement in the 1990s.* Lexington: University Press of Kentucky, 1996, pp. 9–37.

Hafez, Kai. *Radicalism and Political Reform in the Islamic and Western Worlds.* Cambridge: Cambridge University Press, 2010.

Hafez, Mohammed M. "Dying to be Martyrs: The Symbolic Dimension of Suicide Terrorism," in Ami Pedahzur (ed.), *Root Causes of Suicide Terrorism.* London: Routledge, 2006, pp. 55–80.

Manufacturing Human Bombs: The Making of Palestinian Suicide Bombers. Washington, DC: U.S. Institute of Peace Press, 2006.

Suicide Bombers in Iraq: The Strategy and Ideology of Martyrdom. Washington, DC: U.S Institute of Peace Press, 2007.

Haim, Sylvia G. *Arab Nationalism: An Anthology.* Berkeley: University of California Press, 1962.

Halbwachs, Maurice. *On Collective Memory.* Chicago: University of Chicago Press, 1992.

Halevi, Leor. "The Consumer Jihad: Boycott Fatwas and Nonviolent Resistence on the World Wide Web," *International Journal of Middle East Studies* 44 (2012), pp. 45–70.

Hall, Stuart G. "Women among the Early Martyrs," in Dian Wood (ed.), *Martyrs and Martyrologies.* Cambridge, MA: Blackwell Publishers, 1993, pp. 1–21.

The Hamas Covenant. N.p., August 1988.

Hamzeh, Ahmad. *In the Path of Hizbullah.* Syracuse: Syracuse University Press, 2004.

Harel, Efrat. *Mobilizing Iranian Society during the War with Iraq, 1980–1988.* PhD dissertation; Tel Aviv: Tel Aviv University, 2003 (in Hebrew).

Harris, Sam. *The End of Faith: Religion, Terror, and the Future of Reason.* New York: W.W. Norton, 2004.

Hartman, David. *Crisis and Leadership: Epistles of Maimonides.* Philadelphia: Jewish Publication Society of America, 1985.

Hassan, Nasra. "An Arsenal of Believers: Talking to Human Bombs," *New Yorker* (November 2001), pp. 36–41.

"Are You Ready? Tomorrow You Will Be in Paradise," *Times,* July 14, 2005. Available at: http://www.timesonline.co.uk/tol/life_and style/article543551.ece (accessed July 11, 2011).

Hatina, Meir. "Iran and the Palestinian Islamic Movement," *Orient* 38 (March 1997), pp. 107–120.

Islam and Salvation in Palestine. Tel Aviv: The Moshe Dayan Center, 2001.

"Theology and Power in the Middle East: Palestinian Martyrdom in a Comparative Perspective," *Journal of Political Ideologies* 10 (October 2005), pp. 241–254.

"Restoring a Lost Identity: Models of Education in Modern Islamic Thought," *British Journal of Middle Eastern Studies* 33 (November 2006), pp. 179–197.

"'Ulama' and the Cult of Death in Palestine," *Israeli Affairs* 12 (January 2006), pp. 29–51.

"Introduction," in idem. Guardians of Faith in Modern Times: the Ulama in the Middle East. Leiden: Brill, 2008, pp. 1–21.

"Redeeming Sunni Islam: al-Qaʿida's Polemic against the Muslim Brethren," *British Journal of Middle Eastern Studies* 39/1 (April 2012), pp. 101–113.

Hegghammer, Thomas. *Jihad in Sadui Arabia.* Cambridge: Cambridge University Press, 2010.

Henten, J. W. van (ed.). *Die Entstehung der Jüdischen Martyrologie [The Emergence of Jewish Martyrology].* Leiden: Brill, 1989.

Herr, Moshe D. "Persecution and Martyrdom in Hadrian's Days," *Scripta Hierosolymitana* 23 (1972), pp. 85–125.

Hoare, Quintin, and Geoffrey Nowell-Smith (eds.). *Selections from the Prison Notebook of Antonio Gramsci*. New York: International Publishers, 1971.

Hobsbawm, Eric. "Introduction: Inventing Traditions," in E. Hobsbawm and T. Ranger (eds.), *The Invention of Tradition*. Cambridge: Cambridge University Press, 1983, pp. 1–14

"Mass-Producing Traditions: Europe 1870–1914," in E. Hobsbawm and T. Ranger (eds.), *The Invention of Tradition*. Cambridge: Cambridge University Press, 1983, pp. 263–307.

Hoffman, Bruce. *Inside Terrorism*. New York: Columbia University Press, 2006.

Hoffman, Bruce, and Gordon H. McCormick, "Terrorism, Signaling, and Suicide Attack," *Studies in Conflict and Terrorism* 27 (2004), pp. 243–281.

Holmes, Stephen. "Al-Qaeda, September 11, 2001," in Diego Gambetta (ed.), *Making Sense of Suicide Missions*. Oxford: Oxford University Press, 2005, pp. 131–172.

Holt, P. M. *A Modern History of Sudan*. 2nd ed., London: Weidenfeld and Nicolson, 1967.

Holtmann, Philipp. *Abu Mus'ab al-Suri's Jihad Concept*. Tel Aviv: Moshe Dayan Center, 2009.

Hopgood, Stephen. "Tamil Tigers 1987–2002," in Diego Gambetta (ed.), *Making Sense of Suicide Missions*. Oxford: Oxford University Press, 2005, pp. 43–76.

Hurvitz, Eli. *The Military Wing of Hizballah: A Social Profile*. Tel Aviv: Moshe Dayan Center, December 1999 (in Hebrew).

Ibrahim, Raymond. *The al-Qaeda Reader*. New York: Broadway Books, 2007.

İmset, İsmet G. *The PKK: A Report on Separatist Violence in Turkey, 1973–1992*. Ankara: Turkish Daily News, 1992.

"The PKK: Terrorists or Freedom Fighters?" *International Journal of Kurdish Studies* 10/1–2 (1996), pp. 45–100.

Israeli, Raphael. "A Manual of Islamic Fundamentalist Terrorism," *Terrorism and Political Violence* 14 (Winter 2002), pp. 23–40.

Islamikaza: Manifestations of Islamic Martyrology. London: Frank Cass, 2003.

Jaber, Hala. *Hizballah: Born with a Vengeance*. New York: Columbia University Press, 1997.

Jacoby, Susan. *Wild Justice: The Evolution of Revenge*. New York: Harper & Row, 1983.

Jacquard, Roland. *Fatwa contre l'Occident*. Paris: A. Michel, 1998.

Jalal, Ayesha. *Partisans of Allah*. Cambridge, MA: Harvard University Press, 2008.

Jansen, Johannes J. G. *The Dual Nature of Islamic Fundamentalism*. Ithaca, NY: Cornell University Press, 1997.

Jean-Klein, Iris. "Palestinian Martyrdom Revisited: Critical Reflections on Topical Cultures of Explanation," *Pragmatism, Law and Governmentality*. Paper 5 (2000), pp. 1–35. Available at: http://scholarship.law.cornell.edu/ealccs_plg/5. (accessed April 7, 2013).

Johnson, James T., and John Kelsay (eds.). *Cross, Crescent and Sword: The Justification and Limitation of War in Western and Islamic Traditions*. New York: Greenwood Press, 1990.

Johnson, Nels. *Islam and the Politics of Meaning in Palestinian Nationalism.* London: Kegan Paul International, 1982.

Jones, Chris. "Women, Death, and the Law during the Christian Persecutions," in Dian Wood (ed.), *Martyrs and Martyrologies.* Cambridge, MA: Blackwell Publishers, 1993, pp. 23–34.

Juergensmeyer, Mark. "The World-Wide Rise of Religious Nationalism," *Journal of International Affairs* 50/1 (Summer 1996), pp. 1–20.

"Terror in the Name of God," *Current History* 100 (November 2001), pp. 357–361.

Terror in the Mind of God. Berkeley: University of California Press, 2001.

Kalpakian, Jack. "Building the Human Bomb: The Case of the 16 May 2003 Attacks in Casablanca," *Studies in Conflict and Terrorism* 28 (2005), pp. 113–127.

Kassimir, Ronlad. "Complex Martyrs: Symbols and Catholic Church Formation and Political Differentiation in Uganda," *African Affairs* 90 (1991), pp. 357–382.

Kedar, Benjamin Z. *Crusade and Mission: European Approaches toward the Muslims.* New Jersey: Princeton University Press, 1984.

Kelsay, John. *Islam and War: A Study in Comparative Ethics.* Louisville, KY: John Knox Press, 1993.

Kenney, Jeffery T. *Muslim Rebels: Kharijites and the Politics of Extremism in Egypt.* Oxford: Oxford University Press, 2006.

Kepel, Gilles. *The Prophet and the Pharaoh.* London: Dar al-Saqi, 1985.

Jihad: The Trail of Political Islam. Cambridge, MA: Harvard University Press, 2002.

Kerr, M. H. *Islamic Reform.* Berkeley: University of California Press, 1966.

Khadduri, Majid. *War and Peace in the Law of Islam.* Baltimore: John Hopkins Press, 1955.

"Maslaha," *The Encyclopaedia of Islam* 6 (1991), pp. 738–740.

Khalili, Laleh. *Heroes and Martyrs of Palestine: The Politics of National Commemoration.* Cambridge, UK: Cambridge University Press, 2007.

Khosrokhavar, Farhad. "Toward an Anthropology of Democratization in Iran," *Critique: Critical Middle Eastern Studies* 9/16 (2000), pp. 3–29.

Suicide Bombers: Allah's New Martyrs. London: Pluto Press, 2005.

Kiefer, Thomas. *The Tausug: Violence and Law in a Philippine Moslem Society.* New York: Holt, Rinehart and Winston, 1972.

Kierkegaard, Søren. *Either/Or,* trans. by David F. Swenson and Lillian M. Swenson. New York: Doubleday, 1959, vol. 1.

Klausner, Samuel. "Martyrdom," *The Encyclopedia of Religion* 9 (1987), pp. 233–238.

Kleinberg, Aviad. *Prophets in Their Own Country.* Chicago: Chicago University Press, 1992.

Flesh Made Word: Saints' Stories and the Western Imagination. Cambridge, MA: Belknap Press of Harvard University Press, 2008.

Klob, Robert. *For All the Saints: Changing Perceptions of Martyrdom and Sainthood in the Lutheran Reformation.* Macon, GA: Mercer University Press, 1987.

"Lutheran Martyrology in the Reformation Era," in Johan Leemans (ed.), *More than a Memory: The Discourse of Martyrdom and the Construction of Christian Identity in the History of Christianity.* Leuven: Peeters, 2005, pp. 295–313.

Kohlberg, Etan. *Suicide and Self-sacrifice in Islamic Tradition.* Jerusalem: Institute for Asian and African Studies, 1987 (in Hebrew).

"Martyrdom and Self-sacrifice in Classical Islam," *Pe'amim* 75 (Spring 1988), pp. 5–27 (in Hebrew).

"Taqiyya in Shi'i Theology and Religion," in H. G. Kippenberg and G. G. Stroumsa (eds.), *Secrecy and Concealment: Studies in the History of Mediterranean and Near Eastern Religions*. Leiden: Brill, 1995, pp. 345–380.

"Martyrs and Martyrdom in Classical Islam," in A. Destro and M. Pesce (eds.), *Religions and Cultures*. Binghamton, NY: Global Publications, 2000, pp. 91–120.

Koopmans, Ruud et al. *Contested Citizenship: Immigration and Cultural Diversity in Europe*. Minneapolis: University of Minnesota Press, 2005.

Kostiner, Joseph. *The Making of Saudi Arabia 1916–1936*. New York: Oxford University Press, 1993.

Krämer, Gudrun, and Sabine Schmidtke. "Introduction: Religious Authority and Religious Authorities in Muslim Societies: A Critical Overview," in Gudrun Krämer and Sabine Schmidtke (eds.), *Speaking for Islam: Religious Authorities in Muslim Societies*. Leiden: Brill, 2006, pp. 1–14.

Kramer, Martin. "The Moral Logic of Hizballah," in W. Reich (ed.), *Origins of Terrorism*. Cambridge: Cambridge University Press, 1990, pp. 131–157.

"Sacrifice and Fratricide in Shiite Lebanon," in Mark Jurgensmeyer (ed.), *Violence and the Sacred in the Modern World*. London: Frank Cass, 1992, pp. 30–47.

Kupferschmidt, Uri M. *The Supreme Islamic Council: Islam under the British Mandate for Palestine*. Leiden: Brill, 1987.

Kurz, Robert W., and Charles K. Bartles. "Chechen Suicide Bombers," *Journal of Slavic Military Studies* 20 (2007), pp. 529–547.

Lacroix, Stephane. *Awakening Islam: The Politics of Religious Dissent in Contemporary Saudi Arabia*. Cambridge, MA: Harvard University Press, 2011.

Lahoud, Nelly. "In Search of Philosopher-Jihadis: Abu Muhammad al-Maqdisi's Jihadi Philosophy," *Totalitarian Movements and Political Religions* 10/2 (June 2009), pp. 205–220.

Landau-Tasseron, Ella. *"Non-Combatants" in Muslim Legal Thought*. Washington, DC: Hudson Institute, December 2006, pp. 1–25.

Landkford, Adam. "Ten Years after 9/11: The Suicidal Angel," in: dam-landkford/ten-years-after-911-the-s_b_956462.html (accessed date March 4, 2013).

The Myth of Martyrdom: What Really Drives Suicide Bombers, Rampage Shooting and other Self-Destructive Killers. New York: Palgrave Macmillan, 2013.

Larzillièr, Pénélop. "Le 'martyre' des jeunes Palestiniens pendant l'intifada Al Aqsa: analyse et comparaison," *Politique étrangère* 4 (octobre–décembre 2001), pp. 937–951.

Lauzière, H. "Post-Islamism and the Religious Discourse of 'Abd al-Salam Yasin," *International Journal of Middle East Studies* 37 (2005), pp. 241–261.

Lav, Daniel. "Jihadists and Jurisprudents: The 'Revisions' Literature of Sayyid Imam and Al-Gama'a Al-Islamiyya," in Joseph Morrison Skelly (ed.), *Political Islam from Muhammad to Ahmadinejad*. Santa Barbara, CA: Praeger Security International, 2010, pp. 105–146.

Radical Islam and the Revival of Medieval Theology. Cambridge: Cambridge University Press, 2012.

Leemans, Johan. "Martyr, Monk and Victor of Paganism: An Analysis of Basil of Caesarea's Panegyrical Sermon on Grodius," in Johan Leemans (ed.), *More than a Memory: The Discourse of Martyrdom and the Construction of Christian Identity in the History of Christianity*. Leuven: Peeters, 2005, pp. 45–79.

Levi Della Vida, G. "Khāridjites," *The Encyclopaedia of Islam* 4 (1997), pp. 1074–1077.

Lewinstein, Keith. "The Revaluation of Martyrdom in Early Islam," in Margaret Cormack (ed.), *Sacrificing the Self: Perspectives on Martyrdom and Religion*. Oxford: Oxford University Press, 2002, pp. 78–91.

Lewis, Bernard. *The Assassins: A Radical Sect in Islam*. New York: Basic Books, 1976. "The Revolt of Islam," *New Yorker*, November 19, 2001, pp. 50–63.

Lia, Brynjar. *The Muslim Brotherhood: The Rise of a Mass Movement*. London: Ithaca Press, 1991.
Architect of Global Jihad: The Life of al-Qaida Strategist Abu Musʿab al-Suri. New York: Columbia University Press, 2008.

Lichtenstein, Yechezkel S. *Suicide: Halakhic, Historical and Theological Aspects*. Tel Aviv: Hakibbutz Hameuchad, 2008 (in Hebrew).

Lilla, Mark. *The Stillborn God: Religion, Politics and the Modern West*. New York: Knopf, 2007.

Litvak, Meir. "The Islamization of the Palestinian-Israeli Conflict: The Case of Hamas," *Middle Eastern Studies* 34 (1998), pp. 148–163.
"'More Harmful than the Jews': Anti-Shiʿi Polemics in Modern Radical Sunni Discourse," in Mohammad Ali Amir-Moezzi, Meir M. Bar-Asher, and Simon Hopkins (eds.), *Le shiʿisme imamite quarante ans après*. Turnhout: Brepols, 2009, pp. 293–314.

Litvak, Meir, and Esther Webman. *From Empathy to Denial: Arab Responses to the Holocaust*. New York: Columbia University Press, 2009.

Luke, Allan. *Literacy, Textbooks and Ideology*. London: Falmer Press, 1998.

Lybarger, Loren D. *Identity and Religion in Palestine: The Struggle between Islamism and Secularism in the Occupied Territories*. Princeton, NJ: Princeton University Press, 2007.

Lynch, Marc. "Islam Divided between Salafi-Jihadi and the Ikhwan," *Studies in Conflict and Terrorism* 33/6 (May 3, 2010), pp. 467–487.

Maalouf, Amin. *In the Name of Identity: Violence and the Need to Belong*. New York: Penguin Book, 2000.

McAdam, Doug et al. (eds.). *Comparative Perspectives on Social Movements: Political Opportunities, Mobilizing Structures, and Cultural Framings*. Cambridge: Cambridge University Press, 1996.

MacAuley, Denis. "Ideology of Osama Bin Laden: Nation, Tribe and World Economy," *Journal of Political Ideologies* 10/3 (October 2005), pp. 269–287.

MacDermott, Terry. *Perfect Soldiers: The Hijackers – Who They Were, Why They Did It*. New York: HarperCollins, 2005.

Madelung, Wilfred. *Religious Trends in Early Islamic Iran*. Albany, NY: Bibliotheca Persica, 1988.

Majul, Cesar Adib. *Muslims in the Philippines*. Quezon City: University of the Philippines Press, 1973.

Makiya, Kanan, and Hassan Mneimneh. "Manual for a Raid," in R. B. Silvers (ed.), *Striking Terror: America's New War*. New York: Publishers Group West, 2002, pp. 303–327.

Mandaville, Peter G. "Reimagining the Umma?" in Ali Mohammadi (ed.), *Islam Encountering Globalization*. London: Routledge, 2002, pp. 61–90.

Global Political Islam. London: Routledge, 2007.

Mansfield, Laura. *His Own Words: Translation and Analysis of the Writings of Dr. Ayman al-Zawahiri*. Old Tappan, NJ: TLG Publications, 2006.

Maréchal, Brigitte. *The Muslim Brothers in Europe: Roots and Discourse*. Leiden: Brill, 2008.

Martin, R. C. "The Religious Foundation of War, Peace, and Statecraft in Islam," in John Kelsay and James T. Johnson (eds.), *Just War and Jihad*. New York: Greenwood Press, 1991, pp. 91–117.

Martin, Vanessa. *Islam and Modernism*. London: Tauris, 1989.

Marvin, Carolyn, and David W. Inge. "Blood Sacrifice and the Nation: Revisiting Civil Religion," *Journal of the American Academy of Religion* 64/4 (1996), pp. 767–780.

Masalha, Shafiq. "Children and Violent Conflict: A Look at the Inner World of Palestinian Children via Their Dreams," *Palestinian-Israeli Journal* 10 (2003), pp. 62–70.

Masud, M. K., B. Messick, and D. S. Powers. "Muftis, Fatwas and Islamic Legal Interpretation," in M. K. Masud, B. Messick, and D. S. Powers (eds.), *Islamic Legal Interpretation: Muftis and Their Fatwas*. Cambridge, MA: Harvard University Press, 1996, pp. 3–26.

Mauss, Marcel. *The Gift: The Form and Reason for Exchange in Archaic Societies*. London: Routledge, 1990.

Mawdudi, Sayyid Abul A'la. *Towards Understanding the Qur'an*. 7 vols. Leicester: Islamic Foundation, 1990.

Maxwell, Margaret. *Narodniki Women: Russian Women Who Sacrificed Themselves for the Dream of Freedom*. New York: Pergamon Press, 1990.

McGregor, Andrew. "'Jihad and the Rifle Alone': 'Abdullah 'Azzam and the Islamist Revolution," *Journal of Conflicts Studies* 33/2 (Fall 2003), pp. 92–113.

Meital, Yoram. "The Struggle over Political Order in Egypt: The 2005 Elections," *Middle East Journal* 60/2 (Spring 2006), pp. 257–279.

Melucci, Alberto. "The Process of Collective Identity," in Hank Johnston and Bert Klandermans (eds.), *Social Movements and Culture*. Minneapolis: University of Minnesota Press, 1995, pp. 41–63.

Challenging Codes: Collective Action in the Information Age. Cambridge: Cambridge University Press, 1996.

Merari, Ariel. "The Readiness to Kill and Die," in Walter Reich (ed.), *Origins of Terrorism*. Cambridge: Cambridge University Press, 1990, pp. 192–207.

"Social, Organizational and Psychological Factors in Suicide Terrorism," in Tore Bjørgo (ed.), *Roots Causes of Terrorism*. London: Routledge, 2005, pp. 70–86.

Driven to Death: Psychological and Social Aspects of Suicide Terrorism. New York: Oxford University Press, 2010.

Millard, J., and Robert Collins. *Revolutionary Sudan: Hasan al-Turabi and the Islamist State 1989–2000*. Leiden: Brill, 2003.

Milstein, Michael. *Mukawama: The Challenge of Resistance to Israel's National Security Concept*. Tel Aviv: Institute for National Security Studies, December 2007 (in Hebrew).

Milton-Edwards, Beverley, and Stephen Farrell. *Hamas: The Islamic Resistance Movement*. Cambridge: Polity, 2010.

Mishal, Shaul. "Al-Qaeda as a Dune Organization: Toward a Typology of Islamic Terrorist Organizations," *Studies in Conflict and Terrorism* 28/4 (2005), pp. 275–294.

Mishal, Shaul, and Avraham Sela. *The Palestinian Hamas: Vision, Violence and Coexistence*. 2nd ed. New York: Columbia University Press, 2006.

Mitchell, R. P. *The Society of the Muslim Brothers*. London: Oxford University Press, 1969.

Moghadam, Assaf. "Palestinian Suicide Terrorism in the Second Intifada: Motivations and Organizational Aspects," *Studies in Conflict and Terrorism* 26/2 (2003), pp. 69–76.

The Globalization of Martyrdom: al-Qaeda, Salafi Jihad and the Diffusion of Suicide Attacks. Baltimore: Johns Hopkins University Press, 2008.

Molloy, Rebecca. "Deconstructing Ibn Taymiyya's Views on Suicidal Missions," *CTC Sentinel* 2/3 (2009), pp. 16–19.

Morris, Colin. "Martyrs on the Filed of Battle before and during the First Crusade," in Diane Wood (ed.), *Martyrs and Martyrologies*. Cambridge, MA: Blackwell Publishers, 1993, pp. 93–104.

Mosse, George L. *Fallen Soldiers: Reshaping the Memory of the World Wars*. New York: Oxford University Press, 1990.

The Nationalizations of the Masses: Political Symbolism and Mass Movements in Germany from the Napoleonic Wars through the Third Reich. New York: Howard Fertig, 1975.

Mottahedeh, Roy P., and Ridwan al-Sayyid. "The Idea of the Jihad in Islam before the Crusade," in Angeliki E. Laiou and Roy P. Mottahedeh (eds.), *The Crusades from the Perspective of Byzantium and the Muslim World*. Washington, DC: Dumbarton Oaks, 2001, pp. 23–29.

Al-Mubarak, Khalid. *Turabi's Islamist Venture and Implications*. Cairo: El Dar El Thaqafia, 2001.

Mutahhari, Murtada. "Shahid," in M. Abedi and G. Legenhausen (eds.), *Jihad and Shahadat: Struggle and Martyrdom in Islam*. Houston, TX: Institute for Research and Islamic Studies, 1986, pp. 125–148.

Jihad: The Holy War of Islam and Its Legitimacy in the Qur'an, trans. by Mohammad S. Tawhidi. Tehran: Department of Translation and Publication, 1998.

Nachmani, Amikam. "The Palestinian Intifada: The Dynamics of Symbols and Symbolic Realities – The Role of Symbols, Rituals and Myths in National Struggles," *Alpayim* 24 (2002), pp. 75–118 (in Hebrew).

Najjar, Orayb A. "The Editorial Family of al-Kateb Bows in Respect: The Construction of Martyrdom Text Genre in One Palestinian Literary Magazine," *Discourse and Society* 7/4 (1996), pp. 499–530.

Nasr, Seyyed Vali Reza. *The Vanguard of the Islamic Revolution: The Jama'at-i Islami of Pakistan*. Berkeley: University of California Press, 1994.

Mawdudi and the Making of Islamic Revivalism. New York: Oxford University Press, 1996.

Nazemi, Nader. "Sacrifice and Authorship: A Compendium of the Wills of Iranian War Martyrs," *Iranian Studies* 30 (1997), pp. 263–271.

Neria, Yuval, et al. "The al-Qaeda 9/11 Instructions: A Study in the Construction of Religious Martyrdom," *Religion* 35 (2005), pp. 1–11.

Netzer, Miriam. "One Voice? The Crisis of Legal Authority in Islam," *al-Nakhla* (Spring 2004), pp. 1–5.

Neusner, Jacob. *The Talmud of Babylonia*. Atlanta, GA: American Scholars Press, 1996.

Newman, Hillel. *Proximity to Power and Jewish Sectarian Groups of the Ancient Period*. Leiden: Brill, 2006.

Nietzsche, Friedrich. *The Will to Power*. 2 vols. New York: Russell & Russell, 1964.

Nivat, Anne. "The Black Widows: Chechen Women Join the Fight for Independence – and Allah," in Cindy D. Ness (ed.), *Female Terrorism and Militancy: Agency, Utility, and Organization*. New York: Routledge, 2008, pp. 122–130.

Nora, Pierre. *Realms of Memory: Rethinking the French Past*, trans. by Arthur Goldhammer. New York: Columbia University Press, 1996–1998.

Norton, Augustus R. *Amal and the Shiʿa: Struggle for the Soul of Lebanon*. Austin: University of Texas Press, 1988.

Hezbollah: A Short History. Princeton, NJ: Princeton University Press, 2007.

Ohnuki-Tierney, Emiko. *Kamikaze, Cherry Blossoms and Nationalisms*. Chicago: University of Chicago Press, 2002.

Oliver, Anne Marie, and Paul F. Steinberg. *The Road to Martyrs' Square: A Journey into the World of the Suicide Bomber*. New York: Oxford University Press, 2005.

Oron, Israel. *Death, Immortality and Ideology*. Tel Aviv: Ministry of Defense, 2002 (in Hebrew).

Owens, Cóilín. "A Literary Preamble," in Rona M. Fields et al. (eds.), *Martyrdom: The Psychology, Theology and Politics of Self-sacrifice*. Westport, CT: Praeger Publishers, 2004, pp. 3–21.

Özcan, Ali Kemal. *Turkey's Kurds: A Theoretical Analysis of the PKK and Abdullah Öcalan*. London: Routledge, 2006.

Pape, Robert A. "The Strategic Logic of Suicide Terrorism," *American Political Science Review* 97 (August 2003), pp. 343–361.

Dying to Win: The Strategic Logic of Suicide Terrorism. New York: Random House, 2005.

Pargeter, Alison. *The New Frontiers of Jihad: Radical Islam in Europe*. London: I.B. Tauris, 2008.

Pauly, Robert J. *Islam in Europe: Integration or Marginalization?* Aldershot: Ashgate, 2004.

Paz, Reuven. "The Saudi Fatwah against Suicide Terrorism," *PeaceWatch*, May 2, 2001. Available at: http://www.ict.org.il/Articles/tabid/66/Articlsid/63/currentpage/34/Default.aspx (accessed August 13, 2010).

Peteet, Julie. "Male Gender and Rituals of Resistance in Palestinian Intifada: A Cultural Politics of Violence," in Samir Khalaf and Roseanne Saad Khalaf (eds.), *Arab Youth: Social Mobilization in Times of Risk*. London: Dar al-Saqi, 2011, pp. 197–219.

Peters, Rudolph. "Wasiyya," *The Encyclopaedia of Islam* 1 (1960), pp. 171–172. *Jihad in Classical and Modern Islam*. Princeton: Markus Wiener Publishers, 1996.

Piscatori, James P. *Islam in a World of Nations States*. Cambridge: Cambridge University Press, 1986.

Pitcher, Linda M. "The Divine Impatience: Ritual, Narrative, and Symbolization in the Practice of Martyrdom," *Medical Anthropology Quarterly* 12/1 (1998), pp. 8–30.

Platt, Larry A., and V. Richard Persico. *Grief in Cross-Cultural Perspectives*. New York: Garland Publishers, 1992.

Podeh, Elie. *The Arab-Israel Conflict in Israeli History Textbooks 1948–2000*. Westport, CT: Bergin and Garvey, 2002.

Pritchard, Colin. *The Ultimate Rejection? A Psycho-Social Study*. Buckingham: Open University Press, 1995.

Ul-Qadri, Muhammad Tahir. *Fatwa on Terrorism and Suicide Bombings*. London: Minhaj ul-Qur'an International, 2001.

Qasim, Na'im. *Hizbullah: The Story from Within*. London: Dar al-Saqi, 2005.

Rahman, H.R. "The Concept of Jihad in Egypt – A Study of Majallat al-Azhar 1936–1982," in Gabriel R. Warburg and U.M. Kupferschmidt (eds.), *Islam, Nationalism and Radicalism in Egypt and the Sudan*. New York: Praeger, 1983, pp. 249–261.

Rahnema, Ali. *An Islamic Utopian: A Political Biography of Ali Shari'ati*. London: I.B. Tauris, 1998.

Rahner, Karl. *On the Theology of Death*. New York: Herder and Herder, 1961.

Ram, Haggai. *Myth and Mobilization in Revolutionary Iran*. Washington, DC: American University Press, 1994.

Iranophobia: The Logic of an Israeli Obsession. Stanford, CA: Stanford University Press, 2009.

Ranstorp, Magnus. "Terrorism in the Name of Religion," *Journal of International Affairs* 50/1 (Summer 1996), pp. 41–62.

Al-Rasheed, Madawi. *Contesting the Saudi State*. New York: Cambridge University Press, 2007.

Reich, Wilhelm. *The Mass Psychology of Fascism*. Harmondsworth: Penguin Books, 1970.

Rein, Ra'anan. *Populism and Charisma: Peronist Argentina 1943–1955*. Tel Aviv: Modan, 1998 (in Hebrew).

Reiter, Yitzhak. *War, Peace and International Relations in Islam*. Brighton: Sussex Academic Press, 2011.

Reuter, Christoph. *My Life Is a Weapon: A Modern History of Suicide Bombing*. Princeton: Princeton University Press, 2004.

Riddle, Donald W. *The Martyrs: A Study in Social Control*. Chicago: University of Chicago Press, 1931.

Riemer, Jeffrey W. "Durkheim's Heroic Suicide in Military Combat," *Armed Forces and Society* 25 (Fall 1998), pp. 103–120.

Riley-Smith, Jonathan. *The First Crusade and the Idea of Crusading*. Philadelphia: University of Pennsylvania Press, 1986.

Rinder, Michael T. *The Evolution of Religion Nationalism in Pakistan: Islamic Identity, Ideology and State Power*. PhD dissertation; Cambridge, MA: Harvard University, 2007.

Robinson, Glenn E. "Hamas as Social Movement," in Quintan Wiktorowicz (ed.), *Islamic Activism: A Social Movement Theory Approach*. Bloomington: Indiana University Press, 2004, pp. 112–139.

Rosental, Franz. "On Suicide in Islam," in idem, *Muslim Intellectual and Social History*. London: Variorum, 1990, pp. 239–246.

Rosourx, Valérie. "The Politics of Martyrdom," in Rona M. Fields et al. (eds.), *Martyrdom: The Psychology, Theology and Politics of Self-sacrifice*. Westport, CT: Praeger Publishers, 2004, pp. 83–116.

Rotenberg, Mordechai. *From Mikdash to Midrash: Psychology of Fundamentalism and Judaism*. Tel Aviv: Schocken Publishing House, 2001 (in Hebrew).

   Heaven, Hell and Immortality: Christianity, Islam and Judaism. Jerusalem: Rubin Mass Ltd., 2008 (in Hebrew).

Roth, Cecil. "Religion and Martyrdom among the Conversos," in *Holy War and Martyrdom*. Jerusalem: Israeli Historical Society, 1968, pp. 93–105 (in Hebrew).

Rouleau, Éric. "Politics in the Name of the Prophet," *Le Monde diplomatique* (English edition, November 2001). Available at: http://mondediplo.com/2001/11/09prophet (accessed May 25, 2010).

Russell, Bertrand. *On Education*. London: Unwin Books, 1964.

Russell, Frederick H. *The Just War in the Middle Ages*. Cambridge: Cambridge University Press, 1975.

Safrai, Shemuel. "Martyrdom in the Teachings of the Tannaim," in Th.C. de Kruijf and H. van de Sandt (eds.), *Sjaloom*. Arnhem: B. Folkertsma Stichting voor Tamudica, 1983, pp. 145–164.

Sageman, Marc. *Leaderless Jihad: Terror Networks in the Twenty-First Century*. Philadelphia: University of Pennsylvania Press, 2004.

   Understanding Terror Networks. Philadelphia: University of Pennsylvania Press, 2004.

Salt, J. "An Islamic Scholar-Activist: Mustafa al-Sibaʿi and the Islamic Movement in Syria 1945–1954," *Journal of Arabic, Islamic and Near Eastern Studies* 3 (1996), pp. 103–115.

Sande, Hans. "Palestinian Martyr Widowhood: Emotional Needs in Conflict with the Role Expectations," *Social Science and Medicine* 34 (1992), pp. 710–716.

Savinkov, Boris. *Memoirs of a Terrorist*. New York: Kraus Reprint Co., 1972.

Sayigh, Yezid. *Armed Struggle and the Search for State: The Palestinian National Movement 1949–1993*. Oxford: Clarendon Press, 1997.

Schalk, Peter. "Resistance and Martyrdom in the Process of State Formation in Tamililam," in Joyce Pettigrew (ed.), *Martyrdom and Political Resistence: Essays from Asia and Europe*. Amsterdam: VU University Press, 1997, pp. 61–83.

Scheuer, Michael. *Osama bin Laden*. Oxford: Oxford University Press, 2011.

Schleifer, S. Abdallah. "Izz al-Din al-Qassam: Preacher and Mujahid," in Edmund Burke and David N. Yaghoubian (eds.), *Struggle and Survival in the Modern Middle East*. London: I.B. Tauris, 1993, pp. 164–178.

Schmucker, Werner. "Iranische Märtyretestamente," *Die Welt des Islams* 27 (1987), pp. 185–249.

Schumann, Christoph. "Freiheit und Staat im islamistischen Diskurs," in *Islam und Moderner Nationalstaat*. Paderborn: Wilhelm Fink Verlag, forthcoming.

Schuster, Henry. "al-Qaeda's Media Strategy," in Karen J. Greenberg (ed.), *al-Qaeda Now: Understanding Today's Terrorists*. New York: Cambridge University Press, 2005, pp. 112–134.

Schwartz, Barry. "The Social Context of Commemoration: A Study in Collective Memory," *Social Forces* 61 (December 1982), pp. 374–376.

Schwedler, Jillian. *Faith in Moderation: Islamist Parties in Jordan and Yemen*. Cambridge: Cambridge University Press, 2006.

Schweitzer, Yoram. "Palestinian Female Suicide Bombers: Virtuous Heroines or Damaged Goods?" in Cindy D. Ness (ed.), *Female Terrorism and Militancy: Agency, Utility, and Organization*. New York: Routledge, 2008, pp. 131–145.

"Suicide Bombings: The Ultimate Weapon?" in *International Policy*. Hertzlia: Institute for Counter-Terrorism, August 7, 2001. Available at: http://www.ict. org.il/Articles/tabid/66/Articlsid/68/Default.aspx (accessed June 23, 2010).

Scott, James C. "Protest and Profanation: Agrarian Revolt and the Little Tradition," *Theory and Society* 4 (1977), Parts 1–2, pp. 1–38, 211–245.

Sears, David. *At War with the Wind: the Epic Struggle with Japan's World War II Suicide Bombers*. New York: Citadel, 2008.

Seely, Robert. *Russo-Chechen Conflict 1800–2000: A Deadly Embrace*. Portland, OR: Frank Cass, 2001.

Seery, John. E. *Political Theory for Mortals*. Ithaca, NY: Cornell University Press, 1996.

Seyed-Goharb, Asghar. "Martyrdom as Piety: Mysticism and National Identity in Iran-Iraq War Poetry," *Der Islam* Bd. 87 (2010), pp. 248–273.

Shari'ati, 'Ali. *Martyrdom: Arise and Bear Witness*, trans. by Ali Asghar Ghassemy. Tehran: Ministry of Islamic Guidance, 1981.

Man and Islam, trans. by Fatollah Marjani. Houston, TX: Free Islamic Lit, 1982.

"Shahadat," in M. Abedi and G. Legenhausen (eds.), *Jihad and Shahadat: Struggle and Martyrdom in Islam*. Houston, TX: The Institute for Research and Islamic Studies, 1986, pp. 153–229.

"A Discussion of Shahid," in M. Abedi and G. Legenhausen (eds.), *Jihad and Shahadat: Struggle and Martyrdom in Islam*. Houston, TX: Institute for Research and Islamic Studies, 1986, pp. 230–241.

"Expectations from the Muslim Women," in Laleh Bakhtiar, *Shariati on Shariati and the Muslim Women*. Chicago: ABC International Group, 1996, pp.51–73.

"Fatima is Fatima," in Laleh Bakhtiar, *Shariati on Shariati and the Muslim Women*. Chicago: ABC International Group, 1996, pp. 75–213.

Shay, Shaul. *The Shahids: Islam and Suicide Attacks*. New Brunswick: Interdisciplinary Center, 2004.

Sheffer, Gabriel. *Diaspora Politics: At Home Abroad*. New York: Cambridge University Press, 2003.

"Diasporas, Terrorism, and WMD," *International Studies Review* 7/1 (March 2005), pp. 160–162.

Shirazi, Faegheh. *The Veil Unveiled: The Hijab in Modern Culture*. Gainesville: University Press of Florida, 2001.

"The Islamic Republic of Iran and Women's Images: Masters of Exploitation," in Faegheh Shirazi (ed.), *Muslim Women in War and Crisis: Representation and Reality*. Austin: University of Texas Press, 2010, pp. 109–138.

Shoshan, Boaz. *Popular Culture in Medieval Cairo*. Cambridge: Cambridge University Press, 1993.

Silber, Ilana F. "Echoes of Sacrifice? Repertoires of Giving in the Great Religions," in Albert I. Baumgarten (ed.), *Sacrifice in Religious Experience*. Leiden: Brill, 2002, pp. 291–312.

Silverman, Adam L. "Just War, Jihad and Terrorism: A Comparison of Western and Islamic Norms for the Use of Political Violence," *Journal of Church and State* 44/1 (Winter 2002), pp. 73–92.

Singer, Amy. *Charity in Muslim Societies*. Cambridge: Cambridge University Press, 2008.

Singerman, Diane. "The Networked World of Islamist Social Movements," in Quintan Wiktorowicz (ed.), *Islamic Activism: A Social Movement Theory Approach*. Bloomington: Indiana University Press, 2004, pp. 143–163.

Sivan, Emmnuael. *Radical Islam*. New Haven: Yale University Press, 1990.

The 1948 Generation: Myth, Profile and Memory. Tel Aviv: Ministry of Defence, 1991 (in Hebrew).

The Clash within Islam. Tel Aviv: Amm Oved, 2000 (in Hebrew).

Sizgorich, Thomas. *Violence and Belief in Late Antiquity: Militant Devotion in Christianity, and Islam*. Philadelphia: University of Pennsylvania Press, 2009.

Skovaard-Petersen, Jakob. *Defining Islam for the Egyptian State*. Leiden: Brill, 1997.

"Fatwas in Print," *Culture and History* 16 (1997), pp. 73–88.

"In Defence of Muhammad: 'Ulama', Da'iya and the New Islamic Internationalism," in Meir Hatina (ed.), *Guardians of Faith in Modern Times: 'Ulama' in the Middle East*. Leiden: Brill, 2008, pp. 291–309.

Smith, Anthony. *National Identity*. London: Reno: University of Nevada Press, 1991.

Smith, Sebastian. *Allah's Mountains: The Battle for Chechnya*. Revised ed. London: Tauris Parke Paperbacks, 2006.

Speckhard, Anne, and Khapta Ahkmedova. "Mechanisms of Generating Suicide Terrorism: Trauma and Bereavement as Psychological Vulnerabilities in Human Security – The Chechen Case," in Jill Donnelly et al. (ed.), *Developing Strategies to Deal with Trauma in Children*. Amsterdam: IOS Press, 2005, pp. 54–69. Available at: http://ebooks.iospress.nl/volume/developing-strategies-to-deal-with-trauma-in-children (accessed July 6, 2010).

"The Making of a Martyr: Chechen Suicide Terrorism," *Studies in Conflict and Terrorism* 29/5 (2006), pp. 1–65.

"Black Widows and Beyond: Understanding the Motivations and Life Trajectories of Chechen Female Terrorists," in Cindy D. Ness (ed.), *Female Terrorism and Militancy: Agency, Utility, and Organization*. New York: Routledge, 2008, pp. 100–121.

Springer, Devin R., James L. Regens, and David N. Edger. *Islamic Radicalism and Global Jihad*. Washington, DC: Georgetown University Press, 2009.

Sprinzak, Ehud. "Rational Fanatics," *Foreign Policy*, no. 120 (September–October 2000), pp. 66–73.

Stein, Rebecca L., and Ted Swedenburg. "Popular Culture, Rational History and the Question of Power in Palestine and Israel," *Journal of Palestinian Studies* 33/4 (Summer 2004), pp. 5–20.

Stein, Ruth. "Vertical Mystical Homoeros," *Studies in Gender and Sexuality* 4/1 (Winter 2003), pp. 38–58.

Stock, Brian. *The Implications of Literacy: Written Language and Models of Interpretation in the Eleventh and Twelfth Centuries*. Princeton, NJ: Princeton University Press, 1983.

Stories from the Thousand and One Nights, trans. by Edward William Lane. New York: P.F. Collier, 1909.

Stork Joe. *Erased in a Moment: Suicide Bombing Attacks against Israeli Civilians*. New York: Human Rights Watch, October 2002.

Sviri, Sara. *The Sufis: An Anthology*. Tel Aviv: Tel Aviv University, 2008 (in Hebrew).

Swenson, Jill D. "Martyrdom: Mythro-Cathexis and Mobilization of the Masses in the Iranian Revolution," *Ethos* 13/2 (Summer 1985), pp. 121–149.

Szanjder, Mario, and Luis Roniger. *The Politics of Exile in Latin America*. New York: Cambridge University Press, 2009.

Szyska, Christian. "Martyrdom: A Drama of Foundation and Tradition," in Friederike Pannewick (ed.), *Martyrdom in Literature: Visions of Death and Meaningful Suffering in Europe and the Middle East From Antiquity to Modernity*. Wiesdanden: Reichert, 2004, pp. 29–46.

Tabataba'i, Muhammad Husayn. *Shi'ite Islam*. 2nd ed. Albany: State University of New York Press, 1977.

Taheri, Amir. *Holy Terror: The Inside Story of Islamic Terrorism*. London: Hutchinson Ltd., 1987.

Taji-Farouki, Suha. "Islamists and the Threat of Jihad: Hizb al-Tahrir and the Muhajiroun on Israel and the Jews," *Middle Eastern Studies* 36 (October 2000), pp. 21–46.

Taleqani, Mahmud. "Jihad and Shahadat," in M. Abedi and G. Legenhausen (eds.), *Jihad and Shahadat: Struggle and Martyrdom in Islam*. Houston: Institute for Research and Islamic Studies, 1986, pp. 47–80.

Tamimi, Azzam. *Hamas: A History from Within*. Northampton, MA: Olive Branch Press, 2007.

Taylor, Christoph S. *In the Vicinity of the Righteous: Ziyara and the Veneration of Muslim Saints in Late Medieval Egypt*. Boston: Brill, 1999.

Teitelbaum, J. *Holier than Thou: Saudi Arabia's Islamic Opposition*. Washington, DC: Washington Institute for Near East policy, 2000.

Terner, Bryan S. "Religious Authority and the New Media," *Theory, Culture and Society* 24/2 (2007), pp. 117–134.

"Thomas Aquinas on Martyrdom," in Brian Wicker (ed.), *Witnesses to Faith? Martyrdom in Christianity and Islam*. Appendix 1. Aldershot, Hants: Ashgate, 2006, pp. 139–146.

Tilly, Charles. *Social Movements 1768–2004*. Boulder: Paradigm Publishers, 2004.

Timni, Hussam S. *Modern Intellectual Readings of the Kharijites*. New York: Peter Lang, 2008.

Tzoref, Mira. "The Palestinian Shahida," in Yoram Schweitzer (ed.), *Female Suicide Bombers: Dying for Equality*. Tel Aviv: Juffe Center for Strategic Studies, 2006, pp. 13–22.

The Maccabean Martyrs as Saviours of the Jewish People. Leiden: Brill, 1997.

Varzi, Roxanne. *Warring Souls: Youth, Media, and Martyrdom in Post-revolutionary Iran*. Durham: Duke University Press, 2006.

Venturi, Franco. *Roots of Revolution: A History of the Populist and Socialist Movements in Nineteenth Century Russia*. London: Weidenfeld and Nicolson, 1960.

Victor, Barbara. *Army of Roses: Inside the World of Palestinian Women Suicide Bombers*. Emmaus, PA: Rodale, 2003.

Vilozny, Roy. "A Šīʿī Life Cycle According to al-Barqī's Kitab al-Maḥāsin," *Arabica* 54/3 (2007), pp. 362–396.

Voll, John O. "Relations among Islamist Groups," in John L. Esposito (ed.), *Political Islam: Revolution, Radicalism or Reform?* Boulder: Lynne Rienner, 1997, pp. 231–247.

Von Sivers, Peter. "The Realm of Justice: Apocalyptic Revolts in Algeria," *Humaniora Islamica* 1 (1973), pp. 47–60.

Wabuda, Susan. "Henry Bull, Miles Coverdale and the Making of Foxe's Book of Martyrs," in Dian Wood (ed.), *Martyrs and Martyrologies*. Cambridge, MA: Blackwell Publishers, 1993, pp. 245–258.

Wagemakers, Joas. "Reclaiming Scholarly Authority: Abu Muhammad al-Maqdisi's Critique of Jihadi Practices," *Studies in Conflict and Terrorism* 34/7 (2011), pp. 523–539.

" 'Seceders' and 'Postponers'? An Analysis of the 'Khawarij' and 'Murji'a' Labels in Polemical Debates between Quietist and Jihadi-Salafis," in Jeevan Deol and Zaheer Kazmi (eds.), *Contextualising Jihadi Thought*. New York: Columbia University Press, 2011, pp. 145–164.

A Quietist Jihadi: The Ideology and Influence of Abu Muhammad al-Maqdisi. Cambridge: Cambridge University Press, 2012.

Walter, Christopher. *The Warrior Saints in Byzantine Art and Tradition*. Aldershot: Ashgate, 1988.

Waltz, James. "The Significance of the Voluntary Martyrs of Ninth-Century Cordova", *Muslim World* 60 (1970), pp. 143–59, 226–236.

Warner, Dennis. *The Sacred Warriors: Japan's Suicide Legions*. New York: Van Nostrand Reinhold Co., 1982.

Wax, Emily. "The Mufti in the Chat Room," *Washington Post*, July 31, 1999.

Weber, M. "Politics as a Vocation," in H. H. Gerth and C. W. Mills (eds.), *From Max Weber: Essays in Sociology*. New York: Oxford University Press, 1946, pp. 77–128.

Weimann, Gabriel. *Terror on the Internet: The New Media, the New Challenges*. Washington, DC: U.S. Institute of Peace Press, 2006.

Wein, Peter. *Iraqi Arab Nationalism: Authoritarian, Totalitarian, and Pro-fascist Inclinations 1932–1941.* London: Routledge, 2006.

Weiner, Eugene, and Anita Weiner. *The Martyr's Conviction: A Sociological Analysis.* Atlanta, GA: Scholars Press, 1990.

Weinrich, William C. *Spirit and Martyrdom.* Washington, DC: University Press of America, 1981.

Weir, Fred. "Chechen Rebels Go Kamikaze," *Christian Science Monitor*, June 7, 2000.

Weismann, Itzchak. "Modernity from Within: Islamic Fundamentalism and Sufism," *Der Islam* 86 (2011), pp. 142–170.

Wendell, Charles. *Five Tracts of Hasan al-Banna.* Berkeley: University of California Press, 1978.

Wensinck, Jan Arent. *The Oriental Doctrine of the Martyrs.* Amsterdam: Koninklijke Akademie van Wetenschappen, 1921.

Wiktorowicz, Quintan. "Introduction: Islamic Activism – A Social Movement Theory," in Quintan Wiktorowicz (ed.), *Islamic Activism: A Social Movement Theory Approach.* Bloomington: Indiana University Press, 2004, pp. 1–34.

Wilson, Stephan. "Introduction," in Stephan Wilson (ed.), *Saints and Their Cults.* London: Cambridge University Press, 1985, pp. 1–53.

Winder, Bayly. "Islam as the State Religion – A Muslim Brotherhood View in Syria," *Muslim World* 44 (1954), pp. 215–226.

Winter, Jay, and Emmanuel Sivan. "Setting the Framework," in J. Winter and E. Sivan (eds.), *War and Remembrance in the Twentieth Century.* Cambridge: Cambridge University Press, 1999, pp. 6–37.

Wolf, Kenneth B. *Christian Martyrs in Muslim Spain.* New York: Cambridge University Press, 1988.

Woods, David. "The 60 Martyrs of Gaza and the Martyrdom of Bishop Sophronius of Jerusalem," in Michael Bonner (ed.), *Arab-Byzantine Relations in Early Islamic Times.* Aldershot, Hant: Ashgate 2004, pp. 429–450.

Young, Frances M. *Sacrifice and the Death of Christ.* London: SPCM Press, 1975.

Zahavi, Amotz and Avishag. *The Handicap Principle: A Missing Piece of Darwin's Puzzle.* New York: Oxford University Press, 1997.

Zamel, Abdulaziz I. *The Rise of Palestinian Islamist Groups.* MA thesis; Tampa: University of South Florida, 1991.

Al-Zayyat, Muntasir. *The Road to al-Qaeda: The Story of Bin Laden's Right Hand.* London: Pluto Press, 2004.

Zedalis, Debra D. *Female Suicide Bombers.* Honolulu, HI: University Press of the Pacific, 2004.

Zerubavel, Yael. *Recovered Roots: Collective Memory and the Making of Israeli National Tradition.* Chicago: Chicago University Press, 1995.

   The Nation and Death: History, Memory and Politics. Tel Aviv: Dvir, 2002 (in Hebrew).

   "Battle, Self-sacrifice, Sacrifice: Recompense in the Ideology of Patriotic Self-sacrifice in Israel," in Avner Ben-Amos and Daniel Bar-Tal (eds.), *Patriotism: Homeland Love.* Tel Aviv: Hakibbutz Hameuchad, 2004, pp. 61–99 (in Hebrew).

Žižek, Salvoj. *Welcome to the Desert of the Real.* New York: Verso, 2002.

Internet Sites

www.alarabiya.net
www.almasryalyoum.com
www.aqsa.org.uk/activities
www.alsunnah.info
www.assabeel.net
www.azzam/afgan/html/afghanfatawahmmoudl.htm
www.al-fateh.net.
www.hizballah.org
www.ikhwanonline.com
www.islamonline.net
www.lailatalqadr.com
www.maktabah-alsalafiyah.org/english/military-operations.htm
www.moqawama.org
www.palestine-info.info
www.palestine-info.info/arabic/hamas/shuhda
www.pkkonline.com
www.pwhce.org/textaq.html
www.saraya.ps/index.php?act
www.ssnp.info
www.tawhed.ws

Index

Lightning Source UK Ltd.
Milton Keynes UK
UKOW06f1903180616

276557UK00008B/194/P